Introducing Pragmatism

This unique introduction fully engages and clearly explains pragmatism, an approach to knowledge and philosophy that rejects outmoded conceptions of objectivity while avoiding relativism and subjectivism. It follows pragmatism's focus on the process of inquiry rather than on abstract justifications meant to appease the skeptic. According to pragmatists, getting to know the world is a creative human enterprise, wherein we fashion our concepts in terms of how they affect us practically, including in future inquiry. This book fully illuminates that enterprise and the resulting radical rethinking of basic philosophical conceptions like truth, reality, and reason.

Author Cornelis de Waal helps the reader recognize, understand, and assess classical and current pragmatist contributions—from Charles S. Peirce to Cornel West—evaluate existing views from a pragmatist angle, formulate pragmatist critiques, and develop a pragmatist viewpoint on a specific issue.

The book discusses:

- Classical pragmatists, including Peirce, James, Dewey, and Addams;
- Contemporary figures, including Rorty, Putnam, Haack, and West;
- Connections with other twentieth-century approaches, including phenomenology, critical theory, and logical positivism;
- Peirce's pragmatic maxim and its relation to James's Will to Believe;
- Applications to philosophy of law, feminism, and issues of race and racism.

Cornelis de Waal is Professor of Philosophy at Indiana University–Purdue University Indianapolis and Editor-in-Chief of the *Transactions of the Charles S. Peirce Society*. Previously he was one of the editors of *The Writings of Charles S. Peirce: A Chronological Edition*. In addition to numerous journal articles, he authored *Charles S. Peirce: A Guide for the Perplexed* (2013) and *On Mead* (2002). He is currently editing *The Oxford Handbook of Charles S. Peirce*.

Introducing Pragmatism

A Tool for Rethinking Philosophy

Cornelis de Waal

Routledge
Taylor & Francis Group

NEW YORK AND LONDON

First published 2022
by Routledge
605 Third Avenue, New York, NY 10158

and by Routledge
2 Park Square, Milton Park, Abingdon, Oxon, OX14 4RN

Routledge is an imprint of the Taylor & Francis Group, an informa business

Library of Congress Cataloging-in-Publication Data
A catalog record for this book has been requested

ISBN: 978-1-138-36716-6 (hbk)
ISBN: 978-1-138-36718-0 (pbk)
ISBN: 978-1-003-19973-1 (ebk)

Typeset in Bembo
by Apex CoVantage, LLC

To Kelly, Sophia, Olivia

Contents

Preface

The German language draws a distinction between *Einführung* and *Einleitung*. Both are indiscriminately rendered into English as "introduction." There is, though, an important difference. An *Einführung* is an introduction in the sense that it gives the reader an accessible overview of something that is thought to be already established. An *Einleitung*, in contrast, is an introduction in the sense of a prelude, a first chapter of what is still to come.[1] *Introducing Pragmatism* aims to be both. It aims to present an overview of an approach to doing philosophy, called pragmatism, and it aims to be a prelude of what is still to come, since we are still very much in the beginning phase of that approach. In short, the aim of this book is to familiarize readers with the contributions made by pragmatists so as to enable them to evaluate existing views—whether in philosophy, science, or religion—from a pragmatist angle, formulate a pragmatist critique, or develop a pragmatist viewpoint on a specific subject. Much of the book discusses the development of pragmatism from the 1870s onward. It is not, however, a mere chronological account of who wrote what when, and who learned what from whom. Rather, it is a natural history of the development of a certain cluster of ideas. The triumvirate of classical American pragmatism—Charles Peirce, William James, and John Dewey—is well represented. But they are only the tip of the iceberg, and as we will see, it is an iceberg that runs deep and wide. There are far more pragmatists than can with reasonable lucidity be treated within the confines of a small volume, and painful choices had to be made. Part of what motivated the choices was to present the diversity of pragmatism while remaining close to its core idea, which is Peirce's 1878 pragmatic maxim.

The British pragmatist Ferdinand Schiller once remarked that there are as many pragmatisms as there are pragmatists. And since many pragmatists shifted their opinions, this estimate may even be called conservative. To make matters worse, the many strands of pragmatism often seem ill at ease with one another, if not straightforwardly contradictory. Of course, that is not necessarily a bad thing. Peirce once optimistically called pragmatism "a house at war against itself concerning not inconsiderable questions," adding that "perhaps this will not endanger its stability, and it certainly renders the discussions more interesting."[2] So far, it has not endangered its stability. Today, pragmatism is not just alive and kicking; it is arguably one of the most promising approaches to doing philosophy. It is the aim of this volume to outline that approach.

The current book is a significantly updated and expanded edition of *On Pragmatism*, which appeared with Wadsworth in 2005. Added to the revised and updated chapters of the old book are brand new discussions on the reception of pragmatism in Europe that detail the relations between pragmatism and central tenets in twentieth-century philosophy, such as phenomenology, logical positivism, philosophical anthropology, and critical theory. The book also contains a discussion of legal pragmatism, from Justice Oliver Wendell Holmes Jr. to the present, as well as a chapter on issues of race and gender, including the work of Alain Locke and Cornel West. In the concluding chapter, I try to show that to be a good philosopher, you really need to be a pragmatist.

In addition to all who helped me pull the old volume off the ground, I would like to thank my students, especially Heather Anderson, Aubrey Kenefick, Michael Seidel, and Nicolas Tedla for their valuable feedback while reworking the old material and breaking new ground. Most importantly, this work would not have existed without the constant support of my essential companion, Kelly de Waal, the delightful distractions of my daughters, Sophia and Olivia, and the ferocious barking of our two dogs, Lucy and Licorice, who kept us all safe while I had my nose deep in the books.

Note on References and Quotations

References to frequently cited sources are given in-line, combining an abbreviation of the title with a page number. The "References and Select Bibliography" at the close of the book contains the keys to the abbreviations used. Cross-references are made by chapter and section number. Unless stated otherwise, emphasis in quotations is as found in the original.

Notes

1. For an example of the latter, Helmuth Plessner, *Die Stufen des Organischen und der Mensch: Einleitung in die philosophische Anthropologie* (Berlin, 1928).
2. Charles Peirce, *Charles Sanders Peirce: Contributions to the* Nation (Lubbock, 1975), 3:234.

Chapter 1

Introduction

Philosophically, what characterizes the twentieth century is that old ways of thinking could no longer be relied upon. Theories of evolution, most prominently Darwin's, opened up ways of looking at the world that no longer demanded fixed categories or a divine creator to explain the order of nature. Independently, advances in logic showed that traditional logic—which was long considered to represent rationality as God had bestowed it on us—is woefully out of touch with what is happening in the sciences. To make things worse, there appear to be numerous equally acceptable logics, so that one must choose which logic to apply. Something similar happened in Euclidean geometry, long considered the only way physical space could be. Mach and Einstein further showed that the very idea of absolute space and time—a core presupposition of Newtonian mechanics that carried deeply into modern philosophy—cannot be maintained. With it, we had to give up on the idea that the universe is some big empty space where things happen at set locations in a set order, as if in a watchmaker's workshop. In consequence, the traditional notion of reality as a ready-made world created especially for us, and truth as how an all-knowing God takes it all in, can no longer be taken for granted. This has resulted in a rather peculiar situation. The nineteenth century witnessed enormous progress in the applied sciences, while at the same time, the foundations of science began to crumble. When it appeared that we got a better grip on the world, it became more difficult to argue that we can know its true nature.

It is not just in our conception of the external world that we see dramatic changes. When Descartes famously concluded "I think, therefore I am," he assumed that he had an immediate, full, and transparent access to his own mind. Because how could it be otherwise? After Freud, however, this is no longer so obvious. Not only do we have only limited access to our own mind (merely the tip of the iceberg), but our mind is also very skilled at deceiving us, *even* (perhaps especially) when we reason. During the twentieth century it also becomes increasingly clear that rationality, though immensely powerful (especially when reinforced by technology) is neither neutral nor intrinsically good. As is well documented, both the natural and social sciences are painfully implicated in industrialized warfare, mass propaganda, genocide, and the creation of weapons that are capable of unprecedented destruction.

In brief, great shifts have been taking place in how we understand ourselves and the world we encounter. In this book, we look at pragmatism, an approach to philosophy that embodies one response to these shifts. The chapters that follow give you a thorough familiarity with the origin and history of pragmatism and guide you through some of the challenges of the twentieth century. The intention is not just to give you a working knowledge that will enable you to engage in current debates—both within pragmatism and in philosophy more generally—but also to set the stage for new strategies that will enable you to engage with the problems we face today.

Pragmatism originated in the early 1870s, when a small group of young men from Cambridge, Massachusetts, began to meet regularly to talk philosophy. The group includes William James, Charles Sanders Peirce, Oliver Wendell Holmes Jr., and Nicholas St. John Green. As Peirce later writes, "we called ourselves, half-ironically and half-defiantly 'The Metaphysical Club,'—for agnosticism was riding its high horse, and was frowning severely upon all metaphysics" (EP2:399).[1] At some point their discussions congregate on Alexander Bain's definition of belief as "that upon which a man is prepared to act." Once we settled on that definition, Peirce later recalls, pragmatism follows almost instantly as its natural outcome.[2] This is not to say that the Metaphysical Club members think that this pragmatism is something entirely new—a revolutionary method that had never before been discovered. Rather, they see it as a conscious and systematic adoption of a method that philosophers have been practicing from antiquity onward, even if often unawares. To put it briefly, pragmatism originated from a certain fermentation of ideas within a small group of people that came together in the early 1870s in Cambridge, Massachusetts.

Since pragmatism is generally considered to be an approach to philosophy, or a school within philosophy, we should first ask what philosophy is, or at least what pragmatists think it is. Returning to the Greek origin of the term, philosophy can be described as the exercise of a love of wisdom that is being engaged in for its own sake. According to Immanuel Kant, its main concern centers on three questions: What can I know?, What must I do?, and What may I hope?[3] To this we can add a fourth question, one that becomes especially prominent within the twentieth century: Who, or what, are we?

Charles Peirce, who is generally acknowledged as having given birth to pragmatism, defines philosophy by contrasting it to the specialized sciences. He describes it broadly as the discipline that "contents itself with a more attentive scrutiny and comparison of the facts of everyday life, such as present themselves to every adult and sane person" (EP2:146; see also Chapter 6). Its aim, Peirce continues, is that of developing a comprehensive conception of the world and our relationship to it—in short, a *Weltanschauung*. Consequently, it seeks to address questions such as, What is truth?, What makes something real?, What do we mean by "a thing"?, etc. This view is partially reflected in the *Oxford English Dictionary*, which currently defines philosophy as the discipline that studies "the fundamental nature of knowledge, reality, and existence, and the basis and limits of human understanding"—a definition that oddly leaves out ethics and a critical reflection on the human condition, something Peirce's does not. In fact, within twentieth-century philosophy we see a growing divide between the Anglo-Saxon tradition, which is fairly represented by the Oxford dictionary, and the continental European tradition, which puts greater emphasis on the philosophers' responsibility to reflect critically on the human condition. The American pragmatist Richard Rorty wryly observes that, in contrast to Europe, people in British and American philosophy departments who engage in the latter are not thought of as true philosophers. "The Anglo-American notion of what philosophers are good for," he writes, "is at the opposite pole from Husserl's claim, in *The Crisis of the European Sciences*, that only rigorous phenomenological analysis can save us from barbarism."[4] On the whole, pragmatism aims to remain clear from this divide, and when it encounters it, seeks to bridge it. As the pragmatist John Dewey puts it, aligning himself with both Rorty and Husserl, "Philosophy recovers itself when it ceases to be a device for dealing with the problems of philosophers and becomes a method, cultivated by philosophers, for dealing with the problems of men" (MW10:46).

Having defined philosophy as the discipline that "contents itself with a more attentive scrutiny and comparison of the facts of everyday life," Peirce observes that when we engage in it, we should not do it aimlessly, but we should do it deliberately. This means that we need to have some idea of what the outcome is likely to be. Philosophy, Peirce argues, is a deliberate, purpose-directed activity. And that, he continues, naturally leads to pragmatism (R478:4). In brief, for Peirce, pragmatism is what philosophy should be, and in part the aim of the present volume is to bear this out.

It is not Peirce, however, who brings pragmatism to the forefront of philosophy. That honor goes to William James. As a gifted lecturer and writer, James attracts much attention, and by the time of his death in 1910, most philosophers know about pragmatism and have an opinion about it, even if not always a positive one. James's take on pragmatism, however, is quite different from Peirce's, and we can discern in pragmatism a Peircean and a Jamesean strand that still exists today.

In his 1710 *Principles of Human Knowledge*, Bishop Berkeley famously remarks that philosophers are very good at confusing themselves and others. "Upon the whole," he writes,

> I am inclined to think that the far greater part, if not all, of those difficulties which have hitherto amused philosophers, and blocked up the

way to knowledge, are entirely owing to ourselves. That we have first raised a dust and then complain, we cannot see.[5]

It is this propensity to confusion that Peirce's pragmatism seeks to address. Peirce, as we will see, considers pragmatism primarily as a method for doing philosophy, one that aims to guarantee that the concepts we use have meaning. Concepts that have no conceivable practical consequences are to be thrown out as meaningless, and if the conceivable practical consequences of two concepts are the same, they are to be considered synonyms.

When James introduces pragmatism to mainstream philosophy, however, he uses an analogy to describe its core idea—an analogy that proved far too powerful for its own good. What we need to focus on, James writes, is the cash value of our concepts in terms of concrete experiences. James even comes to identify truth as the cash value of our ideas. The analogy sticks, but not in a good way. Pragmatism is quickly associated with crass American capitalism, even by those who are otherwise favorably disposed to it. It is interpreted as the apology of a culture where the value of a painting is settled on the auction block, and where the greatness of a book, movie, or theater production is determined by how much money it brings in. What doesn't generate revenue is meaningless. Martin Heidegger dismissively calls it a *Weltanschauung* for engineers—a utilitarian philosophy that makes everything into an exploitable resource. Bertrand Russell, certainly no fan of Heidegger, similarly complains that it robs life "of all that gives it value, and [makes] man himself smaller by depriving the universe which he contemplates of all its splendour."[6] Similar sentiments are expressed by Max Horkheimer, who sees in it the philosophy of a society that has no time to spare for reflection or meditation. The British author and culture critic G.K. Chesterton sums it all up well when he writes, "Pragmatism is a matter of human needs; and one of the first human needs is to be something more than a pragmatist."[7] Ironically, the main motivation that drove James is exactly the opposite of what he is being accused of. He hoped to restore a place for religious faith in an age that in his view has become overly materialistic and scientistic. Peirce expresses similar sentiments when he calls capitalism "the gospel of greed."

It is fair to say that James's cash-value analogy harmed the early European reception of pragmatism. As we will see, however, it did not stop it. Russell comes to embrace enough of it to make Frank Ramsey call him a pragmatist; the logical positivist Rudolf Carnap converts to pragmatism, thanks to Charles Morris; Horkheimer's intellectual heirs embrace it; there are clear similarities between Heidegger and pragmatism, and so on. Not everyone is on board, though. Quite recently, the American bioethicist Leon Kass dismissed it as a thoughtless advance toward whatever serves expediency,[8] and the Israeli jurist Michal Alberstein calls it "a philosophical discourse that is general, hysteric, external, practical, and progressive."[9]

Unfair as these criticisms may be, the fact that pragmatism originates in America is not without significance. In general, we can say that philosophy is to an important extent always the expression of a culture. The shift from the schoolmen, with their focus on God, to modern philosophy, with its focus on science, is not due to some isolated insight but is intimately intertwined with developments such as the Protestant Reformation, the emergence of cities, the growth of the merchant class, and the invention of the printing press. As John Dewey keenly observes in *Reconstruction in Philosophy*, "The distinctive office, problems and subject matter of philosophy grow out of stresses and strains in the community life in which a given form of philosophy arises" (MW12:256). With regard to the philosophy of pragmatism, opinions are divided on what these stresses and strains are. Suggestions range from puritanism, to the pioneer mentality of the settlers, to the American Civil War. The German sociologist Max Weber draws a direct relation between puritanism and James's views on religion, writing that "James's pragmatic valuation of the significance of religious ideas according to their influence on life is . . . a true child of the world of ideas of the Puritan home of that eminent scholar."[10] Michael Novak attributes pragmatism's distinctive edge to the pioneer mentality that found its way into America's intellectual circles:

> On this at first dark continent, and now in the dark and unknown reaches of technological power, Americans have always sensed that there may not be any rules made up in advance, no finished and a priori world "out there" to operate as an absolute, secure standard by which to measure themselves.[11]

To this, Scott Pratt adds that there is a Native American influence; while Louis Menand, in *The Metaphysical Club*, emphasizes the influence of the American Civil War (1861–5) on the ground that it radically discredited the basic presuppositions and beliefs that defined intellectual life before it.[12] This is also the time during which Darwin's theory of evolution gains widespread influence within the US, in part thanks to John Fiske and Chauncey Wright, both of whom were affiliated with the Metaphysical Club.

In addition, we can say that America emerged as a society of immigrants. Though mostly European initially, those who migrated to the US came from a wide variety of national, social, and cultural backgrounds. The result was an unprecedented comingling of people and a veritable melting pot of ideas. Although philosophy in America begins as a mixture of the philosophies that the European immigrants brought with them, by the middle of the nineteenth century, unhindered by established power structures and faced with the challenges of a young society in an unfamiliar land, a new philosophy starts to emerge—one with its own identity, that focuses on the future rather than the past. This philosophy is pragmatism.

Pragmatism is best described as a way of doing philosophy. In this sense it differs from, for instance, materialism. What makes someone a materialist is the belief that in some form or other matter is the primordial, or fundamental, constituent of the universe. Materialism is thus a theory about what the universe is like. Pragmatism makes no such claims. Instead, it concerns itself with the question of how we should conduct our business as philosophers, scientists, homicide detectives, accountants, etc., whenever we engage in inquiry. Originally, pragmatism was devised as a method for determining the meaning of words, most significantly philosophical and scientific terms. Its initial impetus was polemic. The aim was to show that numerous of our most basic terms had no meaning at all and that several key problems in science and philosophy were products of terminological unclearness—the dust Berkeley so forcefully complained about earlier. In this sense, the main objective of pragmatism is not unlike that of the nineteenth-century positivists and the logical positivists that follow in their footsteps. They too sought to eradicate meaningless philosophical verbiage, in their case by replacing metaphysical speculations by what they considered (as we will see, mistakenly) solid empirical science. One of the arguments of this book is that the pragmatists fare much better in cleaning up philosophy than the positivists did.

It is often argued that pragmatism encompasses a theory of truth, and a bad one at that. As we will see, however, the pragmatists are themselves divided on the question of whether the principle that defines pragmatism is to be taken only as a criterion of meaning, or whether it is also a criterion of truth. Peirce maintains that these are two different issues and that pragmatism is strictly about meaning. What is often referred to as the pragmatist theory of truth, then, results from applying the pragmatist criterion of meaning to the existing concept of truth. For Peirce, "truth," like "hardness," "identity," "simultaneity," etc., is just one of those concepts that one should have a pragmatist conception of. What is called the pragmatist theory of truth is thus an outgrowth of the desire to clean up philosophical discourse. Hence, it is a product of pragmatism, and certainly an important one, but it is not a defining characteristic. Nonetheless, much of the criticism of pragmatism, especially early on, is directed specifically against various pragmatist conceptions of truth. Broadly speaking, the criticism is that pragmatists confuse truth with gratification. In the pages that follow, we will address this accusation. If justified, it undermines all forms of pragmatism, because even those who, with Peirce, see pragmatism merely as a doctrine of meaning hold that "truth" is one concept to which this doctrine applies.

Before moving on, it may be helpful to first ask why this way of doing philosophy is called pragmatism, and why the early pragmatists were so reluctant to truly embrace the term (as we will see, James prefers practicalism, Schiller humanism, and Dewey instrumentalism). The term pragmatism most likely originates within the Metaphysical Club, and it may have been used just as much tongue-in-cheek as the name of the club itself. James uses the term at least once in a draft of a paper written around that time, while there is no evidence that Peirce does. In fact, in the early 1890s, when defining over 16,000 philosophical terms for the twelve-volume *Century Dictionary*, Peirce does not include a definition for pragmatism. Part of the explanation may be what the colloquial term meant at the time. The same *Century Dictionary* defines pragmatism as "busy impertinence" and a pragmatist as someone "who is impertinently busy or meddling" (CD:4667). Perhaps (and this is mere speculation), the youthful Metaphysical Club members saw themselves as deliberately "meddling impertinently" with metaphysics—a discipline Peirce decades later still considers "a puny, rickety, and scrofulous science" (EP2:375). All this suggests that pragmatism was a word better suited for a conversation among friends than for print publication—something Peirce later hints at as well (CP5.414n1).

One way of extracting meaning from the term pragmatism is to follow the same recipe we used earlier for the term philosophy, by examining its roots. Both Peirce and James did so. In the *Century Dictionary* entry for "pragmatic" (Peirce does not ignore the term altogether), he describes its use in Kantian philosophy and defines *pragmatic method* as "the treatment of historical phenomena with special reference to their causes, antecedent conditions, and results. Also *pragmatism*" (CD:4667). The reference to Kant is not accidental. It is Kant's use of the German *Pragmatisch* that Peirce credits as the source of his own use (R329:9). The word itself, however, is far older, and both Peirce and James return to the original Greek πραῖγμα (*pragma*) to explain what pragmatism is about. What they find is quite different, however, and we will see this difference play out in the history of pragmatism until today. In his explication of the term, Peirce writes,

> When I gave the doctrine of "pragmatism" the name it bears . . . I derived the name by which I Christened it from πραῖγμα "behavior,"— in order that it should be understood that the doctrine is that the only real significance of a general term lies in *the general behavior which it implies.*[13]

James, in contrast, takes πραῖγμα to mean action (WJ:377), later adding that *Pragmata* "are things in their plurality," so that what pragmatism truly stands for is that "the meaning of any proposition *can always be brought down to some particular consequence* in our future practical experience" (MT:113; emphasis added). James further drives home the point by emphasizing that the key issue is "that the experience must be particular [rather than] that it must be active" (ibid).

Returning to ancient Greece, we see the word πραῖγμα appear in Plato's *Apology* when Socrates is asked, "What is your occupation?" and again in the *Phaedo*, where Plato has Socrates respond, "philosophy is my business."[14] To this Peirce and James, and those following in their footsteps, will now add that it is the business of the philosopher to be a pragmatist.

Notes

1. On the Metaphysical Club, see also Louis Menand, *The Metaphysical Club: A Story of Ideas in America* (New York, 2001).
2. See e.g., Max Fisch, "Alexander Bain and the Genealogy of Pragmatism," in Max Fisch (ed), *Peirce, Semeiotic, and Pragmatism* (Bloomington, 1986), pp.79–109.
3. Immanuel Kant, *Critique of Pure Reason* (New York, 1965), A805/B833.
4. Richard Rorty, "The Professor and the Prophet," *Transition* (1991): 70–8, p.72.
5. A.A. Luce and T.E. Jessup (eds), *The Works of George Berkeley, Bishop of Cloyne*, vols. 9 (London, 1949), 2:26.
6. Bertrand Russell, *Philosophical Essays* (New York, 1966), p.110.
7. G.K. Chesterton, *Orthodoxy* (London, 1908), p.64.
8. Leon Kass, *Toward a More Natural Science* (New York, 1985), p.98. For a more nuanced view, Glenn McGee (ed), *Pragmatic Bioethics*, 2nd ed. (Cambridge, 2003).
9. Robert Innis, *Pragmatism and Law: From Philosophy to Dispute Resolution* (Dartmouth, 2002), p.2.
10. Max Weber, *The Protestant Ethic and the Spirit of Capitalism* (New York, 1958), p.232.
11. Michael Novak (ed), *American Philosophy and the Future* (New York, 1968), p.87; also, Waldo Frank, *Our America* (New York, 1919), pp.26–9.
12. Scott Pratt, *Native Pragmatism: Rethinking the Roots of American Philosophy* (Bloomington, 2002), p.19f; Menand (2001), p.x.
13. Letter to Howes Norris Jr., May 28, 1912 (RL:321); emphasis added.
14. *Apology* 20c5 (Jowett translation), *Phaedo* 61a (Hackforth translation).

Chapter 2

Peirce and the Principle of Pragmatism

Peirce's pragmatism can be roughly divided into two periods. The first is discussed here, whereas the second is postponed to Chapter 6. What motivates this division is historical circumstance: Peirce's influence on the early stages of pragmatism is almost exclusively confined to his 1878 essay "How to Make Our Ideas Clear." In other words, the division is inspired by the reception of Peirce's pragmatism, not by a change in his own thought. Peirce's views do evolve over time, but these changes are more gradual and multifaceted and relate only tangentially to his objections to the other pragmatists.

The first period, which is the subject of this chapter, covers pragmatism's initial formulation. This period culminates in Peirce's second "Illustrations of the Logic of Science" paper entitled "How to Make Our Ideas Clear." In this paper, which appears in 1878, Peirce develops a method for determining the meaning of a concept, which he summarizes in the form of a maxim. It is this maxim that William James makes famous twenty years later, calling it "the principle of pragmatism." This principle, we will see, forms the core of pragmatism.

The second period, which is treated in Chapter 6, starts around the turn of the century. Motivated by the popularity of pragmatism, but disappointed by how its proponents interpret it, Peirce seeks to explain how his own version differs from those that have become mainstream. In 1903, he delivers six lectures on pragmatism at Harvard. Two years later, he publishes three papers in the *Monist* outlining his views: "What Pragmatism Is," "Issues of Pragmaticism," and "Prolegomena to an Apology for Pragmaticism." However, living in relative isolation in the small town of Milford, Pennsylvania, and without any students of his own to carry his views forward, Peirce's later attempts have a more limited impact for much of the twentieth century.

2.1 The Limits of Thought

At the age of twelve, Peirce finds in his brother's bedroom a copy of Richard Whately's *Elements of Logic*.[1] As he later recalls, he immediately stretched himself out on the floor and started reading. Peirce quickly devours the book, and from then on logic remains his passion. Although logic is his passion, Peirce is no dry, bookish logician. As he likes to remind his readers, he developed his views on logic and philosophy in the laboratory. The scope of that laboratory work is staggering. Far from being an armchair scientist, Peirce makes significant contributions to gravimetry, geodesy, astrophysics, and spectroscopy. Because of his scientific background, his approach to philosophy, and to pragmatism in particular, is that of a scientist at work. It is no accident that Peirce's first statement of pragmatism—even though the word itself does not occur there—appears in a series of articles called "Illustrations of the Logic of Science."[2]

Peirce opens his "Illustrations of the Logic of Science" series with a paper titled "The Fixation of Belief." Peirce there continues the criticism of Cartesian philosophy that he began in a series of articles for the *Journal of Speculative Philosophy* almost a decade earlier. In these articles, Peirce argues that we have no power of intuition, we have no power of introspection, we cannot think otherwise than in signs, and we have no conception of the absolutely incognizable (EP1:30). By taking this position, Peirce goes radically against the grain of established opinion. Because Peirce's pragmatism develops largely out of these four denials, I will discuss them each briefly.

Peirce's first denial is to the claim that we have any intuitive knowledge. The notion of intuitive knowledge goes back at least to Plato and draws heavily on a comparison with the faculty of vision. Just as we see sensory objects when light shines upon them, so do we "see" intelligible objects when they are "illuminated" by what some have called the "light of reason." On this view, you have intuitive knowledge when you immediately "see" that something is true. Classic examples are the claim that the whole is always greater than any of its parts, that whenever we think we must also exist, etc. This notion of intuitive knowledge is intimately tied up with Descartes's conception of clear and distinct ideas, which to him is simultaneously a criterion of meaning and a criterion of truth. In his *Meditations*, Descartes argued that whatever is clearly and distinctly perceived is true.[3]

It would lead us too far astray to examine in detail Peirce's objections to the notion of intuitive knowledge, but they are empirical, not a priori. He points to a number of circumstances where claims of intuitive knowledge are shown to be wrong or compromised beyond repair. Peirce argues, for instance, that our direct perception is seriously compromised by the ease with which magicians make us "see" things that do not happen. It also happens quite frequently that what seems absolutely clear and true at the outset later turns out to have been deceptive and false. Take the thesis that the whole is always greater than any of its parts. This thesis is constantly confirmed in simple and convincing ways. Just try to cut up a birthday cake in a way that defies it. In fact, this thesis is so deeply ingrained in our understanding that it seems altogether impossible to conceive of anything for which it would not hold, suggesting it is a simple, self-evident, and universal truth.

However, suppose that rather than a birthday cake, we take the set of natural numbers and divide it into two equal parts—say, the odd and the even numbers. Does the principle hold here too? Let's look at the even numbers. First, it can be established that they form a genuine subset of the natural numbers. In fact, even numbers seem to make up exactly half of the natural numbers, with odd numbers making up the other half. This follows from the simple fact that there is an odd number in between any two subsequent even numbers. But although the set of even numbers is thus truly a part of the set of natural numbers, and one that is equal in size to the set of numbers not included (the set of odd numbers), the set of even numbers, far from being smaller than the set of natural numbers, turns out to be of exactly the same size: there are precisely as many even numbers as there are natural numbers. For this we only have to multiply each natural number by two. This will give us a set of numbers that has just as many members as the set of natural numbers (as for each natural number, there is exactly one number that is its double), but which is also identical to the set of even numbers, as the double of each natural number (whether the original is odd or even) is always even. Consequently, the thesis that the whole is always greater than any of its parts, which was believed to be self-evident for over two millennia, cannot be considered intuitive knowledge. As it turns out, the thesis is false because there are situations where cutting something into equal parts gives us parts that all have the exact same size as what they are parts of.[4]

Peirce's rejection of intuitive knowledge, and of the Cartesian notion of clear and distinct ideas accompanying it, forces him to develop a new criterion of meaning. The pragmatic maxim, or as James calls it, "the principle of pragmatism," is precisely that.

Peirce's second denial is that we have no power of introspection. This again puts Peirce on a direct collision course with Descartes. Descartes's argument in the *Meditations* not only required that we have such a power, but also privileged it. According to Descartes, we are much more familiar with our own mind than the world around us—the so-called external world. For Peirce, in contrast, we *first* learn about this external world, and only *then* derive from our interaction with this external world that we have a self and what this self entails. Hence, for Peirce, our knowledge progresses not from the inside out (which is how Descartes had it), but from the outside in. Peirce's rejection of the power of introspection follows from his earlier denial of intuitive knowledge.

Peirce's third denial is that we can think without signs. This follows straight from his previous denial of introspection. If we have no direct access to our own thoughts, then we can only access our own thoughts indirectly through their external aspects, that is, through how they present themselves to us, as signs. But this is as much as to say that the *only* thought we can *cognize* is thought in signs, and since it belongs to the essence of thought that it can be cognized (incognizable thoughts being a contradiction in terms), all thought must be in signs. In referring to signs rather than ideas, as the modern philosophers have done, Peirce is returning to a rich philosophical tradition that preceded Descartes. It leads Peirce to develop a doctrine of signs, or semiotics, to which we return in Chapter 6. Peirce's third denial and his embrace of semiotics has important ramifications because the meaning of a sign lies in what it points to in the eyes of an interpreter. Consequently, if all thought is in signs, the meaning of any thought lies in the thoughts it calls up. As we will see, this future-directed aspect of thought is central to pragmatism.

Peirce subsequently concludes from this that the absolutely incognizable is absolutely inconceivable. What cannot in any way be perceived or apprehended (including imagination, instinct, etc.), cannot convey any meaning because we cannot form any conception of it. Peirce is here directing his criticism against those who maintain that we can only say that we truly know something if it is grounded in something that we cannot possibly know—Kant's things in themselves, or Herbert Spencer's unknowable—a view that leaves the door wide open to the skeptic. It is in this context that Peirce first introduces his pragmatic maxim:

> There can be no conception of the absolutely incognizable, since nothing of that sort occurs in experience. But *the meaning of a term is the conception which it conveys*. Hence, a term can have no such meaning.
>
> (EP1:24; emphasis added)

Although this is Peirce's first published formulation of the maxim (albeit not the one that James would later refer to), the idea behind it was entertained already a few years earlier in a notebook entry dated November 20, 1866. On that day, Peirce concluded, "What is not a question of a possible experience is not a question of fact" (W1:9). Peirce hereby rejects Kant's distinction between phenomena and noumena—the things as they are in themselves, beyond our cognition—as the very presupposition that there are such things is meaningless.

Peirce's four claims concerning the limits of our thought (that we have no power of intuition, that we have no power of introspection, that we can think only in signs, and that we have no conception of the absolutely incognizable) pave the way for Peirce's own philosophy—a philosophy that is later called pragmatism.

2.2 The Purpose of Thought

Returning to Peirce's "Illustrations of the Logic of Science" papers, we can see that his starting point differs dramatically from the approach of Descartes or Locke. Descartes began by doubting everything in an almost desperate attempt to see whether anything was beyond doubt. What he found was that when he was doubting, he could not possibly doubt that he was doubting, which led him to his famous conclusion, "I think, therefore I am," which he subsequently made the unshakable foundation of his philosophical system.

Locke rejected this kind of reasoning, arguing instead that we can analyze all our thoughts and perceptions and break them down into their most basic components, which he called "simple ideas." These simple ideas—analogous to the atoms of classical physics in that they are discrete and cannot be divided further—Locke took to be the basic building blocks of all our ideas, ranging all the way from our ideas of gold and lithium to those of honesty and democracy. Locke called these "complex ideas." According to Locke, we cannot doubt the simple ideas we have. Either we have a simple idea, or we don't. We can only raise doubts about what the simple ideas we have represent. For instance, we can have the simple ideas that are commonly associated with gold but doubt whether the object in front of us is really made of gold. In sum, Locke made "simple ideas" the unshakable foundation of all our knowledge.

Peirce breaks radically with both traditions. Instead of singling out specific ideas as absolutely certain and building his philosophy upon them, he commences with the beliefs we actually have when we start examining our beliefs. Any inquiry—any question we ask—always takes place against a backdrop of beliefs that we take for granted. The archeologist who wants to know more about the pyramid of Cheops takes it for granted not only that there is an external world and that the pyramid is part of it, but also that much of what we know about ancient Egypt, and about the human condition more generally, is more or less correct.

Like Descartes, Peirce begins by contrasting doubt with belief. According to Peirce, these are two states of mind that are relatively easy to distinguish. The state of doubt, Peirce writes, is "an uneasy and dissatisfied state from which we struggle to free ourselves" (EP1:114). In contrast, the state of belief is "a calm and satisfactory state" (ibid). Not only do we feel a strong desire to change doubt into belief, but we even do our very best to maintain the beliefs we have to avoid lapsing back into doubt. As he puts it, "We cling tenaciously, not merely to believing, but to believing just what we do believe" (EP1:114).

There is another important difference between states of doubt and belief, and this has to do with action. Doubt and belief each lead to action, but they do so quite differently. Doubting is very much like having an itch. It requires immediate action directed to its relief. Doubt is thus a direct stimulus to inquiry, and we stop inquiring as soon as the doubt is gone, just as we stop scratching when the itch is gone.

Belief, Peirce observes, does not make us act with the same immediacy. Instead, it puts us into "such a condition that we shall behave in some certain way, when the occasion arises" (EP1:114). That is, for Peirce, belief is the establishment of a certain *habit* that will determine how we will act when appropriately stimulated. As we see later on, this notion of beliefs as habits, or dispositions to act, is crucial to Peirce's pragmatism and marks a major difference between his view and the views of James and Schiller, who focus instead on the particular consequences of a belief, or the particular sensations we should expect if the belief is true.

Since, for Peirce, the very motive of inquiry is to clear ourselves from the discomfort of doubt, the ultimate aim of all inquiry is nothing other than to regain a state of belief. The belief thus arrived at, however, is not necessarily *true* belief. *Any* belief that alleviates doubt will work, no matter whether it is true or false. By taking this course, Peirce declares the attainment of belief, or the settlement of one's opinion, the sole purpose of inquiry.

Peirce's doubt–belief theory fits nicely with the views expressed about two decades earlier by Darwin in *The Origin of Species*. Inquiry, or the exercise of reason, is no longer the godlike feature that separates man from beast but is a mechanism by which certain organisms adapt themselves to concrete changes in their environment so as to regain (or maintain) their homeostatic equilibrium. We will see this shift to the biological most clearly in Mead (7.3).

2.3 The Fixation of Belief

Given Peirce's account of inquiry and belief, the central question becomes, how can we fix our beliefs so that we are unlikely to lapse back into a state of doubt? In "The Fixation of Belief," Peirce discusses four methods: the method of tenacity, the method of authority, the a priori method, and what he calls "the scientific method." For each of these methods, Peirce examines how well it succeeds in fixing belief.

The first and most primitive method is the method of tenacity. Here, opinion is settled purely by obstinately holding on to one's beliefs with all one's might. One way of doing this is to seek out people one agrees with and avoid those with different opinions, or one can develop a habit of despising or belittling everything that challenges one's own beliefs. Conspiracy theorists often think this way. They fully embrace all evidence in support of their view (say, that an alien spaceship crashed near Roswell) and reject or reinterpret everything that goes against it.

In Peirce's view, this first method works only up to a point. Our confidence in our own beliefs, he argues, is too easily shaken in the interaction with others or when we are confronted with brute facts. As Peirce puts it,

> the social impulse is against it. The man who adopts it will find that other men think differently from him, and it will be apt to occur to him, in some saner moment, that their opinions are quite as good as his own, and this will shake his confidence in his belief.
>
> (EP1:116)

Moreover, when faced with opposing beliefs or recalcitrant facts, the method itself provides no guidance on how to settle the issue. Consequently, Peirce argues, doubt inevitably creeps in. Especially in today's diverse society where we are frequently confronted with views very different from ours, the first method is unlikely to render stable belief. Nonetheless, there are still heroic efforts, like that of Vicki Frost who sued her daughter's elementary school because, in teaching her to respect the views of others, they diverted her from "the one true way."[5] Most cases, however, are not that deliberate. Being in denial, making one's beliefs unfalsifiable in the way Popper accused the Marxists of doing,[6] or letting them float in an ever-changing quicksand of vague generalizations and half-baked opinions, are also examples of this method. Both rigid fundamentalism and freewheeling bullshitting are ways through which beliefs can be maintained according to the first method.

The second method for fixing belief aims to solve this problem by elevating the method of tenacity to the social level. This results in what Peirce calls the method of authority. Here, belief is fixed not by individuals themselves but by a social institution such as the church or state. Individuals no longer need to shield themselves from contrary evidence, as with the method of tenacity, but contrary evidence is purposely withheld from them by a regulating institution through censorship and the oppression, or even elimination, of so-called subversive elements.

The method of authority has a far better chance of success, as the history of organized religion testifies: "Except the geological epochs, there are no periods of time so vast as those which are measured by some of these organized faiths" (EP1:118). However, as no institution can undertake to regulate opinion on *every* subject, this method too is unlikely to fix belief in the long run. To give one example, when Galileo attended mass as a young boy, he was fascinated by a continuously swinging lamp in the cathedral. This stimulated his interest in physics, which in turn led to the destruction of the long-held and authoritatively fixed belief that the sun revolved around a stationary earth positioned at the center of the universe. For the second method, it is not required that the believer realizes that his belief is grounded in authority. Good propaganda makes people freely believe what the authorities want them to believe, and good advertising makes people freely choose products because of what manufacturers say about them.

The third method of fixing belief, which Peirce calls the a priori method, operates by the sanction of thought alone. By this method belief is fixed by the beliefs being "agreeable to reason." With this, Peirce is thinking not of beliefs that agree with empirical facts, but beliefs we find ourselves inclined to believe because they, so to speak, "make sense." An example is the long-held but false belief that heavy bodies fall faster than light ones. Peirce credits Descartes for "passing, in the directest way, from the method of authority to that of apriority," by having our own self-consciousness "furnish us with our fundamental truths, and to decide what was agreeable to reason" (EP1:124).

Other adherents include Kant, who grounded our beliefs in sensory and pure intuition, and Hegel, who, Peirce writes, "simply launches his boat into the current of thought and allows himself to be carried wherever that current leads" (CP5.382n).

The third method differs from the first two in an important respect. Not only does it provide us with an impulse to believe, as did the others, but it also determines *what* is to be believed, namely, that one should believe what is agreeable to reason. Consequently, this time there is an intrinsic relation between the belief and how adherence to the belief is secured. Such a relation is absent in the previous two methods, where the content of the belief is wholly immaterial to how the belief is attained. What secured belief in the first two methods is not the content of the belief, but the willpower and the ability of individuals (or, with the second method, the authorities) to entrench existing beliefs and suppress dissenting opinions (including one's own). Alternatively, one could argue that whereas the method of authority involves censorship and indoctrination, the a priori method involves something similar, namely self-censorship and self-indoctrination. In a way this makes the a priori method a more refined version of the method of tenacity. Part of what lies behind Peirce's criticism of the a priori method is his earlier rejection of intuitive knowledge. If we have no intuitive knowledge, then a mere inclination to believe, however strong, can never be a sufficient ground for knowledge.

Since it is now the *content* of the belief that steers the process of fixation, the a priori method (like the scientific method to which I turn next) is properly a method of inquiry. This notwithstanding, the method is not likely to result in stable belief. As Peirce observes, "The opinions which today seem most unshakeable are found tomorrow to be out of fashion" (CP5.382n). And since the method lacks the means by which competing views can be critically compared, it is rather to be expected that the pendulum of taste will endlessly swing back and forth between a number of alternatives (EP1:119).

The fourth and final method Peirce distinguishes is the scientific method. This method differs from the first three in that the fixation of the belief is no longer fixed by what we wish to believe. Instead, our beliefs are determined "by something upon which our thinking has no effect" (EP1:120). The scientific method, Peirce writes, proceeds from the hypothesis that,

> There are real things, whose characters are entirely independent of our opinions about them; those realities affect our senses according to regular laws, and, though our sensations are as different as our relations to the objects, yet, by taking advantage of the laws of perception, we can ascertain by reasoning how things really are; and any man, if he have sufficient experience and he reason enough about it, will be led to the one true conclusion.
>
> (EP1:120)

About fifteen years later, when preparing his papers for a book, Peirce further explicates this method by contrasting it with the a priori method discussed earlier. With the scientific method, he explains,

> changes of opinion are brought about by events beyond human control. All mankind were so firmly of opinion that heavy bodies must fall faster than light ones, that any other view was scouted as absurd, eccentric, and probably insincere. Yet as soon as some of the absurd and eccentric men could succeed in inducing some of the adherents of common sense to look at their experiments—no easy task—it became apparent that nature would not follow human opinion, however unanimous. So there was nothing for it but human opinion must move to nature's position.
>
> (CP5.384n)

In contrast to the first three methods, where we set the terms, the scientific method proceeds upon the recognition that nature does not accommodate itself to our beliefs, but that our beliefs must accommodate themselves to nature. True, nature accommodates itself to some extent to human action, but it does so only up to a point and only on its own terms. Hence, by the fourth method, we fix our beliefs by having external realities guide our thoughts as opposed to having our thoughts guide themselves. This process only results in a fixed belief, however, when these external realities do not pull us in many directions at once but exert a truly centripetal force upon our thoughts. That there is such a permanent externality that exhibits such a centripetal force Peirce sees confirmed in the enormous progress that was being made by science:

> Who would have said, a few years ago, that we could ever know of what substances stars are made whose light may have been longer in reaching us than the human race has existed? Who can be sure of what we shall not know in a few hundred years? Who can guess what would be the result of continuing the pursuit of science for ten thousand years, with the activity of the last hundred? And if it were to go on for a million, or a billion, or any number of years you please, how is it possible to say that there is any question which might not ultimately be solved?
>
> (EP1:140)

Later, Peirce comes to acknowledge that there might be important questions that in the end remain unanswered. But that does not take away the need that we should always proceed upon the "*hope* that the particular question into which we are inquiring is susceptible of an approximate answer in a reasonable time" (R422:16). That is, for Peirce, the idea that there is a reality becomes a practical postulate of reason.

Peirce not only believes that inquiry would eventually lead us to the right answer, but he also maintains that in many cases we already found the right answer, even though we cannot say for any *particular* question that we found it. In this way, Peirce seeks to wedge a third option between skepticism and dogmatism, which he names fallibilism. The skeptics insist that we can never know anything for sure, and that therefore we should suspend our judgment. The dogmatists, in turn, believe that some truths are self-evident and then ground their philosophic edifices upon them. Peirce rejects the dogmatist's claim that we know with certainty that some particular beliefs are true, while at the same time dismissing the skeptic's conclusion that it follows from this that all our beliefs must be regarded as untrustworthy. Instead, Peirce argues that overall we can trust our beliefs, but we should not bet our lives on any single one of them; a view he later refers to as critical common-sensism (6.4). In Peirce's eyes, the skeptic makes the basic mistake of concluding from the fact that any belief can be doubted that all beliefs can be doubted. But these are very different things. If at an intersection you can go in any direction, it does not mean that you can go in all directions at once. With fallibilism—or, as he also calls it, anti-cock-surism—Peirce introduces a mindset that has become common in the sciences into philosophy, which historically had been hostile to it.

These are the four ways Peirce thinks belief can be fixed or stabilized. We have seen that Peirce sees fixing belief as the sole purpose of inquiry, and that for a belief to be fixed it is not required that the belief be true (it suffices that it is *believed* to be true). Now, one might object that the purpose of inquiry is not belief, but action. For instance, when we inquire into the cause of a fever, the aim of the inquiry is not to fix our belief (or to alleviate ourselves from the discomfort of doubt), but to act—in this case, to cure the disease that causes the fever. This objection rests upon a misconception. The purpose of inquiry is a belief, which, being a *disposition* to act, will cause those who hold the belief to act when they are properly stimulated. Peirce rejects what Dewey comes to call the spectator theory of knowledge—the view that knowing something means seeing it as a disinterested spectator would see it (8.2).

There is no doubt that in Peirce's mind the scientific method is the most advanced of the four. At the same time, however, he maintains that each method is legitimate in its own way and may in certain circumstances be preferable to the scientific method. Hence, Peirce does not claim that the scientific method should simply replace all the others. It should moreover be said that when Peirce talks about science, here as well as elsewhere, he has something in mind that is much broader than how the term is used today, especially within the Anglo-Saxon world. It includes any inquiry engaged in with the aim of having one's questions answered.

2.4 The Fixation of Meaning

In the second of his "Illustrations of the Logic of Science" papers, called "How to Make Our Ideas Clear," Peirce develops what is best described as a theory of meaning. In this paper, Peirce argues that there are three different grades of clearness that our ideas can obtain. Peirce's conception of meaning follows directly from the doubt–belief theory of inquiry he developed in "The Fixation of Belief." If the sole purpose of inquiry is to establish belief, and if belief is a habit or a disposition to act, then the meaning of a word, sentence, or road sign must naturally be understood in terms of the habits connected with it; that is to say, in terms of how it leads us to act. I know what words like "chair" or "cauliflower" mean when I associate with them certain reasonably well-defined habitual responses or attitudes. Peirce goes even further. For him, those responses or attitudes actually determine what those words mean—they constitute their *entire* meaning. Nothing else is required, such as an intuition of chairness or cauliflowerhood. As Peirce puts it concisely, "What a thing means is simply what habits it involves" (EP1:131).

The first and lowest grade of clearness Peirce distinguishes is obtained when an idea is "so apprehended that it will be recognized wherever it is met with, and so that no other will be mistaken for it" (EP1:124). Our idea of "chair" is of this kind. We recognize a chair the moment we see one. Similarly, a pawnbroker, who instantly recognizes whether a piece of jewelry is made of gold, has a clear idea of gold. Of course, the pawnbroker could be mistaken and call something gold when it is not. To know what a word means does not entail that one is infallible when applying it. All that is required for this first grade of clearness is a certain familiarity. Though it is primarily a sensuous clearness (R254:6), it need not be narrowly empirical. One can obtain a clear idea of unicorns, electrons, or God by becoming familiar with how these concepts feature in our language and culture.

For many of our conceptions, the clearness with which we apprehend them does not go beyond this first level. In Peirce's view, however, this first grade of clearness cannot act as a *criterion* of meaning. We may know what chairs are, but we will be hard pressed to come up with any solid criteria that would enable us to explicitly identify certain objects as chairs. All we get with this first grade of clearness, Peirce argues, is "a subjective feeling of mastery," and one that "may be entirely mistaken" (EP1:125).

The second grade of clearness is obtained when the idea does not merely seem clear at the outset, as with the first method, but can also be demarcated with enough precision to sustain the test of dialectical examination, meaning that subsequent discussions will not bring to light any points of obscurity connected with it (EP1:125). This second grade of clearness is traditionally obtained by developing abstract criteria that unambiguously determine what falls under the conception and what does not. The scientific definition of gold is an example of an idea that has reached this second grade of clearness. On this definition, gold is defined as the element that has atomic number 79, meaning that it has exactly 79 protons in its nucleus. This definition is taken to uniquely determine gold, as no other element has this atomic number. Peirce's second grade of clearness comes close to the traditional notion of clear and distinct ideas that is found with Descartes, Leibniz, and others.[7]

This second grade of clearness often builds on the first. Talking about gold in terms of its atomic number is in essence an attempt to speak in more precise terms about the stuff the pawnbroker calls gold. But it does not always work this way. Sometimes we come to know something first through abstract definition. For instance, when Dmitry Mendeleyev published his periodic table, it defined several elements in terms of their atomic number that were only later found to exist.

A key problem with framing definitions like the one that identifies gold with its atomic number is that it does not really give us a reason for why *that* criterion should be used and no other for determining whether the pawnbroker has it right or wrong. Why is it the atomic number that binds all our uses of the word together? This becomes even more problematic when we abstract definitions from our experience for such things as justice, race, gender, or democracy. To put it more generally, a problem with framing definitions this way is that, though they may be formally precise, they come at the cost of becoming disconnected from lived experience. With his third grade of clearness, Peirce aims to accommodate for this by returning to the world of experience while trying to retain the precision gained at the second grade. It is here that Peirce introduces what becomes later known as the pragmatic maxim:

> Consider what effects, that might conceivably have practical bearings, we conceive the object of our conception to have. Then, our conception of these effects is the whole of our conception of the object.
>
> (EP1:132)

Unless the maxim proves a conception vacuous, applying it to the second grade of clearness gives us what Peirce calls a *pragmatistic definition*, which he defines as, "a definition by means of characters that might conceivably influence rational conduct" (R1170). We will return to this in Chapter 6, when we discuss Peirce's later philosophy. For the moment, it suffices to say that pragmatism, for Peirce, is a method for ascertaining the meaning of concepts, ideas, beliefs, claims, propositions, etc.—that is, of anything that can act as a sign. Peirce maintains this view his entire life. As he explains it to the audience of his 1903 Harvard Lectures on Pragmatism: "One of the faults that I think [the new pragmatists] might find with me is that I make pragmatism to be a mere maxim of logic instead of a sublime principle of speculative philosophy" (EP2:134). In the end pragmatism, Peirce explains, boils down to the ability to say, "here is a definition and it does not differ at all from your confusedly apprehended conception because there is no *practical* difference" (EP2:141).

As with the four ways of fixing belief, Peirce holds that pursuing the third grade of clearness is not always the best option. There are situations where the first or second suffices or may even be preferable. To be a successful pawnbroker, you do not need a pragmatic definition of gold. Other philosophers have argued that something like the first grade of clearness is best suited for certain basic philosophical concepts. G.E. Moore, for instance holds that goodness is a primitive and that any explanation of what it means is doomed to fall short;[8] Donald Davidson holds a similar view with respect to truth.[9] This suggests that in their view, in contrast to Peirce, the highest grade of clearness for terms such as good and true is the first grade, not the third.

2.5 Applications of the Pragmatic Maxim

Immediately after introducing the pragmatic maxim, Peirce seeks to further explicate the maxim by applying it to several concepts. One of them is the concept of weight. "To say that a body is heavy," Peirce writes, "means simply that, in the absence of opposing force, it will fall," adding that this is "evidently the whole conception of weight" (EP1:133). Similarly, when the physicist speaks of "natural force," what is meant "is completely involved in its effects" (ibid). Applying the pragmatic maxim to scientific concepts such as weight and force, Peirce argues, results in more well-defined conceptions than we would otherwise have.

Not all concepts come out so well. The notion of transubstantiation—the change of bread and wine into the body and blood of Christ during the Eucharist—fails the pragmatic test. According to Catholic dogma, the bread and wine literally change into the body and blood of Christ, but they do so without changing any of their perceptible qualities: they still look, taste, and smell like ordinary bread and wine.

It is quite easy to obtain an idea of transubstantiation at the second grade of clearness, as it fits in very well with the classic substance-attribute view. On this view, the object, or substance, is distinguished from its qualities, or attributes. This distinction is made in part to allow for accidental change. For instance, when we say that "Socrates is bearded," "Socrates" is the substance, and "being bearded" is the attribute. Now, were Socrates to shave his beard, he would no longer be bearded, but he would still be Socrates.

The substance-attribute view has given us the widely accepted notion of transformation. What happens in a transformation, say from caterpillar to butterfly, is that the attributes change, while the substance—that which *has* the attributes—remains the same. The exact same animal that had the attributes of a caterpillar now has the attributes of a butterfly.

What happens in transubstantiation can easily be explained along the same lines. As opposed to a change of attributes that leaves the substance unaffected—as with the change from caterpillar to butterfly—transubstantiation involves a change of substance that leaves the attributes unaffected. This is precisely what Catholics claim happens to the bread and wine during the Eucharist. However, when we apply Peirce's pragmatic maxim to the concept of transubstantiation, the idea is immediately shown to be devoid of any meaning, because *by its very definition*, transubstantiation can have no conceivable practical bearings.

Peirce's criticism of transubstantiation is part of a deeper criticism based on the view, referred to earlier, that what is absolutely incognizable is absolutely inconceivable. This view does away with the philosophical notion of an incognizable substance (known only through its attributes) on which the idea of transubstantiation trades. The same argument can be used against the brain-in-a-vat hypothesis—the idea that we cannot be certain that we have hands, eyes, and feet, that there is sunlight and the sound of a schoolground in the distance, etc., because we may be only a brain in a vat connected to a large computer programmed to make us "see," "feel," and "hear" those things. Again, as the hypothesis is often phrased, it makes no conceivable practical difference whether we are a brain in a vat or a brain in a body sitting on a park bench, making the hypothesis meaningless.

Interestingly, William James reaches the exact opposite conclusion, arguing that transubstantiation does have practical effects and is thus pragmatically meaningful, even though the underlying philosophical concept of substance has none and must be dismissed as meaningless. However, there is an important difference between the views of Peirce and James: whereas Peirce is thinking of the practical consequences caused by *the belief being true*, James is thinking of the practical consequences of *the belief being believed to be true*. We return to this in the next chapter.

The application that raises most dust, however, is not the one on transubstantiation, but the one on the concept of hardness. What do we mean when we say that a diamond is hard?, Peirce asks, and he replies with confidence:

> Evidently that it will not be scratched by many other substances. The whole conception of this quality, as of every other, lies in its conceived effects. There is absolutely no difference between a hard thing and a soft thing so long as they are not brought to the test.
>
> (EP1:132)

In this passage Peirce not only reduces the meaning of "hardness" to the practical effects we associate with certain objects (for instance, that we cannot scratch them with a knife), but he reduces it still further by limiting it strictly to the *actual* effects experienced. Only when objects are *brought to the test*—for instance, by trying to scratch them with a knife—can we say that they are hard or soft, depending on whether the knife leaves a mark. As long as an object is *not* brought to the test, Peirce continues, we cannot truly say whether it is hard. For all we know, all untouched objects are soft, with some of them hardening under pressure, their hardness increasing with pressure exerted upon them until they are scratched. This causes Peirce to conclude "that the question *of what would occur* under circumstances which do not actually arise is not a question of fact, but only of the most perspicuous arrangement of [these facts]" (EP1:132; emphasis added). As we see later, the logical positivists run into similar problems with their verification principle (9.5).

It is worth noting that Peirce's view at this point *differs* from the one he held in the early 1870s, and to which he would later return. In one of his numerous attempts to write a logic book, Peirce concludes with respect to the hardness of a diamond:

> But though the hardness is entirely constituted by the fact of another stone rubbing against the diamond yet we do not conceive of it as beginning to be hard when the other stone is rubbed against it; on the contrary, we say that it is really hard the whole time, and has been hard since it began to be a diamond. And yet there was no fact, no event, nothing whatever, which made it different from any other thing which is not so hard, until the other stone was rubbed against it.
>
> (W3:30)

What happens in "How to Make Our Ideas Clear," however, is not a mere slip of the pen. Around that time Peirce comes to reject the view that is tacitly implied in his earlier account, namely that what *would* occur when certain circumstances were to take place is a real fact. Because of this, Peirce comes to reject the use of subjunctive and counterfactual conditionals when trying to clarify our ideas. A *subjunctive conditional* is a claim like the following: "Were I to fly to Rome, I would land in Italy." This statement is generally considered true, even if I never were to fly to Rome. What suffices is that the antecedent can be materialized—that we can make the antecedent true by taking a plane to Rome. With *counterfactual conditionals*—or counterfactuals for short—the situation is different. When I say, "Had I flown to Rome last fall, I would have landed in Italy," this claim also rings true. However, whereas with subjunctive conditionals the antecedent could be made true, with a counterfactual the antecedent cannot possibly be made true as it would no longer be a counterfactual. Furthermore, calling the *objects* of counterfactuals real facts seems especially problematic, as counterfactuals by their very nature *counter* the facts. Quite the opposite: it is a real fact that I did *not* fly to Rome last fall.

Accepting subjunctive conditionals allows us to say that certain objects that have not yet been brought to the test can still be called hard on the grounds that *if* they were to be brought to the test, then they *would* not get scratched. Allowing for counterfactual conditionals would even enable us to call something hard that has not been tested and can no longer be tested, say, because it no longer exists or because it has changed considerably in a way that is irreversible. Accepting counterfactual conditionals allows us to call certain objects hard on the grounds that *had* they been brought to the test, they *would not have been* scratched.

Peirce later comes to repudiate this radical dismissal of subjunctive and counterfactual conditionals. The step to remedy this, however, is by no means a small one. It involves the acceptance of real possibilities and real habits; or, as Peirce also puts it, of real can-bes and real would-bes. It may even involve the acceptance of certain real would-have-beens, real might-have-beens, etc. According to Peirce, the denial of real possibilities results from the erroneous view that the potential, or possible, "is nothing but what the actual makes it to be" (CP1.422). Peirce denies that possibilities can be thus reduced, remarking that "it is sheer insanity to deny the reality of the possibility of my raising my arm, even if, when the time comes, I do *not* raise it" (CP4.579).

Accepting that some possibilities are real, Peirce later comes to regard as indispensable for pragmatism. For this reason, Peirce holds that one can be a pragmatist only if one is also a realist, meaning one believes there is more to reality than existing individuals alone. We return to this in Chapter 6. It is important, though, to keep Peirce's later view in mind when examining the views of James and Schiller, as both reject this type of realism.

Pragmatism differs from empiricism proper, in that whereas the empiricist is content to rely on an individual's detached and disinterested observation, the pragmatist emphasizes the practical. The empiricist's reliance on observation makes it private and subjective, whereas the pragmatist's emphasis on practical consequences makes it both public and objective. Whether something is hard cannot be settled by whether it generates a certain publicly inaccessible mental state within a certain individual, but it can be determined only through certain practices, procedures, or rules that are accessible to the members of a community. Peirce further argues that it is hard to think of meaning as anything but practical:

> Man is so completely hemmed in by the bounds of his possible practical experience, his mind is so restricted to being the instrument to his needs, that he cannot, in the least, *mean* anything that transcends those limits.
>
> (CP5.536, c.1905)

In light of this, we can now say that the shift from the third to the fourth method of fixing belief, discussed earlier, also marks a shift toward pragmatism, as it is in terms of its practical consequences that this "something upon which our thinking has no effect," which fixes our belief, appears to us (EP1:120). Looked at this way, we can say that it is precisely Peirce's pragmatism that enables him to escape the instability that plagues the a priori method.

The application of the pragmatic maxim, however, is by no means confined only to scientific or religious concepts, such as hardness, weight, transubstantiation, and force. It should be applied equally to the most basic philosophical conceptions. The philosophical conception that Peirce picks as an example in "How to Make Our Ideas Clear" is that of reality. As it turns out, however, this conception is closely related to that of truth. Since the pragmatists' conception of truth comes to play a prominent role in the development of pragmatism, and still does, I will discuss Peirce's application of the pragmatic maxim to the concept of truth instead.

2.6 The Pragmatic Conception of Truth

As we saw in the previous sections, the pragmatic maxim is for Peirce a criterion of meaning, *not* a criterion of truth. Having said this, I should add that the maxim can and even should be applied to the notion of truth. Our conception of truth seems to have reached the second grade of clearness most prominently with Aristotle's famous definition: "To say of what is that it is not, or of what is not that it is, is false, while to say of what is that it is, and of what is not that it is not, is true."[10] Applying the pragmatic maxim to our notion of truth is what is often referred to as the pragmatic conception of truth. It is important, though, to realize that this new conception of truth does not stand all on its own, as if philosophy could be saved simply by furnishing it with a pragmatic conception of truth. The pragmatic maxim should be applied not just to the concept of truth, but to all core philosophical conceptions, such as identity, reality, equality, personhood, autonomy, necessity, freedom, etc.

In "How to Make Our Ideas Clear," Peirce does not directly apply the pragmatic maxim to the concept of truth. Instead, he applies it to the concept of reality, which is intimately connected with that of truth. About the relation between the two, Peirce writes later in response to a criticism by *Monist* editor Paul Carus, "My view is that the real is nothing but the immediate object in a true cognition"; it is that which a true cognition (whether it's an idea, belief, statement, etc.) is about (R958:205).

According to Peirce, our conceptions of truth and reality attain the first grade of clearness. We use both terms with perfect confidence, not doubting even for a moment that we know what they mean. According to Peirce, our concept of reality reaches the second grade of clearness with a definition that can be traced back to the medieval philosopher Johannes Duns Scotus, who introduced the term into philosophy. On Scotus's definition, something is real when it is independent of what you or I or anyone in particular thinks it to be. This definition furnishes a precise demarcation by delineating, clearly and unambiguously, the difference between reality and its opposite, fiction.

As we saw earlier, the third grade of clearness is obtained by applying the pragmatic maxim to the definition that constitutes the second grade, as the latter gives us the most precise rendition of the concept. If we apply the pragmatic maxim to Scotus's definition, our conception of reality becomes the conceivable practical bearings we conceive real objects (that is, those objects that are independent of what you or I or anyone in particular thinks them to be) to have. Now, the *only* effect such objects *can* have upon us, Peirce claims, is to produce belief. Therefore, *if* our conception of these effects is the whole of our conception of "real object," as the pragmatic maxim asserts it is, then the *belief* these real objects *can* effect upon us is our whole conception of those real objects (see W3.271f). To put it briefly, "reality" can mean nothing *other* than the object of permanently settled belief or opinion.

It is through inquiry that we seek to attain such permanently settled belief. In inquiry, we start from the beliefs we happen to have at the time. There is no Archimedean point or indubitable foundation to which we can first go. Consequently, we enter any inquiry, scientific or other, with all our biases and predispositions, many of which are products of the first three methods of fixing belief. Because of this, Peirce insists that science is an inherently social affair. The interaction with fellow inquirers is essential to filtering out the various idiosyncrasies that individual inquirers bring to the table—it allows us, as he puts it, "to grind off the arbitrary and the individualistic character of thought" (R969:3f). The solitary genius, so favored in popular culture, is to Peirce not a scientist at all. In fact, not even his observations count: "one man's experience is nothing if it stands alone. If he sees what others cannot see, we call it hallucination" (CP5.402n). Hence, in contrast to the first three methods for fixing belief, error plays a central role in science, as it is precisely when we are wrong that we are given the strongest evidence that there is a world out there that is independent of what we may think it to be, and with which we are somehow in immediate contact. Hence, error is to be encouraged rather than avoided. This too speaks to the idea that science is a communal enterprise, and one that should involve people with different backgrounds, inclinations, and talents, so that the greatest variety of angles is explored. Part of what is at play here are Peirce's conceptions of self and mind, which are decidedly anti-Cartesian. Peirce defines the private self not in terms of anything exquisite or divine, but in terms of error and ignorance. What makes us unique is that we differ from others in what we are ignorant and wrong about. Hence, for Peirce, inquiry—which seeks to alleviate this error and ignorance—rather than a process of self-assertion, is a process of self-effacement.

Returning to the claim that a cognition is true when its immediate object is real, the above derivation can be used to derive a pragmatic definition of truth, which is that truth is nothing more, and also nothing less, than permanently settled opinion. As Peirce put it in "How to Make Our Ideas Clear," "The opinion which is fated to be ultimately agreed to by all who investigate, is what we mean by the truth, and the object represented in this opinion is the real" (EP1:139).

The aforementioned account, however, should not be taken as the prediction of a future empirical fact—i.e., the reaching of a final agreement among those who investigate the matter—but as the claim that the terms "truth" and "final opinion" are in fact synonyms. On this view, to say that a proposition P is true means nothing other than that if P were inquired into long enough, this will eventually result in the settled belief that P. For example,

> The truth of the proposition that Caesar crossed the Rubicon consists in the fact that the further we push our archeological and other studies, the more strongly will that conclusion force itself on our minds forever—or would do so, if study were to go on forever.
>
> (CP5.565)

Similarly, to say that it is true that there was once life on Mars is to say that if that issue were to be inquired into long enough, those that inquired into it would come to agree on whether that claim is true.

Application of the pragmatic maxim to Peirce's conceptions of truth and reality gives the following pragmatic definition of truth when applied to propositions:

> Proposition P is true if and only if, if inquiry into P (by an indefinite community of inquirers) continues long enough, this inquiry will eventually result in a permanently settled belief that P (within an indefinite community of inquirers).

The underlying idea is that this ultimate belief is reached when all that can be inquired into is inquired into, so that no future inquiry can possibly reveal anything new of it. Therefore, the ultimate belief—or, as Peirce also phrased it, the final opinion—is a permanently settled belief. The phrase "permanently settled belief" refers in this context to a belief that no future inquiry can undermine; that is, no future inquiry can show it to be false or cast any doubt on it (other than temporary confusion). The locution "by an indefinite community of inquirers" is added to filter out any distorting elements that may result from the peculiarities that individual inquirers may carry with them, such as a propensity for conspiracy theories, a general distrust of mathematics, or a desire to interpret everything as part of the overall plan of an all-powerful and benevolent God.

The pragmatic conception of truth thus arrived at does not commit Peirce to maintain that there is one mammoth super story, "The Truth," which contains the last word on all there is to know about life, the universe, and everything. Peirce's aim is far more modest, as the following analogy of his makes clear:

> The fact that I try to get well of each given bodily malady I may suffer from, is no argument that I am cherishing any hope to escape from *every* malady that I may ever suffer from. So the fact that I try to find the truth in respect to each doubt that presents itself involves no assumption on my part that there is any real truth about *all* questions.
>
> (R787:11)

Peirce's conception of truth (as the final opinion) and of reality (as the object of this final opinion) received much criticism. It has been argued, for instance, that we will never reach such final opinion; that if we would, we would not know that we reached it; and that it does not adequately reflect what we generally mean with "truth."[11]

Objections that fall within the first category often hinge on what type of conditional is used. When Peirce published "How to Make Our Ideas Clear," he identified truth with the opinion that *will* be reached in the long run.[12] The problem with putting it this way is that it makes the truth of a statement today conditional upon a contingent future event that may never occur. What if the human race ceases to exist next year, bringing all inquiry abruptly to an end? Bertrand Russell even suggests, erroneously, that pragmatists commit themselves to the absurd view that the opinions held *at that point* would determine whether a statement that is made today is true or false, as it is there that inquiry comes to an end. A crucial part of the pragmatic definition is that it makes truth the natural outcome of an inquiry that is unrestricted both in scope and in time.

In agreement with the prior discussion of hardness, Peirce seeks to accommodate for this type of objections by shifting to the subjunctive mood, identifying truth with the opinion that *would* be reached if inquiry . . . etc. This circumvents the problem that contingent events (such as the annihilation of the human race), that are unrelated to the content of the statement in question, preclude us from ever reaching a final opinion about it, or that we have to count as true whatever is believed when inquiry comes to its premature demise. This is because the subjunctive mood does not require that such a point is ever reached, just as it did not require us to try to scratch the diamond in order to say that it is hard. It only requires us to maintain that reaching it is at least in principle possible.

Peirce touches upon these types of problems when he raises the so-called buried-secrets objection. What about the truth of facts that are long forgotten? It is surely conceivable that Cleopatra sneezed five times on her fifth birthday, making the claim that she did true on most accounts, including Aristotle's. At the same time, however, it is almost certain that if we were to begin investigating this issue today, we would never reach the permanently settled opinion that she did, as it is most likely (and if not likely, at least possible) that we will never have sufficient data to establish this fact beyond doubt. On Peirce's theory, on which the final opinion is the truth and its object reality, we would have to classify the claim that she sneezed five times that day as not true and the sneezes themselves as not real, even when as a matter of fact she did sneeze five times that day.

Peirce's shift to the subjunctive mood does not help us here, as what now precludes us from reaching a final opinion is not that inquiry came to an end prematurely, but that it lacked a timely beginning—we simply waited too long. But this again should have no bearing on the question whether a statement or belief is true. This suggests that for Peirce's pragmatic definition of truth to work, we need to seriously entertain the idea of putting it in terms of a counterfactual conditional. However, whereas a subjunctive conditional can at least be seen as representing a real possibility, this is not so for counterfactuals. Since the moment has passed for doing the inquiry needed to reach a final opinion, reaching that opinion is no longer a real possibility. In brief, for Peirce's theory of truth to work, he may have to commit himself to real counterfactuals as well.

Put in more general terms, Peirce's revisions with respect to the pragmatic conception of truth indicate a shift away from nominalism—the view that only actually existing individual things are real—toward a realism, which holds that reality encompasses more than what actually exists. We will see this tension between nominalism and realism recur when discussing the work of the various pragmatists.

To conclude, pragmatism originates as a new approach to philosophy that involves a radical rejection of the traditional Cartesian viewpoint and a more radical critique of pure reason than is found in Kant. This new approach centers on a method for determining, or fixing, the meaning of our conceptions that, when consistently applied, requires us to seriously rethink what philosophy is or can be. Hidden in old issues of *Popular Science Monthly*, it takes two full decades until William James, in a lecture called "Philosophical Conceptions and Practical Results," propels Peirce's view into the world. In the process, pragmatism does not remain unaffected, as James's take on it is in important ways different from Peirce's. It is to this that we turn next.

Notes

1. For a biography of Peirce, see Joseph Brent, *Peirce: A Life,* revised and enlarged edition (Bloomington, 1998); for an accessible introduction to Peirce, see Cornelis de Waal, *Peirce: A Guide for the Perplexed* (London, 2013).

2. A complete edition of the Illustrations series, including later revisions made by Peirce, is found in Charles Peirce, *The Illustrations of the Logic of Science by Charles S. Peirce* (Chicago, 2014).

3. René Descartes, *The Philosophical Writings of Descartes*, 3 vols. (Cambridge, 1984–91), 2, p.24.

4. This thesis is one of the axioms in Euclid's *Elements* (c.300 BC) and was refuted only in the nineteenth century by Georg Cantor.

5. *Mozert v. Hawkins County Public Schools*, United States Court of Appeals, Sixth Circuit.

6. Karl Popper, *Conjectures and Refutations* (London, 1972), pp.34–9.

7. René Descartes, *Principles of Philosophy*, Part 1, Art.45 (*The Philosophical Writings of Descartes*, op. cit., 1:207f); G.W. Leibniz, "Reflections on Knowledge, Truth, and Ideas," in Philip Wiener (ed), *Leibniz Selections* (New York, 1951), pp.283–90.

8. G.E. Moore, *Principia Ethica* (Cambridge, 1903), Ch.1, §10, ¶1.

9. Donald Davidson, *Subjective, Intersubjective, Objective* (Oxford, 2001), p.155.

10. Aristotle, *Metaphysics,* 1011b26.

11. For some of these criticisms, see e.g., Cornelis de Waal, "Eleven Challenges to the Pragmatic Theory of Truth," *Transactions of the Charles S. Peirce Society: A Quarterly Journal in American Philosophy* 35 (1999): 748–66.

12. It is worth noting that since Peirce's death, various editions of this paper have been published where "will" is silently emended into "would." Though this fairly represents Peirce's final intention, it is not what he originally published.

Chapter 3

William James
Pragmatism and the Will to Believe

William James (1842–1910) studies medicine at Harvard, after which he slowly drifts from physiology to psychology to philosophy. He makes a name for himself with his monumental two-volume *Principles of Psychology*, which appears in 1890, and which influences philosophers as diverse as Husserl and Wittgenstein. However, his philosophical interests date from much earlier. Like Peirce, James is a member of the Metaphysical Club, and he develops an alternative strand of pragmatism that is well beyond its infancy when he begins working on the *Psychology*, a book in which he draws a tight connection between mind and purpose-directed behavior. Especially early on, James's *Psychology* is often cited as a key text in pragmatism. Hence, it is to this that we turn first.

In the *Psychology*, James sets out to describe, as accurately as he can, mental phenomena as we actually encounter them, arguing that such a description is indispensable to doing psychology and, by extension, epistemology. This makes the *Psychology* essentially a work in phenomenology; more specifically, a study of consciousness as it is experienced from the first-person point of view. James's focus on phenomenology causes him to reject traditional philosophies that start with either mind or matter, replacing them with what he later calls a neutral monism. In what follows, I focus specifically on the issue of reality, a topic we will repeatedly come back to. A central theme of pragmatism revolves around the question of what we are left with when traditional notions such as truth and reality are no longer tenable. Traditionally, reality is seen as something that precedes our thoughts about it. We discover it, and when our thoughts faithfully represent or copy it, we say that what we think is true. James has a very different take on this.

James begins his discussion of reality by distinguishing what he imagines to be the experiences of a very young child with those of an adult. When the child sees "a lighted candle against a dark background, and nothing else," he observes, what the child sees "constitutes the entire universe known to the mind in question" (PP2:287). In this sort of situation, James argues, the child will think that the candle is real, because there is no possible ground for suspecting it to be otherwise; the candle is simply there. Now, if *we* were to respond and say that the child is hallucinating because there is no candle present, James continues, what we mean is something quite definite; we mean "that there is a world known to *us* which *is* real, and to which we perceive that the candle does not belong" (PP2:287f). But we can draw this conclusion only by observing that what the child sees conflicts with *other* beliefs that we have about the situation. This causes James to conclude that "Any object which remains uncontradicted is ipso facto believed and posited as absolute reality" (PP2:289). That is, so to speak, our default. We only depart from it when the object fails to fit in with other things that we also believe to be real. When that happens, we are forced to make a choice—we must either stick with the object or stick with those other things.

In its first encounter with the world, James writes, "the baby, assailed by eyes, ears, nose, skin, and entrails at once, feels it all as one great blooming, buzzing confusion" (PP1:488). Over time, this confusion becomes domesticated. James rejects, however, the assumption that there is only one (correct) way of doing this. And he sees our practice bearing this out. We commonly find ourselves residing, James observes, in multiple universes, each "a consistent system, with definite relations among its own parts" (PP2:292), often being at ease *even* when they conflict. Most of us, for instance, happily accept both the sensory and the scientific view of a table—the former a solidly filled object with continuous, colored surfaces, etc.; the latter a mostly empty region through which numerous, sparsely scattered electric charges traverse at great speed.[1] As James explains, each such world, "*whilst it is attended to* is real after its own fashion; only the reality lapses with the attention" (PP2:293). For James, we thus live in a different universe depending on whether we are dining out or doing physics. Or, more accurately put, as each such universe is self-contained, we live in a multiverse, confidently traveling between universes. Later, James calls our world a pluralistic universe.

Because "everything that can be thought of at all exists as *some* sort of object," James concludes that merely appearing as an object is not enough to constitute reality: "an object must not only appear, but it must appear both *interesting* and *important*" (PP2:295). In effect, this makes the subjective individual the origin of all reality. This is especially true for objects that relate to our will. James calls these our living realities:

> Reality, starting from our Ego, thus sheds itself from point to point—first, upon all objects which have an immediate sting of interest for our Ego in them, and next upon the objects most continuously related with these. It only fails when the connecting thread is lost. A whole system may be real, if it only hang to our Ego by one immediately *stinging* term. But what contradicts any such stinging term, even though it be another stinging term itself, is either not believed, or only believed after settlement of the dispute.
>
> (PP2:297)

To pass for true, such a system "must at least include the reality of the sensible objects in it, by explaining them as effects on us, if nothing more" (PP2:312). And if there are rivals, that system will generally be believed which "besides offering us objects able to account satisfactorily for our sensible experience, also offers those which are most interesting, those which appeal most urgently to our aesthetic, emotional, and active needs" (ibid). What happens, James argues, is that the individual agent

> looks at the object and consents to its existence, espouses it, and says "it shall be my reality" . . . The rest is done by nature, which in some cases *makes* the objects real which we think of in this matter, and in other cases does not.
>
> (PP2:320)

It makes them real by not confronting the individual with anything that contradicts them—and the more they excite us, the more real they will be. In brief, for James, the individual is a "fighter for ends" who sculpts her experience according to her interests (PP1:141). As we will see, this view closely aligns both with James's so-called will-to-believe argument and with his pragmatism.

3.1 Birth of the Term "Pragmatism"

James is the first to use the term "pragmatism" in print. He had used it in a lecture on August 26, 1898, at the Philosophical Union of Berkeley University. Shortly afterward, the lecture appears in *The University Chronicle* under the title "Philosophical Conceptions and Practical Results."[2] In this lecture, James tries to show his audience "the most likely direction in which to start upon the trail of truth"; he introduces the "principle of pragmatism" as his compass, and he explicitly attributes it to Peirce (WJ:347). In fact, the principle is nothing other than James's interpretation of the maxim that Peirce formulated earlier in "How to Make Our Ideas Clear." In the lecture, James paraphrases Peirce's maxim as follows:

> To attain perfect clearness in our thoughts of an object . . . we need only consider what effects of a conceivably practical kind the object may involve—what sensations we are to expect from it, and what reactions we must prepare. Our conception of these effects, then, is for us the whole of our conception of the object, so far as that conception has positive significance at all.
>
> (WJ:348)

James's rendition of the maxim differs in several respects from Peirce's 1878 original. Recall that the idea Peirce sought to convey with his maxim was that our conception of an object (its meaning, or the *idea* we have of it) cannot be anything other than the effects we conceive that object to have, adding that those effects must be such that they might conceivably have practical bearings (2.4).

In his restatement of Peirce's maxim, James widens the maxim by identifying our conception of an object with the effects that the object "may involve." However, objects of our conception often "involve" many effects that we would not consider to be part of our conception of those objects. For example, the act of snatching someone's purse may involve tripping and getting a bloody knee, but that does not make getting a bloody knee part of our *conception* of purse snatching. In brief, not all effects belong to the concept.

With respect to what he has in mind with these "effects," James's rendition of the maxim is more explicit than Peirce's original. For James, the effects are the sensations we are to expect and the reactions we must prepare. Here, too, there is a crucial difference with Peirce. Whereas Peirce aims to relate the meaning of an idea with the habits to which the idea gives rise (which are *generals*, not particulars), James relates the meaning of an idea strictly to *particulars*—namely, sensations and reactions. As shown in the previous chapter, this reading of the maxim agrees with Peirce's own reading in 1878, as was clear from Peirce's discussion of "hardness," but it does not agree with Peirce's later reading, in which he strongly rejects such an interpretation, dismissing it as nominalistic. Peirce rejects *nominalism*, the view that only particulars are real, in favor of *realism*—the view that some generals are also real. In fact, we can say that Peirce's realist interpretation of the pragmatic maxim marks a crucial difference between his pragmatism and James's.

In his treatment of the maxim, James also draws a closer connection with our practical lives than Peirce does. For James, the pragmatist is interested primarily in those effects that can be conceived to make a *practical* difference, rather than those that are of mere theoretical value. For this reason, James prefers to call Peirce's maxim the "principle of practicalism" rather than the "principle of pragmatism" (WJ:348).

The 1898 Berkeley Union address is not James's first reference to Peirce's maxim. He did refer to the maxim before, drawing similar conclusions. There is an explicit reference to Peirce's maxim in "Reflex Action and Theism" of 1881, which is reprinted in *The Will to Believe* (WTB:99), and in "The Function of Cognition" of 1885 (WJ:151). It is unlikely, though, that James's pragmatism is the product of him simply misinterpreting Peirce. James uses a principle similar to Peirce's in a paper that appeared in the very same month as "How to Make Our Ideas Clear." In this paper, "Quelques considérations sur la méthode subjective," which appeared only in French, James discusses what he calls the "subjective method." In this method, James's own brand of pragmatism is already clearly visible.[3] James writes, for instance,

> that every question is significant and is propounded with propriety, from which an obvious practical alternative results in such sort that accordingly as it be answered in the one way or the other, one, or the other line of conduct should be followed.
>
> (EPh:335)

Moreover, in the same paper, while reflecting upon two rival hypotheses on the nature of the universe, James calls the distinction between the two hypotheses a significant one, *precisely because* "it admits of conclusions so opposite in the conduct of life" (EPh:336).

Around this time, we also find James's first use of the phrase "the principle of pragmatism." In manuscript notes for his 1879 "The Sentiment of Rationality," James writes, "The general principle of pragmatism proves every thing by its result," and, a little later, "the principle of 'pragmatism' . . . allows all assumptions to be of identical value so long as they equally save the appearances" (EPh:352, 364). The term, however, does not make it into the published essay. In contrast, not a single instance of the term is found in Peirce's work until James's 1898 Berkeley address, neither in his published nor his unpublished writings.

James's early use of the term pragmatism, and the similarity of the approaches of Peirce and James in "How to Make Our Ideas Clear" and in "Quelques considérations sur la méthode subjective," cast doubt on the thesis, advocated most prominently by Ralph Barton Perry in *The Thought and Character of William James*, that "the modern movement known as pragmatism is largely the result of James's misunderstanding of Peirce."[4] It seems rather that by the time Peirce publishes his famous maxim, James's emphasis on conduct and practicalness is already firmly in place. In sum, James does not take Peirce's pragmatism for a ride; rather, their views represent two different strands of pragmatism that both find their origin in the discussions that took place within the Metaphysical Club in the early 1870s.

Before discussing James's pragmatism, however, some attention should be given to his 1896 "The Will to Believe." In the previous chapter, we saw that Peirce's "The Fixation of Belief" formed a prelude to his pragmatism. To a large extent the same is true for James's "The Will to Believe."

3.2 The Will to Believe

In his famous but often misunderstood "The Will to Believe," which is the opening essay of a book of the same title, James argues that in certain circumstances one has a right to believe something even when there is no sufficient evidence for its truth.[5] James is in part responding to the British mathematician William Kingdom Clifford, who, in an 1877 essay entitled "The Ethics of Belief," concluded that "it is wrong always, everywhere, and for anyone, to believe anything upon insufficient evidence."[6]

Clifford opens his essay with the example of a shipowner who manages to convince himself that an old ship that is about to sail is seaworthy:

> Doubts had been suggested to him that possibly she was not seaworthy. These doubts preyed upon his mind and made him unhappy; he thought that perhaps he ought to have her thoroughly overhauled and refitted, even though this should put him to great expense. Before the ship sailed, however, he succeeded in overcoming these melancholy reflections. . . . He would put his trust in Providence, which could hardly fail to protect all these unhappy families that were leaving their fatherland to seek for better times elsewhere. He would dismiss from his mind all ungenerous suspicions about the honesty of builders and contractors. In such ways he acquired a sincere and comfortable conviction that his vessel was thoroughly safe and seaworthy.[7]

The ship sinks, of course, mid-ocean. Clifford concludes that although the shipowner managed to make himself *genuinely believe* that the ship was safe, *he had no right* to believe this given the evidence he had before him.

It is unlikely that James would disagree with Clifford on this point. What James does disagree with is Clifford's extrapolation that this holds for all situations, i.e., that no one is ever allowed to believe anything on insufficient ground. According to James, in certain situations, one not only has the right to believe when there is no conclusive evidence, but it would even be wrong not to do so.[8]

James starts his argument with some technical distinctions. First, he reserves the term "hypothesis" for anything that may become an object of our belief. Such a hypothesis is either a living hypothesis or a dead one. The hypothesis that humans will someday land on Venus is for many a living hypothesis. In contrast, the hypothesis that centaurs once roamed the Greek countryside is for most of us a dead one. We do not consider it seriously or have any stake in it. Next, James calls the decision between two rival hypotheses an "option." Such options, he continues, are either living or dead, depending on whether the hypotheses one has to choose from are living hypotheses or not. In addition, options can be forced or avoidable, and they can be momentous or trivial. Momentous options are those that deeply affect one's life. Some of them will be once-in-a-lifetime affairs, whereas others, such as breaking one's professional career to go to graduate school, can be postponed. However, to postpone a choice (say, until one is absolutely certain it is the right one) is itself also a choice, and for a once-in-a-lifetime opportunity, it comes down to rejecting it. In a sense, momentous options are thus always forced. By insisting that some options are momentous, James shows that we cannot always simply suspend our belief until we are better informed, which is basically what Clifford asked us to do. For James, to suspend belief is also a choice, and that choice may very well not be the best one.

A living option which is both forced and momentous, James calls a genuine option. For genuine options that cannot be decided on intellectual grounds, James accepts that we may, or even must, make up our mind even when there is not enough evidence to support our choice. According to James, we must be willing to take the risk and be prepared to face the consequences. In the words of Fitz James Stephen, with which James concludes his essay,

> In all important transactions of life we have to take a leap in the dark. . . . Each must act as he thinks best; and if he is wrong, so much the worse for him. . . . If death ends all, we cannot meet death better.
>
> (WJ:735)

James explicitly *rejects*, however, and this part is often forgotten, that such leaps in the dark are permitted in science:

> But in our dealings with objective nature we obviously are recorders, not makers, of the truth; and decisions for the mere sake of deciding promptly and getting on to the next business would be wholly out of place.
>
> (WJ:728)

Such leaps are also not really needed in science, James continues, as the options faced by scientists are not genuine options (options that are living, forced, and momentous). What difference does it make whether dinosaurs were feathered, whether dark matter exists, or how many types of butterflies there are? Because the questions raised by scientists are generally trivial options involving hypotheses that are barely living, and for which the choice between believing their truth or falsehood is seldom forced, a disinterested quest into their truth is not only possible but even requisite.

Note that James appears to be advocating two different and independent arguments at this point. His first argument proceeds from the premise that science deals with "objective nature," and that in such matters we are "obviously" only the "recorders, not the makers, of truth," to the conclusion that "deciding promptly" is "wholly out of place." Put differently, for issues relating to objective nature, James concedes that Clifford is right, and relegating it to Peirce's "scientific method" would be the appropriate way of dealing with them.

James's second argument is based on the altogether different premise that scientific options are not truly genuine options. This raises the immediate objection that such a view leaves us at a complete loss when we are confronted with momentous issues, such as finding a vaccine for a new disease or ways of reducing global warming—certainly issues that fall within the domain of science. James seeks to avoid such objection by restricting the "freedom to believe" solely to genuine options *that cannot be resolved by the intellect*. The genuine options faced by scientists are, James continued, such that they can be resolved by the intellect, as it is precisely this aspect that allows them to be scientific problems to begin with. This response only goes so far. It does not really apply to cases that *could* eventually be resolved intellectually, but where immediate action is called for. Peirce sought to resolve the matter by distinguishing between the science of discovery and the practical sciences, relegating such things as finding a vaccine and reducing global warming to the latter. However, whether this distinction can be drawn so sharply is not clear.

James's strongest argument for why we should sometimes believe something even when there is insufficient evidence, is that some things become true precisely because we believe them. To illustrate his point, James gives the following example. Suppose that I am grappling with the question of whether you like me or not. Many times, James argues, the answer to this question will depend on what we believe that answer to be. If I am *willing* to believe that you must like me, then I am much more likely to be nice to you myself, thereby increasing the chance that you will indeed like me. In contrast, when I decide to wait until I have objective evidence that clearly points one way or the other, I am much more likely to cause your dislike by my aloof attitude. More in general, James observes, "The desire for a certain kind of truth here brings about that special truth's existence; and so it is in innumerable cases of other sorts" (WJ:730). Note that James is not implying here that evidence is irrelevant for determining the truth of such beliefs. We can be mistaken. What he rejects is that evidence should always precede the belief.

We may call this the argument of self-fulfilling prophecies. Not all living, momentous, and forced options, however, are self-fulfilling prophecies. In "The Will to Believe," James mentions three areas where genuine options are numerous, without taking the form of a self-fulfilling prophecy: law, morality, and religion. First, in a court of law, the options are often momentous, and it is generally imperative that decisions are made expediently. As James puts it somewhat uneasily, "Few cases are worth spending much time over: the great thing is to have them decided on any acceptable principle, and get them out of the way" (WJ:728). James holds a similar view on moral issues: "Moral questions immediately present themselves as questions whose solution cannot wait for sensible proof" (WJ:729). However, James's discussion of moral issues in "The Will to Believe" remains brief and unsatisfactory. He moves too soon to his argument from self-fulfilling prophecies and leaves it at that. James's discussion of the third area, religious faith, is more thorough. He begins by reaffirming that he will limit his discussion specifically to genuine options. Hence, he does not concern himself with dusty dogmas or with metaphysical proofs for the existence of God that are so complicated and removed from life that they are of no use to anyone. Any affirmation of faith must be part of an option that is at once living, momentous, and forced.

After discussing the various scenarios, James cuts short the skeptic by arguing that skepticism is only the expression of a certain conservative epistemic temperament, namely that it is always better to risk a loss of truth than to chance an error (WJ:732). The issue is thus not one of the intellect against the passions, but of one passion against another. For James, the religious believer is simply more adventuresome than the skeptic.

James continues his argument with a variant on Pascal's wager. In the *Pensées*, Pascal argued that it is better to accept what Scripture tells us because it is our best bet.[9] A belief in the Scripture carries the promise of an infinite gain (to be included in the Kingdom of Heaven) at only a minimal cost (going to church and saying our prayers). Hence, should we be mistaken, the worst that can happen to us is that we have wasted some of our time. On the other hand, if we refuse to believe what Scripture tells us, we get only minimal gains (we would not have to go to church) while running the risk of eternal damnation. Pascal directed his wager against the skeptic who would not be convinced otherwise. The wager aimed, moreover, to provide a *rational* argument for why the skeptic should accept what Scripture says. Genuine belief would come later, Pascal envisioned, as the natural outcome of practicing the religion.

Pascal's argument fails, James argues, because the option he presents is not a live option to those he is addressing. It is unlikely to convince the staunch skeptic, and it is even less likely to convince a Hindu or a Buddhist. However, James continues, if the option is a truly genuine one—one that is forced, living, and momentous—Pascal's argument would work. The skeptic "who should shut himself up in snarling logicality and try to make the gods extort his recognition willy-nilly, or not get it at all," James argues, "might cut himself off forever from his only opportunity of making the gods' acquaintance" (WJ:733).

In his discussion of Pascal's wager, James puts a creative spin on the self-fulfilling prophecy argument that he used before. Instead of the belief contributing to its truth, as with the self-fulfilling prophecy, here the belief contributes to the future well-being of the believer: one is better off when one believes it to be true. Being better off by holding a belief, James considered sufficient ground for believing it, even when there is no sufficient evidence for doing so. James goes even further and argues that it would be absurd to force someone who shows a strong will to believe to assume the skeptic's temperament. It is important, though, to keep in mind the restrictions that James has put on his argument. The freedom to believe is far from absolute. It concerns only genuine options, and of these it may concern only those "which the intellect of the individual cannot by itself resolve" (WJ:734).

James's doctrine of the will to believe aligns neatly with his *Psychology*. Recall that James calls an object real when it excites us and does not conflict with other objects that also excite us. In the case of a conflict, we essentially face a genuine option. This option may not always be all that momentous, but it does constitute a situation that cannot be resolved on purely intellectual grounds. Moreover, once we have made our choice, and act upon it, it is we who will reap or pay the consequences—evidently not everything that "excites" us is good (like burning your finger). In fact, what James is thinking of is essentially the biological notion that certain stimuli occasion a response whereas others do not—something that can be extrapolated, for instance, from his discussion of melancholy (PP2:298). The *Psychology* also explains James's penchant for having the will to believe settle grand metaphysical disputes, like that between idealism and materialism—two competing ways of extracting a reality from the phenomena we encounter.

In all of this, the individual remains front and center. This because James relates beliefs directly to the individual's motives for holding them. This is true both for the will-to-believe argument and the *Psychology*. In this sense, James differs from Peirce, who holds that knowledge and belief are rather communal affairs. This is evident from Peirce's claim that other people's testimony can be "a stronger mark of fact than *the facts themselves*, or rather than what must now be thought of as the *appearances* themselves"—and he gives the example of a mother warning her child that the stove is hot, even though it does not seem so to the child (EP1:19f). Peirce draws from this the radical conclusion that what defines the self, what makes each of us unique, is our errors and our ignorance—the idiosyncrasies that are to be filtered out within inquiry (2.6). Knowledge belongs not to the individual, but to the community. Such a social theory of knowledge, however, had little appeal to the individualistic James.

3.3 The Principle of Pragmatism

As noted, the central purpose of James's 1898 Pragmatism lecture is to lead his audience upon the "trail of truth," using Peirce's principle as its compass. In his explanation of Peirce's principle, James acknowledges that Peirce considers it a method for determining the meaning of our thought but feels that the principle "should be expressed more broadly than Mr. Peirce expresses it." James then continues by giving his own version of Peirce's principle:

> The ultimate test for us of what a truth means is indeed *the conduct it dictates or inspires*. But it inspires that conduct because it first foretells some *particular* turn to our *experience* which shall call for us just that conduct for us.
>
> (WJ:348; emphasis added)

James departs from Peirce at several points, and for the purpose of comparison, it may be helpful to repeat Peirce's original maxim:

> Consider what effects, that might conceivably have practical bearings, we conceive the object of our conception to have. Then, our conception of these effects is the whole of our conception of the object.
>
> (EP1:132)

To begin, we should note that James replaces Peirce's "object of our conception" with "truth"—a term James seems to use as an equivalent to "thought" and "philosophical proposition." The result, as we will discover, becomes a rather volatile mixture of truth and meaning.

James next restricts Peirce's maxim in at least two ways. First, he explicitly confines the meaning of a thought, truth, or philosophical proposition to its *particular* effects. This is James's nominalist interpretation of pragmatism, mentioned earlier. James is fully aware of his nominalism and thinks it a good thing. The requirement that meaning is related to particular experiences, James sees as an important safeguard for avoiding the abuses of the old metaphysicians. The second restriction is James's demand that these particular effects be experiential. There is no such demand in Peirce's original maxim, and Peirce later repeatedly emphasizes that what he had in mind was the establishment of habits, and habits are very different from particular experiential effects.

At the same time, James radically broadens the maxim. For James, the effects in question are not, as with Peirce, related to the *object* of our conception, but to the *individual* who believes that a thought or proposition is true. As James explains, "The whole function of philosophy ought to be to find out what definite difference it will make to you and me, at definite instants of our life, if this world-formula or that world-formula be the one which is true" (WJ:349).

Take, for instance, the notion of transubstantiation discussed in Chapter 2. There, we saw that Peirce's maxim revealed it to be meaningless because there are no conceivable practical differences between ordinary bread and wine, and bread and wine that have been transubstantiated into the body and blood of Christ. James's conclusion is the exact opposite. He agrees with Peirce that the scholastic notion of substance, on which the notion of transubstantiation trades, is void, writing that, "few things would seem to have fewer pragmatic consequences for us than substances, cut off as we are from every contact with them" (WJ:391). But he immediately proceeds by saying that it is precisely in the mystery of the Eucharist that this otherwise useless notion comes to life. Within the Eucharist, James contends, the notion of substance accrues "momentous pragmatic value." Granted, it does not have such a value for everyone, but it does have it for those to whom Christ is a live option. Transubstantiation, James adds, "will only be treated seriously by those who already believe in the 'real presence' on independent grounds" (WJ:392).

Thus, for James, the "pragmatic value" of the notion of transubstantiation is not, as with Peirce, a function of the conceivable practical consequences related to the process of transubstantiation itself, but of the practical consequences that belief in it has for the person that believes it. If the belief that transubstantiation occurs during the Eucharist has practical consequences for the believer, then that belief has pragmatic value. In this manner, James ties in his pragmatism with the course he set out earlier in the *Psychology* and in "The Will to Believe."

It is important to realize, however, that James reaches his contrary conclusion not because he rejects Peirce's argument, but because he gives a different interpretation to the maxim and how it should be applied. Peirce argues that we should use only terms, etc., whose meaning can be cast entirely in terms of conceivable practical consequences. Thus, for Peirce, "hardness" is meaningful precisely because we can say that an object is hard when it will not be scratched by a knife edge. For Peirce, no such conceivable practical consequences can be connected with "transubstantiation," which is therefore to be rejected as meaningless. For James, a philosophical proposition or theory is pragmatically meaningful if it has conceivable practical consequences *in the lives of those who believe in it*. Many propositions that are meaningless on Peirce's maxim will make a difference in some people's lives, making those propositions meaningful to them. For James, "The effective meaning of any philosophical proposition can always be brought down *to some particular consequence, in our future practical experience*, whether active or passive" (WJ:349; emphasis added). Thus, instead of making the meaning of a concept depend on the conceivable practical consequences we conceive that concept to have, which is what Peirce argues for, James makes the meaning of a concept (or a philosophical proposition, as James calls it here) depend on "some particular consequence in our future practical experience." This is indeed much broader than what Peirce intended the principle to convey.

3.4 Applications of the Principle

Like Peirce, James too gives several examples to illustrate how the principle works. James's examples, however, are of a grander scale than Peirce's, as he illustrates his version of the principle by evaluating entire metaphysical systems. James's first example concerns the choice between materialism and theism as alternative and incompatible hypotheses on the origin and nature of the universe. Should we believe that the universe is a chance product of the random motion of bits of matter (materialism), or should we believe that the universe is created by a god (theism)?

James rejects that a purely retrospective approach can settle the issue. With such an approach, one would examine which of the two hypotheses would best account for the world as it currently is. Were the two alternatives to be thus examined, James argues, the choice would cease to be a live option. As James puts it,

> If no future detail of experience or conduct is to be deducted from our hypothesis, the debate between materialism and theism becomes quite idle and insignificant. Matter and God in that event *mean exactly the same thing*—the power, namely, neither more nor less, that can make just this mixed, imperfect, yet uncompleted world.
>
> (WJ:351; emphasis added)

In other words, when the examination is purely retrospective, then there will be no *practical* difference between the two; there is only a nominal difference—that is, a difference in name only. What matters for James is not how these rival hypotheses explain the past, but how they direct us to the future. We live in a universe that is still evolving, James argues, and in the face of such an unfinished universe, the choice between materialism and theism becomes, as he puts it, an "intensely practical" one because both alternatives give us a radically different outlook on life (WJ:352). As for the materialist outlook, James quotes a rather somber passage from James Balfour:

> The energies of our system will decay, the glory of the sun will be dimmed, and the earth, tideless and inert, will no longer tolerate the race which has for a moment disturbed its solitude. Man will go down into the pit, and all his thoughts will perish.[10]

Compared to this dismal prospect, theism has what James calls a "practical superiority"; it "guarantees an ideal order that shall be permanently preserved." As he explains,

> A world with a God in it to say the last word, may indeed burn up or freeze, but we then think of Him as still mindful of the old ideals and

sure to bring them elsewhere to fruition; so that, where He is, tragedy is only provisional and partial, and shipwreck and dissolution not the absolutely final things.

(WJ:354)

Thus, where materialism would cut off all ultimate hope, "theism means the affirmation of an eternal moral order and the letting loose of hope" (ibid). In doing so, theism can make the world a much more hospitable place for those to whom it is a living hypothesis. Consequently, James argues, they have a right to believe that it is true even in the absence of any evidence that favors this option to the materialist one. This aligns with James's phenomenology, with which we opened the chapter. As with the child's candle, we can hold it to be real *as long as* it does not conflict with anything else that we find also important (or even more so). Recall that James wrote that,

> A whole system may be real, if it only hang to our Ego by one imme-diately *stinging* term. But what contradicts any such stinging term, even though it be another stinging term itself, is either not believed, or only believed after settlement of the dispute.
>
> (PP2:297)

In this manner James uses the principle of pragmatism to transform a rather abstruse metaphysical dispute between dogmatic theologians and transcendent materialists into a genuine option. In doing so he secures for us, in accordance with the argument he presented in "The Will to Believe," the right to believe in theism even though there is no sufficient evidence that the universe is the product of a god. Having obtained that right, it is then up to us to gather the willpower to believe it.

Later, in his 1906–7 Lowell lectures, James adds a few examples, includ-ing the question of whether the universe is designed, and the long-standing controversy between determinism and free will. Physics, with its insistence that every event must have a sufficient cause, generally sides with the deter-minist; whereas ethics, with its insistence on accountability, tends to hold that we have a free will. Pragmatism, James argues, not only points us to the free-will alternative, but also tells us how to interpret it. This leads to James's doctrine of *meliorism*, in which the doctrine of free will is developed into a general cosmological theory that allows for novelty and improvement in the universe. This doctrine has pragmatic value, because we are seeking to position ourselves within an imperfect world.

3.5 Rationalism, Empiricism, Pragmatism

James's *Pragmatism* appears in 1907, well after Peirce's 1903 Harvard Lectures on pragmatism (which James not only attended but also helped organize) and Peirce's 1905–6 *Monist* papers on pragmatism. We return to both in Chapter 6. In contrast to James's earlier book, *The Will to Believe*, which he dedicated to Peirce, *Pragmatism* is dedicated to someone Peirce is most critical of, the late John Stuart Mill. Moreover, when positioning himself within the pragmatic tradition, James no longer seeks the company of Peirce, but rather that of Schiller, Papini, and Dewey.[11]

In *Pragmatism*, James develops his own views largely as a criticism of what he considers the two dominant tendencies within philosophy: rationalism and empiricism. James sees this opposition foremost as a clash of temperaments, which he calls the tough-minded and the tender-minded.

James's criticism of the rationalists is most severe, accusing them of escapism. Rationalists, he argues, create a beautiful and self-contained system and then fall in love with it, turning their backs to the world we encounter in experience, and which this system is supposed to represent. In their carefully designed systems there is no room for the messy and gritty details, the cruelties, the unfinishedness, and the bewildering surprises of the world of experience. Still prevalent in James's own days, the rationalist attitude goes at least back to ancient Greece. It can be detected in Plato, who, insisting that the object of true knowledge must be unchanging, denied that it can be known through the senses. For Plato, the horses we see compete in the Kentucky Derby are but imperfect imitations, or shadows, of the ideal horse—a horse that is never felt, heard, or seen, but that is somehow grasped intellectually.

The empiricists, in turn, do take experience seriously and explicitly seek to develop their system of thought from it. But for James, the empiricists do not go far enough. They often cling dogmatically to materialism, causing them to offhandedly dismiss everything that cannot be accounted for in terms of senseless matter. Most significantly, for James, this includes all religious beliefs. In a letter to his former student Arthur Lovejoy, James explains that he had written *Pragmatism* "to make air and room for an empirical philosophy that might not necessarily be irreligious, to breathe in."[12] Briefly put, James faults empiricism for failing to sufficiently free itself from rationalist influences.

To these traditional forms of empiricism, James contrasts his own brand, an outgrowth of the position he developed in the *Psychology*, which he calls "radical empiricism." James's empiricism is radical in that it does not take anything for granted, but only accepts the experienced, finite facts as given. James even leaves open the question of whether those facts all belong to a single universe. *Pragmatism* comes close to this radical empiricism, although James stops short of equating the two. He does so largely because he wants to keep open the possibility of being a pragmatist without being a radical empiricist.

For James, pragmatism continues to be primarily a method for choosing between rival hypotheses, and the arguments he presents in his 1906–7 Lowell lectures are largely the same as those he gave in his 1898 Berkeley address. But it is more than just a method. It is the expression of a philosophical temperament—a way of looking at the world and our place within it.

In part, James is envisioning a change of temperament as to what is important in philosophy. The old enterprise of making our thoughts somehow mimic reality, James considers misguided. In *The Meaning of Truth*, he phrases the issue succinctly by asking the following question: "Why may not thought's mission be to increase and elevate, rather than simply to imitate and reduplicate, existence?" (MT:50). The result is a radical reinterpretation of the notion of truth.

Especially in the sixth lecture of *Pragmatism*, James develops a pragmatic conception of truth.[13] He does so, as Peirce before him, by applying the principle of pragmatism to the existing notion of truth. Although there are strong similarities between James's and Peirce's understandings of the notion of truth, there are also important differences. James begins by accepting the traditional dictionary definition of truth, on which an idea, belief, or statement is true when it agrees with reality and false when it disagrees with reality. The point where pragmatists, in James's view, depart from the rationalist and the empiricist is in their interpretation of this notion of agreement. To both the rationalists and the empiricists, James ascribes a notion of agreement on which our thoughts, etc., agree with reality when they are faithful copies of reality. In short, James first attributes to them a copy theory of knowledge (or a correspondence theory of truth) and then continues by arguing that such a copy theory of knowledge is far too restrictive.

Close to the beginning of the lecture, James draws a distinction between those ideas or beliefs that can copy their object in thought and those that cannot—a distinction that returns in his preface to *The Meaning of Truth*. In the next section we look at James's conception of truth for those ideas that can copy their object, where we will see that he is in effect arguing for a wider notion of agreement. The section thereafter is devoted to James's discussion of ideas that cannot copy their object.

3.6 Truth as Agreement With Reality

According to James, the rationalist proceeds from the set opinion that there is a fixed reality that is "complete and ready-made from all eternity" (WJ:439). This conception of reality then becomes the basis for the rationalist's conception of truth. The rationalist, James argues, sees truth as the full and correct representation in thought of this ready-made and eternal reality. Science was long looked upon as an attempt to obtain such a true description of the world. Galileo, for instance, famously held that God had written the "great book of nature" in the language of mathematics. Consequently, a scientific treatise, like a treatise in celestial mechanics, can be seen as copying certain passages from this "book of nature," using the very same language in which God had written the heavens themselves. In using the language of mathematics, the heavenly phenomena are grasped intellectually, rather than just perceiving them through the senses.

A similar stance was taken by the empiricists. For instance, the early members of the Royal Society, whose practices Locke sought to justify in his *Essay Concerning Human Understanding*, came to reject scientific speculation, and limited scientific inquiry strictly to presenting what they called natural histories—detailed descriptions of groups of phenomena that ideally would be entirely devoid of any thoughts on how these phenomena had come to be, what they are for, etc.

By the nineteenth century, however, scientists have come to reject this notion of science as a correct description of reality, moving to a more instrumental conception of scientific theories. As James observes, they have come to the position that "no theory is absolutely a transcript of reality, but that any one of them may from some point of view be useful. . . . They are only man-made language, a conceptual shorthand, as some one calls them, in which we write our reports of nature" (WJ:381).

The downfall of Euclidean geometry—the mathematical language Galileo had ascribed to God—as the obvious and true language for describing physical space relations, surely contributed to this change in attitude. Naturally, we can still employ Euclidean geometry in physics and astronomy, but we must no longer consider this an attempt to give a true description of reality (say, a true description of the orbit of the planet Mars), but as a tool by which we can handle certain facts in thought. James writes, "You must bring out of each word its practical cash-value, set it at work within the stream of your experience. . . . *Theories thus become instruments, not answers to enigmas, in which we can rest*" (WJ:380).

If scientific theories are tools rather than efforts to describe reality, the copy theory of knowledge is no longer tenable as a full-fledged theory of knowledge. Truth can no longer be seen as a detached reflection upon a ready-made world but is now related to action. As James puts it, "Ideas (which themselves are but part of our experience) become true just in so far as they help us to get into satisfactory relations with other parts of our experience" (WJ:382). We thus get an instrumental theory of truth. This instrumental theory of truth holds not only for abstruse scientific topics that remain far removed from our daily lives, but holds equally for the most commonsense ways in which we think about things. Basic conceptions, such as "space," "time," "cause," "mind," and "body," were once created by our remote ancestors as tools for dealing with concrete problems they faced. In James's words, "The common-sense categories . . . are but sublime tricks of human thought, our ways of escaping bewilderment in the midst of sensation's irremediable flow" (WJ:425).

Despite his adherence to an instrumental theory of truth, James does not give up on the notion that a belief, statement, or theory is true when it agrees with reality. What he does give up is the notion that the only way in which our thoughts can agree with reality is by making some sort of copy of this reality in thought:

> To copy a reality is, indeed, one very important way of agreeing with it, but it is far from being essential. The essential thing is the process of being guided. Any idea that helps us deal, whether practically or intellectually, with either the reality or its belongings, that doesn't entangle our progress in frustrations, that fits, in fact, and adapts our life to the reality's whole setting, will agree sufficiently to meet the requirement. It will hold true of that reality.
>
> (WJ:434f)

Hence, the crucial aspect of our thoughts or beliefs agreeing with reality is not that they *copy* reality, but that they lead us in the right way. As James put it,

> To "agree" in the widest sense with a reality *can only mean to be guided either straight up to it or into its surroundings, or to be put into such working touch with it as to handle either with it or something connected with it better than if we disagreed.*
>
> (WJ:434)

In short, James does not at all *deny* that there is a reality that is independent of our thought and with which we are forced to reckon. He fully acknowledges that there are things that are beyond our control, and that to the extent that we can control them, we can do so only on their terms, not on ours. We can surely enrich reality with a new suspension bridge, a skyscraper, or spacecraft, but we can do so only when we carefully observe the laws of nature. What James denies is that this reality is something that lies hidden behind our experiences, like the sort of reality he thinks Plato and Galileo believed in. For James, reality is the reality we experience. It is the "total push and pressure of the cosmos" that brought us to philosophize in the first place (WJ:362), and that sets the limits upon our thought: "the only real guarantee we have against licentious thinking is the circumpressure of experience itself" (MT:47). In a letter to Dickinson Miller, James adds the following simile to illustrate his view:

> The world *per se* may be likened to a cast of beans on a table. By themselves they spell nothing. An onlooker may grasp them as he likes. He may simply count them all and map them. He may select groups and name these capriciously, or name them to suit certain extrinsic purposes of his. Whatever he does, so long as he *takes account* of them, his account

is neither false nor irrelevant. If neither, why not call it true? It *fits* the beans-*minus*-him and expresses the *total* fact, of beans-*plus*-him.[14]

This aligns very well the phenomenological stance we encountered in the *Psychology*. As any simile, however, it only goes so far, and this may be worth pointing out. Though one could say that James is implying here that there is a deeper, true reality of finite objects (the beans), it is unlikely that this is what he aimed to convey.

A key element of James's theory of truth is that when we say that something is true, we just as much introduce a new fact into the world as when we erect a new bridge or knock over a glass of lemonade. Taken by themselves, facts are never true. It is only when we say something *about* them that truth and falsity come in. As James puts it, "The 'facts' themselves . . . are not *true*. They simply *are*. Truth is the function of the beliefs that start and terminate among them" (WJ:439). Truth is neither a property of certain ideas, nor a property of facts, but involves the *agreement* of our ideas with facts. Consequently, James argues, when we say that a certain fact is true, we have *added* something to that fact. As he puts it elsewhere,

> Truth we conceive to mean everywhere, not duplication, but addition; not the constructing of inner copies of already complete realities, but rather the collaborating with realities so as to bring about a clearer result.
>
> (MT:41)

In other words,

> On pragmatistic principles, if the hypothesis of God works satisfactorily in the widest sense of the word, it is true. Now whatever its residual difficulties may be, experience shows that it certainly does work, *and that the problem is to build it out and determine it so that it will combine satisfactorily with all the other working truths.*
>
> (WJ:471f; emphasis added)

We don't truly find God, we add him—we bring him into existence.

James fully acknowledges, though, that we cannot add just about anything. In fact, he is quite conservative, explaining that a "new truth" is always "a go-between, a smoother-over of transitions. It marries old opinion to new fact so as ever to show a minimum jolt, a maximum of continuity" (WJ:383). Scientific theories may be "man-made" systems, yet

> In the choice of these man-made formulas we can not be capricious with impunity any more than we can be capricious on the common-sense

practical level. We must find a theory that will work; and that means something extremely difficult; for our theory must mediate between all previous truths and certain new experiences. It must derange common sense and previous belief as little as possible, and it must lead to some sensible terminus or other that can be verified exactly. To "work" means both these things; *and the squeeze is so tight that there is little loose play for any hypothesis.*

(WJ:436; emphasis added)

In this process of smoothing-over, truth is fluid. New experiences lead to changes, often very minute, in the truths we already have. The result of this process is, as James explains, "the new equilibrium in which each step forward in the process of learning terminates" (WJ:419). In short, the old truths are not permanent, as the rationalists claim, but they change over time in the face of new experiences. Truths are temporary equilibriums in the process of learning. James's explicit acknowledgement that the squeeze is really tight has not precluded others from accusing him of epistemic licentiousness.

All of this raises the question of why James insists on calling them truths rather than beliefs. Nobody denies that our beliefs can change over time. We may, for instance, no longer believe that Julius Caesar crossed the Rubicon. But why imply that this means that whereas it used to be *true* that he crossed the Rubicon, it is now *false*? Intuitively, the *truth* of the belief that Caesar crossed the Rubicon seems to be determined, not by what we believe, but by whether he actually crossed the river. The same holds for nonempirical truths, such as whether in a Euclidean plane the angles of a triangle always add up to the sum of two right angles.

The answer to this question is related to James's radical empiricism. As noted earlier, James is critical of the metaphysical prejudices of the empiricists. One of these prejudices is that of a single, fixed reality that lies behind our experiences and precedes our beliefs about it, such as Locke's "the real Being, and Existence of Things."[15] In this view, our beliefs are true when they correspond to this reality. James contrasts this type of empiricism with what he called "pluralistic pragmatism," in which "truth grows up inside of all the finite experiences," where those experiences "lean on each other, but the whole of them, if such a whole there be, leans on nothing" (WJ:457). Such a "bundle theory of experiences" was also entertained by the classical empiricists, but they quickly abandoned it, causing them to relapse in old presuppositions about what hides behind the "veil of ideas."

In James's pluralistic pragmatism, the only meaning that can be given to a statement or belief being true is that it fits within our experience. In this manner, James's pragmatism leads to some sort of coherence theory of truth, albeit one that does not focus on the ivory-tower professor who in his brown study merely reflects upon human experiences, but one that focuses on the *acting* individual who is situated in the midst of a world of experience, where experience is to be interpreted broadly, and for whom true ideas are those that lead to successful action (the latter being cast again in terms of experience).

In short, James's notion of coherence is not a matter of looking backward and trying to fit together the pieces of a preexisting puzzle (like a jigsaw puzzle that has its solution already printed on it), but it is the fitting together of the pieces of a puzzle that is still in the making, that is evolving without any preconceived plan, and without the requirement that the puzzle is supposed to represent anything. Moreover, within this process we are to some degree in control of what the new pieces will look like, and, in contrast to traditional jigsaw puzzles, the new pieces may force changes upon what is already on the table.

In opposing the notion of an unchanging truth, James takes a stance against the fixedness of the rationalists' reality. James seeks to emphasize instead that the world we live in is in a profound way unfinished. With this, James does not mean to refer to the still-evolving cosmos, but that the world as we experience it in our daily lives is still a work in progress. Our future is an open future. More than merely reflecting upon reality, we are required to act in it—we are forced to help shape it. By taking this course, James moves toward a humanist view of reality "as something resisting, yet malleable, which controls our thinking as an energy that must be taken 'account' of incessantly (tho not necessarily merely *copied*)" (WJ:456f).

At the same time, James remains well aware that we have very little wiggle room and that many of our truths are pretty much fixed:

> Truth independent; *truth* that we find merely; truth no longer malleable to human need; truth incorrigible, in a word; such truth exists indeed superabundantly . . . but then it means only the dead heart of the living tree, and its being there means only that truth also has its paleontology.
> (WJ:384)

This fixedness, however, does not indicate that there must be an independent world out there, and that we have found the truth when our ideas adequately mirror this world, but it indicates that we are very entrenched within the world of our experiences, so that certain opinions invariably lead us to desired results.

James opposes not only the fixedness of truth, but also its singularity. For rationalists and empiricists, to whom truth is the perfect copy of reality in thought, there is just one truth. Presumably, there is only one way that our ideas can *copy* reality. In contrast, if agreement means that our beliefs "fit in," the requirement that there is only one truth quickly loses its force. Multiple, altogether different beliefs may equally fit in, especially since the universe is yet unfinished and malleable. As James explains, "Our account of truth is an account of truths in the plural, of processes of leading, realized *in rebus*, and having only this quality in common, that they *pay*" (WJ:436).

So far, we have concentrated mainly on ideas that can somehow copy their object, such as Socrates drinking the hemlock, the orbit of the planet Mars, Newton's law of gravity, etc., and we saw that, for James, the traditional notion of truth as the perfect copy of an independent and unchanging reality is misguided, and that we must broaden our notion of representation.

3.7 Taking Truth Further

For the empiricist James, not all our ideas can copy their object (WJ:430). The question then becomes whether any of those ideas could be true. To answer this question, we need to ask whether ideas that cannot copy an object can still agree with that object, and if so, what agreement means in such cases. The previous section has already done much of the footwork for answering this question. This led to the view that agreement must be understood more broadly than that of copying something. Ideas are true when they fit in.

Neither in the sixth lecture nor in the preface to *The Meaning of Truth*, where this is made a central issue, are there any clear examples of what sort of ideas James has in mind here. It is quite evident, though, that they are primarily moral and religious ideas. Moral ideas—expressing how things should be, for instance—may differ widely from how things are. However, when we see that a certain moral imperative fails to copy its object, we generally do not conclude that it must therefore be false. This point was expressed quite succinctly by John Locke about two centuries earlier. The moral rules Cicero laid out in *On Moral Obligation*, Locke observes, are not any less true, "because there is no Body in the World that exactly practices his Rules, and lives up to that pattern of a vertuous Man, which he has given us, and which existed no where, when he writ, but in *Idea*."[16]

With regard to ideas that cannot copy their object, James writes, "pragmatism asks its usual question. 'Grant an idea or belief to be true,' it says, 'what concrete difference will its being true make in any one's practical life?' . . . What, in short, is the truth's cash value?" (WJ:430). Put differently, ideas that cannot copy their object can still be true depending on what the consequences of believing it are for the believer. This notion leads James to his famous and often misinterpreted conclusion:

> "The true," to put it very briefly, is only the expedient in the way of our thinking, just as "the right" is only the expedient in the way of our behaving. Expedient in almost any fashion; and expedient in the long run and on the whole of course.
>
> (WJ:438)

James takes this to mean that "on pragmatic principles we can not reject any hypothesis if consequences useful to life flow from it" (WJ:461). Whatever works is true. For example, "if the hypothesis of God works satisfactorily in the widest sense of the word," then it will be a true hypothesis (WJ:471). James is quite aware of the skepticism this view is likely to encounter:

> I am well aware how odd it must seem to some of you to hear me say that an idea is "true" so long as to believe it is profitable to our lives. That it is *good*, for as much as it profits, you will gladly admit.
>
> (WJ:388)

At this point it is almost impossible to avoid seeing a close connection with James's earlier approach in "The Will to Believe." In that paper, James had argued that, under certain circumstances, one has the right to believe something even if there is no sufficient ground for doing so. Recall, however, that in "The Will to Believe," James was quite careful to specify under what sort of circumstances such a move is permissible. One is not entitled to believe just about anything that happens to be expedient, but James specifically restricts himself to only those situations where one is faced with a choice that is forced, living, and momentous, and that cannot be decided on intellectual grounds. In *The Meaning of Truth*, James makes a claim that is very similar to this by requiring that the truth satisfies "some vital human need" (MT:5). Recall, further, that in "The Will to Believe," James also presents moral and religious beliefs as prime examples where one would have such a right to believe. Critics point out that James slides here, perhaps unconsciously, from the view that one sometimes has a right to believe something because one is better off believing it to the view that such beliefs are actually *true*.

Right off the bat, there seems to be at least one situation where such a step is defensible. This is when we are dealing with self-fulfilling prophecies, where believing that something is true actually makes it true or contributes to making it true. As already noted, however, it is hard to defend that this can be maintained for all choices that are forced, living, and momentous, or that are to some degree or other expedient.

Continuing a line of thought begun in the previous section, it seems that expediency can be interpreted as one way of "fitting within reality," and should be treated like that. As James observed,

> If theological ideas prove to have a value for concrete life, they will be true, for pragmatism, in the sense of being good for so much. For how much more they are true, will depend entirely on their relations to the other truths that also have to be acknowledged.
>
> (WJ:387)

Restricting ourselves to those beliefs that cannot copy their object, this would make the *truth* of such beliefs dependent on whether the consequences of my believing it fit within reality. This agrees entirely with the general notion of truth James ascribes to the pragmatist, "as something essentially bound up with the way in which one moment in our experience may lead us toward other moments which it will be worth while to have been led to" (WJ:431f). To put it somewhat differently, beliefs that originate within ourselves, but that do not copy anything without us, will still count as true when they lead us in directions that are worthwhile. What this comes down to is a process of *veri*-fication, in which our beliefs *are made true* by the events to which they lead. James made much of the etymology of "verification." Just as we make something pure when we purify it, or liquid when we liquify it, so we make something true when we verify it (*veritas* being Latin for truth). Thus, if my believing in God leads to good consequences (on the whole and in the long run), then we can say that this belief agrees with reality, and consequently, it can be said to be true (as truth is an agreement of our beliefs with reality).

In his critical review of James, Bertrand Russell remarks that deciding whether we are better off accepting a belief rather than rejecting it is by no means easy. Take something like the doctrine of the Catholic faith, which comes with countless ramifications in many directions. It might, in fact, be easier to ascertain whether the doctrine is true. For instance, Russell contends, it is far simpler "to settle the plain question of fact, 'have Popes been always infallible?' than to settle the question whether the effects of thinking them infallible are on the whole good."[17]

With respect to this "veri-fication," James further insists that such beliefs must be consummated in particular experiences. True beliefs are beliefs that are veri-*fied*, not beliefs that are merely veri-*fiable*. Although James admits that truth lives "for the most part on a credit system," he immediately adds that "beliefs verified concretely by somebody are the posts of the whole superstructure" (WJ:433). We believe that there are tigers in India without bothering to *veri*-fy this ourselves, but it can be true only if someone or other has actually veri-fied it for us (i.e., made it true), or when it fits in with the rest of our (verified) beliefs. Recall that being true, for James, is neither a property of facts nor a property of beliefs, but a certain connection of beliefs to facts. In Chapter 9 we return to the verified/verifiable distinction in the context of logical positivism.

During the nineteenth century we see a growing realization that science, conceived broadly, can be used to shape society, and we see this confirmed in the development of new disciplines such as economics, anthropology, psychology, and sociology, as well as sociopolitical schools of thought like utilitarianism and Marxism. Old-school thinking had it that improvements to society should be preceded by and grounded in a truer description of the world. Its model is pretty much that of Newtonian physics, which, by giving us a better description of the world, enables us to develop such things as steam engines, skyscrapers, and industrial manufacturing. As many begin to realize, however, this approach is ill-suited for addressing the unprecedented rapid societal changes caused by the Industrial Revolution and the widespread social inequities that accompany it. To them, it seems that at the societal level, we are faced with genuine options, where decisions have to be made lest they are made for us—that even if there is a truth to be learned, that truth will come too late. Against Clifford, they argue that ships can also sink because we are suspending our belief. We return to this with Sorel in Chapter 5, with Dewey, Addams, and Bourne in Chapter 8, and later in Chapter 15 when discussing pragmatic feminism and the Afro-American experience. First, however, we direct our attention to the other pillar of the early reception of pragmatism, the British philosopher Ferdinand Schiller.

Notes

1. Sir Arthur Eddington, *The Nature of the Physical World* (Cambridge, 1928), Introduction.
2. Up until 1904, this text has only a limited circulation, and for many James's *Varieties of Religious Experience* (New York, 1902) is the first introduction into James's brand of pragmatism.
3. An English translation of this essay is found in EPh. The essays by James and Peirce are products of the discussions held earlier in the 1870s within the Metaphysical Club.
4. Ralph Perry, *The Thought and Character of William James*, 2 vols. (Boston, 1935), 2:409.
5. In 1905, James laments, "I once wrote an essay on our right to believe, which I unluckily called the Will to Believe" (WJ:457).
6. W.K. Clifford, *Lectures and Essays* (New York, 1901), p.175; first published in the *Contemporary Review* of January 1877, the same year Peirce's "The Fixation of Belief" appears. For a detailed discussion, see Scott Aikin, *Evidentialism and the Will to Believe* (London, 2014).
7. Clifford (1901), p.164f.
8. In "The Fixation of Belief," Peirce paid little attention to the moral aspects of belief, focusing instead on the different ways in which belief can be fixed. It is clear, however, that Clifford would find only Peirce's fourth method of fixing belief acceptable. As for Peirce, he would agree with James that this is too demanding.
9. Blaise Pascal, *Pensées* (London, 1910), §233.
10. WJ:353. The quotation is from Arthur James Balfour's, *The Foundations of Belief* (London, 1894). Fifteen years earlier, in *A Defense of Philosophic Doubt* (London, 1879), Balfour had already tried to show that scientific knowledge depends just as much on an act of faith as does theology.
11. In a March 26, 1907, letter to Théodore Flournoy, James explained that Papini and Schiller had given him "great confidence & courage. I shall dedicate my book, however, to the memory of J.S. Mill"; in Ignas Skrupskelis and Elizabeth Berkeley (eds), *The Correspondence of William James*, vol. 11 (Charlottesville, 2003), p.332.

12. Letter dated September 13, 1907; in Skrupskelis and Berkeley (2003), p.444.
13. On James's theory of truth see, e.g., Hilary Putnam's "James's Theory of Truth" (in Putnam, 1997) and Harvey Cormier's *The Truth Is What Works: William James, Pragmatism, and the Seed of Death* (Lanham, 2001).
14. Letter to Dickinson Miller, August 5, 1907; in Skrupskelis and Berkeley (2003), p.411.
15. John Locke, *Essay Concerning Human Understanding* (Oxford, 1975), II.xxx.1.
16. Ibid., IV.iv.8.
17. Bertrand Russell, *Philosophical Essays* (London, 1910), p.135.

Chapter 4

The Pragmatic Humanism of F.C.S. Schiller

Ferdinand Canning Scott Schiller (1864–1937) is pragmatism's early ambassador in England. His fierce opposition against the absolute idealism of the British Hegelians, no doubt stemming from his own student days, makes him the *enfant terrible* of the Oxford establishment. Schiller is born in the Danish part of Schleswig-Holstein. His father, a Calcutta merchant of German origin, sends his sons to school in England. Schiller attends Rugby School and continues his education at Balliol College, Oxford, which is heavily dominated by idealism. From 1893 until 1897, he lives in the United States, where he is an instructor in logic and metaphysics at another bastion of idealism, Cornell University. During that time, Schiller first comes into contact with James. In 1897, Schiller returns to England, where he joins Oxford's Corpus Christi College. Upon his retirement, in 1926, he spends part of the year at the University of Southern California, first as visiting lecturer and later as professor. In 1935, after marrying for the first time at the venerable age of 71, Schiller makes California his permanent home. He dies less than two years later.

Although Schiller is heavily influenced by James and frequently pays tribute to him, he maintains that he arrived at his own pragmatic stance independently. Indeed, the basic elements of his pragmatism are already present in his first book, *Riddles of the Sphinx*, which appears in 1891 under the pseudonym "a Troglodyte," or cave dweller (the reference is to Plato's famous allegory of the cave). In this book Schiller defends a non-skeptical relativism, arguing that knowledge is always a product of specific human interests. For Schiller, all thoughts and actions are unavoidably the product of individual human beings who are guided by human needs and desires, of which they cannot be abstracted. Schiller considers himself the modern version of Protagoras, the Sophist who proclaimed that "man is the measure of all things."[1] In the book Schiller further advocates for a position close to James's doctrine of the will to believe, writing,

> And in action especially we are often forced to act upon slight possibilities. Hence, if it can be shown that our solution is a possible answer, and

the only possible alternative to pessimism, to a complete despair of life, it would deserve acceptance, even though it were but a bare possibility.[2]

The applicability of this doctrine is significantly broadened when Schiller gets acquainted with James. Schiller's campaign for humanism—which is how he comes to call his own brand of pragmatism—begins with the 1902 essay "Axioms as Postulates," which contains a vigorous attack on the notion of a priori knowledge. It is followed by *Humanism*, in 1903, and *Studies in Humanism*, in 1907. The next year, Schiller publishes *Plato or Protagoras*, in which he examines Protagoras's speech in Plato's *Theaetetus*. In 1924, Schiller publishes *Problems in Belief* in which he traces the epistemological implications of different varieties of belief.

In logic, Schiller's first major contribution is his 1912 *Formal Logic: A Scientific and Social Problem*. In this polemical work, Schiller presents a humanist critique of traditional logic, arguing that the material of logic cannot be meaningfully abstracted from actual use and interest. Seventeen years later, in 1929, Schiller publishes a second book on logic, *Logic for Use: An Introduction to the Voluntarist Theory of Knowledge*, which is meant as a constructive sequel to *Formal Logic*.

Schiller also publishes three books on eugenics, the science that seeks to improve the genetic qualities of the human race through selective breeding: *Tantalus or the Future of Man* (1924), *Eugenics and Politics* (1926), and *Social Decay and Eugenic Reform* (1932). Schiller's defense of eugenics as the savior of society, with its accompanying antidemocratic sentiments, sets him apart from the other pragmatists, although it can be argued that his proactive stance toward eugenics is at least in part a logical outcome of his humanism.[3]

4.1 Broadening the Will to Believe

The essay that most influences Schiller is James's "The Will to Believe." Schiller sees this essay as a clear denouncement of "the cramping rules and regulations by which the Brahmins of the academic caste are tempted to impede the free expansion of human life."[4] According to Schiller, James's approach opens up philosophy by showing that "there are not really any external and non-human truths to prohibit us from adopting the beliefs we need to live by, nor any infallible a priori test of truth to screen us from the consequences of our choice."[5] Schiller's own "Axioms as Postulates" is largely an attempt to vindicate James's "The Will to Believe" by showing how it universally applies to *all* knowledge, even including the so-called self-evident axioms of logic. In this essay, Schiller goes to great lengths to prove that all so-called a priori knowledge ultimately boils down to a set of *postulates*, that is, claims which we hope, desire, or wish to be true. What subsequently makes us stick with these postulates is *that we exercise the will to believe them*, a belief that is reinforced by their success—what James called their cash value. For example,

> Perfect regularity . . . can be postulated; and the temptation to do so is great. . . . If nature is regular, it can be trusted; the future will resemble the past—at least enough to calculate it—and so our past experience will serve as guide to future conduct. There is, moreover, a glorious simplicity about calculating the future by the assumption that out of the hurly-burly of events in time and space may be extracted change-less formulas whose chaste abstraction soars above all reference to any "where" or "when," and thereby renders them blank cheques to be filled up at our pleasure with any figures of the sort. The only question is—Will Nature honour the cheque?
>
> (AP:111)

Schiller has a similar take on the axiom of identity—the logical truism that everything is identical with itself, or that *A* equals *A*. Schiller begins his discussion of this axiom by observing that except for the felt self-identity of consciousness, identity is not a product of sensory impressions. The most that our senses can give us is what Schiller calls a "feeling of likeness." Schiller then gives a different account of the origin of what we call identity, writing that "to obtain identity we must first desire it and demand it" (AP:98). Thus, for Schiller, it is the purpose-directedness of our thought that guides us in the establishment of identities, and it is the felt self-identity of consciousness that makes this possible. Take the following example:

> Edwin meets Angelina in her winter furs whom he admired last summer in fig leaves; he recognizes her identity in the differences of her primitive attire. That such things as the persistence of identity through change should be, and what they mean, he could learn only from the immediate experience of his own identity. That they are *is his postulate*, a postulate that fills his heart with the delicious hope that Angelina will smile on him as bewitchingly as before.
>
> (AP:98)

The identity of Angelina is thus made into a postulate, and it is moreover *Edwin's* postulate: "In recognizing Angelina he had of course (although he realized it not) construed her identity upon the model of his own" (AP:99). Angelina herself, in contrast, changes over time: one day she is glutted, the next day she is hungry; now she likes broccoli, though as a child she didn't; and many years down the line she will be gray, stooped, and wrinkled.

From this living notion of identity, Schiller argues, logicians have abstracted the notion of an identity that *excludes* all differences. However, such an abstract notion of identity, he adds,

> is never found, but has always to be made. It is made . . . in whatever way and to whatever extent it is needed, and remains subservient to the purpose of its maker. It is a postulated ideal which works, though nature never quite conforms to it.
>
> (AP:103)

Hence, though never fully realized, the abstract notion of identity may be adhered to insofar as it is useful, as it is precisely from this usefulness that it originated. This causes Schiller to conclude that "it may therefore blandly be admitted that *A* is *A* is an impotent truism, so long as it is vividly realized that *A* *shall be* *A* is an active truth that remoulds the world" (ibid). In this manner, one of the most fundamental axioms of logic, one that is often proclaimed to be absolutely self-evident, is exposed as a mere postulate in disguise—it is something we *hope* to be true, which makes it distinctly a product of our will to believe.

Schiller gives similar arguments for other classic axioms, such as the principle of non-contradiction, the principle of excluded middle, the principle of causation, the principle of sufficient reason, etc. By thus expanding James's will-to-believe argument, Schiller develops a voluntaristic and contextualist epistemology, where knowledge is always directly related to the particular wills of concrete individuals who find themselves in specific contexts. Logical and scientific principles are *not* extracted from reality as self-evident propositions, nor are they necessary presuppositions, but they are distinctly human products that are imposed upon reality to serve practical ends:

> For the pragmatic theory of knowledge, initial principles are literally ἀρχαί [archai] mere starting points, variously, arbitrarily, casually selected, from which we hope and try to advance to something better . . . truth and reality in the fullest sense are not fixed foundations, but ends to be achieved.
>
> (HP:133)

For Schiller, we are not just observers of reality; we are participants, caught right in the midst of things. This brings us to Schiller's pragmatism, and his view that we *make* truth, and *make* reality.

4.2 Pragmatism

On how pragmatism and humanism relate, Schiller sends out mixed signals. At times he considers them equivalent, arguing that problems associated with the *term* pragmatism are the main reason why he opts for humanism instead.[6] Or, as he later explains, he quickly came to realize "that pragmatism was a very bad name and apt to hang any dog that bore it" and thus is best avoided.[7] On other occasions, however, as in the preface to *Humanism*, Schiller describes humanism as "a greater and more sovereign principle" than pragmatism, adding that pragmatism is "only the application of Humanism to the theory of knowledge" (HP:24). In part, Schiller's motive for separating the two is that he wants to allow that one can be a pragmatist without having to commit oneself to the more comprehensive doctrine of humanism:

> There will . . . be many pragmatists who cannot rise to Humanism; nor indeed is there any logical necessity why they should do so. It is quite possible to accept pragmatism as an *epistemological method* and analysis, without expanding it into a general philosophic principle. No man can be compelled to have a metaphysic . . . or at least be conscious of it. Anyone can, if he chooses, stop short on the epistemological plane, as he can on that of science or that of ordinary life. If, on the other hand, he proceeds to become a Humanist, he will no doubt regard his pragmatism as merely a special application of a principle which he applies all round to ethics, aesthetics, and theology, as well as to the theory of knowledge.[8]

Briefly put, though one can be a pragmatist without committing to humanism, one cannot be a humanist (at least not in Schiller's sense) without also being a pragmatist. Hence, it is with pragmatism that we start.

For Schiller, pragmatism originates as an opposition movement that offers a much-needed antidote to the atrophied intellectualism that reigns over philosophy. Pragmatism arose, Schiller contends, from the recognition that the developments in psychology and biology, in particular the idea of evolution, have profound effects on epistemology (EB:246). The result is that pragmatism is driven by a "thoroughgoing recognition of the influence of the purposiveness of thought on all our cognitive activities."[9] We are not mere spectators; we are actors for whom thought is always related to some purpose that we seek to achieve.

In his construal of pragmatism, Schiller follows James's lead in "Philosophical Conceptions and Practical Results" that pragmatism cannot be seen merely as a device for determining the meaning of a statement or belief, but that it must also determine what makes that statement or belief true. As Schiller points out in his review of the fourth volume of Peirce's *Collected Papers*, "[Peirce's] principle was ostensibly a rule for determining *meaning* and *eliminating* the unmeaning. But it was impossible to overlook its bearing on all attempts to determine *truth*."[10]

It would not be too much to say that Schiller's own view of pragmatism is largely overshadowed by his views on truth. For instance, in his *Encyclopaedia*

Britannica article on pragmatism, he gives the following rendition of Peirce's pragmatic maxim:

> The real difference between two conceptions lies in their application, in the different consequences for the purposes of life which their acceptance carries. When no such "practical" difference can be found, conceptions are identical; when they will not "work," i.e., when they thwart the purpose which demanded them, they are false; when they are inapplicable they are unmeaning (A. Sidgwick). Hence, the "principle of Peirce" may be formulated as being that "every truth has practical consequences, and these are the test of its truth."
>
> (EB:247)

Here, one can discern a marked shift in the meaning of "pragmatism." Whereas for Peirce, the maxim is a principle for determining the meaning of the terms we use, the term "truth" being one of them, Schiller makes it a principle for distinguishing true conceptions (or beliefs) from false ones. True beliefs are those that work, and false beliefs are those that don't.

This view of truth immediately raises the crucial question of what it means for a belief to work. In addressing this question, it is important to keep in mind that, for Schiller, all our thoughts, and hence all our concepts, are always purpose-directed. In fact, the main reason why Schiller embraces pragmatism is its insistence "that the purposive character of mental life must influence and pervade our most remotely cognitive activities" (HP:15). All our conceptions, no matter how abstract and how far removed from our daily lives they might be, are ultimately purpose-directed. This purpose-directedness of all our thought causes Schiller to conclude that the truth of any conception is a function of its use or application. What makes a belief or an assertion true is its effect on "any human interest," and more specifically on "the interest with which it is directly concerned" (HP:58). Hence, Schiller concludes,

> Pragmatism, then, in its wider sense, refers to the way in which our attributions of "truth" and our recognitions of "reality" are established and verified by their working, and sooner or later brought to the definite test of experiments which *succeed* or *fail*, i.e., give or deny satisfaction to some human interest, and are valued accordingly.[11]

This brings us to Schiller's humanism.

4.3 Humanism

Schiller's humanism is best understood as a reaction against the tendency to "de-humanize" knowledge. *Humanism*, for Schiller, is a "systematic protest against the artificial elimination of the human aspects of knowing";[12] or, as he puts it elsewhere, it is "the perception that the philosophic problem concerns human beings striving to comprehend a world of human experience by the resources of human minds" (HP:65). Not only are human minds limited, they are also intrinsically caught up with the whole person with all its desires, fears, hopes, plans, purposes, etc. By dehumanizing thought, philosophers inadvertently severed the link between thought and reality. Schiller repeatedly insists that we should never lose sight of Protagoras's maxim that "man is the measure of all things." Philosophical conceptions such as truth, reality, determinism, etc., must always be kept within our own human perspective and may not be "dehumanized." As Schiller describes it vividly in *Studies in Humanism*,

> It is only as a concrete human being that we know thought to be a real process at all. . . . thought per se, however, "absolute" and "ideal" and "eternal" we may call it, is wafted away from earth into the immense inanity of abstractions which have lost the touch with a reality to which they can never again be applied.

> (HP:125)

When in actual thinking we abstract, this abstraction is not absolute, as something that can be neatly separated from the purposes and conditions that gave rise to it, but is an instrument of thought, designed to help us cope with the world wherein we live (HP:127). Without a context, abstraction is devoid of meaning.

In Schiller's view, Western philosophy took a wrong turn with Plato. In Plato's time, he argues, philosophy faced a dilemma. On one side, there were the followers of Heraclitus, who believed that everything was in a constant flux—a view that was captured famously in the aphorism that you cannot step in the same river twice. On the other side, there were the Eleatics, who claimed that everything was absolutely static so that nothing could ever move. You could not even step in a river once. Both views made knowledge impossible. For the followers of Heraclitus, it was impossible to assert anything of anything, because if everything keeps changing, nothing is stable enough for an assertion to refer to. For the Eleatics, the problem was a different one. Because of their fundamental commitment to the unity of being, the *only* assertion they could make was to declare the being of being: "What is, is." According to Schiller, Plato found a way out when he discovered the function of concepts in the organization of experience. By using a concept, an idea could be predicated of the Heraclitan flux. Whereas the *object* of the idea would continue to change, the *concept* through which the object is lifted out of the flux of experience would remain constant. The sky differs significantly depending on cloud formations and weather conditions, but by calling it "the sky," we identify something that remains constant even though what we see changes continually. Using concepts allowed Plato to attach permanence to the flux of experience in a way that avoided the problems that came with the undifferentiated unity of the Eleatic "one." He did so by replacing the latter with "a well-knit system of knowable ideas."[13] The central problem that Plato subsequently ran into, however, is that of the *interface* between the Heraclitan flux of experience and this stable system of "knowable ideas." Plato's myth of the cave was one attempt to bridge this gap between the eternal world of ideas and the perpetual flux of experience.[14] For Schiller, it was Protagoras who gave Plato the answer, and Plato failed to see it. As Schiller understands it, what connects, for Protagoras, the ideas with the flux of sensory impressions is that they are useful to us humans in our dealings with the world within which we live. This is the true meaning of the claim that man is the measure of all things. The idea of a snow shovel is constituted, not by something otherworldly within the realm of ideas, but simply by the fact that it allows *us* to scoop snow. It is this usefulness that gives our idea of the snow shovel its stability.

The requirement of making ourselves the measure of all things holds not only for philosophy, Schiller contends, but also for the sciences. All scientific knowledge is intimately related to human needs and desires, and the world shaped by science is ultimately a human world. "Pure science," he writes, "is pure bosh, if by purity be meant abstraction from all human purposes and freedom from all emotional interest."[15] As Schiller adds a few pages later, this should not be taken as derogatory to science. Quite the opposite. The idea of a humanized science leads to "a much-needed vindication of the rights of man, the maker of all sciences."[16]

This discussion brings to light the following difference between pragmatism and humanism, assuming that we follow the strategy for distinguishing the two laid out in the previous section. Pragmatism focuses specifically on the idea that beliefs must have practical consequences to be meaningful, and that if those practical consequences come about, the belief is not just meaningful but also true. Humanism is broader than this, in that it focuses on the *whole* individual that is holding the belief, including all its fears, frailties, desires, etc., and emphasizes that in determining the meaning or the truth of a belief, we may never abstract from this. According to humanism, philosophers should always keep the whole person in mind—a view that aligns Schiller with a view called personalism. Pragmatists do not need to go this far. They may still dehumanize truth as long as they keep sight of the fact that truth is an inherently practical affair.

4.4 The Making of Truth

Before discussing Schiller's views on the making of truth and reality, we should reflect briefly on what he means by "making." Three different verbs come into play in Schiller's discussions about truth and reality: to discover, to make, and to create. In "The Making of Reality," Schiller seeks to draw a pragmatic distinction between the processes of discovering and making:

> A reality is said to be discovered, and not made, when its behavior is such that it is practically inconvenient or impossible to ascribe its reality for us entirely to our subjective activity. And as a rule the criteria of this distinction are plain and unmistakable. To wish for a chair and find one, and to wish for a chair and make one, are experiences which it is not easy to confuse.
>
> (HP:131)

What is more, when we say that a carpenter *makes* a chair, we do not mean that he is creating the chair *ex nihilo*, that is, out of nothing. Rather, the carpenter makes the chair from material that is already at hand, such as wood, fabric, and nails. Making the chair is not a creation "out of nothing" but a transformation of things that already exist (meaning that they are either found or made at an earlier stage). Similarly, when speaking of the *making* of truth and reality, Schiller is not suggesting that we are *creating* truth and reality "out of nothing." Rather, our making of truth and reality is more like how the carpenter makes a chair. As Schiller put it, "We do not make reality out of nothing . . . we are not 'creators,' and our powers are limited" (HP:146). We make truths just as we make mistakes.

Schiller does observe that in practice, the distinction between making and finding is not as sharp as is typically suggested, and he is quick to point out that finding "often involves a good deal of 'making'" (HP:132), suggesting that finding is essentially a limiting case of making. This raises the question whether it is even possible to *just find* anything.

Let us now turn to Schiller's view on truth-making. Schiller argues that we make truth for several reasons. Most importantly, he aims to ensure that the notion of truth remains within the realm of human capability. With his theory of truth, Schiller opposes especially the nineteenth-century idealists who deny that truth is ever made—holding instead that truth is eternal. On their view, that the earth is round is not something "made true" by those who first discovered it, but something that was true all along, and something that would have been equally so had it never been discovered. According to the idealists, the best we humans can aim for is to approximate this eternal truth insofar as our easily distracted and finite minds allow us to do it. In Schiller's opinion, this is an odd sort of view. First, the idealists remove "the truth" from its human context by abstracting it from everything that is important to us (so that we would not be biased), and then they set up this alien notion of truth as an ideal—calling our ideas true only insofar as they conform to that ideal—only to conclude that our ideas must always hopelessly fall short of it, so that the truth can never be known.

4.5 Three Pragmatic Views on Truth

Within pragmatism, Schiller distinguishes three different views on truth, which he attributes respectively to Peirce, James, and himself. Not quite grasping the purport of Peirce's pragmatic maxim, which for the longest time he seems to have known only vicariously through James, Schiller attributes to Peirce the view that "the difference between the truth and the falsehood of an assertion must show itself in some visible way."[17] Schiller dismisses this view as philosophically uninteresting and laments that Peirce was unable to keep up with the development of pragmatism. Peirce may have originated the doctrine, Schiller observes, but "also exhibited extensive inability to follow the later developments, and now calls his own specific form of Pragmatism 'pragmaticism'" (HP:59). Consequently, Schiller adds, the greater majority of Peirce's work remains at a "pre-pragmatic" level.[18]

The second pragmatic view on truth is James's. On this view, which Schiller considers an improvement on Peirce's, truths not only *have* consequences, but the truth of an assertion actually *consists in* the purported consequences of the assertion, adding that these consequences must be "good" (HP:59). For Schiller, this second view follows naturally from the first:

> For to say that a truth has consequences and that what has none is meaningless, must surely mean that it has a bearing upon some human interest; they must be consequences *to* someone *for* some purpose. But now, we may ask, *how are these "consequences" to test the "truth" claimed by the assertion?* Only by satisfying or thwarting that purpose, by forwarding or baffling that interest. If they do the one, the assertion is "good" and *pro tanto* "true"; if they do the other, "bad" and "false." Its "consequences," therefore, when investigated, always turn out to involve the "practical" predicates "'good" or "bad,'" and to contain a reference to "practice" in the sense in which we have used that term.[19]

James denies that Schiller correctly represented his view, arguing that the idea that the truth of any claim consists in its consequences goes well beyond pragmatism, and he advised that Schiller's proposal to call this wider view "humanism" be adopted (MT:37).

Lastly, Schiller's own view, which he considers the logical outcome of the view he ascribes to James, rests on the idea that there is nothing more to the truth of an assertion than the consequences that are claimed by it. Consequently, Schiller argues,

> We may effect a transition from the original assertion that the truth expresses itself in the "consequences" to the more advanced conclusion that it so expresses itself *fully,* i.e., "consists" in them, and that if it is really "true" those consequences are "good."[20]

In short, for Schiller, an assertion is true when it has good consequences, meaning that it satisfies the purpose that was (tacitly) expressed in it (recall that, for Schiller, all thought is purpose-directed). In contrast, an assertion is false when it has bad consequences, meaning that the purpose that is (tacitly) expressed in the assertion is not satisfied. Take a man who just spent the evening drinking and concludes he is still sober enough to drive home. For Schiller, whether his belief is true consists entirely in the consequences of that belief, thus making the belief true if he manages to get home without problems and false when he gets arrested, causes an accident, etc. To this one can object that this is far too crude an analysis. One way to refine it is to say that the realization that one is too drunk to drive really means that one believes that there is a heightened probability that something bad will happen—and this belief is not proven wrong by getting home safely. However, here, too, what justifies the belief is still cast in terms of consequences, albeit that it is now an adjudication of the likelihood that certain consequences will follow. We encountered this same issue earlier in Peirce, when discussing the meaning of the term hardness (2.5), and we will return to it with Rudolf Carnap's discussion of a brittle vase (9.5). What is at play here is not so much Schiller's consequentialist conception of truth, but rather the question of nominalism versus realism (is the world just a bunch of individual, concrete things or events, or is there more to it than that?). As we will see further down, Schiller sides with the former, which means he has to reject our refinement.

There is still the further issue that Schiller explicitly requires the consequences to be good. This suggests that a correct prediction that certain bad consequences will follow, would not count as true, so that the statement "you are too drunk to drive" would always be false. This, however, would be a misconception, as it ignores the reasons for making that claim, which is to prevent a potentially bad outcome (an accident), which is something good.

This brings us to the contextual aspect of truth. When Schiller speaks of "success" in validating a truth, this must be understood as a relative term; it is success "*relative to the purpose* with which the truth was claimed" (HP:245). For instance, when I am looking for a place to sit, the belief that a certain object is a chair is true if I can sit in it. However, were I to be a collector of fragile seventeenth-century Baroque furniture, that same judgment—I can sit in it, hence it is a chair—may not be applicable. More in general, for Schiller, truth depends "very essentially upon context, on who says what, to whom, why, and under what circumstances" (HP:62). This is true even for our most abstract claims. If we want to know whether it is true that $2 + 2 = 4$, Schiller argues, we first need to know what the "twos" and the "fours" stand for: "It would not be true of lions and lambs, nor of drops of water, nor of pleasures and pains" (HP:62). Now if we were to object that addition requires that the addenda be the same, Schiller would not deny this. However, if we add two animals to two animals that we already have, we still end up with only two animals if the first are lions and the second are lambs. Context matters.

Because Schiller relates the truth of an assertion to its consequences, while adding that they must be good consequences, truth, for Schiller, is a value. To say that an assertion is true is to say that believing it leads to good consequences, and this is nothing other than making a value judgment about that assertion. This connects with Schiller's postulational approach discussed earlier, as well as James's will-to-believe argument in the previous chapter. For Schiller, we always have some reason for claiming that something is true, and we maintain its truth by exercising our will to believe. To say that a particular assertion is true is not a mere statement of fact made by a disembodied, disinterested, dehumanized god-like observer, but a normative claim made by a human being in some context for some purpose. In a deep sense, all that we say or think is performative. As we will see in Chapter 6, Peirce too considers pragmatism as a normative doctrine, albeit that he approaches the issues of truth, pragmatism, and normativity from a very different angle.

Given Schiller's insistence that all our thought, no matter how abstract, is purposive, it follows that even our most basic notions, such as "reality" and "fact," are not disinterested descriptions of a world of which we are merely spectators, but are expressions of value. To call something real is to give it value. There are no objective facts in the sense of being value neutral. As Schiller puts it elsewhere, pragmatism is "the doctrine that 'truths' are values and that 'realities' are arrived at by a process of valuation, and that consequently our 'facts' are not independent of our 'truths,' nor our 'truths' of our 'goods.'"[21]

Schiller consequently dismisses any attempt to develop the pragmatist theory of truth along Peircean lines, in which meaning and truth could be cast in subjunctive or even counterfactual conditionals (2.6). For Schiller, truth claims must be actually verified to be true:

> All "truths" must be verified to be properly true. . . . On its entry into the world of existence, a truth claim has merely commended itself (perhaps provisionally) to its maker. To become really true it has to be tested, and it is tested by being *applied*. Only when this is done, only, that is, when it is *used*, can it be determined what it really means, and what conditions it must fulfill to be really true.
>
> (HP:61)

When trying to come to grips with Schiller's conception of truth, it is important not to slide back into the old notion of a fixed, eternal truth, for which there is no longer any place. For Schiller, truths are relative and temporal. New discoveries reveal that certain existing truths are no longer tenable, which means literally that a new truth is made. This making of new truth is accompanied by a re-valuation of old truths. The old truths are now called "false," and the new truth is generally "antedated" and said to have been "true all along" (EB:247).

Although Schiller firmly rejects the idea of a rigid, static, and incorrigible truth, his process of truth-making and the revaluation of old truths does allow for something like an ideal, or absolute, truth. Such an absolute truth—and here Schiller remains quite close to Peirce and James—would be a truth that is adequate to every purpose and can accommodate every contingency, so that it would no longer change. Schiller explains that we can conceive of "an ideal completion of the making of truth, in the achievement of a situation which would provoke no questions and so would inspire no one with a purpose to remake it," adding that, "on this ideal the name absolute truth may be bestowed" (HP:247).

However, whereas this conception of absolute truth was central to Peirce's conception of truth, it plays little or no role in Schiller's humanistic outlook. Schiller does recognize it as an implication of his pragmatism, but he does not consider it a particularly interesting one, as it remains too far removed from concrete individuals and their dealings with reality. In his personal copy of Hartley Grattan's *The Three Jameses*, published in 1932, Schiller wrote next to Grattan's explanation of Peirce's view of truth as the opinion with which all who investigate are ultimately fated to agree (2.6), that such a state would be realized only in heaven, when all those that disagree have been damned.[22] Later, we'll see Richard Rorty make a similar move.

4.6 The Making of Reality

Although Schiller maintains what he calls a "voluntaristic metaphysic," he does not deny that there is an external world that is to a large extent independent from what we think or want it to be. As he explains,

> Humanism has no quarrel with the assumptions of common-sense realism; it does not deny what is popularly described as the "external" world. . . . It insists only that the "external world" of realism is still dependent on human experience, and perhaps ventures to add that the data of human experience are not completely used up in the construction of a real external world.
>
> (HP:66)

In other words, for Schiller, the external world—or reality—is plastic, incomplete, and thoroughly anthropomorphic. What the physical scientist calls "real" is largely a product of the questions she is interested in and the experiments she performs.

How, then, is reality made? To this question Schiller gives one answer that is not so controversial and another one that is. The not-so-controversial answer is that making a new truth, or gaining new knowledge, alters our *subjective* reality; it changes how we see reality (HP:139). Gaining a new truth also changes the knower, and since the knower is herself part of reality, this changes reality as well. Since in Schiller's terminology changing reality comes down to making reality, this means that a new reality is made (recall that making reality is not the same as creating it).

The second, and more controversial, answer is that gaining a new truth alters not only the knower but also the object known. The paradigm case is the self-fulfilling prophecy, already discussed in Chapter 3. My belief that I can jump over a stream may give me the strength to do so, and thereby it makes the object of the belief (my ability to jump over the stream) real. Schiller is aware that this is a special case, but he sees it as much less of a special case than it appears at first sight. Schiller agrees that pure perception, or mere knowing, would not at all affect its object, and would thus not make any reality apart from the changes it establishes in the knower. But he denies that there can be such a thing as pure perception or mere knowing:

> Mere knowing does not seem capable of altering reality, merely because it is an intellectualistic abstraction, which, strictly speaking, does not exist. In the pragmatic conception, however, knowing is a prelude of doing. . . . Hence to establish the bearing on reality of the making of truth, we must not confine ourselves to this fragmentary "mere knowing," but must consider the whole process as completed, i.e., as issuing in action, and as sooner or later altering reality.
>
> (HP:141)

For Schiller there is no such thing as "mere knowing"; rather, knowing always has an active component. The mind is not wholly passive, as if sensations were to leave their impressions in us like a signet ring imprints its seal in a piece of wax, but we actively contribute to all we perceive. To experience is either to experiment or to react, and in the process we affect what we experience. For Schiller, this holds even for our most passive perceptions. Referring to the history of thought, he observes, "Our most passive receptivity of sensations can, and should, be constructed as the effortless fruition of what was once acquired by strenuous effort, rather than as the primal type to which all experience should be reduced" (AP:56). Passive perception is perception where the active component has grown habitual or reflex-like. What is true of perception, Schiller argues, equally applies to knowledge in general. With a pun at the Hegelians' expense, Schiller concludes that the true method of philosophy is not *dia*-lectic but *trial*-ectic; our knowledge advances not by an inner dynamic of thought, as with Hegel's dialectic, but by trying things (AP:58). Were there to be a pure knower, or mere spectator, Schiller concludes, it "would be the most negligible thing in the universe" (HP:141).

Schiller's account of the making of reality steers him in a perspectivist direction. For Schiller, reality is always the reality of some knower, and it makes little sense to speak of a knower-independent reality. For Schiller, absolute reality, if there even is such a thing, would be a bundle of different perspectives encroaching upon one another. In *Studies in Humanism*, he examines three such perspectives, that of Newton, his dog, and a stone. Although Newton's dog no doubt loved his master, the latter's theory of gravitation would not have entered its world. Newton, in turn, was most likely similarly oblivious of many of the finer delights of canine rabbit hunting. Now, in contrast to the dog, a stone cannot even apprehend us as spiritual beings. But does this mean, Schiller asks, that the stone cannot apprehend us at all? Not so: "It is aware of us and affected by us on the plane on which its own existence is passed, and quite capable of making us effectively aware of its existence in our transactions with it" (HP:142). The plane at which the perspectives of Newton and the stone intersect—the "world" they have in common—is the physical realm of bodies. The initial reality from which all these perspectives ultimately emerged, Schiller characterizes as "sheer potentiality" with an explicit reference to Aristotle's *hyle*—the primary substratum or yet fully undifferentiated primeval matter from which all that is takes shape (HP:134). This view is not all that far removed from James's phenomenology, on which reality emerges from pure experience, and also resonates with Mead's perspective realism (7.7).

Based on his perspectivist interpretation, Schiller comes to the following conception of what is generally called "the external world":

> It seems clear that we are not the sole agents in the world, and that herein lies the best explanation of those aspects of the world which we, the present agents, i.e., our empirical selves, cannot claim to have made.
>
> (HP:146)

Put differently, for Schiller, I make my own reality. But I am apparently not the only one to do so, and the work of others enters into my reality where my perspective (or my reality) intersects with theirs. At those intersection points, I am confronted with things for which I cannot really claim any substantial authorship. For instance, when I trip on a stone, this is because my perspective intersects with that of the stone, as a result of which the stone becomes present to me.

Overall, we can say that Schiller is closer to James than to Peirce, and we also see a continuation of the tension between pragmatism proper and the will-to-believe argument that originated with James. We further find both James and Schiller trying to safeguard pragmatism by separating it from their more metaphysical claims—radical empiricism for James, and humanism for Schiller. Moreover, as we will see in Chapter 9, the approaches of James and Schiller presage Lewis's conceptual pragmatism, as well as the discussions about conceptual schemes by the logical positivists and others. Schiller's perspectivist view of reality further bears close similarities to George Herbert Mead's principle of sociability, to which we turn in Chapter 7.

Notes

1. For Protagoras's main argument, see Plato's *Theaetetus* 166A–168B.
2. F.C.S. Schiller, *Riddles of the Sphinx: A Study in the Philosophy of Evolution* (London, 1891), p.5.
3. An extensive collection of Schiller's work is found in John Shook and Hugh McDonald (eds), *F.C.S. Schiller on Pragmatism and Humanism: Selected Writings, 1891–1939* (Amherst, 2008).
4. Review of *The Will to Believe, Mind* (1897): 547–54, p.548.
5. Ibid.
6. F.C.S. Schiller, "William James and the Making of Pragmatism," *The Personalist* (1927): 81–93, esp. pp.89–92.
7. F.C.S. Schiller, "Humanism and Humanisms," *The Personalist* (1937): 352–69: esp. pp.363–7; see also F.C.S. Schiller (1927), p.89f.
8. F.C.S. Schiller, "The Definition of 'Pragmatism' and 'Humanism,'" *Mind* (1905): 235–40, p.239. This essay returns in a revised version as the opening chapter of *Studies in Humanism*.
9. F.C.S. Schiller, "Pragmatism and Pseudo-Pragmatism," *Mind* (1906): 375–90, p.377.
10. F.C.S. Schiller, "Peirce and Pragmatism," *The Personalist* (1935): 169–73, p.171.
11. F.C.S. Schiller (1905), p.237f.
12. F.C.S. Schiller, "Why Humanism?" in J.H. Muirhead (ed), *Contemporary British Philosophy* (New York, 1924), pp.385–410, p.397.
13. F.C.S. Schiller, *Studies in Humanism* (London, 1912), p.53.
14. *Republic* 514A–517A.
15. F.C.S. Schiller (1897), p.548.
16. Ibid., p.551.
17. F.C.S. Schiller (1905), p.236f.
18. F.C.S. Schiller, "Peirce and Pragmatism," *The Personalist* 16.2 (1935): 169–73.
19. F.C.S. Schiller (1905).
20. Ibid., p.237.
21. Ibid.
22. See Wallace Nethery, "Schiller in the Library," *The Personalist* 45.3 (1964): 326–8, p.327.

Chapter 5

European Reception
France and Italy

Notwithstanding vocal opposition by leading European philosophers, pragmatism gained significant inroads into European thought. In this, we can distinguish between the influence of their specifically pragmatist views and the influence of their views more broadly. As we saw earlier, Peirce made a name for himself as a scientist and a logician, and James's *Psychology* helped shape phenomenology. In this chapter, I focus on the early influence of pragmatism on French and Italian philosophy. Pragmatism's influence in Britain and Germany is postponed to Chapter 10. As it turns out, there was a healthy appetite for pragmatism among European anti-establishment thinkers, especially for the views of James and Schiller. Peirce's contributions to pragmatism were much less known.

5.1 French Philosophy of Action

Independently of the Anglo-American pragmatism of Schiller and James, a philosophy of action emerges in France that is affiliated with the Catholic modernist movement. As early as 1888, Maurice Blondel (1861–1939) coins the term "pragmatism" to describe this view.[1] Five years later, Blondel publishes his influential *L'Action: Essai d'une critique de la vie et d'une science de la practique*,[2] in which he aims to make action an integral part of philosophy. Blondel specifically objects to the one-sided focus of philosophers on either reason or experience. Those that focus on reason end up looking narrowly for single, abstract uniformity; those that focus on experience remain trapped in a plurality of experienced, qualitative wholes. For Blondel, it is only when reason and experience are reconciled that we can attain genuine knowledge, and this, he claims, can be done only through action. This action is not something extraneous to the other two—it is not a dumb, mechanical affair—but action encapsulates the response of the whole person to a problem or situation. In other words, thought and experience are inherent to action—they culminate, or get their consummation, within action. Moreover, this action is not reducible to either reason or experience. This significantly affects how we should understand the human condition.

As Blondel observes in *L'Action*: "I act, but without even knowing what action is, without having wished to live, without knowing exactly either who I am or even if I am."[3] Because of this, our actions are at once voluntary and necessary. Finding ourselves in a situation where we are continuously obliged to act without ever fully appreciating either the sources of our acts or their consequences, any discussion of the meaning of life should center on action. It cannot be settled in rational reflection (by giving reasons) or through passive experience (as if watching a play), but can be resolved only through action, that is, by actually living life, as a freely chosen experiment.

Despite clear affinities between the two approaches, Blondel abandons the term pragmatism when he learns of James and Schiller, as he takes them to espouse an impoverished form of empiricism, one that values only expediency. Writing to Dominique Parodi, he explains that between the pragmatists and his own view, there is "no factual dependency, no logical affiliation, and no essential analogy."[4] William James, in contrast, writes to Blondel that although *L'Action* is so abstruse, esoteric, and complex that it is almost a foreign tongue to him, its results are very similar to his own *Pragmatism*.[5]

Before pragmatism enters the European scene, two other groups of French intellectuals had been developing views quite similar to it. On the one hand there are scientific constructionists, including Henri Poincaré and Pierre Duhem, and on the other there is the neo-critical school inspired by Blondel's dissertation advisor Émile Boutroux, Charles Renouvier, and Henri Bergson. Although there are significant differences, there is also a close affinity between the views of James and Bergson (1859–1941). Like the pragmatists, Bergson advocates for an instrumentalist view of knowledge. In *Creative Evolution*, for instance, he explicitly identifies the understanding as "an appendage of the faculty of action." For Bergson, the understanding is a very recent product of evolution—most of our instincts being far older—and, though our understanding is *practically* useful, it can never tell us how things really are. In fact, eager to serve our purposes, the intellect masks key aspects of reality, such as its continuity and fluidity, by breaking up the world that surrounds us into timeless (hence stable and workable) pieces that are of its own making. Put differently, to cope with life, we have construed for ourselves a world of our own making, one that is designed specifically to assist us in our actions. Consequently, it is not through the understanding, but through an immediate, private, and non-discursive intuition—which Bergson describes as metaphysical—that we can get in touch with the things themselves. Hence, like the pragmatists, Bergson ascribes to some form of anti-intellectualism. However, whereas the pragmatists agree with Bergson that the understanding is subservient to action, they reject his notion of an immediate intuition that can somehow reveal how things really are. Though Peirce too carves out a space for intuition—and at times calls it superior to our deliberative understanding—Peirce's intuition functions more like our instincts, and he denies that it can give us some sort of privileged access to how things really are (2.1). In fact, in a way very contrary to Peirce, Bergson's anti-intellectualism and his reliance on intuition developed into a celebration of the irrational. In certain political circles this was taken as a sign that revolutionaries should follow their instincts rather than their understanding, a position that appealed, for instance, to Georges Sorel (1847–1922), a French social philosopher and political activist who comes to associate himself somewhat with pragmatism, most specifically with James.

Extrapolating on the work of Marx, Bergson, and Vico, Sorel develops in his 1906 *Réflexions sur la violence* a position of revolutionary syndicalism.[6] The syndicalist movement, which was popular both in France and Italy, represented a strand of socialism that focused on the trade union (*syndicate tavailleurs*). Their main weapon was the strike, and with the idea of a general strike—one that would halt all economic activity—the syndicalists thought they could bring about a political revolution that would bring an end to capitalism and would allow them to take control of industries and even the state. Such a general strike, however, can be carried out successfully only when people really believe in it. What is thus needed, Sorel concludes, is a good myth. As he explains in a July 15, 1907 letter to Daniel Halévy: "As long as there are no myths accepted by the masses, one may go on talking of revolts indefinitely, without ever provoking any revolutionary movement."[7] In Sorel's view, one needs a myth to stir the masses and a good myth makes itself true by being believed in and acted upon. Sorel calls a social or political movement driven by a myth a *ricorso*, and he considers the first Christians as a paradigm case. Myths are in part instinctive, Sorel argues—they emerge as a communal motivating force out of the loves, fears, and hatreds of a group. Sorel's theory of myths broadly comes down to a social version of James's will-to-believe argument discussed in Chapter 3. Sorel, however, remains critical of pragmatism. For instance, in a 1908 letter to Benedetto Croce, he writes of James's pragmatism:

> There is something frightening in that idea of making success the touchstone for the legitimacy of a belief! That is very English, but not very philosophical, in the sense in which that noble term is commonly employed.[8]

For Sorel, a myth may make itself true in a Jamesian fashion, but that is not what legitimates it. Which myth to push and why to push for it are to be established on very different grounds. About a decade later, however, Sorel warms up to pragmatism. In a book on James and Bergson entitled *De l'utilité du pragmatisme* (1921), he aims to transform James's pragmatism into a doctrine of social criticism. In Sorel's view, James's pragmatism needed to be rethought by a European brain, and that is what he set out to do.[9]

Sorel's search for a *ricorso* and his revolt against materialistic and mechanistic thinking drew him into a current of voluntarism and activism that was already well underway in Italy. Before moving on to Italy, however, a few words on the French sociologist Émile Durkheim (1858–1917), who lectured on pragmatism just before the outbreak of the First World War.[10] In twenty lectures, Durkheim—who, like Blondel, had been a student of Boutroux— seeks to distance himself from pragmatism despite substantial similarities with his own view. Focusing on pragmatism as a theory of truth rather than a method for making our ideas clear, Durkheim dismisses pragmatism as a "logical utilitarianism" where truth is made subservient to psychological gratification, just as the utilitarians, with their pleasure-pain calculation, had done for morality.[11] As a result, Durkheim argues, the pragmatists fail in their moral obligation to seek truth, satisfying themselves instead with what is useful and pleasurable. In contrast, we must accept truths *also* when they are useless or painful, and only rationalism can guarantee that. In line with this, Durkheim writes that pragmatism is "much less of an undertaking to encourage action than an attack on pure speculation and theoretical thought."[12] The identification of pragmatism with utilitarianism, and also positivism, is a common trope among its critics during the first part of the twentieth century.[13] Though Durkheim explicitly attacks the American pragmatists, his criticisms are truly directed against his fellow countrymen Bergson and Sorel.

There is another important distinction between pragmatism and utilitarianism that needs pointing out—a distinction often missed by critics of pragmatism, and, as we will see, by some adherents (14.5). Consequentialist theories, like utilitarianism, judge actions based on whether the consequences that they are expected to have meet certain criteria, criteria that are determined *prior to and independently of* the actions to which they are applied. This is not so for pragmatism. For the pragmatists, there are no preset expectations that must be met; quite the contrary, they are an intrinsic part of it. This is especially clear in Peirce's theory of inquiry for which the criteria for what counts as good inquiry and what inquiry should strive for (its goal) are both products of inquiry.

5.2 The *Leonardo* Movement

The classic period of Italian pragmatism centers in Florence, where at the beginning of the century a particularly vocal group of pragmatists emerges. In Chapter 1, I suggested that pragmatism as it developed within the United States is in important respects a product of its time. This is true too for the development of pragmatism in Italy. Although the Italian pragmatists— especially Giovanni Papini and Giuseppe Prezzolini—draw heavily on James and Schiller, Italian pragmatism originates, and also flourishes, as a criticism of the Italian political scene, which was dominated by strong displays of oratorical skills and a distinctive lack of action.[14]

When William James visits Rome to attend the Fifth International Congress of Psychology in April 1905, he is overwhelmed by the attention given to his philosophy by the Italian avant-garde. As he puts it in a letter to his wife Alice:

> I have been having this afternoon a very good and rather intimate talk with the little band of pragmatists, Papini, Vailati, Calderoni, Amendola, etc. most of whom inhabit Florence, publish the monthly journal *Leonardo* at their own expense, and carry on a very serious philosophical movement, apparently *really* inspired by Schiller and myself . . . and show an enthusiasm, and also a literary swing and activity that I know nothing of in our own land.[15]

The Florentine pragmatists, or the *Leonardini*, as they are also called, may have formed a "very serious philosophical movement," but they do little to systematize their pragmatism or define its limits. In a short essay entitled "What Pragmatism Is Like," Papini simply concludes that "there *is no such thing as pragmatism*, but there are only *pragmatic theories*, and *thinkers who are more or less pragmatic*."[16] And he continues by saying that: "Pragmatism is a *coalition* of theories coming from various sources and temperaments rather than a handsome system sprung from the brain of a single philosopher, or from a homogeneous and well-organized school."[17] This attitude toward pragmatism, which is found in both Papini and Prezzolini, follows directly from their attitude to philosophy in general. For Papini and Prezzolini, pragmatism is first and foremost the proclamation that thought should be free and that it should not be restrained within some rigid philosophical system like that of a Hegel or Spinoza. If philosophy is to genuinely reflect the complexities of life, we should expect a corresponding diversity of theories.

Interestingly, the Florentine pragmatists divided themselves roughly along Peircean and Jamesian lines. Papini and Prezzolini are staunch supporters of James and Schiller. They show a strong literary inclination and feel particularly attracted to James's doctrine of the will to believe. On the Peircean side we find the more scientifically minded Giovanni Vailati and Mario Calderoni. In fact, James's meeting with the Florentine pragmatists coincides with the culmination of a debate between Prezzolini and Calderoni that is unfolding itself on the pages of *Leonardo*—the former representing the Jamesian strand in pragmatism, the latter the Peircean one.

The journal *Leonardo* is founded in 1903 under the leadership of Papini as a militant review for young Italian intellectuals. Its founders are young indeed. Papini is twenty-two, while Prezzolini is twenty-one. As Papini later testifies, the journal was meant to "reveal to the masters of the present (to men no longer young, to men of thirty and forty) that the real youngsters, the new youngsters of twenty, have also come of age and at last acquired the right to speak."[18] The review is named after one of Florence's most illustrious natives, Leonardo da Vinci. The choice of name also reflects the desire of its founders to restore that combination of science, art, and a great personality that characterized the great Renaissance master. In contrast to the philosophy professors that the Leornardini encounter, da Vinci did not approach nature in a bookish fashion but sought to live it. "The divine Leonardo," Papini explains,

> did not compose treatises methodically divided into sections, in the manner of pedants who study only ancient books, but he takes his stand before the universe as a new man, as an explorer of unknown lands, and above all as an artist who knows better than the pure scientists themselves, how to penetrate to the depths and grasp the aspects and secrets of things.[19]

Leonardo's first issue appears on January 4, 1903. Its eight folio-size pages are printed on handmade paper, and detailed attention is given to its artistic appearance. In a programmatic statement the editors explain that, "in thought they are idealists and individualists, superior to any system and to any limits; they are convinced that any philosophy is nothing but a personal mode of living," adding that they deny "any other form of existence outside of thought."[20] In their individual contributions, Papini and Prezzolini embrace the radical voluntarism of the Italian idealist Benedetto Croce, who wrote in his 1902 *Estetica* that the creative powers of humanity are so vast we can create our own history like an artist creates a piece of art. Papini and Prezzolini further reject all prefabricated ideas or theories, believing that each individual is capable of developing his or her own theory of life.

Briefly put, the Leonardini are iconoclasts. As Papini reminisces in his autobiography *The Failure*, "we demolished, destroyed, dismembered, striking to right and left, sometimes with perfect holy justice, then again, as our maturer judgment admitted, too precipitously, but always in good faith and in the name of a greater love."[21] The ferocious beardless conquistadores, as Papini at one point characterizes the group, radically opposes the philosophic establishment:

> Philosophy hitherto had always been rational: we set out to combat intellectualism with might and main. Philosophy had always been speculative and contemplative: we decided it should become

something active, creative, taking its part in a necessary reformation of the world.

(ibid)

The movement's main mission is to stir people up rather than present them with a new ideology. As Papini writes in 1906:

> I want to awaken the drowsy ones, but I do not, at least right now, want to say what they must do when they do awaken. It is enough for me that they no longer lie about on the beds of habit or in the grass of mediocrity.[22]

Positivism, which dominated Italian philosophy for over thirty years, is the Leonardini's main target. Whereas pragmatism means power, positivism means impotence—man is reduced to a mere passive observer of the world. Benedetto Croce, who at the time shares the Leonardini's sentiments, writes of the positivists:

> These new directors of social life are entirely insensitive to art, they ignore history, they sneer like drunken bumpkins at philosophy and they satisfy their religious needs, if at all, in . . . masonic lodges and electoral committees. The philosophical and cultural reawakening will have to put the naturalists, doctors, physiologists, and psychiatrists in their place and destroy their arrogance.[23]

Parallel to their dismissal of positivism runs a rejection of academic philosophy in general, which the Leonardini see as lacking in originality and passion.

5.3 The Magical Pragmatism of Giovanni Papini

The Florentine pragmatist movement begins roughly with Giovanni Papini's 1903 "Death and Resurrection of Philosophy."[24] In this essay, Papini argues that philosophical principles are valuable only insofar as they enable us to transform or master reality. Man is active by nature, Papini argues, and it is the distinct aim of philosophy to spur him into action. Action leads to power, which for Papini means the satisfaction of our desires. In the attainment of power, Papini continues, we attain a state of divinity, which in essence makes his pragmatism a doctrine that teaches us how to become God. A few years later, Papini develops this view further in a celebrated essay entitled "*Dall'uomo a Dio*" (from man to God). In part, what he is trying to do in these essays is to formulate a response to Nietzsche's claim that God is dead. In doing so, Papini replaces James's will to believe with Nietzsche's will to power. The result is a view that proves all too attractive to the early Italian fascists.

James feels a strong attraction to Papini. James's "G. Papini and the Prag-matist Movement in Italy"[25] is all about Papini and mentions the others only in passing. As James confesses to Papini:

> It is your *temper of carelessness*, quite as much as your particular formulas, that has had such an emancipating effect on my intelligence. You will be accused of extravagance, and *correctly* accused; you will be called the Cyrano de Bergerac of Pragmatism, etc., but the abstract program of it *must* be sketched extravagantly.[26]

And Papini's pragmatism is extravagant indeed. It is an exuberant embracing of the will to believe, while being intoxicated by the creative spirit. It is a philosophy of action. Dismissing the rational and detached contemplation of traditional philosophers, Papini calls for a total and unconditional immer-sion. If we want to know reality, he writes later in *The Failure*:

> We must . . . become living realities in a living reality. We should not just stand in its presence like so many thinking machines, so many microscopes, so many rubber stamps, so many tape measures; rather we should dive into it headlong, penetrate into it and be penetrated by it, feel within our own selves the external multicolor, multi-sound, and multisavor of its flux, putting its pulse in rhythm with the pulsation of our blood, with our own heartbeat, so completely identifying ourselves with reality that it becomes wholly of us, all of us within it.
>
> (Papini, 1972, p. 201)

Put briefly, just as we can only discover the meaning of life by living it to the fullest, we can only discover the meaning of the world by living *in it* to the fullest. This magical pragmatism (*pragmatismo magico*), as Papini calls it, has close affinities with the pragmatism of Schiller. As with Schiller, it is a philosophy of the whole individual, not just the part we call reason. Like Schiller, it is hostile to positivism, which sees reality as something to be measured with an air of detachment rather than to be lived in. Pragmatism, Papini continues in *The Failure*, is:

> A philosophy of action, a philosophy of doing, of rebuilding, trans-forming, creating! . . . No more wild goose chasing down roads leading nowhere save into the snares and traps of visionary logicians. The *true* is the *useful*. To *know* is to *do*. Among many uncertain truths, choose the one best calculated to raise the tone of life and promising the most last-ing rewards. If something is not true but we wish it were true, we will *make* it true: by *faith*.[27]

Pragmatism, Papini exclaims, is a "tool-philosophy, a hammer-and-anvil idea, a theory that produces, a practical promotion and exploitation of the spirit!"

In a nutshell, Papini's pragmatism becomes a program for men to become gods. This is far from a humble undertaking, and Papini realizes this: "Great in very deed, my dream; but I did not despair of realizing it. Had men ever before set out deliberately to become God?"[28] It is crucial to realize that Papini did not seek to become *like* God, or that like the mystics he sought to lose himself *within* God, since both would already presuppose the existence of God and Papini did not at the time believe (or was unwilling to accept) that God existed. Instead, he sought to *create* God by first returning "to complete nudity, to the terrifying freedom of the absolute universal atheist," and, having thus rid himself of "all kinds of trumpery," by transforming himself, "a poor, weak, wretched man," into "a supreme and sovereign Being, all-rich and all powerful."[29] A few years later, Papini's rather megalomaniacal pragmatism reduces to a devout Catholicism.

It is easy to say that Papini carries pragmatism too far, but his criticism of the detached view of the positivists—who look upon reality as an object that is somewhere out there, and that it is the philosopher's task to measure it precisely—is well taken. In "G. Papini and the Pragmatist Movement in Italy," James gives a somewhat toned-down account of Papini's pragmatism:

> Tristan and Isolde, Paradise, Atoms, Substance, neither of them copies anything real; all are creations placed above reality, to transform, build out and interpret it in the interest of human need or passion. Instead of affirming with the positivists that we must render the idea world as similar as possible to the actual, Sig. Papini emphasizes our duty of turning the actual world into as close a copy of the idea as it will let us.[30]

Papini's message is clear. We must not accept reality "as is." Our responsibility is not to *describe* reality, but to shape it according to our own ideals. It is not we who must bend to reality, but reality must make way for us. Papini, James explains, holds that we should treat our desires "as *ideal limits* towards which reality must be ever more approximated" (ibid). It is in action that our ideals are real-ized; that is, made real. We find very similar sentiments in Prezzolini, to whom I return later.

In 1926, in a *Sunday Times* interview with André Révesz, the fascist dictator Benito Mussolini identifies Nietzsche, Sorel, and James as his three main sources of inspiration, explaining that he found in James "that faith in action, that ardent will to live and fight, to which fascism owes a great part of its success."[31] However, when two American philosophers, Herbert Schneider and Horace Kallen, each independently interview Mussolini the following year, they both find that the Italian dictator knows very little of pragmatism.[32] Earlier in the same interview with Révesz, however, Mussolini also remarks that, "to fight for the establishment of that social order that at a given moment best corresponds to our *personal* ideal is one of the worthiest of human activities."[33] Mussolini does not mention any names here, but it is tempting to read in this statement a Papini–Prezzolini style pragmatism, which would make Mussolini's rise to power perhaps the fullest, even if diabolical, incarnation of the Man-God. The anti-democratic sentiments of Papini and Prezzolini (both favored an intellectual aristocracy),[34] and Prezzolini's later associations with Mussolini, support such a reading. One year after the demise of *Leonardo*, Prezzolini starts a new journal, *La Voce*, with a strong focus on politics and social issues. Mussolini considers his encounter with *La Voce* decisive. It taught him, he later tells his biographer, Margherita Sarfatti, that it was his calling to "announce a new epoch."[35] In 1914, Prezzolini helps Mussolini found *Il Popolo d'Italia*, which becomes the central intellectual mouthpiece of the Fascists. Not long afterward, Arcangelo di Staso explicitly credits Prezzolini with having discovered Mussolini, and concludes that without *La Voce*, Italy would have "fewer men of action."[36]

Overall, what characterizes the magical pragmatists is that they combine an excessive skepticism about the powers of reason with an excessive optimism about the ability of the will to generate truth through action. This is very different from the logical pragmatism of Giovanni Vailati and Mario Calderoni, to which we turn next.

5.4 Giovanni Vailati's Logical Pragmatism

Papini's magical pragmatism, with its focus on human's godlike creative functions, stands in stark contrast with the more subdued logical pragmatism of Giovanni Vailati and Mario Calderoni. Vailati and Calderoni seek their inspiration in Peirce rather than James and Schiller, and they join Peirce in keeping the scope of pragmatism mostly limited to a doctrine of meaning.

Vailati's background and interests are very different from those of the more literary and artistically inclined Papini. In 1892, having completed his degree in engineering at the University of Turin, Vailati becomes an assistant of Giuseppe Peano, a pioneer in mathematical logic and the axiomatization of mathematics, and he contributes to the latter's ambitious *Formulario Mathematico*. The aim of the *Formulario* is to collect all known mathematical theorems and formulas and express them in Peano's logic notation. The last edition, which appears in 1908, contains no less than 4,200 formulas and theorems, all completely stated and most of them proved.[37] The *Formulario* greatly influences Bertrand Russell and Alfred North Whitehead in their *Principia Mathematica* (1910–13).[38] Vailati feels especially attracted to Peano's postulational approach and his use of the logic of relations that was developed earlier by Charles Peirce and, partly in Peirce's footsteps, by the German logician Ernst Schröder.

In 1895, Vailati becomes an assistant of the projective geometer Vito Vol-terra (1860–1940). After being promoted to honorary assistant the following year, Vailati initiates a course on the history of mechanics. Like Peirce before him, Vailati develops a great interest in the history of science, which sets him apart from most of his positivist colleagues who simply dismiss the history of science as a menagerie of refuted theories, useful at best as a resource for anecdotes.[39] It is at this time that Vailati begins to investigate the role of axioms and postulates in systems of geometry.

Vailati's academic career, however, is short-lived. In 1899, the same year in which he publishes two reviews of James's *The Will to Believe* (a third review is to follow the next year), he leaves academia to become a high school mathematics teacher. He remains actively engaged in pragmatism, however. In 1904, Vailati moves to Florence, where he meets Papini and Prezzolini. Also while in Florence, he meets Mario Calderoni, who soon becomes his main philosophic ally.

It was primarily Vailati's study of the history of mechanics as an assis-tant of Volterra that leads him to philosophy. Vailati quickly discovers that the sequence of scientific theories is not a fortuitous product of accidental circumstances (chance discoveries, practical demands, private inclinations, etc.), but that the history of science has an inner logic. Hence, the history of science must not be looked upon as an accumulation of isolated theories and problems but one should "analyze and consider from a general point of view the various methods of scientific investigation and the part each of them has effectively had in augmentation of the various realms of knowl-edge."[40] According to Vailati, it is by studying the *history* of science that one discovers the *logic* of science. Especially from the seventeenth century onward, scientists have dismissed the importance of the history of science, emphasizing that good science should always be a direct product of empiri-cal observations. In their hostility to the history of science, early modern scientists were particularly reacting against the schoolmen who, as they saw it, put too much faith in the ideas found in the books of their predecessors. Galileo, for instance, has the central character of his *Dialogue on the Two World Systems* firmly declare that only the sensible world mattered and not, what he disparagingly called the *mondo di carta*—the world of paper.

Vailati, living in an age that had developed a new appreciation for this "world of paper," argues that science is cumulative: today's science contains the successful parts of the science of yesterday. This is most evident in math-ematics and mechanics, but it is equally true for the basic concepts in phys-ics, chemistry, psychology, etc. The symbols and formulas that have become second nature for today's mathematicians embody the work of countless generations of scholars. Their work, Vailati remarks, has been "concentrated and stored in those symbols and formulas which through habit we handle with great facility and rapidity."[41] Our faith in these symbols and formulas—which is evident, for instance, in the confidence with which we use logarithms or imaginary numbers—has become so great that we trust these formulas even more than our senses. In taking up the cause of the "world of paper" that Galileo had so firmly rejected, Vailati sides with the eighteenth-century mathematician Leonard Euler, who boldly declared that "our pencil is more to be trusted than our judgments." At the same time, Vailati is careful to warn against a too-exaggerated respect for formalisms.

Vailati's discovery that one cannot separate the "world of paper" from the science of mechanics directs his attention to the role of concepts, axioms, and arguments in science. Following partly in the footsteps of the physicist Ernst Mach, Vailati develops an instrumentalist view of science. Concepts, mathematical symbols, hypotheses, etc., are not meant to represent anything, nor are they intended to be true, but they are tools, or instruments, for organizing observational data. In Vailati's words: "The concepts of which mechanics makes use, and the suppositions upon which mechanics is based, clearly come to assume the character of instruments whose value depends solely on the service they render for attaining some proposed end."[42]

Vailati's instrumentalist approach is further confirmed by his rejection of the two dominant schools of thought about the nature of science: empiricism and rationalism. The empiricists rejected all theorizing and hypothesis formation on the ground that science should build directly upon observations. From our observations we subsequently derive, through induction by enumeration, general truths such as the laws of nature. Newton, with his famous dictum *hypotheses non fingo*, belongs to this school. The rationalists, in contrast, saw science as built upon unshakable foundations (or axioms), which were often believed to be self-evident and which were connected with our observations through irrefutable deductive chains of arguments. To this second view Vailati objects that even in a science so well ordered and developed as mechanics, there are no unshakable axioms. As he explains in *Leonardo*:

> Notwithstanding contrary suggestions, arising from images representing premises as "pillars" or "pegs" by which conclusions are "upheld," . . . the opposite case, in which the truth or certainty of conclusions, deducible from given premises, is apt to increase and consolidate the certainty of the premises themselves, is no less frequent nor less important to be kept in view . . . There is hardly any branch of knowledge in which the premises are so indubitably secure that they cannot receive further plausibility from their leading to conclusions which are immediately verifiable.[43]

For Vailati, the relation between premises and conclusions is not as one-directional as the rationalists make it out to be. Not only do premises support conclusions, but conclusions also support, and modify, their premises. Even deduction is a reciprocal control that propositions exert upon another.

In a process of successive approximation, Vailati explains, the premises gain in precision and generality while simultaneously "correcting those crude interpretations of experience from which they originally were suggested."[44] Like Peirce, Vailati sees science as a dynamic, self-correcting enterprise.

Instead of grounding science in indubitable self-evident axioms, Vailati seeks to ground it in its ability to control the world within which we live and act. For Vailati, scientific concepts, whether they represent zoological species, mathematical operations, or physical constants, must be interpreted not as high-level abstractions from observational data, but as instruments that prove successful in bringing order to the manifold of sense impressions:

> Only with great effort and after long apprenticeship do we reach the point of seeing in such words as "force," "cause," "production," "agent," symbols useful for summarizing and classifying the results of our experience and which serve us to introduce order and discover analogies and laws among the congeries of data that we have before us. We do not even know, for example, whether the concept corresponding to the word "matter" and the distinction based on it are destined to acquire or lose importance with the progress of our knowledge.[45]

Vailati's interest in the role of concepts and his instrumentalist attitude make him particularly receptive to pragmatism, especially Peirce's maxim which connects the meaning of our conceptions explicitly with their conceivable practical consequences. Vailati firmly rejects, however, the tendency of some pragmatists to mingle the question of meaning with that of truth. For Vailati, as with Peirce, the question of meaning must be clearly separated from, and should precede, the question of truth:

> The question of determining what it is we *want to say* when we enunciate a given proposition, not only is an entirely distinct problem from that of deciding *whether it is true or false;* it is a question that, in one way or another, must be decided before the treatment of the other can be initiated.[46]

Vailati sharply distinguishes concepts from sensory representations, arguing that, "while sensations or representations are something purely passive or receptive, concepts are essentially a product of our selective or constructive activity."[47] Concepts are not derived from experience but are created by the mind in its purposive and interpretive activity, and then we impose them on our experience. As Vailati explains: "All 'facts' or 'things' in general to which we address our thoughts or attention are 'created' or 'constructed' by ourselves by processes which are in a certain measure arbitrary and partial."[48] Though one can hear in this a faint echo of Schiller's conception of the making of reality, Vailati cautions that, "one must not restrict the world to the narrowness of the intellect, but it is the intellect which must expand and enlarge itself in order to be able to contain the image of the world as is."[49] Moreover, the arbitrariness Vailati allows in the formation of concepts does not extend to the truth or falsity of the assertions that are formed with them. Our concept of a leg may be a product of our understanding, but, once we have created this concept, the question of how many legs we have is not.

Although concepts are products of our own making, it is not through an analysis of how they were formed that we come to understand what they mean. Concepts are justified by their use, and we can only say that we know what a concept means when we know how to use it:

> The not knowing how to use a concept, the not knowing how to apply it, the not being in the position to recognize the facts included in the concept from other contrasting facts, finally, the not being able to connect to the eventual particular cases the consequences indicated in the general statements in which the concept figures as a term (deduction and prediction), is equivalent to not possessing the concept and to not having acquired it, whatever be the ability that one has to repeat the words that claim to define it.[50]

In line with this, Vailati rejects the idea that concepts can have meaning in isolation. To determine the meaning of a concept, one must see it in action. That is to say, one must see the concept used in assertions, and it is through that use that concepts accrue meaning. Vailati goes even further. Assertions, or propositions, have no meaning in isolation either, that is, independent from the context within which they appear. This is because it is the context that determines what the practical consequences of a proposition will be. Different contexts will lead to different consequences. The result is a sort of meaning holism that well antedates Quine's (9.6):

> A proposition is always more or less a member, a part of a theoretical organism, just as a word is a part of a sentence or proposition. To determine the meaning or to judge the truth of a proposition without attaching it, explicitly or implicitly, to a system of other propositions, constitutes a problem as insoluble and absurd as that of determining the position of a body without referring to other bodies or guide marks. But this does not prevent one's asking what is the meaning of a proposition given *by reference to other propositions*, and one can find answers to this question by the examination of consequences that can be drawn from a given system of propositions when one adds the proposition which is in question.[51]

Hence, regarding the question of meaning, Vailati's pragmatism involves the choice of a conceptual framework. As with the concept, the meaning of a proposition is a function of the "logical medium" within which it plays its role rather than of the principles through which it was construed. This can be said even of something as fundamental as the laws of logic. The laws of logic are not true or false depending on whether they conform to the "reality of things," but they are "opportune or not opportune to follow, according to the purpose for which they are proposed."[52] For Vailati, there can be alternative logics, just as there can be alternative geometries, and those logics can depart as dramatically from our logical intuitions as non-Euclidian geometries have departed from our intuitions of space. Moreover, we can choose between those alternative logics just as we can choose between different systems of measurement, and for both we make our choice on pragmatic grounds. A similar line of argument surfaces with C.I. Lewis (9.1) and Rudolf Carnap (9.3).

In his theory of truth Vailati also remains close to Peirce, rejecting the Jamesian alternative. In Vailati's view, James, Schiller, and the magical pragmatists Papini and Prezzolini were all too cavalier in their dismissal of the positivists' correspondence theory of truth, which resulted in an alternative that becomes itself too easy a target for criticism. Vailati denies that the notion of correspondence requires a passive and detached attitude, which is what James and his close allies seemed to assume. Rather, Vailati claims:

> To represent, for example, the properties that a given body *has*, is not to represent some present facts, but rather some facts that it *will have*, or *would have*, if the body in question were placed in such and such circumstances.[53]

Thus, to discover the truth goes beyond a mere gathering of facts. It involves, Vailati argues, "the exercise of those organizing and elaborating activities of experience, which, while artificially simplifying, impoverishing and schematizing reality, have no other purpose than that of making possible the representation and more perfect mastery of it."[54] To represent reality is to master it, not to mirror it in thought. We must go beyond passive experience. We must act, that is, interrogate the world through active experimentation. Consequently, for Vailati, the divide between the pragmatic and the correspondence conception of truth is more apparent than real.

As we have seen, pragmatism is taken by its critics as a justification for the subject to believe anything one wants to believe. Vailati maintains that pragmatism ought to go in the opposite direction. Far from suggesting a subjective turn, pragmatism should embody a quest for greater objectivity by an unrelenting insistence on experiments and hard facts. The pragmatic maxim is not a personal criterion but a public criterion, one where meaning and truth are interpreted in terms of the scientific method.

In sum, Vailati is looking for a middle way between the hot-tempered will-to-believists, who found in pragmatism the Midas touch that could transform any desire into truth, and the cold detachment of the positivists, for whom our ideas, whether true or false, remain utterly detached from the world. Vailati agrees with the will-to-believists that our passions and interests play a role in the acquisition of knowledge, and a necessary one at that, but at the same time he emphasizes that their role is a restricted one.

5.5 The Prezzolini–Calderoni Debate

When James visits Rome in 1905 and meets with the Florentine pragmatists, the debate between the magical and the logical pragmatists just reached its apex. The two main voices in this debate are Prezzolini and Calderoni. Like Papini, Prezzolini directs most of his arrows against the positivists, finding much of his inspiration in Bergson and the voluntarism of the early Croce. Well before Papini, Prezzolini had been the first to maintain that through the free exercise of our creative power we attain a state of divinity, a view he expanded upon in the essay "*L'Uomo Dio*."[55] Prezzolini also remains close to Schiller's humanism, including its Protagorean dictum that man is the measure of all things.

Not surprisingly, Prezzolini also sides with Schiller in his hostility to formal logic, and he does so on the ground that logic unnecessarily restricts our thought. In "*La miseria dei logici*," Prezzolini calls logic the greatest idol of contemporary philosophy, and one that desperately needs to be smashed. Far from being the epitome of thought, formal logic is forced upon us because of our mental limitations and our lack of imagination.[56] According to Prezzolini, the assumption that consciousness is inherently logical and that we generally act from rational motives is wholly mistaken, and he rejects the idea that there is a single universal logical system. "All our rational expressions," Prezzolini contends, "are nothing but expressions of sentimental states, signs of moral tendencies, manifestations of personal character and temperament."[57] Formal logic, which ignores all of this, is thus an impoverishment of our thought. It is something we need (often for practical purposes), but it is hardly something to be proud of; and whenever we can, we should avoid becoming dependent on it.

Having thus dispensed with the philosophical establishment, Prezzolini outlines his own view while calling himself a Sophist, even writing under the pen name Giuliano il Sofista (recall that Schiller called the Sophist Protagoras the first pragmatist). Against the positivist—whom Prezzolini sees as restricting thought within the narrow confines of reason—the sophist stresses that we should follow our imagination and our dreams. Against the skeptic, the sophist urges us to embrace everything with a youthful enthusiasm: "*everything is true, because I desire it. Man is able to be the creator of his truth.*"[58]

To a large extent Prezzolini's sophism is James's will-to-believism turbocharged with Machiavellian tendencies. In his book *L'Arte di persuadere*, Prezzolini even goes so far as saying that, since we make truth, we can make others believe whatever we want them to believe, as long as we possess the art of persuasion. The aim of language, Prezzolini contends, is not to convey truth but to excite the will of another, and for this a beautiful parable often works better than a perfect syllogism. Vailati called it a "manual for liars."[59]

It is Calderoni, however, and not Vailati, who takes up the challenge that is posed by Prezzolini's polemic essays in *Leonardo*. Like Vailati, Calderoni came to pragmatism primarily through Peirce, and it is from his Peircean background that he opposes the Prezzolini–Papini flavor of pragmatism. Prezzolini and will-to-believists in general, Calderoni complains, have distorted pragmatism by giving the will far too much power over our beliefs. In his criticism of Prezzolini, Calderoni aims to stay close to the pragmatism of Peirce. According to Calderoni, Peirce's pragmatism is "only a request, expressed in a particularly suggestive form, to introduce experimentalism not only in the solution of questions but also in the choice of the questions to be treated."[60] What is more, Calderoni continues, the central idea behind Peirce's pragmatism is precisely to discourage the kind of intellectual practices that are seemingly allowed by James's will-to-believism and which are carried to new heights by Papini and Prezzolini. It is important to add the qualifier "seemingly," as James, in contrast to Papini and Prezzolini, explicitly restricted the application of his will-to-believe argument to pressing and momentous choices in situations that do not allow for a scientific solution or where we do not have the luxury of waiting (3.2).

Prezzolini replies to Calderoni by distinguishing two varieties of pragmatism. The first is the Peircean kind, which Prezzolini seeks to confine strictly to the realm of science and logic. The second, which was proposed by James and Schiller, focuses instead on the realm of morality. It was this second variety, Prezzolini explains, that he adhered to, so that Calderoni's criticisms are misdirected. In his rejoinder, Calderoni rejects Prezzolini's division between the two varieties of pragmatism, which he sees as inspired by a mere caricature of positivism. In turn, Calderoni distinguishes *three* varieties. The first is a straightforward application of Peirce's principle. On this view, the purpose of pragmatism is to eliminate useless philosophical questions, which is an aim it shares with positivism. The second is the doctrine of the will to believe taken in the radical sense, where the will exercises some sort of supreme power over our beliefs. The *Uomo-Dio* doctrine of Papini and Prezzolini falls under this second variety. Calderoni's third variety is a methodological pragmatism where the will has some power over how inquiry will proceed, implying that it has some power over the progress of knowledge.

The pragmatism of Prezzolini, which Calderoni argues falls under the second variety, is antagonistic not only to positivism (Prezzolini's main target) but also to the first variety of pragmatism. In contrast, the third variety, which Vailati and Calderoni himself adhere to, fits nicely with the first variety of pragmatism and with positivism while also having distinct advantages over positivism. Based on his triadic division, Calderoni concludes that "pragmatism" should be reserved either for the first and the third variety combined, or for the will-to-believe argument that is expressed in the second variety. By putting it this way, Calderoni's division becomes a methodological one rather than one that, like Prezzolini's, relies on a prior distinction between two different and mutually exclusive domains, the scientific and the moral.

The debate between Prezzolini and Calderoni comes to an end with an essay called "*Il Pragmatismo messo in ordine*," which is signed by "The Florence Pragmatist Club," although it is really written by Papini.[61] This essay opens with the claim that although no precise definition of pragmatism can be given, one can specify its main character, which is that pragmatism "unstiffens" our theories and beliefs by recognizing their purely instrumental value, making them susceptible to change when the circumstances alter. Hence, pragmatism does not stand for a certain type of theory but for a certain attitude toward theories.

Within the context of the Prezzolini–Calderoni debate, Papini divides pragmatism into three areas that he considers complementary. The first contains all those varieties of pragmatism that focus on the relation between the particular and the general. Papini distinguishes two subgroups within this area. The first is a pragmatism with respect to the formation of general propositions. Here pragmatism stands for the view that the meaning of a general proposition is determined by the particular consequences that someone who believes the proposition would expect. The second is a pragmatism with respect to the testing of general propositions. This is the view that general propositions must be verified in terms of their particular consequences. For the first subgroup, Papini lists Peirce and James by name; for the second, one might think of Schiller. With their focus on *particular* consequences, both subgroups have a distinctly nominalistic flavor.

Papini's second area involves those varieties of pragmatism that focus on the choice of representative conventions and ways of expression (definitions, classifications, abstractions, points of reference, units of measurement, etc.). What choices we make depend on what purposes we have set for ourselves. These purposes are in the end products of our sentiments and our will. The principal purposes found in the sciences include: practical application, the economy of thought (Ernst Mach), mental peace, and overcoming fear. Papini mentions no names, but one can think of Vailati as fitting this description.

Finally, Papini's third area concerns those varieties of pragmatism that focus on the influence of faith and belief on truth and action. This includes, in particular, those varieties that study the *cause* of belief (such as James's will to believe) or the *effects* of belief on action or on its own verification. Papini considers this third area of special importance, not only because it teaches us how to attain beliefs but also because it teaches us how to transform reality through those beliefs. James's will-to-believe argument and the magical pragmatism of Papini and Prezzolini fall within this third area.

Papini sees the three areas not only as complementary but also as intimately connected:

> Their common aim is to act, that is, to strengthen our power of modifying things. But to act, you must also predict and to predict with confidence [*sicurezza*] you must have well-developed sciences, that is sciences that are at once expedient and verifiable.[62]

For Papini, the will to believe is thus largely a prelude to the will to act. Although Papini does not mention Nietzsche by name, he does use the phrase "will to power," suggesting that Nietzsche might have been close to his mind when he was writing this.

In a phrase made famous by James, Papini calls pragmatism a corridor-theory (*una teoria corridoio*). It is with this metaphor that Papini closes the Prezzolini–Calderoni debate. The entire passage is worth quoting:

> Pragmatism is a collection of methods; from a certain point of view, it is the positive method made perfect, refined, and complete, and this is why one of its main features is its *armed neutrality*. This means that it does not decide upon questions, but it only says: given certain goals, I suggest you to use certain means rather than others. It is, thus, a *corridor theory*—a corridor of a large hotel where a hundred doors open into a hundred rooms. In one of those rooms there is a kneeler and a man who wants to reconquer the faith; in another there is a desk and a man who wants to kill all metaphysics; in a third there is a laboratory and a man who seeks new "handles" to grasp the future . . . But the corridor belongs to all and everybody walks through it: if from time to time conversations start among the guests, no waiter will be so impolite as to break them up.[63]

For Papini, pragmatism is thus an attitude, or a collection of methods, but it is distinctly not a philosophy; its "armed neutrality" precludes that. In fact, pragmatism is averse to philosophy. As Papini observes: "Pragmatism is really *less a philosophy than a method of doing without philosophy*."[64] As we will see, similar sentiments later return with Richard Rorty (11.5).

It does not take long before Papini realizes that he can do without pragmatism as well. The magical pragmatism of Papini and Prezzolini quickly proves untenable, even to its own proponents, and it does so mainly because of its extreme individualism. In the absence of an independent criterion of truth, the solution to any intellectual or practical problem can only be a product of caprice. *Leonardo* ceased its publication in August 1907 and with its demise pragmatism quickly disappeared from the Italian landscape.

In recommencing their "intellectual lives," Papini falls into a religious crisis and returns to Catholicism, while Prezzolini embraces the idealism of Croce, who by that time had moved away from his earlier voluntarism. For about a decade the magical pragmatism of Papini and Prezzolini survives in the futurist movement, but then it is over. The Peircean strain in Italian pragmatism also came to a sudden end, but for different reasons—its two main proponents died prematurely. Vailati died in 1909 at the age of forty-six, and Calderoni died five years later at thirty-five. Although the writings of both were posthumously collected in monographs, their publication had little impact.[65]

As this chapter shows, after the turn of the century pragmatism is beginning to attract some lively opinions. It is views like these that make Peirce distance himself from pragmatism. "At present," he writes, "the word begins to be met with occasionally in the literary journals, where it gets abused in the merciless way that words have to expect when they fall into literary clutches" (EP2:334). Consequently, he thinks it is time "to kiss his child goodbye," and he opts for the term pragmaticism instead, declaring that this new term "is ugly enough to be safe from kidnappers" (EP2:335). In the next chapter, we therefore return to Peirce and his attempts at introducing his own take on pragmatism to the world.

Notes

1. For an extensive discussion of Blondel's use of the word pragmatism, see Michael Conway, "Maurice Blondel and Early Anglo-American Pragmatism—The Consideration of Religion in a Pragmatic Setting," *Ephemerides Theologicae Lovanienses* 79.1 (2003): 72–96.
2. Paris: F. Alcan, 1893.
3. Published in English as *Action (1893): Essay on a Critique of Life and a Science of Practice* (South Bend, 1984), p.3.
4. Letter dated "May 1908"; quoted in Conway, p.84.
5. Letter to Blondel, dated 24 February 1908; quoted in Conway, p.84.
6. Georges Sorel, *Reflections on Violence* (Cambridge, 1999).
7. Ibid., p.28.
8. Meisel, p.42, quoted from Croce, *La Critia,* 1928, p.107; letter dated May 27, 1908.
9. Georges Sorel, *De l'utilité du pragmatisme* (Paris, 1921), p.21f.
10. Published in English as Émile Durkheim, *Pragmatism and Sociology* (Cambridge, 1983). See also Neil Gross, "Durkheim's Pragmatism Lectures: A Contextual Interpretation," *Sociological Theory* 15.2 (1997): 126–49.
11. Durkheim (1983), p.72.
12. Ibid., p.64.
13. E.g. René Berthelot denounced pragmatism as a "romantic utilitarianism" in his three-volume *Un romantisme utilitaire: Étude sur le movement pragmatiste* (Paris, 1911–22).
14. There is some familiarity with the work of John Dewey, in particular *Studies in Logical Theory* (Chicago, 1903), which is edited by Dewey and contains essays by him and his students. However, references to Dewey during this period are extremely rare.

15. Henry James (ed), *The Letters of William James* (Boston, 1920), 2:227.
16. Giovanni Papini, "What Pragmatism Is Like," *Popular Science Monthly* 71.10 (1907), p.354. Papini had been working on a book on pragmatism that was intended to come out in 1906, with prefaces by James and Bergson. However, the book, *Il Pragmatismo* (Milan, 1913), did not appear until much later, and by then it had transformed itself from platform for the future into a record of the past.
17. Ibid.
18. Giovanni Papini, *The Failure* (Westport, 1972), p.103. When he writes this, Papini is in his early thirties.
19. Florence, *Flower of the World* (New York, 1951), p.135. See also Papini's essay on da Vinci in *Four and Twenty Minds* (New York, 1971), pp.15–25. In this essay, Papini finds the historical Leonardo too much of a positivist and replaces him with his own image of Leonardo, one that better satisfies Papini's own needs and desires (what he calls the "living Leonardo," as opposed to the "historical Leonardo").
20. From the program statement, *Leonardo* I.1 (1903): 1.
21. Papini (1972), p.119.
22. Giovanni Papini, "Campagna per il forzato risveglio," *Leonardo* (August 1906): 193–9, p.194.
23. B. Croce, "Il risveglio filosofico e la cultura italiana," in *Cultura e vita morale* (Bari, 1955), pp.22f; translation Edmund Jacobitti, "Hegemony Before Gramsci: The Case of Benedetto Croce," *The Journal of Modern History* 52.1 (1980): 66–84, p.71.
24. Giovanni Papini, "Morte e resurrezione della filosofia," *Leonardo* 1.11/12 (December 1903): 1–7.
25. William James, "G. Papini and the Pragmatist Movement in Italy," *Journal of Philosophy* 3.13 (1906): 337–41.
26. Letter of April 27, 1906; in Ignas Skrupskelis and Elizabeth Berkeley (eds), *The Correspondence of William James*, vol. 11 (Charlottesville, 2002), p.214.
27. Papini (1972), p.204.
28. Ibid., p.206.
29. Ibid., pp.130, 207.
30. James (1906), p.339.
31. Interview with André Révesz, *Sunday Times,* April 11, 1926 (Late London Edition): 15–16, p.15, col. 2. Mussolini's apparent enchantment with pragmatism did not prevent him from ordering a deadly assault on Giovanni Amendola (1882–1926), one of the pragmatists James mentions as having met in Florence and who had become a central figure in the political opposition. Amendola coined the term "totalitarian," using the phrase *sistema totalitario* to describe Mussolini's fascism, in "Maggioranza e minoranza," *il Mondo*, May 12, 1923.
32. See Herbert Schneider, *Making the Fascist State* (New York, 1928), p.310. On Schneider's own sympathies with fascism, see Peter Vogt, "Herbert Schneider and the Ideal of an Intelligent Society," *TSCPS* 38.3 (2002): 393–411. For Kallen's interview, "Fascism: For the Italians," *New Republic* 49 (January 12, 1927): 211.
33. Révesz (1926), p.15, col.1; emphasis added. On Mussolini's relation to pragmatism, see e.g. H.S. Thayer, *Meaning and Action: A Critical History of Pragmatism*, 2nd ed. (Indianapolis, 1968), pp.321–3; W.Y. Elliott, *The Pragmatic Revolt in Politics: Syndicalism, Fascism, and the Constitutional State* (New York, 1968), esp. pp.313–50; Schneider (1928), esp. pp.230–42; Horace Kallen, "Mussolini, William James, and the Rationalists," *Social Frontier* 4 (May 1938): 253–6.
34. See e.g. Walter Adamson, *Avant-Garde Florence: From Modernism to Fascism* (Cambridge, 1993), esp. pp.79–94; Paul Colella, "Philosophy in the Piazza: Giovanni Papini's Pragmatism and Italian Politics," *Journal of Speculative Philosophy* 11 (1997): 125–42.

35. See Yvon De Begnac, *Palazzo Venezia. Storia di un regime* (Rome, 1950), p.111. On the relation between Mussolini and *La Voce,* see also Emilio Gentile, *Il mito dello Stato nuovo* (Rome, 1982), pp.103–34; Adamson (1993), pp.139–43.
36. *Il Popolo d'Italia,* November 28, 1914.
37. For a complete edition, see Giuseppe Peano, *Formulario mathematico: Riproduzione in facsimile dell'edizione originale. Con introduzione e note di Ugo Cassina e col contributo del comune di Cuneo* (Roma, 1960).
38. See e.g. Bertrand Russell, *The Autobiography of Bertrand Russell,* 3 vols. (Boston, 1967–9), 1:218.
39. Ernst Mach is a notable exception, and a clear inspiration for Vailati.
40. *Scritti,* p.66; translation, Zanoni, p.47.
41. *Scritti,* p.72; translation, Zanoni, p.50.
42. *Scritti,* p.75f; translation, Zanoni, p.51.
43. G. Vailati, "On Material Representations of Deductive Processes," *Journal of Philosophy* 5 (1908): 309–16, p.311.
44. M. Calderoni, "L' 'arbitrario' nel funzionamento della vita psichica," *Rivista di Psicologia Applicata* 6 (1910): 166–83, 234–48, 385–416, 403; tr. Zanoni, p.185. The "L'arbitrario," was published posthumously by Calderoni, based on notes he and Vailati had made before Vailati's death, and combined with passages from Vailati's earlier writings. It is not included in the *Scritti.*
45. *Scritti,* p.61; translation, Zanoni, p.35.
46. *Scritti,* p.923; translation, Zanoni, p.77.
47. "L'arbitrario," p.245; translation, Zanoni, p.175.
48. "L'arbitrario," p.247; translation, Zanoni, p.175.
49. *Scritti,* p.53; translation, Zanoni, p.194.
50. *Scritti,* p.573; translation, Zanoni, p.176.
51. *Scritti,* p.758; translation, Zanoni, p.149.
52. *Scritti,* p.152; translation, Zanoni, p.172.
53. *Scritti* p.578; translation, Zanoni, p.154.
54. *Scritti,* p.578; translation, Zanoni, p.155.
55. *Leonardo* I.3 (January 1903), pp.3–4.
56. Giuseppe Prezzolini, "La miseria dei logici I & II," *Leonardo* 1.4 (February 8, 1903): 5–7; I.6 (March 8, 1903): 7–8.
57. Prezzolini, cited in Colella (1994), p.870f.
58. Ibid., p.872.
59. G. Vailati, "Un Manuale per i bugiardi: Prezzolini, *L'Arte di persuadere,*" *Rivista de Psicologia Applicata* 2 (1907); *Scritti,* pp.770–6.
60. Calderoni, quoted in Colella (1994), p.878.
61. *Leonardo* III (April 1905): 45–8.
62. Ibid.
63. *Leonardo* III (April 1905): 47 (ellipsis in original).
64. Papini (1907), p.354.
65. Calderoni edited Vailati's writings in *Scritti* (Florence, 1911). Seven years later, Papini edited a selection of writings by Calderoni and Vailati under the title *Il Pragmatismo di Mario Calderoni e Giovanni Vailati* (Lanciano, 1918). In 1924, a two-volume edition of Calderoni's works, with an introduction by Papini, appears as *Scritti* (Florence, 1924).

Chapter 6

Peirce Revisited

The Normative Turn

During the final fifteen years of his life, Peirce spends much time and effort explaining, defending, and even proving pragmatism. In part, this effort comes from his sincere belief that if one introduces a new concept, one must say what it stands for. Peirce strongly believes that the success of the sciences was to a large extent due to the development of a technical nomenclature in which each term had a single, definite, and generally accepted meaning. Even more than had been the case with botany and zoology, Peirce believes that philosophy was in desperate need of a proper taxonomy. With views not easily checked by experience, if at all, a precise nomenclature for basic philosophical concepts, such as "reality," "self," "necessity," "universal," etc., becomes essential for molding the divergent views of philosophers into a fruitful philosophical debate. Earlier, Peirce had put this belief into action by uncovering the meaning of thousands of philosophical terms for the twelve-volume *Century Dictionary*, thereby *de facto* establishing the beginning of such a taxonomy.[1]

Peirce even envisions a system of prefixes and suffixes, as is common in chemistry. For example, the prefix "prope-" could mark "a broad and rather indefinite extension of the meaning of the term to which it was prefixed," and the suffix "-ism," which is already used to designate a doctrine, could be supplemented with the suffix "-icism," to mark, as Peirce phrases it, "a more strictly defined acception of that doctrine" (EP2:334). Applying this to pragmatism, Peirce first identifies pragmatism as a form of prope-positivism and then introduces "pragmaticism" to denote a more strictly defined use of the term pragmatism. On this stricter definition, pragmatism—or *pragmaticism*, as it is now called—must be understood as a maxim of logic:

> Pragmatism makes or ought to make no pretension to throwing positive light on any problem. It is merely a logical maxim for laying the dust of pseudoproblems, and thus enabling us to discern what pertinent facts the phenomena may present. But this is a good half of the task of philosophy.
>
> (CP8.186)

Peirce thus rejects the broadening of the doctrine we encountered with James and Schiller. As he sees it, they carry the doctrine too far by making it a speculative principle of philosophy. This stricter definition of pragmatism is the subject of this chapter. We do this by looking at three sets of documents: Peirce's 1898 Cambridge Conference lectures, his 1903 Harvard lectures, and his 1905–6 *Monist* papers. In the last, Peirce introduces the term pragmaticism to distinguish his view from the pragmatism popularized by James and Schiller.

6.1 Peirce's Later Years

In 1878, when "How to Make Our Ideas Clear" (the paper that contains the pragmatic maxim) is published, Peirce is in the prime of his life and in the midst of a promising career. In 1879 he joins the newly established Johns Hopkins University, which was conceived primarily as a graduate school. Peirce actively participates in the academic community. He begins a philosophical club, and together with some of his students, he publishes an influential book in logic: *Studies in Logic; By Members of the Johns Hopkins University*. John Dewey, who took courses with Peirce at the time, would later do the same with his *Studies in Logical Theory*. However, in the decade that follows, Peirce loses his job at Johns Hopkins and is forced to resign from the US Coast Survey. In 1888, ten years after his influential 1878 article in *Popular Science Monthly*, Peirce retreats to Milford, a small town in eastern Pennsylvania, where he spends the remainder of his life in increasing isolation.

The premature demise of Peirce's academic career is due to his personality (as one of his students later puts it, there was an air of irresponsibility about him), powerful enemies, and his second marriage to the mysterious Juliette Froissy Pourtalais, then his mistress, two days after divorcing his first wife, Zina Fay. (In his defense, Zina had left him six years earlier.) Juliette's mysterious background adds to the problem. She claims that she is of European nobility, but there is a persistent rumor that she had been a French prostitute. Even today, hardly anything is known about her. Shortly after their marriage, Peirce loses his position at Johns Hopkins University—its president declared that he didn't want to be under the same roof with "so immoral a man"—and Peirce never again holds an academic position. In 1891, after thirty years of service, Peirce is forced to resign from the Coast Survey, in part because of troubles surrounding his gravity report, the result of many years of swinging gravity pendulums at different locations. The report was criticized for being composed in an illogical manner. As Simon Newcomb, then America's leading physicist, puts it in his peer evaluation,

> A remarkable feature of the presentation is the inversion of the logical order throughout the whole paper. The system of the author seems

to be to give first concluded results, then the method by which these results were obtained, then the formulae and principles on which these methods rest, then the derivation of these formulae, then the data on which the derivation rests, and so on until the original observations are reached. The human mind cannot follow a course of reasoning in this way, and the first thing to be done with the paper is to reconstruct it in logical order.

Today, this mode of presentation is standard.

By the time Peirce resigns from the Coast Survey, the Peirces had already retreated to Milford, a few hours by train from New York City, where they purchased a large property with a small farmhouse. Driven by grandiose but impractical plans, and stimulated by the booming economy, they quickly transform the farmhouse into a mansion. Soon afterwards, however, following the Panic of 1893, America suffers an economic depression. Nothing comes of any of Peirce's plans, and the property quickly becomes too expensive for them to maintain. Often going for days without food or firewood, the Peirces live in poverty until Charles Peirce's death in 1914.

6.2 Response to James's *Will to Believe*

William James dedicated *The Will to Believe* to "my old friend, Charles Sanders Peirce, to whose philosophic comradeship in old times and to whose writings in more recent years I owe more incitement and help than I can express or repay." Peirce is clearly touched by James's tribute, and he sends him a long letter of thanks. In this letter, Peirce also explains how his own views have shifted over the years. Commenting in particular on the essay that gave the book its title, Peirce writes,

> That everything is to be tested by its practical results was the great text of my early papers; so, as far as I get your general aim in so much of the book as I have looked at, I am quite with you in the main. In my later papers, I have seen more thoroughly than I used to do that it is not mere action as brute exercise of strength that is the purpose of all, but say generalization, such action as tends toward regularization.[2]

Peirce's comments reveal a sharp divide between the pragmatisms of Peirce and James, and one that is of a metaphysical nature: Peirce is a realist and James a nominalist. For nominalists, only what exists is real and what exists are particulars. Consequently, a nominalist interpretation of the pragmatic maxim, which is what James gives us in his 1898 Berkeley lecture (3.1), relates the meaning of our conceptions to *particular* effects or concrete experiences. Peirce, on the other hand, holds on to a form of realism—the view that some generals are also real. Not only that, but on a realistic interpretation of the pragmatic maxim, the meaning of a conception should be connected with a general—i.e., a habit—not just with particulars, such as particular experiences. Thus although Peirce agrees with James that "the individual deed [is] the only real meaning there is in the Concept," he immediately adds that "it is not the mere arbitrary force in the deed but the life it gives to the idea that is valuable."[3]

Whereas James focuses on experiences, Peirce is thinking primarily in terms of what he calls "habits." Habits are rules of action. They determine what our acts will be when we find ourselves in certain circumstances. Thus, on Peirce's reading of the pragmatic maxim, the meaning of the word "chair" is related *not* to certain concrete sensory impressions, but to the circumstance that the object of this conception invokes in us the *habit* to sit in it, etc. This should not be interpreted as a simple stimulus-response routine—if SEE CHAIR, then SIT—because situations are generally multi-faceted. Sometimes seeing a chair causes one to behave very differently. When we see the chair in which Thomas Jefferson drafted the Declaration of Independence, we react differently than when we just need something to help us get a book from the top shelf. However, without some general tendency, without some regularization that puts the concept in context, any connection with brute experiential facts will be completely lacking in meaning.

Shortly after Peirce wrote his letter of thanks to James, James invites him to deliver a series of lectures in Cambridge. Peirce agrees enthusiastically and mails James a proposal for a series of lectures called "On the Logic of Events." In these lectures, Peirce writes, he will discuss his system of logical graphs, the logic of relatives, the theory of the categories, the law of the association of ideas, and the logic of abduction (or hypothesis formation), deduction, and induction.

James replies quickly, trying hard to dissuade Peirce from the idea of devoting the lectures to logic:

> I am sorry you are sticking so to formal logic. . . . *You* can hardly conceive how little interest exists in the purely formal aspects of logic. Things on that subject ought to be *printed* for the scattered few. You are teeming with ideas—and the lectures need not by any means form a continuous whole. Separate topics of a vitally important character would do perfectly well.[4]

Peirce's response is not without sarcasm. With a direct reference to James's letter, he proposes to rename the lectures "Detached Ideas on Vitally Important Topics." The first lecture, he continues, "is about Vitally important topics, showing that where they are Vital there is little chance for philosophy in them."[5]

Having addressed James's insistence that the lectures deal with *vital* issues, Peirce moves to James's second comment, that the lectures "need not by any means form a continuous whole." Peirce explains,

> The second lecture is about detached thoughts & is intended to show that however little time people may have for connected thought outside their business, yet it is better to make it as connected as possible, not shunning detached ideas but seeking to assimilate them.[6]

For the third lecture, Peirce indicates that he will take James's will-to-believe argument directly by the horns: "My third lecture is to be upon the highest maxim of logic,—which is that the only strictly indispensable requisite is that the inquirer shall want to learn the truth."[7] Against James's "will to believe," Peirce proposes to argue for a "will to truth."

Soon Peirce sends drafts of the first four lectures to James for feedback. The result is a change of heart on James's part. In a letter of January 23, 1898, James writes that he would no longer object if Peirce were to reestablish his original title "The Logic of Events." The title Peirce eventually settles on is "Reasoning and the Logic of Things."[8] After the opening lecture, entitled "Philosophy and the Conduct of Life," follow four lectures on logic, one on causation and force, one on habit, and one on the logic of continuity.

It is clear from the lectures that James's "will to believe" remains close to Peirce's mind. What James called genuine options (options that are living, forced, and momentous), Peirce terms "matters of vital importance." And, like James, Peirce separates them from scientific questions. However, whereas James focuses most of his attention on genuine options, Peirce outright rejects the idea that philosophy is of any use when we are faced with genuine options, that is, with matters of vital importance. Philosophy, at least in its present state, is too ill equipped to help us. Peirce even goes so far as to state that practical applications of philosophy to religion and conduct, which is precisely what James thinks are most important, are "exceedingly dangerous" (EP2:29). Peirce is especially skeptical of our ability to use reason for resolving practical issues that we believe to be of great importance—we are just too skillful in rationalizing everything we do or want. As Peirce puts it,

> Men many times fancy that they act from reason when, in point of fact, the reasons they attribute to themselves are nothing but excuses which unconscious instinct invents to satisfy the teasing "why's" of the ego. The extent of this self-delusion is such as to render philosophical rationalism a farce.
>
> (EP2:32)

Since in the end reason appeals to sentiment, Peirce continues, we are better off relying directly on our instinct, as this is, though certainly fallible, less likely to lead us as easily and as far astray as reasoning. Because of this, Peirce argues that a philosophy that is too heavily dominated by practical considerations is corrupting:

> In philosophy, touching as it does upon matters which are, and ought to be, sacred to us, the investigator who does not stand aloof from all intent to make practical applications, will not only obstruct the advance of the pure science, but what is infinitely worse, he will endanger his own moral integrity and that of his readers.
>
> (EP2:29)

None of this is to say that Peirce thought reasoning useless. Quite the contrary, reasoning is very helpful, indispensable even, in those cases where we are not directed by practical motives. Logic may be of little help when trying to decide whether to marry someone (surely a genuine option in James's sense), but logic is certainly essential for anyone who is developing a metaphysical system or who is engaged in scientific inquiry.

An important feature of reasoning is that, when given enough time and left to run its own course (two conditions unlikely to be met in matters of vital importance), reasoning will eventually correct itself. Reasoning not only corrects its conclusions; it also corrects its premises and its methods. It even gives us a more solid basis for empirical data than observation:

> Every astronomer . . . is familiar with the fact that the catalogue place of a fundamental star, which is the result of elaborate reasoning, is far more accurate than any of the observations from which it is deduced.
>
> (EP2:43)

From the circumstance that inquiry has the vital powers of self-correction and growth, Peirce draws the conclusion that "there is but one thing needful for learning the truth, and that is a hearty and active desire to learn what is true" (EP2:47). What we need, Peirce argues, is not a will to believe, but a will to learn.

Peirce's analysis of reason leads him to the following important conclusion, which he calls the first rule of reason: "in order to learn you must desire to learn and in so desiring not be satisfied with what you already incline to think" (EP2:48). From this first rule of reason, Peirce derives the important corollary "Do not block the way of inquiry" (EP2:47). Blocking the way of inquiry is, for Peirce, the worst sin one can commit against inquiry, as it obstructs the self-correctiveness of reasoning. Classical obstructions include claiming that certain facts can never be known, that certain facts are ultimate (meaning they cannot be explained in terms of anything else), and that certain facts have already attained their final and perfect formulation.

All of this shows that Peirce does not see pragmatism as a device for solving practical problems, nor does he consider our ability to solve such problems the justification of pragmatism, or of philosophy in general. Peirce's views differ in this respect significantly from the pragmatisms of James and Schiller, and even more so from the magical pragmatism of Papini and Prezzolini. Peirce does not see the world as an obstacle that is to be overcome, as something we must mend and tinker with to make it conform to our goals, but as "something great, and beautiful, and sacred, and eternal, and real" (EP2:55). We must be willing to learn the lesson the world is trying to teach us.

Peirce delivers his Cambridge Conference lectures in the winter of 1898. It appears, though, that Peirce did not get his message across. Half a year later, on August 26, James delivers his famous Berkeley address in which he introduces "pragmatism," while at the same time insisting that it should really be called "practicalism" (3.1).

6.3 The Harvard Lectures on Pragmatism

Five years after the Cambridge Conference lectures, in the spring of 1903, Peirce returns to Cambridge to deliver two sets of lectures: the Harvard lectures on pragmatism and the Lowell lectures "Some Topics of Logic."[9] In the Harvard lectures, Peirce again spells out how his views differ from James's, who again organized the lectures. The lectures contain, Peirce informs his audience, "an examination of the *pros* and *cons* of pragmatism" (EP2:133). Moreover, since Peirce sees pragmatism as a maxim of logic rather than a handy instrument for obtaining desirable practical results, he finds it requisite that pragmatism be proven, and the development of a proof of pragmatism becomes a focal point of the lectures.[10] Peirce does not spare his audience, and James later famously described the lectures as "flashes of brilliant light relieved against Cimmerian darkness."[11]

Again, Peirce takes the maxim of his 1878 "How to Make Our Ideas Clear" as his starting point. He rejects, however, the proof that is latent in that paper and in "The Fixation of Belief," which preceded it. In those early papers, Peirce began by observing that we constantly seek belief, defining belief as "that upon which we are prepared to act." Peirce is now asking what justified him to define belief that way. In "How to Make Our Ideas Clear" he had come to this definition after an analysis of our psychological constitution. Our minds just happen to work like this.[12] In 1903 Peirce finds this answer no longer acceptable. What if human nature were different? What if a prolonged use of pesticides causes a chemical modification in the human brain so that we feel euphoria and satisfaction every time we are in doubt, and bored and restless when in a state of belief? Would pragmatism no longer be true? And there is more. If pragmatism is derived from the principles of psychology, which is a descriptive science that studies how we think, then how are we to distinguish how we *should* think from how we actually *do* think?

Consequently, Peirce now seeks to develop a proof of pragmatism that does not depend on the accidental circumstance that our minds happen to work in a particular way. He begins by observing that pragmatism contains a normative component. The pragmatic maxim tells us how we *should* define our terms for them to have meaning. The discovery that the pragmatic maxim is normative leads Peirce to consider pragmatism as a special application of ethics.

Ethics, Peirce continues, presupposes a distinction between what is admirable and what is not, so that we must first determine what we are prepared to admire and what not. This leads Peirce to something more basic, namely esthetics, which studies what is admirable in itself without any reference to anything else. In short, ethics depends on esthetics, with ethics being a specialized subcategory of esthetics, namely that subcategory that confines itself solely to what is admirable in human conduct. As Peirce explains in a draft for one of the lectures,

> An ultimate end of action *deliberately* adopted,—that is to say, *reasonably* adopted,—must be a state of things that *reasonably recommends itself in itself* aside from any ulterior consideration. It must be an *admirable ideal*, having the only kind of goodness that such an ideal *can* have, namely esthetic goodness. From this point of view, the morally good appears as a particular species of the esthetically good.
>
> (EP2:201)

Esthetics, Peirce continues, depends in turn on a pre-normative discipline—one that merely contemplates phenomena as they emerge within consciousness without making any distinction as to their being good or bad, beautiful or ugly, desirable or undesirable, real or unreal, etc. Peirce labels this science *phenomenology* or *phaneroscopy*. According to Peirce, the phenomenologist just opens her eyes and describes what she sees. Here we see Peirce making a move similar to James in his *Psychology*.

For Peirce, phenomenology is the most basic of what he calls the positive sciences. By the latter he means sciences that make categorical assertions, such as "The Nile is a river in Africa," or "DNA is a molecule composed of two polynucleotide chains that coil around each other to form a double helix carrying genetic instructions." The positive sciences differ in this respect from mathematics, which seeks knowledge that is expressed in conditional or hypothetical propositions. Mathematicians, Peirce explains, do not seek to discover how things are, but only how they might be supposed to be (EP2:144).

Having distinguished the positive sciences from mathematics, Peirce divides them into philosophy and the special sciences (physics, psychology, chemistry, political science, etc.). Philosophy, he adds, "contents itself with a more attentive scrutiny and comparison of the facts of everyday life, such as present themselves to every adult and sane person, and for the most part in every day and hour of his waking life" (EP2:146). In this sense philosophy differs from the special sciences, which actively seek out new experiences, often with the use of special instruments (microscopes, spectrometers, cyclotrons, etc.), or with specially developed techniques, such as statistics or psychoanalysis. For Peirce, as we saw already in the Introduction, philosophy's main purpose is to give us a general conception of the universe, a *Weltanschauung*, which can form a basis for the special sciences. Philosophy, Peirce continues, consists of phenomenology, the three normative sciences (esthetics, ethics, and logic), and metaphysics. Next, and building on the insights of philosophy, follow the special sciences.

Division of the Sciences of Discovery

MATHEMATICS	Studies how things can be supposed to be
POSITIVE SCIENCES	Studies of how things are
PHILOSOPHY	Studies the most general facts of everyday life
Phenomenology	Studies phenomena as they appear in their immediacy
The Normative Sciences	Study phenomena in their relation to ends
Esthetics	Studies phenomena whose ends are to embody qualities of feeling
Ethics	Studies phenomena whose ends lie in action
Logic	Studies phenomena whose end is to represent something
Metaphysics	Seeks a general conception of the universe that can act as a basis for the special sciences
THE SPECIAL SCIENCES	Studies facts that are deliberately sought out and often removed from everyday life

---

6.4 In Search of a Proof

Peirce's insistence that pragmatism be proven, even though the method had already proved itself capable of resolving many difficult issues, stems from a fact familiar to scientists and philosophers that simple rules like the pragmatic maxim often "had to be greatly complicated in the further progress of science" (EP2:139). Put differently, it is quite safe to say that, *as a rule of thumb*, our conception of the conceivable practical consequences of a concept is the meaning of that concept, but can we truly say that no concept whatsoever has any meaning *apart* from those consequences? Are there no strange cases that require the rule to be fine-tuned? Is it not true that our most dependable beliefs sometimes fail when applied to specialized fields such as astronomy or quantum physics? Since genuine doubt regarding the maxim can be raised, it is appropriate to demand a proof.

This demand for a proof fits in nicely with Peirce's critical commonsensism. Peirce agrees with Scottish common-sensists, such as Thomas Reid, that Hume's empiricism was too narrowly conceived, which caused it to lead to skepticism. According to the common-sensists, our knowledge of external objects is not a product of sensations alone (as Hume had argued), but of sensations in combination with intuitively known general principles that are considered indubitable. Peirce agrees, but has quite a different take on why these commonsense beliefs are indubitable. They are indubitable, not because they are the product of an infallible intuition, but because we so firmly believe in them that we cannot really make ourselves doubt them. For Peirce, and here he differs from Descartes, you cannot make yourself doubt what you firmly believe to be true. It is in this sense, which matches Peirce's earlier views in "The Fixation of Belief," that Peirce maintains that we have indubitable commonsense beliefs (2.3). This does not mean that those beliefs are above criticism, and Peirce emphasizes repeatedly that we must actively seek to criticize them whenever the opportunity arises. This is why Peirce's common-sensism is called a *critical* common-sensism.

As the earlier sketch of the division of the sciences suggests, any proof of pragmatism should begin with phenomenology and then run through the normative sciences. This is precisely what Peirce sets out to do. The division also reveals that the truth of pragmatism cannot be derived from the laws of psychology, as he had tried to do in the 1870s, or from metaphysics. Given the position of pragmatism within Peirce's classification of the sciences, no metaphysical or psychological truth can be used to support pragmatism without falling into vicious circularity.

Peirce's proof is not an argument in the old rationalist sense, where each proposition follows deductively from those preceding it. As we saw, Peirce rejects not only Descartes's division between facts that are self-evident and those that are not (2.1), but also his portrayal of reasoning as if it were a chain of syllogisms in which each link is perceived clearly and distinctly. Peirce rejects this notion of reasoning, which he sees as a product of two fundamental mistakes he ascribes to Descartes: his method of doubt, and his faith in the infallibility of reasoning.

Dismissing the Cartesian chain argument, Peirce turns to the schoolmen whom Descartes so fiercely rejected, opting for what he calls "the multiform argumentation of the middle ages" (EP1:28). Peirce characterizes this type of argumentation as follows:

> Philosophy ought to imitate the successful sciences in its methods, so far as to proceed only from tangible premises which can be subjected to careful scrutiny, and to trust rather to the multitude and variety of its arguments than to the conclusiveness of any one. Its reasoning should not form a chain which is no stronger than its weakest link, but a cable whose fibers may be ever so slender, provided they are sufficiently numerous and intimately connected.
>
> (EP1:29)

For us humans, who are fallible but have an instinct for guessing right, this "rope reasoning" is far more secure than even the simplest chain argument. Whereas a single broken link will rupture the entire chain, a rope remains in place even if several of its fibers were to break.

The proof of pragmatism Peirce develops in the Harvard lectures is an example of rope reasoning. As he explains roughly two years after the lectures,

> Just as a civil engineer, before erecting a bridge, a ship, or a house, will think of the different properties of all materials, and will use no iron, stone, or cement, that has not been subjected to tests; and will put them together in ways minutely considered, so, in constructing the doctrine of pragmatism the properties of all indecomposable concepts were examined and the ways in which they could be compounded. Then the purpose of the proposed doctrine having been analyzed, it was constructed out of the appropriate concepts so as to fulfill that purpose. In this way, the truth of it was proved. There are subsidiary confirmations of its truth; but it is believed that there is no other independent way of strictly proving it.
>
> (CP5.5)

In the Harvard lectures Peirce largely follows this recipe, entrenching pragmatism firmly within phenomenology and the normative sciences. The main fibers of Peirce's proof of pragmatism include his doctrine of the categories (the "indecomposable concepts"), his argument that logic is a normative science (establishing "the purpose of the doctrine"), his doctrine of perception, and his treatment of deduction, induction, and abduction. It would lead us far beyond the scope of this brief introduction to attempt to spell out Peirce's multifaceted and elaborate proof. Instead, I will limit myself to a few of its core elements, as they will help us understand what this pragmatism is that Peirce is trying to prove.

6.5 Phenomenology and the Normative Sciences

For Peirce, the phenomenologist's central task is to bring order to the manifold of her observations. One way she can do this is by determining whether there are any general characteristics that are found in all phenomena, no matter whether they are forced upon us by outward experience, highly abstract conclusions of theoretical physicists, or colorful products of the most vivid nightmares. Such characteristics, Peirce calls, following Aristotle, Kant, and Hegel, *categories*. Thus, for Peirce, it becomes the business of phenomenology "to draw up a catalogue of categories and prove its sufficiency and freedom from redundancies, to make out the characteristics of each category, and to show the relations of each to the others" (EP2:148). The catalogue of categories Peirce ultimately arrives at is remarkably short. There are only three, and, in an effort to avoid contamination with existing metaphysical systems, he calls them firstness, secondness, and thirdness.

Firstness is the pure presentness of the phenomenon—i.e., without any reference to anything that it might be presented to. As Peirce puts it, it is the phenomenon "such as it is, utterly ignoring anything else," like, for example, a simple, self-effacing, positive quality of feeling. *Secondness* is the category of resistance or struggle. For Peirce, this second characteristic is also found in all phenomena. It is, moreover, not reducible to firstness, as secondness always involves two phenomena, whereas firstness involves only one. This second category, however, concerns otherness only in its purest form, that is, without any notion of its relation to the first, as doing so unavoidably introduces a third element, namely, the relation. This notion of a relation between two objects then brings us to Peirce's third category, that of *thirdness*, or mediation. It is especially the acceptance of this third category that distinguishes the realists, among whom Peirce reckons himself, from the nominalists, among whom he classifies James. For the realist, relations are as real as the individual objects they relate. (To be fair, James does allow for relations to be real, but when he does so, he tacitly treats them as individuals.)

The preceding account shows that you cannot have thirdness without secondness and no secondness without firstness, as you need a first before you can relate it to a second and you need two before you can relate them. But, for Peirce, it also works the other way around. You cannot have a first *without* also having a second, and you cannot have two *without* also having a third. The three categories are all-pervasive; they are present in all we can possibly think of. For instance, when you conceive of something purely in isolation (i.e., as a first), you are already also conceiving something else, namely that what it is not (which is second to it) that stands in a particular relation to it, namely that of negation, thereby bringing in a third. Peirce devotes two full lectures to an extensive defense of the categories, including a defense of why there are not more than three. Peirce's focus on developing a categoriology distinguishes his phenomenology from James's, as well as from the later phenomenologies of Husserl and others (10.4).

Although phenomenology is the most basic of the positive sciences, it can appeal to mathematics, which, as we saw, is not a positive science but only studies hypothetical states of things. In fact, the preceding derivation of the categories does precisely that. It draws conclusions from *hypothetical* pure firsts, pure seconds, and pure thirds—hypothetical, because, as we saw, all three are present in all phenomena.

An important conclusion that can be drawn from this analysis is that generality (or thirdness) is a basic constituent of *all* phenomena. This is an important result for Peirce, because his pragmatism seeks to relate the meaning of terms, etc., not to *particular* effects, as with James, but to the habits they inspire. These habits, however, must be *real* habits, not mere products of our fancy, which is what the nominalists contend. The habits must be real because otherwise Peirce's pragmatism would only relate terms to mental constructs, which is precisely what the pragmatists are seeking to avoid. Since habits are generals, and not particulars, the pervasiveness of thirdness in the phenomena we encounter becomes an important argument in support of Peirce's version of pragmatism, while it is at the same time a strong argument against a nominalistic interpretation of pragmatism.

By itself, however, the discovery of real generals does not prove pragmatism. Peirce's pragmatic maxim is a *normative* principle; it tells us how we should define our terms, or what we should expect from our beliefs, for them to have meaning. Hence, the proof of pragmatism must continue with an investigation of the normative sciences.

Whereas phenomenology studies phenomena as they appear in their immediacy (that is, in their firstness), the normative sciences study phenomena in their relation to specific ends, or, as Peirce puts it elsewhere, "in so far we can act upon it and it upon us."[13] That is to say, the normative sciences study phenomena in their secondness (metaphysics, the third and final branch of philosophy, then studies phenomena in their thirdness). Traditionally, the ends of the normative sciences have been beauty, goodness, and truth. Interpreted this way, Peirce explains, "esthetics considers those things whose ends are to embody qualities of feeling, ethics those things whose ends lie in action, and logic those things whose end is to represent something" (EP2:200).

Peirce goes into great detail showing not only that logic is a normative science, but also how deeply it is intertwined with and depends upon the two more basic normative sciences, esthetics and ethics.

Thomas Hobbes once famously called reason the faculty that enables us, unlike the brutes, "to multiply one untruth by another."[14] Peirce is not as cynical as Hobbes, but he acknowledges that the instincts of the lower animals "answer their purposes much more unerringly than a discursive understanding could do" (R969:3). For Peirce, the singularly most important advantage of reasoning is that it can critically evaluate itself:

> Reason is inferior to Instinct in several respects. It is less subtle, less ready, less unerring. The one respect in which it is superior is in being controlled, checked, criticized. This supposes, or constitutes,—the existence of bad reasoning. There is no such thing as bad instinct, unless it be bad in the eyes of something else. But there is reasoning that reason itself condemns; and were it not so, reason would be without its solitary advantage.
>
> (R832:2)

Put differently, reasoning is subject to self-control. It is precisely because of this that we can call our inferences good or bad. Inferences that are unconscious, and thus uncontrollable, are not subject to this kind of normative evaluation, just as acts that occur outside of our control, like the knee-jerk reflex or the dilation of our pupils, are not subject to moral approbation or reprobation. To put it briefly, for Peirce, reasoning is essentially self-controlled thought in the same way that moral conduct is essentially self-controlled action.

A year after the lectures, in a draft for a review of Herbert Nichols's *Treatise on Cosmology*, this emphasis on self-control explicitly enters the pragmatic maxim:

> The method prescribed in the maxim is to trace out in the imagination the conceivable practical consequences,—that is, the consequences for deliberate, self-controlled conduct,—of the affirmation or denial of the concept; and the assertion of the maxim is that herein lies the *whole* of the purport of the word, the *entire* concept.
>
> (CP8.191)

In the 1903 Lowell lectures, Peirce further explains the notion of self-control when applied to reasoning in terms of rule-following:

> A person who draws a rational conclusion, not only thinks it to be true, but thinks that similar reasoning would be just *in every analogous case*. If he fails to think this, the inference is not to be called reasoning. It is merely an idea suggested to his mind and which he cannot resist thinking is true.
>
> (CP1.606; emphasis added)

Thus emerge general patterns of reasoning that come to act like norms, against which our reasoning in new or complex situations is to be measured. In short, reasoning by its very nature involves the application of rules or norms, so that for each particular inference we must ask ourselves whether it satisfies those rules or not. Peirce's argument is in a way very Kantian. The individual act, in this case the act of assertion, involves (even if only tacitly) a *commitment* to repeat the act when at some other time we find ourselves in the same situation, or one sufficiently like it, *even* if we have at that time an inclination to do otherwise (which is where self-control comes in). For example, when I decide to set my alarm at 4:00 a.m. because I want to catch an early flight, this decision extends beyond the particularities of the current situation in that it involves the general rule, or habit, that in comparable situations I should set my alarm as well. Similarly, the purpose of logic is to develop good habits of reasoning.

The next question to ask, then, is, what is the aim of reasoning? What constitutes logical goodness? Identifying logic with the critic and classification of arguments, Peirce examines three answers to this question, each corresponding with one of the three categories. If we stick to the category of firstness, the end of argumentation would be pure esthetic satisfaction. Good arguments would be those that are esthetically pleasing. This is the attitude of the Platonic idealist. For Peirce, this option is unsatisfactory. It may be feasible for an all-powerful God, but not for us humans. Our ideals are all too easily shattered by the brute force of experience.

Alternatively, we could center on secondness, and make the brute force of experience our ultimate aim and benchmark. Good arguments would be those that lead us to certain preordained brute experiences. This is in essence the attitude of the nominalist. This view also lies behind the pragmatism of James and Schiller, and that of Papini and Prezzolini.

For Peirce, this second option is also unsatisfactory. When we rely solely on blind compulsion, we make ourselves utter strangers to the world. We would never be able to *know* anything. Because pure secondness leaves no residue (as that would invariably require thirdness), we would be caught entirely within a web of our own making without being able to connect it to the world. In a way, Kant's transcendental philosophy with its distinction between the phenomena and the noumena (the things themselves) also falls in this category.

The two choices just described are the only options open to the nominalist. The realist, who accepts the reality of relations, also has a third option. This option is to hold that there are real relations within nature—relations "to which we can train our own reason to conform more and more" (EP2:212). Put differently, the realist can hold that there is an element of reasonableness in what we experience, and that the aim of reasoning is to draw this out.

Admittedly, the claim that the universe that enters our experience is organized such that it agrees with our reason is merely a postulate; it is a claim that we *hope* to be true. But no more is needed, Peirce argues, as our only hope of ever knowing anything *presupposes* that this postulate is true, as does the very distinction between logical goodness and badness. Moreover, if we accept, with Peirce, an evolutionary account of the human species, this agreement can be explained quite adequately in terms of adaptation. Reasoning is not something that is *external* to the universe—something like a divine infusion—but over the course of its development, the human organism (like any other organism) *internalizes*, however imperfectly, part of the dynamic order of the universe—a universe that is itself still evolving.

On the realist's interpretation of pragmatism, the meaning of a concept is thus not some singular experience or act, but how such practical effects contribute to the development of the reasonableness of the universe (CP5.3). Understanding is not gained by gathering disconnected facts, but by getting in tune with the concrete reasonableness of the cosmos.

Whether James truly understood what Peirce was up to in the Harvard lectures is doubtful, as the following exchange of letters reveals. At issue is again a clash between James's nominalism and Peirce's realism. Not long after the lectures, James writes in "Humanism and Truth," "The serious meaning of a concept, says Mr. Peirce, lies in the concrete difference to someone which its being true will make" (MT:37). James sends a copy of the paper to Peirce, who writes back,

> I do not think I have often spoken of the "meaning of a concept" whether "serious" or not. I have said that the concept itself "is" *nothing more* than the concept, not of any concrete difference that *will* be made to someone, but, is nothing more than the *concept* of the *conceivable* practical applications of it.[15]

James replies instantly, and not without some irritation, about what he sees as Peirce making a lot of fuss about a minor point: "I am very sorry that the brief paraphrase by which I summed up what seemed to be the essential practical outcome of your view should seem to you so to belie it."[16] For Peirce, however, it is not a minor point at all; it is the central message of his Harvard lectures, which leads Peirce to reply to James with no less irritation: "My Harvard lectures were chiefly bringing out the point which you seem surprised I should attach any importance to."[17]

6.6 *Pragmatism* Versus *Pragmaticism*

The Harvard lectures weren't published, but in 1905–6 Peirce publishes three articles in the journal *Monist*: "What Pragmatism Is," "Issues of Pragmaticism," and "Prolegomena to an Apology for Pragmaticism." As with the

Harvard lectures, Peirce is again developing his own branch of pragmatism while distancing himself from the other pragmatists. Again, the development of a proof of pragmatism is central, albeit that it is now called an apology in the old Greek sense of a speech made in defense of something (as the speech Socrates gave at his trial in Plato's *The Apology*).

In the third paper, the prolegomena to his apology of pragmatism, Peirce goes into great detail discussing his graphical logic (a geometric rather than an algebraic approach to logic) which he subsequently sets out to use in his proof. The proof itself, however, is never fully completed and does not make it into print. Many manuscripts related to it have survived, but it would lead us too far astray to try to wade our way through this mass of material. Instead, we concentrate on Peirce's general account of pragmatism in "What Pragmatism Is" and Peirce's later reflections on the doctrine.

As already noted, disappointed with what pragmatism has become Peirce renames his view pragmaticism. Recall that the suffix "-icism" indicates that what he has in mind is a more strictly defined reading of pragmatism. It is important to keep in mind, however, that Peirce embraces the new term not to mark a departure from his earlier view, but because he wants to distance himself from how the term has been taken up by those who made pragmatism fashionable.

The centerpiece of pragmaticism remains the 1878 pragmatic maxim (2.4). Continuing the course that he set out in the Harvard lectures, Peirce spends much time and effort ensuring that the maxim is interpreted in realist terms. In the process he revises the maxim as follows:

> Consider what effects, that might conceivably have practical bearings, we conceive the object of our conception to have. Then, ~~our concep-tion~~ *the general mental habit that consists in the production* of these effects is the whole of our conception of the object.
>
> (R318:346; emphasis added)

The idea behind this, Peirce explains elsewhere, is that "every concept (in contrast to qualities of feeling, images, experiences, etc.) is definable in terms of a possible purpose of conduct under hypothetical general conditions" (RL107:7).

At times Peirce also interjects brief clauses to spell out what he means by "conceivable practical consequences." They are "consequences for deliberate, self-controlled conduct" (CP8.191), or, in a letter to F.W. Frankland, "consequences for rational conduct."[18] In a 1906 draft letter to Schiller, Peirce similarly elaborates on his choice of "practical" by explaining, "by 'practical' I mean apt to affect conduct; and by conduct, voluntary action that is self-controlled; i.e., controlled by adequate deliberation" (CP8.322). And, in a passage that inspired the revision in the previous block quotation, Peirce explains that "since pragmatism . . . relates to intellectual concepts exclusively, and since these are general, the mental element we seek must be general," and this naturally leads him to habits, which are general, rather than feelings or sense impressions, which are particular (R318:346). And around 1908, he writes James: "the point I wished to make as supremely important in philosophical inquiries was that an idea which *cannot conceivably result in a general effect upon conduct* can have no intellectual significance whatsoever" (RL224:168).

For Peirce, what constitutes meaning is thus not the "effects" qua sensory impressions, nor the singular act of bringing these effects about, but the deliberate, self-controlled behavior that is elicited by the concept. To make meaning consist exclusively of the concrete acts that the conception brings about, Peirce explains, would make brute force the *summum bonum* of pragmatism (R284:3). For Peirce, this is absurd. Drawing an analogy with music, he observes, "nobody conceives that the few bars at the end of a musical movement are the purpose of the movement" (CP5.402n3). Or, to give another analogy of his: one might as well contend that "the artist-painter's living art is applied to dabbing paint upon canvas, and . . . that art-life consists in dabbing paint, or that its ultimate aim is dabbing paint" (ibid).

Peirce's general model is still that of the experimenter or laboratory worker. The experimenter has a tendency to interpret the meaning of an assertion as a prescription for an experiment that, if carried out correctly, will result in an experience of a given description. As Peirce puts it,

> When you have found, or ideally constructed upon a basis of observation, the typical experimentalist, you will find that whatever assertion you may make to him, he will either understand as meaning that if a given prescription for an experiment ever can be and ever is carried out in act, an experience of a given description will result, or else he will see no sense at all in what you say.
>
> (EP2:332)

Now one could object, as Peirce has an imaginary opponent do (EP2:339), that this is a nominalist view because an experiment always concerns a *particular* operation upon a *particular* object, leading to a *particular* result, thereby reducing meaning to particulars. To take such a position, Peirce counters, betrays a serious misunderstanding of what experiments are about. The meaning of an experiment lies not in any of these particulars, nor in all of them together, but in the *phenomenon* that this particular event exemplifies, which is not a particular at all:

> Indeed, it is not in an experiment, but in *experimental phenomena*, that rational meaning is said to consist. When an experimentalist speaks of a *phenomenon*, such as "Hall's phenomenon," "Zeeman's phenomenon" and its modification, "Michelson's phenomenon," or "the chessboard

phenomenon," he does not mean any particular event that did happen to somebody in the dead past, but what *surely will* happen to everybody in the living future who shall fulfill certain conditions.

(EP2:340)

Now, "what *surely will* happen to everybody in the living future who shall fulfill certain conditions" is certainly something quite different from singular experiences or discrete sensory data. The scientist, Peirce argues, is always tacitly a realist; she cannot be otherwise, as without a commitment to realism, the entire enterprise of empirical science becomes void. Why experiment if all that matters is the particular effects the experiment brings about?

What makes experiments valuable is that they are recipes for action. For Peirce, the meaning of a proposition is always again a proposition. That is to say, it is a translation. Now there are countless ways in which a proposition can be translated. So, which of them would we call "its meaning"? The pragmatist has an answer. It is, Peirce observes,

> that form in which the proposition becomes applicable to human conduct, not in these or those special circumstances, nor when one entertains this or that special design, but *that form which is most directly applicable to self-control under every situation, and to every purpose.*

> (EP2:340, emphasis added)

Recall that pragmatism, for Peirce, is a maxim of logic and that logic, being a branch of ethics, studies how we should act.

6.7 Logic and Semiotics

Peirce claims that we can think only in signs (2.1), calls pragmatism a maxim of logic, and draws a close connection between logic and semiotics—at times considering them equivalent. Consequently, a brief excursion into Peirce's semiotics, or doctrine of signs, is called for. In line with the doctrine of the categories we looked at earlier, Peirce's semiotics is triadic: it connects what he calls an immediate object with a dynamic object through an interpretant. It is triadic, not just because it consists of three elements, but because the relation between them cannot be reduced to a combination of dyads, or pairs.

First, some terminology. By immediate object, Peirce means what is "presented in the Sign" (EP2:498), or "cognized in the Sign" (EP2:492). The *dynamic object*, in contrast, refers *not* to what is presented in the sign, but to what occasions the presentation—its cause. The dynamic object forces itself upon the mind while encompassing more than is revealed. To ascertain what that dynamic object is, we must go beyond what appears in the sign and acquire what Peirce calls collateral experience (CP8.314). Such collateral experience is gained when we interpret various other signs as indicating the very same dynamic object. In fact, given Peirce's earlier dictum that the absolutely incognizable is absolutely inconceivable (2.5), Peirce even goes a significant step further by arguing that we cannot say, without falling into absurdity, that there might be aspects of this dynamic object that are inaccessible to us in principle. Finally, the *interpretant* is what connects an immediate object with a dynamic object; for instance, when the darkening sky is connected with a storm.

For Peirce, a sign is thus something cognizable (something capable of being known), that is so determined by something else, while simultaneously determining a third, namely some actual or potential mind (EP2:493). Note that in stating that signs must be cognizable, Peirce allows for something to be a sign even when it never has been, and perhaps never will be, interpreted. If the sign is interpreted, then we have a new sign; i.e., an immediate object that comes with its own dynamic object and interpretant. "Determine" means in this context setting a boundary, or limit. For instance, the immediate object of a footprint on the beach can give rise to a great variety of signs (human presence, the firmness of the sand, etc.), and though any sign can give rise to a variety of interpretations (a spouse's infidelity, a lost child, the direction of the tide), the dynamic object limits, or determines, what can be a sign of it, and each sign similarly limits what can be an interpretant of it. On Peirce's semiotics, everything that enters our mind is a sign, and every sign comes with its triadic structure of immediate object, dynamic object, and interpretant. Moreover, as any interpretant announces itself as an immediate object, any train of thought is a sequence of signs.

Applying this to pragmatism comes down to asking what exactly gives a sign its meaning. On Peirce's semiotics, it is the interpretant. For Peirce, however, we must distinguish three types of interpretants: the immediate, dynamic, and final interpretant. When I tell someone that it is storming outside, and she understands me by conjuring up a vague composite image of storms seen and imagined, then meaning takes the form of an immediate interpretant. The dynamic interpretant is the effect that my comment actually produces on her mind. This can be a sudden urge to close some windows, a feeling of disappointment, or the surfacing of that composite image. But since the dynamic object encompasses more than is revealed in the immediate object, we must go further and incorporate also the corroborating experience that would reveal to us those aspects of the object that did not enter into the immediate object through which it became known initially. Consequently, in line with Chapter 2, Peirce defines the final interpretant as "that which *would finally* be decided to be the true interpretation if consideration of the matter were carried so far that an ultimate opinion were reached" (CP8.184). The idea is that we can get beyond our first impression and get a better interpretation of the dynamic object, even up to the point where there is "no latitude of interpretation at all" (CP5.447).

Identifying symbols as those signs that represent something, Peirce rephrases his original maxim in the following manner:

> The entire intellectual purport of any symbol consists in the total of all general modes of rational conduct which, conditionally upon all the possible different circumstances and desires, would ensue upon the acceptance of the symbol.
>
> (EP2:346)

By casting the maxim in semiotic terms, Peirce avoids one problem that plagued modern philosophy. When we speak of meaning, are we talking about ideas, words, sentences, statements, beliefs, theories? For Peirce, the maxim applies to anything that can become a symbol; a symbol being a sign "whose special significance or fitness to represent just what it does represent lies in nothing but the very fact of there being a habit, disposition, or other effective general rule that it will be so interpreted," where this general rule may be either natural or acquired (CP4.447).

In this new rendition, Peirce seeks to ensure a reading of the maxim that is non-sensationalist, non-emotivist, and realist. It is non-sensationalist in that the meaning of a symbol is not cast in terms of what *sensations* to expect. It is non-emotivist, in that it explicitly focuses on the *intellectual* purport of the symbol and links the meaning of the symbol to *rational* conduct. Finally, it is realist, in that it locates meaning not in particulars but in something general; and it does so in such a way that it blocks all attempts to reduce the general to the particular, as no set of particulars can possibly cover "all the possible different circumstances and desires."

6.8 Pragmatism as the Logic of Abduction

Before continuing, a few words on the relation between pragmatism and abduction, as in the Harvard lectures Peirce calls pragmatism "the logic of abduction" (EP2:226ff).

In the 1860s, taking his cues from the medieval doctrine of *consequentiae*, Peirce comes to distinguish a third type of reasoning besides induction and deduction, which he comes to call abduction. The three types emerge as the three ways in which a rule, a case, and a result can be combined, as the following example of Peirce shows (EP1:188):

Deduction

All the beans in this bag are white (Rule),
These beans are from this bag (Case);
These beans are white (Result).

Induction

> These beans are white (Result),
> These beans are from this bag (Case);
> All the beans in this bag are white (Rule).

Abduction

> All the beans in this bag are white (Rule),
> These beans are white (Result);
> These beans are from this bag (Case).

Note that, in contrast to deduction, for neither induction nor abduction does the truth of the premises (the first two claims) guarantee the truth of the conclusion (the third claim). For induction, it is still possible that some beans in the bag are not white; for abduction, it is still possible that the beans did not come from the bag. What happens in an abduction is that the conclusion is a plausible explanatory hypothesis. The conclusion that the beans came from the bag explains that the beans are white given what else we know, namely that the beans in the bag are also white. It is in a way our best explanation for the situation described in the premises. According to Peirce, only through abduction do we truly come to know anything new, and the justification of this mode of reasoning lies in the fact that "if we are ever to understand things at all, it must be in that way" (EP2:205)—neither deduction nor induction can give us such understanding, and those are the only alternatives we have.

Peirce further extracts from these three types of reasoning a general recipe for inquiry. When we encounter a surprising phenomenon—something we do not understand—we first frame an explanatory hypothesis (abduction). Next, using deduction, we determine what would follow if that hypothesis were true. This second step should lead to predictions the truth of which can be verified through induction. This then verifies the hypothesis.

In essence, the formation of a hypothesis is a guess. Now, when Peirce calls pragmatism the logic of abduction, he means to say that not just any guess will do. Quite the contrary, the hypothesis must be framed such that it enables us to trace its conceivable practical consequences; that is, it must be framed in accordance with the pragmatic maxim. Recall that Peirce considers logic a branch of ethics—it is the discipline that teaches us how we should reason. As such, logic comes with its own imperatives, one of which is the pragmatic maxim. In short, for a hypothesis to count as a product of abduction, rather than as a wild guess, the formation of the hypothesis should abide by the principle of pragmatism. It is only in this way that we can hope to regulate our future conduct rationally (EP2:299).

Peirce's logic of abduction also connects his phenomenology with his views about knowledge and inquiry. To identify certain sensory impressions as a bush or a bicycle is to form a hypothesis that ultimately derives its meaning from its conceivable practical consequences. As Peirce explains,

> our first premises, the perceptual judgments, are to be regarded as an extreme case of abductive inferences, from which they differ in being absolutely beyond criticism. The abductive suggestion comes to us like a flash. It is an act of *insight*, although of extremely fallible insight.
>
> (EP2:227)

Though, the formation of a perceptual judgment is "a process not sufficiently conscious to be controlled" (ibid), which distinguishes it from abduction proper, it is still pragmatism that determines which judgments are to be accepted and which are not. This becomes clear when we mistake a distant bush for a bicycle. As we will see in Chapter 9, Peirce's take on verification differs from that of the logical positivists' in that he focuses on practical rather than experiential verification and he never claims that verification is final. All our knowledge of the world is fallible.

Notes

1. A selection of these definitions, in three volumes, is forthcoming as part of the *Writings*. In addition, Peirce's heavily annotated personal copy of the *Dictionary*, which also indicates what entries he wrote, is preserved at Harvard.
2. Perry (1935) 2:222.
3. Ibid.
4. Letter from James to Peirce, December 22, 1897; in Skrupskelis and Berkeley, vol. 8 (2000), p.326.
5. Letter from Peirce to James, January 4, 1898; op. cit., p.334.
6. Ibid., p.335.
7. Ibid.
8. The lectures are published as Kenneth Ketner (ed), *Reasoning and the Logic of Things: The Cambridge Conference Lectures of 1898* (Cambridge, 1992).
9. The Harvard lectures are included in EP2 as selections 10–16; a separate edition, with extensive commentary, is published as Patricia Ann Turrisi (ed), *Pragmatism as a Principle and Method of Right Thinking* (New York, 1997).
10. Not quite demanding a proof, James published the first two of his 1906 Lowell lectures under the umbrella title "A Defense of Pragmatism," *Popular Science Monthly* 70 (1907): 193–206, 351–64.
11. WJ:363. James confuses Peirce's 1903 Harvard lectures on pragmatism with the Lowell lectures on logic Peirce gave later that year. It is quite clear, though, that James has the Harvard lectures in mind.
12. Alternatively, in his 1880 "On the Algebra of Logic," Peirce presents a neurophysiological derivation of logic (W4:163–5).
13. Turrisi (1997), p.66.
14. Thomas Hobbes, *Selections* (New York, 1930), p.23.

15. Letter from Peirce to James, December 6, 1904; in Skrupskelis and Berkeley, vol. 10 (2002), p.511f.
16. Letter from James to Peirce, December 7, 1904; op. cit., p.512.
17. Letter from Peirce to James, December 17, 1904 (RL:224; draft).
18. Letter to F.W. Frankland, February 25, 1907 (RL148).

Chapter 7

Josiah Royce and George Herbert Mead

In this chapter we look at Josiah Royce, who is deeply inspired by Peirce, and George Herbert Mead, a student of Royce and a close friend of John Dewey. (We turn to Dewey in the next chapter.) Royce is a deeply Christian thinker who combines pragmatism with idealism; Mead, on the other hand, is a naturalist who combines pragmatism with biology. Royce is rationalistically inclined, with a strong preference for deduction; Mead is an empiricist with a keen sense for extrapolating upon the findings of the sciences. He is deeply impressed, for instance, by Einstein's theory of relativity, cultural anthropology, and Freud's psychoanalysis, which he seeks to apply to his theory of knowledge and his conceptions of reality and the self.

Josiah Royce (1855–1916) is born in Grass Valley, a remote mining town in California.[1] At age 22, he is the very first to receive a doctorate in philosophy from an American university. After a brief stint at the University of California, Berkeley, Royce moves to Harvard, where he remains. At Harvard, Royce grows very close to William James. They are colleagues at Harvard, live right next to one another, and engage in what becomes a lifelong debate known as "The Battle of the Absolute."[2] Royce is especially critical of James's nominalism and his individualism. In addition to Mead, Royce's students include T.S. Eliot, George Santayana, W.E.B. Du Bois, Norbert Wiener, and C.I. Lewis.

Starting with his dissertation on Kant, and inspired by James, Royce begins as what he later describes as a "pure pragmatist"—a position he comes to reject. However, rather than abandoning his early pragmatism, Royce seeks to modify it, which brings him to a position he calls "absolute pragmatism." The source of Royce's early pragmatism is a combination of his reading of Kant and a strong skepticism about knowledge. As with Peirce, Kant left a deep impression upon Royce at a young age, and like Peirce, Royce gives a pragmatic reading to Kantian philosophy, which (again like Peirce) involves a rejection of the idea of the thing in itself, or *Ding an sich* (2.1).

7.1 Pure Pragmatism and the Absolute Knower

In developing his pure pragmatism, Royce begins by observing that knowledge is a function of judgment. When I judge, say, that rattlesnakes are venomous, I am combining two ideas in my mind: the idea of rattlesnakes and the idea of being venomous. Because these ideas are not themselves already connected, it is the judgment that establishes the connection. Consequently, it is I, and I alone, that draws the connection. For Royce, this means that this connection is in the end an expression of my will. Being expressions of our will, our judgments are also always directed toward action; they are always made, or demanded, for a certain purpose. "The final basis of our thought," Royce writes James in 1880, "is ethical, practical."[3] And over a decade later,

> A thought which has no conscious reference to a deed, which involves no plan of conduct, which joins nothing together that was so far divided, which dissects nothing that was so far whole, which involves no play of active attention from object to object, which voluntarily asserts nothing, and which denies nothing, which neither accepts nor rejects, but only passively contemplates, is no thought at all, but is a vacant staring at nothing in particular.
>
> (EP:119)

When we combine all this, we find that for the early Royce, judgments are purpose-inspired combinations of ideas that express a present need. My judgment that rattlesnakes are venomous, Royce would argue, gives me *knowledge* that rattlesnakes are venomous, albeit that this knowledge is only about the connection that *I* am drawing between ideas that I have within my own mind, and it is moreover strictly confined to the moment when I'm drawing that connection. Since this knowledge is a product of judgments that are always unique and self-enclosed—meaning they can never conflict with other judgments—such knowledge can never be shown wrong, and therefore has to be true. For Royce, this is the only form knowledge can take, and the only source of truth. (Of course, we can form beliefs and opinions that go beyond this, but none of them would qualify as knowledge.) In sum, Royce's early pragmatism, which welds voluntarism onto idealism, is highly nominalistic. All knowledge is about a direct connection of particular, private ideas drawn within a particular voluntary act of judgment by a particular individual at a particular moment and is wholly confined to all of that—it does not extend beyond it. Royce's early view is very clearly a product of a strong penchant for skepticism, accompanied, as skepticism so often is, by a robust desire for absolute certainty.

Royce's early pragmatism quickly runs into problems. These problems do not make him abandon pragmatism, but rather cause him to supplement it.

He can no longer consider himself a *pure* pragmatist. Earlier, when discussing Peirce's four methods for fixing belief, we saw that the method of tenacity proved untenable because the social impulse is against it (2.3). Something akin happens here. As Royce explains,

> Even a pragmatist who wants to be a pure one has an inevitable conception, not only of what he now needs, as he utters this judgment, but of what he ought to need in order to get a warrant for the judgment. And he also has a conception of the need of finding companions who shall be persuaded to agree with him, or who at least ought to be persuaded.
> (EP:129)

Thus, when I judge that rattlesnakes are venomous, I do not merely take this to be a private momentary construction that evaporates the very moment my attention shifts away, but I take it to be something that has authority—something that my future self should also accept, and that others should accept too. In brief, the pure pragmatist has no other option but to recognize "that his truth is something *more* than the result and expression of his present need" (EP:131). For Royce, pure pragmatists thus fall into a performative contradiction: on the one hand, they claim that truth is wholly confined to the individual the moment the judgment is made, while, on the other, they claim that this truth is socially confirmed. Clearly, if you commit to the first, you cannot also commit to the second, and vice versa. In sum, pure pragmatism is refuted by a simple *reductio ad absurdum*.

If pure pragmatism must be supplemented to avoid such a contradiction, the question becomes: what must it be supplemented with? When I judge that rattlesnakes are venomous and that you should agree with this, I'm implying that there is a connection between rattlesnakes and being venomous that is *independent* of whether I happen to draw that connection or not. In fact, to say that the judgment is true implies that rattlesnakes would still be venomous *even* when I fail to draw the connection. The idea that this connection is independent of what I happen to think raises the question of what sustains that connection if it is not my consciousness. Royce's answer is that it has to be sustained in some *other* consciousness. This consciousness cannot be just any other consciousness, but it must be such that entertaining the judgment guarantees that the judgment is true. In Royce's terms, for our ordinary concept of truth to be meaningful, there must be an Absolute Knower, an actual infinite mind that encompasses the totality of all actual truths, as well as all possible errors. This view, Royce comes to refer to as absolute pragmatism. In brief, to Royce's pure pragmatism is now added an absolute reference point, one that is needed to make knowledge, as we generally understand it, possible.

Importantly, what sustains the connections—in this case the connection between rattlesnakes and being venomous—must be some *consciousness*; it cannot be dead matter. The reason for this is that, for Royce, as we saw, the judgments and the ideas connected by them are always purpose directed. They are not passive imprints through which reality reveals itself to us on its own terms. It is the knower that sets the terms. True, Royce acknowledges that "we are accustomed to say that it is the object itself whose nature forces upon us," but, he continues, in truth "nothing can force you except your own need" (EP:123). For Royce, there can thus be no non-idealistic objective reality. He rejects that our ideas correspond to something external to thought, because that would make knowledge inexplicable; he rejects mysticism (like Bergson's; 5.1), because it doesn't explain anything; and he rejects Kant's critical method, because he turns it into a mystery—our relationship to the thing-in-itself that we can never know.

Royce's philosophy remains idealistic and voluntaristic. The result is a monistic worldview, a block universe devoid of real possibility, as the infinite absolute knows all that can be known. As such, Royce's absolute pragmatism contrasts sharply with James's pluralism and with Peirce's notions of real chance and fallibilism. Royce's Absolute Knower must further be distinguished from Peirce's notion of truth as the final opinion (2.6), as Royce requires that there be a true opinion, not as a possibility or perhaps future actuality "at the end of inquiry," but as existing concurrently with any mistake that is being made. A false opinion today *requires* that there be today also the true opinion that it negates. Hence, the very existence of error necessitates that there must be an Absolute Knower. Royce further identifies this Absolute Knower with God, a move that causes Peirce to remark: "I have been studying Royce's book. The ideas are very beautiful [but] I don't think it good taste to stuff it so full of the name of God" (CP8.277).

7.2 Toward a Community of Interpretation

Peirce is not impressed with Royce's absolute pragmatism and the *reductio ad absurdum* argument on which it rests (later, we examine C.I. Lewis's argument for why it fails). Peirce raises four objections. First, the *reductio* argument is deductive, and deduction can never teach us anything about matters of fact, which is what Royce's argument purports to do. Second, it is dilemmatic: it sets up two contradicting views, shows that one is self-refuting, and that therefore we must accept the other. Importantly, we are not given any *positive* reason for why the view that we are left with is correct. Third, outside of pure mathematics, such arguments are seldom decisive. Often all one needs to defeat it is a modification in some inessential detail of the position that is purportedly refuted. Fourth, Royce's argument begs the question. It starts by assuming what it claims to prove, namely the existence of a logically coherent, all-encompassing worldview. Without such assumption, the *reductio* doesn't work, as there will be no reason to insist that contradicting views can't coexist.[4] Peirce's objections drive home the point that Royce's absolute pragmatism remains caught in Peirce's third method for fixing belief, the a priori method (2.3), which means that, for Peirce, it does not amount to pragmatism (2.4).

Overall, Peirce finds Royce's logic so deplorable that he tells him to start studying it—advice Royce takes to heart, and which ends up making him an accomplished logician. However, Royce's main focus remains on deduction, and he stays firm on the absolute. The desire for absolute certainty that drove his early skepticism never really leaves him.

As we saw, Royce's shift from pure to absolute pragmatism involves the notion of community. Knowledge and its acquisition are no longer the prerogative of an individual but is a social affair. In his final years, much due to the influence of Peirce and Peirce's semiotics, the notion of community comes to play a growing role in Royce's philosophy and comes to deeply affect his epistemology and metaphysics. Not only does it change his conception of knowledge, but also that of reality, and even of God.

Historically, philosophers entertained only two sources of knowledge: perception and conception. Empiricists focused largely on the first, rationalists on the second. Kant, aiming to overcome the divide, famously stated that conceptions without perceptions are empty, and perceptions without conceptions are blind. Kant then tried to connect the two by showing, as Royce puts it, "how the 'spontaneity' of the intellect actively combines the perceptual data and brings the so-called 'manifold of sense' to 'unity of conception'" (PC2:122). Pragmatists similarly seek to connect the two, but they do so by referencing the will, action, and practical needs. In all such attempts, however, what is used to connect the two is non-cognitive (PC2:126). We saw this clearly with Blondel, who made action the *tertium quid* that caused knowledge to emerge from perception and conception (5.1).

Instead of connecting perception and conception non-cognitively, Royce introduces interpretation as a *third* source of cognition. In Royce's view, Kant came close to this with his notion of judgment (*Urteilskraft*) but fell short of accepting "a triadic classification of the cognitive processes" (PC2:120). The need for a third source of cognition becomes clear from Royce's description of perception and conception. As Royce observes, we do not have a direct perception-like access to the perceptions of others, nor do we have such access to our own past perceptions. Moreover, conception, which can only give us universals, cannot give us access to them either. As Royce puts it: "Both of ourselves and of our neighbors we have no merely intuitive knowledge, no complete perception, and no adequate conception" (PC2:159). This causes him to conclude that without adding interpretation as a source of cognition, "there would be neither selves nor communities" (PC2:112).

So, what does this third source of cognition look like? Crucially, it does not involve the creation of a mental copy of the object encountered, as if we functioned like a camera; rather, the cognizing individual singles out some aspect(s) of the object encountered to some purpose. This means that the object takes the character of a sign—as something that points someone to something. For Royce, and here he agrees with Peirce, interpretation is by its very nature triadic (6.7). An interpretation always involves an interpreter, the object that is interpreted, and the person to whom the interpretation is addressed (PC2.142). In contrast, perception, as traditionally understood, is dyadic; it directly relates the knower to the known. Now, it may be tempting to say that we do not really need the third, but that quickly leads to problems: if there is nobody to whom the interpretation is directed, it cannot have any meaning. Royce gives the example of an Egyptologist who translates hieroglyphs into English (PC2:140). In doing so she addresses those who speak English. If nobody speaks English, then nobody would be able to understand the translation, so it would be meaningless. Now, one might object and say that the Egyptologist herself would still be able to understand the translation, as she is the one who made it—thus implying that one still only needs the dyadic relation between an interpreter and the object interpreted, and making *that* the more fundamental relation to which the third element can be appended as something that is in the end optional. However, this objection is misguided. At best, it reflects a limit case where the interpreter and the person to whom the interpretation is addressed fully coincide. But, Royce continues, such a case cannot exist. Even when the Egyptologist is reflecting upon her own translation, she is interpreting something that her past self has done while in the process addressing her future self. Put more generally, whenever we think, we engage in an interior dialogue that always involves three parties: our past self, our present self, and our future self (PC2:144)—a view we find in Peirce as well (EP1:53, 2.1).

Since the Egyptologist is addressing a community, it is not her personal interpretation that makes the translation correct (as was the case with Royce's pure pragmatism), but the interpretation that ideally every member of her audience would give it—an audience to which she herself also belongs. Hence, the Egyptologist must conform not only to the object she is interpreting, but also to the comprehension of the minds she is addressing (including her own). Both are necessary to make knowledge possible.

Royce next generalizes this view, again following Peirce, by stating that the world *itself* evolves in a similar vein (recall that Royce is an idealist):

> The relations exemplified by the man who, at a given present moment, interprets his own past to his own future, are precisely analogous to the relations which exist when any past state of the world is, at any present moment, so linked, through a definite historical process, with the coming state of the world, that an intelligent observer who happened to be in possession of the facts could, were he present, interpret to a possible future observer the meaning of the past. . . . In fact, what our

own inner reflection exemplifies is outwardly embodied in the whole world's history.

(PC2:144f)

Briefly put, the current state of the world is an interpretation of its past directed to its future. As Royce puts it, "we can define the present as, potentially, the interpretation of the past to the future" (PC2:147). It is important to note, however, that for Royce, interpretation is intrinsically linked to a mind. This is different from Peirce, who for that reason introduced the neologism "interpretant." This interpretant could be a mind, but that's just one possibility.

Royce's focus on interpretation, and the realization that community is more basic than the individual, also affects his notion of God—the Absolute we were introduced to before. If the individual is a product of, a derivative of, or must be understood in terms of the community, then it makes little sense to continue to think of God as an individual. In line with what was said earlier, God should rather be considered "the world's infinite Community of Interpretation (PC2:418). In contrast to the Absolute Knower, in whose infinite mind all truth about past, present, and future inhered, Royce is now conceiving of God as an infinite Community of Interpretation that at each moment encompasses the present's full potentiality.

7.3 The Social Pragmatism of George Herbert Mead

George Herbert Mead (1863–1931) studies with Royce in the 1880s.[5] He then goes to Germany, where he studies with Wilhelm Dilthey and Wilhelm Wundt. In 1891, he returns to the US to teach at the University of Michigan, where he meets John Dewey. In 1894 Mead follows Dewey to the newly opened University of Chicago, where, together with Dewey and Jane Addams, he becomes a main proponent of pragmatism. In Chicago, Dewey and Mead become actively involved in Hull House—a social settlement founded by Addams with the aim of improving the social conditions of the impoverished industrial working class. We return to Hull House in the next chapter. During his tenure at Chicago, Mead comes to play a key role in two connected currents of thought: pragmatism and behaviorism.

Mead publishes relatively little during his life, and his main influence runs through his students. He is a brilliant lecturer and his most important work, *Mind, Self, and Society*, which appears posthumously, consists of lecture notes taken by professional stenographers hired by his students. For Mead, as with Dewey, the starting point is not some theory, or worldview, but what Mead calls "the problematic situation"—a more developed and biologically inspired version of the experience of real doubt that played such a central role in Peirce's "Fixation of Belief" (2.3). For Mead, our linguistic or communicative capabilities are a derivative of the act, and the mind is again a derivative of our capacity for communication. Mead thereby fits the pragmatist pattern of turning Descartes upside down. The mind does not come first, but last, and knowledge acquisition does not proceed from the inside out, but from the outside in. Moreover, regarding the latter, it is the act with its practical consequences that controls the acquisition of knowledge. For Mead, the core of pragmatism consists essentially of two theses: thought cannot be separated from action, and our minds, just like our bodies, are products of a biological evolution wherein individuals are forced to deal with their environment.

7.4 The Philosophy of the Act

Many philosophers start off with mind, or ideas, and then spend much time and effort trying to connect what is within that mind to the world it finds itself in. Royce belongs in this camp. Others begin with matter, and then devote much of their energy on explaining how unthinking matter could give rise to ideas. Mead takes a third way out, and a deeply pragmatic one. His starting point is neither mind nor matter, but the act. Acts are constrained by the world within which we live, and through interaction with that world (assuming the conditions are favorable) acting leads to awareness, self-awareness, mind, language, and society. In this process, objects, all the way down to subatomic particles, solidify, so to speak, into things that can be acted upon (even if only in principle) or as derivatives thereof.

Mead's general approach closely resembles that of Peirce in "The Fixation of Belief," albeit that Mead, and Dewey too, formulates the issue much more directly in biological terms. Where Peirce speaks of belief, Mead is thinking of homeostatic equilibrium, and where Peirce speaks of doubt, Mead talks about an inhibition to act caused by conflicting impulses on what to do next. The occurrence of conflicting impulses to act Mead terms a "problematic situation." Dewey prefers to call it an indeterminate situation, on the grounds that identifying what the problem is already puts us well on our way to a solution. Within the problematic situation, the organism is, as it were, out of sync with its environment. Mead considers this the fountainhead of awareness. A direct or habitual satisfaction of desires goes by unaware, which is why we often cannot remember whether we turned off the stove or locked the front door. It is when we are confronted with a problematic situation, one where we are forced to make a decision on how to proceed, that we become aware of the world wherein we live.

Mead begins by dividing the act into four subsequent stages: impulse, perception, manipulation, and consummation. The impulse sets the organism in motion, whereas consummation marks the satisfaction of the desire that initiated the act, and thus brings it to a close. For the most part, desires are connected routinely with their consummation. The cow in the meadow just bends over and starts grazing. What happens in a problematic situation is that such habitual connection between desire and its satisfaction—between impulse and consummation—is thwarted. Past habits no longer apply or fail to give the desired result, and the organism, Mead explains, needs to actively determine what it is going to respond to. Though it may not always be momentous, it is faced in a way with a genuine option (3.2).

This brings us to what Mead calls the first intermediary phase that separates the impulse from its immediate consummation: perception. Instead of the traditional distinction between sight, sound, smell, taste, and touch, Mead distinguishes between so-called "contact experiences" and "distance experiences." A contact experience is the immediate presence of the environment as it appears in unmediated physical opposition. It comes close to Peirce's notion of secondness as it appears in Peirce's phenomenology (6.5). A wholly unexpected strike against the back of the head, for instance, which Peirce would identify with secondness, returns in Mead as a pure contact experience. There is no anticipation, and the experience itself gives no indication as to what happened beyond the direct effect upon the recipient. The experience itself cannot reveal what struck you, where it came from, how to avoid it, etc. Consequently, an organism with only contact experiences is entirely at the mercy of its environment. It cannot act; it can only react.

With distance experiences, this changes. Here relatively insignificant contact experiences, such as photons bouncing on the retina or airwaves hitting the eardrum, become signs for possible future contact experiences. Thus, were I to see a baseball barreling right at me, its sight forewarns me of what is to come, and this enables me to adapt my behavior accordingly (catch, duck, jump, scream). Such distance experiences greatly enhance the organism's relation with its environment, not only by presenting it with an array of possible future contact experiences, but also by giving it some time to devise how it will react. Both these aspects are wholly absent for beings that have only contact experiences. This account shows that there is a form of pragmatism at work even at the most rudimentary level of perception: The meaning of distance experiences is determined by their anticipated future contact experiences given such and such courses of action. This is true not only for us but is found throughout the animal world.

Importantly, though contact experiences position the individual against the environment, they also reveal points of connection. In fact, if there is nothing to oppose us, we would not be able to act—it is the *resistance* of the air that allows the bird to fly, it is the *resistance* of the golf ball against my hand that enables me to pick it up, etc.

The third phase of the act is that of manipulation. This is the second intermediary phase, and it is situated between perception and consummation. In this third phase there is a close interplay between contact and distance experience. Things are at once seen and felt, which brings together, as Mead puts it, "both the promise of contact and its fulfillment" (PP:170).

For us humans, this third phase concerns primarily the eye–hand coordination, but for organisms of a different physique, this may play out differently.

Our conception of physical objects is, for Mead, a product of the manipulation phase. It is difficult to overestimate the extent to which the hand regulates how we perceive the world. Distance experiences are almost invariably understood as past or anticipated manipulatory experiences. When we see a hammer, we see it as something we can grasp; when we see a tree, we see it as something we can climb; and even the moon looks like something we could touch if only our arms were long enough. Since Mead sees physical objects as bundles of manipulatory acts, he calls them "collapsed acts" (PA:370).

7.5 The Social Nature of the Act and the Emergence of the Self

The consequences of one's acts are seldom limited to oneself. They boil over. The doe that stirs up and flees from the hunter not only betrays her presence but also leaves the tracks that guide the hunter in his pursuit. The bee that moves from flower to flower not only satisfies its appetite for nectar, but also pollinates the flowers on which it rests. For Mead, acts are by their very nature social.

Organisms routinely enter into situations that involve other organisms. These other organisms can be of the same species, as when a mother cares for her young or a colony of termites builds its nest, or of a different species, as when a lioness hunts down a wildebeest. The mechanism discussed earlier applies equally to both situations. Taking the problematic situation again as his starting point, Mead distinguishes two types of interaction: interaction between organisms without selves, and interaction between organisms with selves. The first, he calls the sign situation; the second, the symbol situation.

In the sign situation, the overt aspects of the acts of one individual enter into the intermediate phases of the acts of other individuals in the form of distance experiences. A favorite example of Mead is the dogfight. When two dogs fight, the first overt signs of the behavior of one dog become a stimulus for the other dog to respond to. What is distinctive about the dogfight is that the acts initiated by the dogs are seldom brought to completion. The first overt aspects of the act already tell the other dog what to expect, so that it will react directly to these early aspects rather than waiting for what is to come. Since the dogs often do not get beyond responding to the first overt phases of their acts, the dogfight reduces to what Mead calls "a conversation of gestures" (MSS:43). This habit of reacting to the first overt signs of the act defines, for Mead, the sign situation.

It is important to see what is *not* happening here. The dogs have no idea how their behavior is *received* by other dogs. It is even unaware that certain aspects of its own acts have a signaling function to begin with. Thus, the gnarling dog associates its display of teeth not with the fear this arouses in *other* dogs, but with the mental states that it has come to associate with the act of gnarling in the presence of other dogs. Especially, when it routinely chases away rival dogs, the sensation that accompanies the gnarling is unlikely ever to be one of fear. Hence, within the sign situation, the gestures that control the interaction lack a shared meaning. What means strength and vigor to one dog means fear to the other. The sign situation works precisely because the different participants understand the gestures differently and react accordingly. The different aspects of the social act of the dogfight fit into each other like cogs in a machine. From Mead's account it is clear, though, that the meaning of the gestures cannot be considered separate from the acts they are part of and the interaction within which they function.

Many human interactions, however, work otherwise. The different participants in a social act, such as throwing and catching a ball, project themselves mentally in the position of others to ensure how their acts are interpreted. The thrower of the ball puts herself mentally in the position of the catcher and adjusts her throw accordingly, while the catcher puts himself in the role of the thrower so as to better receive the ball. According to Mead, this type of interaction requires that the participants have selves.

Earlier, when discussing Mead's philosophy of the act, we saw how objects are formed within the process of interaction. For Mead, the self is also formed this way. Initially, the individual does not experience itself as part of the environment but sees the environment as something that borders on an otherwise autonomous inner world. In the course of one's interaction with the environment, however, one particular object stands out, namely one's own body. This body differs from the rest of the environment in an important way. For instance, when I pinch myself in the arm, I am both the initiator and the recipient of the act. That is to say, the difference between my pinching my arm and my pinching your arm is that when I pinch my arm, I will feel the pain it causes, whereas when I pinch yours, I don't—I can at best witness a change in your behavior. What marks, for Mead, the origin of the self is the individual's discovery that it is itself an object just like the ones that it interacts with—the discovery that, rather than that the world exists wholly outside of me, I am myself an object within that world.

For Mead, key to the development of this self is the hand with the juxtaposition of the thumb. When I push one hand against the other, the second hand resists the first; it pushes back. The same happens when I push with one hand against a heavy door. I push, and the door, so to speak, pushes back. More in general, through the opposition experienced within contact experience, I begin to project my experience into the object that I'm interacting with. The force that I am exerting on the door is projected into the door itself. The harder I push, the harder the door pushes back, up to the point where it relaxes its opposition and gives way. Young children draw this conclusion also for pain, believing that when they feel pain after running into a table, the table must be in pain too.

At first, the individual thus construes what it encounters after its own image. This is due to the circumstance that objects originally emerge as products of a projection by the individual of her inner state in all she encounters. It is only through a prolonged interaction with the environment that the individual comes to distinguish between different kinds of objects. What sets trees apart from squirrels is that they persistently respond differently to our advances. Continued interaction with the tree in our backyard will teach us which aspects of our initial projection can be maintained, and which must be abandoned. The same is true for turtles, walnuts, flashes of lightning, clouds, electrical currents, and our fellow humans. In short, for Mead, objects are differentiated based on their response patterns. As he explains in *Mind, Self, and Society*,

> The physical object is an abstraction which we make from the social response to nature. We talk to nature; we address the clouds, the sea, the tree, and the objects about us. We later abstract from that type of response because of what we come to know of such objects.
>
> (MSS:184)

It is through a prolonged interaction that we learn that trees don't experience pain, but that squirrels, bats, and other humans do; that trees, like squirrels, have solid bodies, but that clouds and flashes of lightning don't, etc.

The individual's understanding of itself and of others is further deepened through a process of role-playing. Although it is the problematic situation, with its demand for a solution, that is the fountainhead of conscious activity, once consciousness has formed itself, its scope is not confined to problematic situations only. Humans, and many animals as well, often engage in mock problematic situations in an activity that Mead calls play. Play is free in that the individual is not subjected to the need of fulfilling some predetermined purpose, like finding food or shelter. Within play, self-endowed individuals project themselves into other objects, most significantly other humans, and play their roles: the pitcher knows how the catcher will receive her ball by playing in her imagination the role of the catcher.

In the early stage of its development, the child plays the roles of mother, doctor, nurse, etc., consecutively, without integrating these roles into a more or less coherent whole within which they all have their designated part. Over time, however, the different roles that are played by the child become integrated into what Mead calls games. In a game, the individual fits the different roles together into a common activity with its own structure. To put it briefly, games are organized play.

The shift from mere play to playing games marks an important step. In a game, roles are connected through the specific rules that moves in the game must abide to. The rules that govern the game thus determine which roles are legitimate (you cannot be a catcher in chess) and how each role should be played (what counts as a valid move within the game). For Mead, games range from very primitive ones that have hardly any rules, such as peekaboo, to highly formalized games, like bridge or chess.

Mead extends his notion of game to cover organized human activity. Not only are chess and football games, but also taxation, open heart surgery, and democracy. In Mead's view, we partake every day in numerous games, and often we play in several at once. For Mead, human interaction comes down to a continued participation in a large variety of games. These games show a certain stratification. Some are more specialized, whereas others are so fundamental that proficiency in them is required for participation in many other games. Linguistic communication is a good example of the latter, as countless games cannot be engaged in without knowing the language of one's community.

Since the self is a product of the individual's interaction with the environment, the self is shaped by the roles that individual comes to play; that is, by the games she comes to participate in. Hence, people understand themselves as students, lovers, parents, bricklayers, doctors, citizens, Christians, and so on. Moreover, because individuals participate in numerous overlapping games, they will not see themselves just as students or just as bricklayers, but as an amalgam of the different roles they played, play, or even only dream of playing (as the bookstore clerk who sees herself as the author she wants to become). In short, for Mead, you are the roles that you play, and a well-balanced self is one where these roles adapt well to one another.

The more fundamental games—which generally comprise large groups—also play an important role in giving structure to the self. For Mead, the largest of such groups is that of rational beings. As he puts it in *The Philosophy of the Act*,

> The self as an object becomes a part of the individual through his having assumed the generalized attitude of a member of the group to which that self belongs, *a group that widens until it takes in all rational individuals*, that is, all individuals who could indicate to one another universal characters and objects in co-operative activity.
>
> (PA:375; emphasis added)

Mead speaks in this context also of the role of the generalized other. When playing the role of the generalized other, one does not view one's affairs, or those of others, from some specialized perspective, such as that of the prelate, the soccer mom, or the prosecutor, but one interprets the situation from the general perspective of being a human being.

For Mead, games are almost invariably social, which means that they cannot be played without the cooperation of others. Moreover, many games have their own purpose, which may be different from the aims of any of the individuals participating in them. In such cases, Mead explains, the object of the game resides "in the life-process of the group, not in those of the separate individuals alone" (SW:280). The stock market is a good example of a game with its own object. Mead called such objects "social objects." Individuals can grasp those objects by distancing themselves from their own role and taking the attitude of the group, which they can do as they can run mentally through the roles of others so as to see how the different roles hang together.

The preceding discussion shows that Mead's pragmatism is distinctly a social pragmatism in that *both the object of the act and its completion* are not the private business of discrete individuals but are ostensibly social affairs.

7.6 Mind, Language, and Pragmatism

To characterize the communication between self-endowed individuals, Mead introduces the "significant symbol." As with the gestures we encountered earlier, the meaning of significant symbols is the response they evoke, but they *differ* in two important respects: significant symbols are understood alike by sign maker and sign receiver, and their significance lies in their contribution to the completion of the social act (or the game) that they are used in.

In his discussion of significant symbols, Mead pays particular attention to what he calls the vocal gesture, a gesture that is perceived alike by sign maker and sign receiver. When I shout to you, "Look out!" I am inadvertently also addressing myself because I too hear what I'm shouting. Given that, on Mead's account, the meaning of a sign is the reaction it evokes, the shout, when meaningful, will evoke the same reaction in me as it does in you. Experience bears this out. When I shout, "Look out!" because a speeding car is rapidly coming at you, my own reaction to the shout is a suppressed form of the act that I want you to do. In Mead's view, all significant symbols, from road signs to romance novels, eventually derive from vocal gestures.

Communication through significant symbols allows for far more intricate and complex forms of interaction than can be attained through a mere exchange of gestures. A mover who carries with two helpers a large bookcase through a narrow winding staircase can put himself mentally in the positions of his helpers and use significant symbols to communicate to them what he wants them to do, anticipate their reactions, etc.

As we saw, the self is for Mead a composite of roles, partially organized in a multiplicity of games, built on the individual's awareness of being an object among objects. In fact, much of the interaction and playing of roles concerns precisely the interaction of the individual with her self. Continuing along this line, Mead interprets mind as a product of the internalization of part of this self-directed interaction. For Mead, like Peirce and Royce before him, thought is largely if not exclusively a conversation one has with oneself. In Mead's view, thought is to be conceived as speech where the use of the vocal cords is all but suppressed and the lips no longer move. Since the outward signs of this internalized speech have all but disappeared, the mind develops as something that is private simply because the acts that make up the mind are no longer accessible to others. Moreover, in the interaction that the individual has with her self, the individual, being at once sign giver and sign recipient, attains a much higher degree of control. As Mead explains,

> The moment an idea arises in our mind, we are aware of our response to it, and our attitude toward the idea determines our social conduct toward ourselves. That constitutes the essential difference between ourselves and others. In the latter the stimulation lies outside our control.
>
> (LEC:64)

Within thought we can envision a problematic situation, run rapidly and with a minimum expenditure of energy through numerous alternative response scenarios, and compare the results for each. Dewey later argues along similar lines that "deliberation is a dramatic rehearsal (in imagination) of various competing possible lines of action" (MW14:132).

The primacy Mead gives to the act, his notion that awareness arises within the problematic situation, and his analysis of the human mind clearly situate Mead within the pragmatist camp. Mead argues not just that thought emerges from action, but he goes significantly further, arguing that thought is nothing but action internalized, so that there is no principal difference between a philosophy of the act and a philosophy of mind.

7.7 Perspective Realism

What characterizes pragmatism for Mead is the "radical position that in immediate experience the percept stands over against the individual, not in a relation of awareness, but in that of conduct" (SW:271). Given Mead's account of self and mind, the notion of a disinterested spectator who, like an omniscient God or the all-knowing narrator of a novel, can see everything "as it truly is" is untenable. Consequently, Mead shows little patience for Royce's Absolute. For Mead, there is not one true description of the world. Rather, how the world is carved out—what the objects will be—depends on the interaction of the individual with her environment; an interaction that is shaped partly by the neurophysiological makeup of the individual's body. For Mead, as with Dewey, we mold our world from what is presented to us through our dealings with what confronts us within the problematic situations that we encounter, and truth is a function of having our problems solved—it is not something independent of that. Importantly, since the solution relates to the problem and not to the mental state of the problem solver, it is *objective*, not subjective. The farthest we can go in this is to systematically devise problematic situations, like the experimental scientist does, and thereby extend the scope of our knowledge beyond what comes at us fortuitously.

The result of this is a perspective realism. On this view, there is a multitude of perspectives, each objective, without there being any guarantee that together they add up to a single comprehensible whole. Instead of the Newtonian picture of the universe as a boundless empty vessel wherein things happen, Mead resorts to Einstein's theory of relativity, especially as it is interpreted by Alfred North Whitehead. Whitehead, Mead writes,

> generalizes the conception of organism to include any unitary structure, whose nature demands a period within which to be itself, which is therefore not only a spatial but also a temporal structure, or a process, Any such structure stratifies nature by its intersection into its perspective . . . there is no world of independent physical entities out of which the perspectives are merely selections. In the place of such a world appear all of the perspectives in their interrelationship to each other.
>
> (PP:163)

A perspective is thus not a *distortion* of reality, but reality is nothing beyond a clustering of intersecting perspectives. And they intersect because acts, and even events more generally, are social. The crying child enters its mother's perspective just like grass enters the ox's. Moreover, since, for Mead, the individual thinks by conversing with itself, the mind too is a clustering of perspectives—which in a way is Mead's take on James's discussion of sub-universes in Chapter 2. For Mead, the "grandiose undertaking of Absolute Idealism" to bring the whole of reality within a single perspective has failed (PP:161). There is no such thing as an absolute vantage point. As Mead keenly realizes, Mach and Einstein have shown that the notions of absolute space and time, a core presupposition of Newtonian mechanics that carried into modern philosophy and shaped its notion of truth, cannot be maintained. As a result, objects do not exist independently of the perspectives they enter into, but it is through the intersecting of perspectives that objects come into existence: "If an animal that can digest grass, such as an ox, comes into the world, then grass becomes food. That object did not exist before, that is, grass as food" (MSS:129). Similarly, it is the eye that endows objects with color. The colors are not in the object, nor are they in the eye of the beholder, but they emerge within the transaction that takes place between the two. And there is nothing subjective about this, because "the same object is food for all animals with a certain digestive apparatus" (PA:258), the same object is red for all animals with a certain optical apparatus, etc.

Objects emerge within transactions that are occasioned by the intersecting of perspectives.

For Mead, we have no access to these other perspectives. All we can do is deepen our own perspective by projecting ourselves into what we encounter, just as we project ourselves into our opponents when playing ball or chess. In line with the pragmatic maxim, the meaning of what we encounter is here again cast in terms of the practical consequences that we can associate with it. The problem Mead sees with absolute idealists, such as Royce, is that they blindly assume that there can be some neutral, external vantage point from which one can survey all perspectives and all that appears within them. For Mead, there is nothing that justifies this assumption; it is merely the echo of a discredited Newtonian universe.

Notwithstanding Mead's emphasis on the consummation of the act, he rejects the idea that truth is what satisfies the individual. As with Dewey (8.5), and remaining close to Peirce's method of science (2.3), Mead relates truth not to the individual's wishes being fulfilled, but to what resolves the problem that is objectively there. And sometimes it is the desires of the individual that are the problem. Moreover, since we are beings with selves, the majority of those problematic situations are not mere personal affairs. They are social objects the meaning of which is not related to the idiosyncrasies of the individual and its circumstances, but to the community within which those individuals live and have their being. As with Peirce and Royce, the community trumps the individual epistemologically. In the next chapter we look deeper into the role of the community, especially with regard to social problems, by exploring the views of Dewey, Addams, and Bourne.

Notes

1. For a more extensive discussion of Royce's life and work, see John Clendenning, *The Life and Thought of Josiah Royce,* 2nd ed. (Nashville, 1999); Bruce Kuklick, *Josiah Royce: An Intellectual Biography* (Indianapolis, 1985).
2. See e.g. Perry (1935), 1:797–808.
3. Letter to James, September 19, 1880; in John Clendenning, *The Letters of Josiah Royce* (Chicago, 1970), p.89.
4. A discussion of 1–3 can be found in CP8.110; of 4 in CP8.130.
5. For an excellent intellectual biography, see Daniel Huebner, *Becoming Mead: The Social Progress of Academic Knowledge* (Chicago, 2014).

Chapter 8

Pragmatism and the Problems of Life

Dewey, Addams, and Bourne

John Dewey is born in 1859 in Burlington, Vermont, in a family that is deeply affected by the Civil War.[1] He attends the University of Vermont and goes to graduate school at Johns Hopkins University. Although he takes several courses with Peirce, it is not until half a century later, when reading Peirce's *Collected Papers*, that Dewey begins to appreciate Peirce. In contrast, Dewey is deeply influenced by James, especially his *Principles of Psychology*. After his graduation, Dewey teaches at the University of Michigan, where he meets George Herbert Mead, before coming to the newly established University of Chicago. Like Mead, Dewey becomes deeply involved with Jane Addams's Hull House.

In 1896, Dewey helps found the Laboratory School at the University of Chicago. The school, which is quickly dubbed the Dewey School, is specifically meant as a laboratory for testing pedagogic and psychological theories. Three years later, Dewey publishes *The School and Society*, a book based in part on his experiences with Hull House and the Laboratory School. In it, Dewey objects to the passive lecture-type format that dominates education, arguing that learning should be an active and collaborative enterprise that is firmly rooted in the students' personal life experiences. Dewey's philosophy of education, with its emphasis on inquiry rather than regurgitating facts, is an early expression of his pragmatism. In 1904, Dewey goes to Columbia University, where he remains until his retirement in 1930. After his retirement, Dewey stays active as a public intellectual. As Henry Commager summarizes it in 1950: Dewey had become "the conscience of the American people: it is scarcely an exaggeration to say that for a generation no major issue was clarified until Dewey had spoken."[2]

8.1 Dewey's Experimental Logic

In 1934, Dewey writes Albert C. Barnes that logic is his "first and last love" (LW12:537). Dewey's logic, however, is an experimental logic and as such has greater affinity with philosophy of science (with a broad conception of science) than with the formal logic that comes from the quarters of Russell and Whitehead, whose monumental *Principia Mathematica* becomes the main competitor to Dewey's own. For Dewey, logic is, as he puts it succinctly, the "inquiry into inquiry" (LW12:12). It should be noted, however, that what Dewey has in mind here is an *empirical* inquiry into inquiry. Dewey strongly believes that most philosophers have lost touch with the methods of inquiry as they are used within the experimental sciences, and he advocates that the experimental method be used in philosophy, including the study of logic. That is, he believes that one can derive norms, rules, and procedures conducive to future successful inquiry by studying past inquiries that paid off and what made them pay off. Consequently, Dewey grounds philosophy, including logic and the theory of inquiry, firmly within psychology. Psychology, Dewey writes shortly after he graduated from Johns Hopkins, "is the ultimate science of reality, because it declares what experience in its totality is; it fixes the worth and meaning of its various elements by showing their development and place within this whole. It is, in short, *philosophic method*" (EW1:144). This approach to logic puts Dewey on a direct collision course, not only with traditional a priori conceptions of logic, but also with Peirce's normative conception discussed in Chapter 6.

This chapter emphasizes Dewey's logic as the theory of inquiry, not just because this is a central thread that runs through Dewey's thought, but also because one cannot really understand Dewey's pragmatism—or, as he prefers to call it, his instrumentalism—without understanding his logic.

While at Chicago, Dewey gathers a group of sympathetic thinkers with whom he publishes *Studies in Logical Theory* in 1903. In the preface, Dewey briefly summarizes five points on which they all agree: judgment is the central problem for logic, logic cannot be separated from psychology, judgments are experienced (so that logic is at least in part an empirical science), reality can be defined only in experiential terms, and there is no universal standard of truth apart from what is required for "readjusting and expanding the means and ends of life" (MW2:296).

In the *Studies*, Dewey is already rejecting the traditional way of philosophizing, which he sees as stuck in pre-scientific habits and modes of thought that draw a sharp but artificial divide between knowing and acting. Dewey hopes to rid philosophy of many pseudo problems that result from the presuppositions and vocabulary of philosophy rather than from its subject matter. Dewey's alternative is that philosophers should embrace the methods used in the experimental sciences, even in traditionally a priori fields like logic, which requires a thoroughgoing reconstruction of philosophy.

Studies in Logical Theory is enthusiastically received by William James, who sees in it the establishment of a genuine school in philosophy which he calls "The Chicago School," and which he predicts would be influential for years to come. Schiller also gives the book a warm welcome, calling it a "weighty contribution to current logical controversy." Peirce is more critical. In an unmailed letter to Dewey, he accuses the Chicago pragmatists of neglecting the normative aspects of logic in favor of a purely historical account of problem-solving techniques. As Peirce explains, "I do not think anything like a natural history can answer the terrible need that I see of checking the awful waste of thought, of time, of energy, going on, in consequence of men's not understanding the theory of inference" (CP8.239). As Peirce sees it, one might as well study the moral practices of Borneo headhunters, Utah Mormons, and Greek cabdrivers to discover the best rules for moral conduct. It is at best a very roundabout way.

James's prediction comes true: the "Chicago School" does indeed flourish for years to come. However, it ends up doing so without Dewey. Shortly after the book is published, Dewey leaves Chicago because of problems surrounding the Laboratory School. Nevertheless, much of Dewey's subsequent thought is shaped by his repeated attempts to clarify and defend the position he took in *Studies in Logical Theory*. The four essays he contributes to the volume reappear with only minor changes as the opening chapters of his 1916 *Essays in Experimental Logic*. It is to this that we now turn.

8.2 A Theory of Knowledge

In *Essays in Experimental Logic*, Dewey further develops the theory of knowledge he had advocated in *Studies in Logical Theory*. Philosophers, Dewey laments, pretty much treat all our experiences as if they are mere objects of contemplation. But when we have the flu or are faced with an overfilled fridge, we are clearly dealing with something other than a mere object of contemplation. What is more, to *conceive* of it as a mere object of contemplation so much alters its nature that it becomes an entirely different experience. One consequence of the traditional practice of reducing all experience to objects of contemplation, Dewey argues, is that knowledge becomes so detached from experience that the question of how this knowledge relates to its objects becomes an inexplicable mystery. In its stead, Dewey argues, our focus should be on lived experience.

It is worth noting that with the *Essays*, Dewey is in particular attacking the new realists, who had replaced idealism as pragmatism's main adversary. Not only have the new realists, or neo realists as they are also called, come to dominate the philosophical scene, but Columbia University, where Dewey is teaching, becomes one of their strongholds.[3]

The new realists are arguably guilty of what Dewey famously calls the "spectator theory of knowledge"—a view of knowledge where the role of the knower is reduced to that of a mere onlooker—someone who studies the world as a detective examines a crime scene—careful not to disturb anything or leave any traces. For Dewey, this ideal may be approximated on occasion, but it cannot and should not be taken as a model for how we acquire knowledge, or for explaining what knowledge is.

Central to the new realists' view is the firm conviction that the *process* of knowledge acquisition is wholly independent of the knowledge that is obtained. For the new realist, neither the truth nor the meaning of the statement, "There are nine planets in our solar system," depends in any way on how we arrived at this conclusion. Consequently, a study of the historical process through which that statement is reached—interesting as it might be as an exercise in the history or anthropology of science—is of no help in determining its meaning or its truth.

Dewey is of an entirely different opinion. The paradigmatic case of knowledge acquisition is not that of the scientist or philosopher who leisurely contemplates this or that subject in his brown study, but the emergence of a concrete problem that requires a concrete response. "Reflection," Dewey writes, "appears as the dominant trait of a situation when there is something seriously the matter, some trouble, due to active discordance, dissentiency, conflict among the factors of a prior non-intellectual experience" (MW10:326). Dewey calls this an indeterminate situation. For Dewey, as with Mead, all reflection is ultimately a product of an indeterminate situation—in a world without trouble, there would be no thought.

An indeterminate situation occurs when conflicting responses are elicited, and we can proceed only when this conflict is somehow resolved. For instance, when I see a hot-dog cart on the other side of a busy street, this may elicit both the hunger-induced response of crossing the street and the life-preserving response to not cross the street. A process of reflection ensues, which will make me either suppress one of the two responses or reconcile them through some plan of action, like taking the pedestrian bridge a block away. Once the conflict is resolved, reflection ceases until we find ourselves within a new indeterminate situation.

By focusing on the indeterminate situation, Dewey follows Peirce's doubt–belief theory, where inquiry is similarly the product of a distress of some kind and which also comes to conclusion once the distress is relieved. Like Peirce, Dewey rejects the idea that we can doubt everything at once as Descartes had assumed. Doubt is always related to a specific indeterminate situation. Dewey gives the example of a man who is lost in the woods. That the uncertainty which confronts the man cannot be separated from the situation within which it arose quickly becomes evident when we try to imagine him remembering the uncertainty *without* remembering the situation. At best, the memory would be a vague, noncognitive feeling of distress (MW4:83).

By recasting the doubt–belief relation in terms of an organism that seeks to maintain homeostatic equilibrium, Dewey puts the problem of knowledge more explicitly than Peirce had done in naturalistic terms. Human behavior, up to the most theoretical endeavor, is continuous with the behavior of the so-called "lower organisms." There is no difference in kind between

Einstein working out his theory of relativity and a lobster trying to catch a small crayfish.

As we saw in the previous chapter, Dewey prefers "indeterminate situation" to "problematic situation," as the latter points already at the existence of a problem. For Dewey, problems are already *products* of inquiry. As the saying goes, a problem well put is a problem half solved. Furthermore, for Dewey, it is very distinctly the *situation* that is indeterminate. As he puts it later in his *Logic* of 1938, "*We* are doubtful because the situation is inherently doubtful," and he immediately adds that "personal states of doubt that are not evoked by and are not relative to some existential situation are pathological" (LW12:109). Moreover, the doubt elicited by indeterminate situations is *not* a subjective affair that can be resolved by manipulating our personal mental states, but is an objective, public relation between means and ends.

Dewey thus empathically denies the accusation—made most prominently by Russell—that he makes personal satisfaction the benchmark of truth and the ultimate aim of inquiry. Mr. Russell, Dewey responds,

> proceeds first by converting a doubtful *situation* into a personal doubt. . . . Then by changing doubt into private discomfort, truth is identified with removal of this discomfort . . . [but on my view] "Satisfaction" is satisfaction of the conditions prescribed by the problem.
>
> (LW14:56)

Thus, for Dewey, inquiry relates to the attempt of resolving the objective conditions of an indeterminate or problematic situation. For instance, if the problem is how to evenly divide five pieces of birthday cake among eleven children, it is not the personal satisfaction of the children or the cake-cutter that determines whether the cake is cut evenly, but whether the eleven children all get the same amount of cake. The same is true for knowledge acquisition in general. There too, the issue is not whether the inquirers feel satisfied with the answer, but whether the answer solves the problem. Of course, solving the problem will generally satisfy the inquirers.

Dewey's views on education are based on the same principle. Hence, the popular claim that Dewey's philosophy of education is child-centered is thoroughly misguided. Dewey does not think that humans are naturally intelligent and rational and that the role of the educator should be limited to that of a facilitator, whose sole task it is to bring out the child's natural development. In *The Child and the Curriculum*, Dewey explicitly criticizes the child-oriented theory of education, which he believes could only be based on a "sentimental idealization of the child's naïve caprices and performances" (MW2:281f). Education should be problem oriented, not child oriented. The child must learn to creatively adapt himself to the indeterminate situations that he is likely to encounter in life and which will set the boundaries of what can or is to be done.

For Dewey, the acquisition of knowledge is thus always a function of a concrete, indeterminate situation. Consequently, for Dewey, knowledge involves the reorganization of an indeterminate situation aimed specifically at resolving conflicting or inhibited responses. Moreover, since for Dewey reflection comes to conclusion only in a successful experimental act (mere contemplation of the problem is not enough), all knowledge is in the end experimental; there is no pure a priori knowledge.

The upshot of all of this is that, for Dewey, for whom reflection emerges within an indeterminate situation that is transformed into a specific problem, and terminates when this problem is solved, knowledge cannot be seen as independent from the conditions wherein it arises and the situation to which it applies. This means that, for Dewey, all knowledge is thoroughly contextual. This is not to deny that different circumstances could have taught us the same, or that the inquiry could have ended with a different solution that is also satisfactory. There are many places from which one can travel to Rome, and for most of these places, there are multiple ways to do so. The same is true for an indeterminate situation.

Dewey further rejects that the object known and the knowing subject are two independent entities. What is experien*ced* cannot be separated from the experien*cing*. According to Dewey, the process of knowledge acquisition is better conceived as a transaction wherein subject and object are formed together through mutual adaptation, rather than that they enter the relation as "irreconcilable separates" that somehow need to be bridged (LW16:67). Without there being anything to know, there would be no knower, and without a knower, there would not be anything to know—the knower and the known reciprocally determine each other.

8.3 Whether All Judgments Are Practical

In the concluding essay of *Essays in Experimental Logic*, "The Logic of Judgments of Practice," Dewey seeks to elaborate his instrumentalist view and see where it will lead. He begins with the noncontroversial claim that science, at least from one angle, is a mode of practice. Scientists do not recline in their armchairs contemplating black holes or pre-Pleistocene life with their eyes closed. They do things. They act. As Dewey observes, "To say that something is to be learned, is to be found out, is to be ascertained or proved or believed, is to say that something is to be done" (MW8:65).

Now in the process of doing things, Dewey continues, scientists make all sorts of practical judgments. Such practical judgments differ from theoretical judgments in that whereas theoretical judgments purport to say how things are, practical judgments assert how we want things to be, and, derivatively, what we should do to make them happen. Questions such as "What should we eat tonight?" and "Where will we go on our next vacation?" are examples of questions that require practical judgments. They cannot be answered by a description of the content of our stomach, however accurate, or by scrutinizing a world atlas, no matter how carefully. Science abounds in practical judgments. They are clearly prominent in the applied sciences, where the purpose could be to cure an infectious disease, or to make cars more energy efficient. But they abound also in the theoretical sciences, where the purpose could be to test an already-existing theory, to explain a specific phenomenon, or to examine the implications of some new or established idea.

Having established the practical component of science, Dewey then asks himself the following daring question:

> Suppose that the propositions arising within the *practice* of knowing and functioning as agencies in its conduct could be shown to present all the distinctions and relations characteristic of the subject-matter of logic: what would be the conclusion?
>
> (MW8:65)

In other words, what if *all* scientific judgments are of the nature of practical judgments, however far removed they might be from our daily lives and however abstract and theoretical they may sound?

If all judgments are practical, thinking would be an art, like boatbuilding or painting watercolors, and all knowledge would be a product of the art of thinking. Now, when we build a boat, Dewey explains, we take raw material such as wood or iron and give it a new shape such that it will serve the purpose for which we had set ourselves to work. For Dewey, the same is true for thinking. Just like boatbuilding, thinking takes certain raw materials (memories, sensory experiences, etc.) and shapes them to make them fit a certain purpose, which in this case is *the purpose of attaining knowledge*. For Dewey, the new realist's ideal of a passive observer is untenable, as even the detached observer has her own agenda, namely the acquisition of knowledge. The astronomer, for instance, is never just passively recording what she sees, but within the act of observation itself, she is already actively molding her observations into objects that further the process of attaining knowledge. And even if for a moment she lets her thoughts wander aimlessly, what she sees is still shaped by past purposes, some of which she may have been long since forgotten or never even have been consciously aware of.

What gives an *observation*—the raw material we encounter in our dealings with the world—its value, Dewey continues, is not something that is inherent in it, antecedent and independent of any motive that we may carry with us, but by how it contributes to the purpose at hand. For instance, in the case of boatbuilding, we will find that certain types of wood are good for

boatbuilding, whereas others are not. That is to say, the antecedent properties of the wood enter into the process of boatbuilding as limiting conditions. The same holds when our purpose is not that of boatbuilding, but that
of attaining knowledge. Here too, some observations will contribute to the
purpose of attaining knowledge, whereas others will not. Dewey considers
the classic distinction between primary and secondary qualities a case in
point. The primary qualities, such as extension, number, and motion, have
proven far more useful in extending our knowledge of physical objects than
secondary qualities, such as colors, smells, and sounds, and for that reason
they have been favored by scientists and philosophers alike. It would be
incorrect though, Dewey insists, to conclude from this, as many have done,
that primary qualities *truly* depict reality whereas secondary qualities do not.
Doing so would be to fully misunderstand how inquiry works and what
its object is. The orchardist, the woodworker, the painter, and the biologist all see an apple tree differently, and it makes no sense to ask which of
these impressions reflects the real apple tree or whether there is something
like "the true apple tree" of which the others are all partial (and partisan)
impressions.

Dewey makes a similar argument for the laws of logic. These laws too
are products of inquiry. As Dewey points out in the *Logic*, "All logical
forms (with their characteristic properties) arise within the operation of
inquiry and are concerned with the control of inquiry so that it may
yield warranted assertions" (LW12:11). Dewey agrees with Peirce that the
aim of inquiry is settled opinion. However, since Dewey focuses much
less on the long run than Peirce, while agreeing with Peirce's fallibilism,
Dewey in effect trades the notion of truth for what he calls "warranted
assertibility."

For Dewey, good logical principles ensue when we discover that certain
inferences (all other things remaining equal) give dependable conclusions—
that is, they are successful. In this respect, the inquirer is no different from
the potter who learns that a certain way of spinning his pottery wheel leads
to good pots. What makes such principles or techniques regulative, or "normative," is that they deliver better results. In a very Peircean manner, Dewey
observes,

> It can hardly be denied that there are habits of inference and that they
> may be formulated as rules or principles. If there are such habits as are
> necessary to conduct every successful inferential inquiry, then the for-
> mulations that express them will be logical principles of all inquiries.
> In this statement "successful" means operative in a manner that tends in
> the long run, or in continuity of inquiry, to yield results that are either
> confirmed in further inquiry or that are corrected by use of the same
> procedures.
>
> (LW12:21)

Although Dewey remains skeptical as to whether a Peircean ultimate opinion is attainable (even in principle), he firmly believes in the convergence of inquiry, at least for practical purposes.

For Dewey, the relationship between knowledge and its object is thus very different from the contention, of new realists and others, that knowledge—the *product* of inquiry—must be a faithful copy of what occasioned the raw material that entered the inquiry. True, we must take account of this raw material, just as in building a boat, we must take account of the wood grain, its buoyance, etc.; but, Dewey argues, this is very different from demanding that our knowledge is a mental replica of something existing in nature. The raw materials we start with, Dewey contends, "are not objects but means, instrumentalities, of knowledge: things by which we know rather than things known" (MW10:347). This is the core of Dewey's instrumentalism.

The analogy with art also points to the fact, often ignored, that both the tools the inquirer uses and the products he creates are, though human-made, not subjective. As Dewey points out, "The tools and works of art are neither mental, subjective things, nor are they antecedent entities like crude or raw material. They are the latter shaped for a purpose" (MW8:68). They are objective both in the sense that they contribute to the purpose at hand—which may be the purpose of gaining knowledge—and in the sense that they depend upon the traits of the objects as they are prior to, or independent of, the act of gaining knowledge. For Dewey, the principles of logic are as objective as the principle that teakwood is the best choice for ship decks—as it is durable, strong, doesn't soak up water, doesn't rot, etc. It is simply a matter of means and consequences.

8.4 Pragmatism and the Problems of Life

What Dewey called "pragmatism" is not all that easy to define, since it is, for Dewey, as with any other intellectual undertaking, a product of concrete perplexities and conflicts faced by philosophers and their ilk. Consequently, it cannot be defined *in abstracto*, nor should we expect it to be clean around the edges. For Dewey, what pragmatism stands for is very much the result of an empirical study of (mostly scientific) inquiry. Like Peirce, Dewey sees pragmatism primarily as a method.

For the pragmatist, Dewey argues, knowledge is in an essential way the product of an indeterminate situation that demands resolution. As he puts it in *How We Think* (1910),

> [Pragmatism] starts from acts, functions, as primary data, functions both biological and social in character; from organic responses, adjustments. It treats the knowledge standpoint, in all its patterns, structures, and

purposes, as evolving out of, and operating in the interests of, the guidance and enrichment of these primary functions.

(MW6:88)

The main deficiency of traditional, intellectualistic philosophy (Dewey also describes his view as anti-intellectualism), is that it mistakenly separates knowledge from its working context. The intellectualist deliberately detaches the acquisition of knowledge from all other human endeavors, declaring it an end in itself that is altogether unaffected by anything else, most specifically our practical interests and our personal desires. What fuels this approach is that it takes the acquisition of knowledge to be a wholly rational affair, and one that depends heavily on the feats of formal logic (the tangible side of rationality) where this rationality itself is seen as something self-sufficient, hovering high above the forever-changing world of experience. What Dewey objects to is this radical separation of knowledge acquisition from its original function, which is to resolve indeterminate situations (which *do* include practical interests, emotions, and desires). Dewey calls this the "intellectualistic fallacy" (MW6:89). Much of Dewey's logic is aimed at debunking this old notion of an autonomous, self-sufficient rationality.

However, while pragmatism may be called anti-intellectual, it is not anti-intelligent. To make this point, Dewey shifts the discussion from talk about reason (as a fixed faculty) to talk about reasonableness:

What is reasonableness? You see a person doing something that is unreasonable. What do you mean? . . . Either he is setting up ends that he hasn't got the means for realizing, or he is using the means in such a way that they won't give him the result he is after. Or, on the other hand, here are these conditions which might be used as means and he isn't using them as means. He isn't forming an end consequently to be reached in terms of the means, the resources that he has got in connection with the obstacles and the obstructions that have got to be overcome.

(LW11:565f)

When reason is not taken as a faculty fixed a priori but is derived from a notion of reasonableness like the one just sketched, Dewey can maintain that pragmatists are rationalists and that they are so in a more sophisticated manner than intellectualists are.

Although pragmatism sees reason as purpose-directed and action-involved, Dewey denies that pragmatism seeks to subordinate knowledge to desired practical results, which, as we saw, is a charge often made against pragmatism. "My pragmatism," Dewey writes, "affirms that action is involved in knowledge, not that knowledge is subordinated to action or 'practice'"

(LW14:13). Pragmatism only seeks to reintegrate knowledge with the world wherein we live.

Dewey's *Essays in Experimental Logic* includes two essays on pragmatism. There, he describes pragmatism as follows:

> [Pragmatism] insists that general notions shall "cash in" as particular objects and qualities in experience; that "principles" are ultimately subsumed under facts, rather than the reverse; that the empirical consequence rather than the *a priori* basis is the sanctioning and warranting factor. But all of these ideas are colored and transformed by the dominant influence of experimental science: the method of treating conceptions, theories, etc., as working hypotheses, as directors for certain experiments and experimental observations.
>
> (MW4:100)

Dewey here agrees with Peirce that pragmatism represents the mental habits we find in the laboratory; that it brings the method of the experimental sciences into philosophy. Dewey agrees with James that the method of pragmatism "should be applied as widely as possible; and to things as diverse as controversies, beliefs, truths, ideas, and objects" (MW4:101).

Pragmatism, Dewey later writes in the syllabus for one of his courses at Columbia, "grows out of the development of experimental methods and of genetic and evolutionary conceptions in science" (MW4:253). As he puts it again years later, it is nothing but "the systematic elaboration of the *logic and ethics of scientific inquiry*" (LW15:24). And although the term is conspicuously absent in the 1938 *Logic*, Dewey calls that book "thoroughly pragmatic" (LW12:4). In brief, Dewey's pragmatism is by and large his experimental logic. However, while Dewey's pragmatism remains empirical, he avoids a reductionist materialism. For Dewey, not only particular things, but also universals, such as natural laws, can be real. Pragmatism, he writes, "gives to thought and thought relations (universals) a primary and constructive function" (MW7:328).

In Dewey's view, pragmatism pans out differently depending on what it is applied to. When we start with an *object* that is empirically given, he follows the German chemist Wilhelm Ostwald's rule—quoted in James's *Pragmatism*—that the meaning of an object is the effects it produces upon us. For instance, when a bee taxonomist discovers a new species of bees and names it, the meaning of this name consists in the practical reactions these newly discovered animals elicit from us or impose upon us.

The situation is different when we begin with *ideas* not yet knowing the objects they are meant to refer to or whether there even are such objects. In Dewey's view, such an idea is in essence "a draft drawn upon existing things." When the draft is honored, he continues—that is, when "existences, following upon the actions, rearrange or readjust themselves in the way the idea intends"—then we can say that the idea is true. For instance, the notions of mutation in genetics and of neutrino in physics were first introduced as ideas, and it was only later that the "objects" were discovered that correspond to them.

Part of what inspires Dewey to embrace pragmatism is a faith in meliorism, a concept we encountered earlier in James (3.4). In Dewey's words, meliorism, or critical optimism,

> is the belief that the specific conditions which exist at one moment, be they comparatively bad or comparatively good, in any event may be bettered. It encourages intelligence to work to improve conditions and it arouses reasonableness and confidence as optimism does not.
>
> (MW12:181)

And we better those conditions, not by wishful thinking, but by applying the scientific attitude to the situations as we encounter them.

Dewey briefly summarizes the difference between the two situations as follows: "the meaning of an *object* is the changes it requires in our attitude, the meaning of an *idea* is the changes it, as our attitude, effects in objects" (MW4:103; emphasis added). The first situation is closely related to Peirce's interpretation of pragmatism; the second resonates, however faintly, James's will-to-believe argument.

8.5 Truth and Warranted Assertibility

In the *Logic* of 1938, Dewey introduces the concept of "warranted assertibility" to replace "belief" and "knowledge" (LW12:15). Dewey seeks to stay away from "belief" because of its ambiguity—it can refer either to the *object* of a belief, or to a *state* of belief. Confusing these two has caused serious misunderstandings in the past. The distinction drawn between Peircean pragmatism, with its emphasis on the object of belief, and Jamesian pragmatism, with its emphasis on the state of belief, is at least in part a product of this confusion. The term "knowledge" is similarly ambiguous, as it can refer to the outcome of an inquiry that satisfactorily came to an end or to the object to which inquiry gravitates. In the second case, Dewey notes, knowledge accrues "a meaning of its own apart from connection with and reference to inquiry" (LW12:15).

The phrase "warranted assertibility" has the added advantage of drawing a clear connection with *inquiry* as what warrants the assertion. What we should be on the lookout for, Dewey observes, are "the *conditions* under which we reach warranted assertibility about particular matters of fact" (LW14:169). It seems that Dewey's prime inspiration comes from judicial language and proceedings. As he remarks in the *Logic*, "When it is ruled that certain evidence is admissible and that certain rules of law (conceptual material) are applicable rather than others, *something* is settled," and the final settlement is in part a product of such intermediary and partial settlements (LW12:125; we return to Dewey's views on the law in Chapter 14). Dewey further notes that "in resolution of problems that are of a looser quality than legal cases we call them opinions *to distinguish them from a warranted judgment or assertion*" (ibid; emphasis added). Hence, the notion of warranted assertibility has much to do with having the (procedural) right to assert something (e.g., to propose something as true or false), where these rights are themselves an intrinsic part of the procedure in question.

One consequence of Dewey's approach is that he rejects that the truth or falsity of a belief is determined by the effects having the belief has on the believer:

> The question of truth-falsity is *not*, on my view, a matter of the effects of *believing*, for my whole theory is determined by the attempt to state what conditions and operations of inquiry *warrant* a "believing," or justify its assertion as true.
>
> (LW14:183)

For Dewey, the issue of truth and falsity is thus not related to whether a belief is good for us, or whether it satisfies our desires, but to the indeterminate situation that spurred the inquiry, and the rules and restrictions intrinsic to the inquiry. Whether a belief is warranted, Dewey observes, is determined by "their pertinency and efficacy in 'satisfying' conditions that are rigorously set by the problem they are employed to resolve" (LW14:183f).

The result is a correspondence theory of truth, but one more sophisticated than the traditional variant that trades on the idea of a disinterested spectator to whom reality is mirrored in true belief. A better metaphor is that of a key that corresponds with a lock; what counts is a congruity—a fitting in. Hence, Dewey concludes, "In the sense of correspondence as operational and behavioral . . . I hold that my *type* of theory is the only one entitled to be called a correspondence theory of truth" (LW14:180).

An important motivation for preferring warranted assertibility rather than truth is Dewey's embracing of Peirce's fallibilism:

> The position which I take, namely, that all knowledge, or warranted assertion, depends upon inquiry and that inquiry is, truistically, connected with what is questionable (and questioned) involves a sceptical element, or what Peirce called "fallibilism." But it also provides for *probability*, and for determination of degrees of probability in rejecting all intrinsically dogmatic statements, where "dogmatic" applies to *any* statement asserted to possess inherent self-evident truth. That the only alternative to ascribing to some propositions self-sufficient, self-possessed,

and self-evident truth is a theory which finds the test and mark of truth in consequences of some sort is, I hope, an acceptable view.

(LW14:171f)

Dewey relates this fallibilism in a fairly Peircean manner to what may be called a probabilistic theory of truth. We can never be certain that something is true, but given the appropriate conditions, we can be warranted in holding it for true. Although Dewey hesitates to equate truth with warranted assertibility, he does maintain that there is no *practical* difference between the two.

8.6 Jane Addams: A Pragmatist in Action

No account of Chicago pragmatism could be complete without Jane Addams (1860–1935).[4] Addams is born in Cedarville, Illinois, as the eighth child of John Huy Addams, a successful miller, banker, and landowner. She loses her mother at the age of two, and a bout with tuberculosis leaves her physically disabled. Raised by a father who supported her intellectual development, Addams attends Rockford Female Seminary, graduating in 1881. This gave her, as a woman, essentially two options: marry and raise a family, or remain single and become a schoolteacher. Addams tries to escape this dilemma by going to medical school, but she is forced to abandon her medical studies because of her health. Unsure how to continue, she travels twice to Europe. In 1888 this lands her in Toynbee Hall, which is part of the British settlement house movement that originated a few years earlier. The settlement house movement aimed to provide education and assistance to the disadvantaged who were filling cities due to rapid industrialization, while simultaneously training teachers and social workers. In showing that "there were other genuine reasons for living among the poor than that of practicing medicine," Toynbee Hall rekindles Addams's sense of purpose.[5]

Returning to Chicago, Addams, together with Ellen Gates Star, rents a run-down mansion that once belonged to Charles Hull, and in 1889 they open what becomes known as Hull House. Initially designed to offer art and literary education to their impoverished neighbors, Hull House quickly becomes much more than that. The curriculum is changed to better fit the needs of the neighborhood, and Hull House comes to offer a large range of services, such as a day care, community kitchen, library, and employment bureau. Hull House also becomes a lively meeting place for labor unions and neighborhood clubs, as well as a safe haven for single women.[6] Modeled after Toynbee Hall, Hull House comes to serve the dual purpose of providing young educated women, who had experienced a women-centered environment at women's colleges, with a place for intellectual and professional development, while providing social and educational opportunities for working-class people in the surrounding, mostly immigrant neighborhood.

Addams lives and works in Hull House until her death in 1935 and writes extensively about her experience.[7] At the time of her death, the settlement expands from the Hull mansion to a complex that fills an entire city block. The Hull House Association continues to provide social services in various locations throughout Chicago, until 2012.

The University of Chicago, which is founded a year after Hull House, was the first American university to have a department of sociology, a science that, as Addams puts it, "had not yet defined its own field."[8] The activities at Hull House and the university (including Dewey's Laboratory School) develop in tandem, and the influence is bidirectional. Mead and Dewey are actively involved in Hull House, and Addams teaches at the university. Prevailing paternalism, however, makes it a very unequal relationship, which results in a suppression of the contributions of the Hull House women.[9] As can be seen, however, from the collaborative *Hull-House Maps and Papers* (Boston, 1885), Hull House is actively engaged in social-science research and becomes a pioneer in progressive education. Following James and Dewey, Addams observes that "the dominating interest in knowledge has become its use, the conditions under which, and ways in which it may be most effectively employed in human conduct," adding that in the settlement, people form themselves into groups "for the purpose of the application of knowledge to life."[10] In Addams's view, the settlement developed into an institute of learning that is very different from a traditional university, one that aims "to express the meaning of life in terms of life itself, in forms of activity."[11] With the women living on site, Hull House aims for immersion, marking a sharp contrast to the ivory tower approach in the universities where the social researchers remain separated from their subjects. Looking back, Addams writes,

> I gradually became convinced that it would be a good thing to rent a house in a part of the city where many primitive and actual needs are found, in which young women who had been given over too exclusively to study might restore a balance of activity along traditional lines and learn of life from life itself; where they might try out some of the things they had been taught and put truth to "the ultimate test of the conduct it dictates or inspires."[12]

The quotation at the end is from one of James's attempts at rephrasing Peirce's maxim. Recalling Peirce's original argument in "How to Make Our Ideas Clear," we can say that it is only within the settlement that ideas regarding social reform approach their third grade of clearness, effectively making the settlement an attempt at creating a pragmatist university. In Addams's words, "The ideal and developed settlement would attempt to test the value of human knowledge by action, and realization, quite as the complete and ideal university would concern itself with the discovery of knowledge in all branches."[13] Put differently, Hull House embodies a shift from the traditional idea of knowing, which was centered on detached individuals contemplating the world from their armchair or from a carefully controlled laboratory setting, to an engaged conception of learning, centered on the community as immersed within the world. Peirce's community of inquiry is here applied to life itself, especially in the domains that interested the Hull House residents. To appropriate a phrase from Kant, knowledge without activism is empty, and activism without knowledge is blind. Old ways of knowing, however, no longer suffice. Knowledge can no longer be looked upon as if disconnected from ethics and responsibility. The key question is not that of proving the truth of a claim by showing how it follows from certain predetermined and well-supported (perhaps even undeniable) general principles and observations, but that of shaping the particular situation encountered so that the claim becomes true. Addams's own involvement in the suffragette movement is not to prove *in abstracto* that women by their very nature possess the requisite qualities to fully participate in democratic processes, but to change the political system and the involvement of American women so that the claim that they do *becomes true*. In this, our ability to engender that change provides the proof. The truth that results is not merely an abstract truth (one that, though theoretically sound, may remain practically impotent) but is a truly pragmatic truth. None of this makes wishful thinking the harbinger of truth. Not everything can be made to work, far from it, and that is why the Hull House approach, which does not separate theory from practice, is so important to Addams. Only thus can we determine what works and what doesn't.

Embedded within a culturally diverse environment defined by imminent needs, the Hull House approach comes to embody an early form of standpoint epistemology, one that focuses on concrete problems rather than abstract frameworks—a view that parallels Mead's perspectivist conception of knowledge and reality, and his focus on the problem situation. By introducing the female perspective to epistemology, Jane Addams and the Hull House residents can further be seen as developing a feminist epistemology, one that highlights aspects of knowing that were traditionally ignored (see also 15.1). The Hull-House approach dovetails nicely with a strong faith in democracy, where the latter is understood not just as a type of government, but as a form of life—as the lifeblood of a community.[14] This view of democracy resonated deeply with Dewey.

8.7 Randolph Bourne: Pragmatism and Romantic Anarchy

Like Papini, whose views we discussed in Chapter 5, Randolph Bourne (1886–1918) is a young radical who finds in pragmatism the means for challenging the established ways of thinking that prove ill-equipped to deal with the rapidly changing world. Bourne's optimistic youthfulness (he dies at thirty-two in the great flu pandemic of 1918), together with his experience as a social outcast (his face is disfigured at birth, and spinal tuberculosis makes him stunted and hunchbacked) turn him into a romantic, idealistic anarchist.

As Bourne points out, "we of the rising generation have to work this problem out alone. Pastors, teachers, and parents flutter aimlessly about with their ready-made formulas, but somehow these are less efficacious than they used to be. I doubt if any generation was ever thrown quite so completely on its own resources as ours is" (YL:38). The new century, he explains, is one of youth:

> It is the glory of the present age that in it one can be young. Our times give no check to the radical tendencies of youth. On the contrary, they give the directest stimulation. A muddle of a world and a wide outlook combine to inspire us to the bravest of radicalisms. Great issues have been born in the last century, and are now loose in the world. There is a radical philosophy that illuminates our environment, gives us terms in which to express what we see, and coordinates our otherwise aimless reactions.
>
> (YL:25)

This radical philosophy is the pragmatism of James and Dewey. Bourne, who studies with Dewey at Columbia, finds in pragmatism a way of thinking that is open-minded, critically affirmative, and experimental. He feels particularly attracted to James's will to believe, which he seeks to merge with Dewey's idea of applying the scientific method (as Dewey and Peirce developed it) to the problems of society. When we are asking, "What makes society just?," abstract answers won't do. Bourne's empiricism entails that we must make our answers true—the proof is in the pudding, not in the recipe. Rejecting abstract talk of liberty and justice, Bourne calls for concrete plans for institutions that are free and just:

> You have been trying so long to reform the world by making men "good," and with such little success, that we may be pardoned if we turn our attention to the machinery of society, and give up for a time the attempt to make the operators of that machinery strictly moral. Indeed, the charm of Socialism to so many of the rising generation is just that scientific aspect of it.
>
> (YL:50)

Recall that part of what inspired James to formulate his will to believe is that there are situations where believing in something can make it happen. James's focus, however, remained on the individual. What we find with

Bourne, Dewey, and Sorel (5.1), is a clear shift to the social. In Bourne's words, "Not personal salvation, but social; not our own characters, but the character of society, is our interest and concern. We feel social injustice as our fathers felt personal sin" (YL:48).

Confronted with a rapidly changing world for which the theories of old have little to offer, and to which we have no choice but to adapt, Bourne, again inspired by James, comes to reject rationalism and traditional logic. "It is good to be reasonable," he admits, "but too much rationality puts the soul at odds with life. For rationality implies an almost superstitious reliance on logical proofs and logical motives, and it is logic that life mocks and contradicts at every turn" (YL:227). In fact, we cannot separate our feelings from our perception of life. For James, Bourne observes, truth "is thoroughly comprehended experience; it is created as we go along, it is what proves its verity by being verified."[15] Truth is not just an issue of intellectual apperception. To understand life, we must feel it, live it. Consequently, Bourne speaks of the experimental life, rather than the experimental method (YL:227ff).

Following Socrates and anticipating Rorty, Bourne identifies irony—the "rub of mind against mind by the simple use of simulated ignorance, and the adoption, without committing one's self, of another's point of view" (YL:101)—as the proper attitude for the experimental life. Without being able to rely upon external standards, Bourne's ironist compares things directly with one another, and "the values that slowly emerge from the process, values that emerge from one's own vivid reactions, are constantly revised, corrected, and refined by that same sense of contrast" (YL:105). In sum, this irony is relativistic, fallible, and forward-looking. Through irony, Bourne adds, we can avoid becoming "encased in a suit of armor . . . invulnerable to our own experience," so that we no longer possess "the faculty of being surprised" (YL:111).

Though Bourne appreciates the "rub of mind against mind," he is deeply troubled by what he calls the American sports culture. "The passion of the American undergraduate for intercollegiate athletics," he writes, "is merely a symbol of a general interpretation for all the activities that come to his attention" (EL:225). As Bourne explains,

> The sporting attitude is a grateful and easy one. Issues are decided cleanly. No irritating fringes are left over. The game is won or lost. Analysis and speculation seem superfluous. The point is that such a philosophy is as different as possible from that which motivates the intellectual world of the modern college, with its searchings, its hypotheses and interpretations and revisions, its flexibility and openness of mind. In the scientific world of the instructor, things are not won or lost. His attitude is not a sporting one.
>
> (EL:226)

Bourne sees this sporting attitude reinforced by university administrators, who make students work "for marks and the completion of schedules rather than for a new orientation in important fields of human interest" (EL:227). As a result, undergraduates are not encouraged to think in any experimental sense. Rather, the sporting attitude fosters docility and lack of creativity—it encases them. In brief, Bourne finds American universities, and modern education more generally, antithetical to the development of the experimental life. This makes him a strong advocate of Dewey's philosophy of education, of which he finds the fullest implementation in the school system of Gary, Indiana.[16] Bourne rejects that children are "empty vessels to be filled by knowledge," or that they are "automatic machines which can be wound up and set running on a track by the teacher"; "they are living, growing things, and they need nothing so much as a place where they can grow" (EL:6). Traditional education, Bourne continues, is ill-equipped for this:

> The bare class-rooms, the stiff seats, the austere absence of beauty, suggest a hospital where painful if necessary intellectual operations are going on [instead] new activities must be woven into a genuine child-community-life . . . They must be opportunities for spontaneous living.
>
> (EL:9)

Sentiments similar to this are found in the work of Michel Foucault, to whom we return when discussing Cornel West's Prophetic Pragmatism (15.4).

The Rise of National Socialism in Germany caused a steady exodus of European intellectuals to the United States, where they found a willing audience, in part because many American university professors did their graduate work in Europe, often Germany. As a result, pragmatism, America's homegrown philosophy, receded to the background. Sometimes this is referred to as the eclipse of pragmatism. According to the eclipse story, pragmatism returns to the fore only with the work of Richard Rorty, to whom we turn in Chapter 11. The following two chapters seek to counter this eclipse story by tracing the debate between pragmatism and logical positivism, which was the dominant import, as well as the often-underhanded reception of pragmatism in Europe, especially in Great Britain and Germany.

Notes

1. For a biography, see George Dykhuizen, *The Life and Mind of John Dewey* (Carbondale, 1973).
2. Henry Steele Commager, *The American Mind* (New Haven, 1950), p.100.
3. British new realism centered around G.E. Moore and Bertrand Russell; American new realism was driven in part by the "Platform of Six Realists," which appeared

in 1910. For an overview of the latter, including Dewey's role in it, see Cornelis de Waal, *American New Realism 1910–1920*, 3 vols. (Bristol, 2001).

4. For a biography, see James Weber Linn, *Jane Addams: A Biography* (Urbana, 2000).

5. Jane Addams, *Twenty Years at Hull House, with Autobiographical Notes* (New York, 1910), p.67.

6. An extensive summary of the activities during the early years is found in *Hull-House Maps and Papers* (Boston, 1885), pp.207–28.

7. First in Addams (1910), later in *The Second Twenty Years at Hull-House, September 1909 to September 1929, with a Record of a Growing World Consciousness* (New York, 1930).

8. Ibid., p.182.

9. For a detailed account, see Mary Jo Deegan, *Jane Addams and the Men of the Chicago School, 1892–1918* (New Brunswick, 1988).

10. Jane Addams, "A Function of the Social Settlement," *Annals of the American Academy of Political and Social Science* 13 (1899): 35.

11. Ibid., p.36.

12. Ibid., p.85.

13. Ibid.

14. Jane Addams, *Democracy and Social Ethics* (New York, 1902).

15. Bourne to Prudence Winterrowd, February 5, 1913, in Eric Sandeen (ed), *The Letters of Randolph Bourne: A Comprehensive Edition* (Troy, 1981), pp.70–2.

16. Randolph Bourne, *The Gary Schools* (Boston, 1916).

Chapter 9

Conceptual Pragmatism
From Lewis to Davidson

In Chapter 7, we saw Royce embrace what he calls a pure pragmatism only to discover that it wasn't tenable. In response, Royce moves to what he calls an absolute pragmatism. In this chapter, we see C.I. Lewis pick up the voluntaristic strain that defines the early Royce, while rejecting Royce's absolute pragmatism. Instead, Lewis proposes a conceptual pragmatism. Following Lewis, we take a closer look at this conceptual pragmatism by comparing it with a parallel approach found in the work of Rudolf Carnap, before turning to the criticisms and elaborations of Quine, Goodman, and Davidson.

9.1 The Given, the A Priori, and Interpretation

Clarence Irving Lewis (1883–1964) spends most of his time at Harvard, connecting the Golden Age of James and Royce with the work of Quine and Goodman, two of his students. Lewis is a contemporary of Rudolf Carnap and actively seeks to connect the pragmatist outlook with the logical positivism, or logical empiricism, that is quickly gaining ground within the United States.[1] Lewis is also deeply influenced by Kant, and he is intimately familiar with Peirce's logical writings, including the mass of manuscripts acquired by Harvard shortly after Peirce's death. In fact, Harvard hires Lewis with the expectation that he oversees the reorganization of the Peirce manuscripts, and Lewis practically lives with them for two years. In his own philosophy, Lewis focuses on a key problem for pragmatism, that of reconciling the observation that our experience is malleable to our purposes with the idea that facts are "hard." He finds his answer in a pragmatic epistemology that brings together what Lewis calls the given (the hard facts that are not subject to our will) and the a priori, which, being a creation of ours, is subject to our will and malleable to our causes.

To understand Lewis, it is helpful to return briefly to Royce. As we saw, Royce rejected pure pragmatism because it involved a performative contradiction, opting instead for an absolute pragmatism. Royce used this very same argument to prove that the fundamental axioms of logic are also absolute. For Royce, the axioms of logic are such that if we try to prove them wrong, we unavoidably end up relying upon them, as without them we would not be able to even frame an argument that could prove them wrong. The axioms of logic are undeniable because any attempt to deny them results in what Royce had called a performative contradiction.

Lewis's own work in modal logic makes him realize that Royce's argument does not work for the simple reason that one can construct rival logical systems that equally pass this test.[2] As Lewis puts it, "there are several logics, markedly different, each self-consistent *in its own terms* and such that whoever, using it, avoids false premises, will never reach a false conclusion" (MWO:248). Briefly put, Lewis finds that Royce's argument works equally well for each and every single one of these alternative logics. When we seek to disprove the fundamental principles of any one of them, and we do it on their terms, then we end up showing these principles equally irrefutable. Hence, there is no such thing as an absolute logic. From this, Lewis concludes that the decision of what logic to choose can be based only on non-logical considerations. Lewis's solution to this problem, to which he is led largely by his reading of Peirce in the early 1920s, is essentially pragmatic: We favor those conceptual structures and ways of categorizing and classifying objects that best fit our plans and purposes. Hence, Lewis concludes, "the ultimate criteria for the laws of logic are pragmatic" (CL:323). He subsequently extends this idea to knowledge more generally.

Lewis's excursions into logic, together with his study of contemporary mathematics, form the basis of his pragmatic notion of the a priori, resulting in a theory of knowledge that combines the free creation of alternative conceptual schemes for interpreting experience with a pragmatic method for determining which one to favor. For Lewis, empirical knowledge is thus in essence a triadic affair. Its three elements are the given, a priori conceptual schemes, and something to connect those schemes to the given. What Lewis calls the given is that element in perception that "remains unaltered, no matter what our interests, no matter how we think or conceive" (MWO:52). It is wholly independent of any activity of thought. Lewis's a priori conceptual schemes furnish the other end of the spectrum. They are entirely products of the free activity of thought. Moreover, for Lewis, the a priori and the given are entirely independent of each other. Neither limits the other nor adds anything to it (MWO:37).

Historically, there has been a wide variety of explanations on how our conceptual schemes connect with the world of brute fact. They run from Plato's allegory of the cave, to Descartes's pineal gland, to Leibniz's idea of a preestablished harmony, to Darwinian ideas of an evolutionary adaptation of the human organism to its environment. Lewis's answer is decidedly pragmatic: what connects a priori conceptual schemes with the given are our human needs and interests. As he puts it, empirical knowledge is "an interpretation, instigated by need or interest and tested by its consequences in action, which individual minds put upon something confronting them or given to them" (CL:241). Application of concepts to the given yields empirical knowledge, but this application is a product not just of the given that confronts the reasoner, but also of her aims and interests. Hence, for Lewis, truth is neither wholly found nor wholly a product of the mind.

Lewis derives his notion of the given from the undeniable fact that there is "such a thing as experience, the content of which we do not invent and cannot have as we will but merely find" (AKV:182). Lewis insists that without the given, all knowledge would be wholly without content and arbitrary (MWO:39). Even the idealists, he observes, hardly mean to deny that "my seeing at this moment a sheet of paper instead of a green tree is a datum which it is beyond the power of my thought to alter" (MWO:45). "Indeed," Lewis writes a few pages later, "an unqualified denial of this element in ordinary cognition is sufficient to put any theory beyond the pale of plausibility" (MWO:48).

In *Mind and the World Order*, Lewis defines the given as what "remains untouched and unaltered, however it is construed by thought" (MWO:53). No matter what our interests are or how we look at it, the given remains unaffected. A scholar, a baby, and a chimpanzee, all *interpret* Lewis's fountain pen differently (as a writing implement, a teething tube, etc.), but at the level of the given, Lewis maintains, all three encounter the same.

Lewis realizes that his use of the phrase "the given" is somewhat misleading, as it hints at a certain unity that can only be conceptual. This is not what he intends with the phrase. What he intends is rather "the *element* of givenness in what we may, for usual and commonplace reasons mark off as 'an experience' or 'an object'" (MWO:59). However, even though we can *isolate* the given in this abstract way, we cannot "describe any particular given *as such*, because in describing it, in whatever fashion, we qualify it by bringing it under some category or other, select from it, emphasize aspects of it, and relate it in particular and avoidable ways" (MWO:52). Consequently, Lewis rejects the idea that the given can be identified through philosophical analysis, as with John Locke's idea of analyzing all that comes before the mind into "simple ideas," or with the "sense data" philosophy of G.E. Moore and Bertrand Russell. Simple ideas and sense data are, for Lewis, not given but sophisticated products of elaborate (a priori) conceptual systems.

Lewis's own approach to the given is phenomenological. On several occasions he compares it with James's "blooming, buzzing confusion" on which the infant first opens her eyes (3.0). The given is what we encounter independently of *any* a priori system through which it can be interpreted.

As with Peirce's category of secondness (6.5), Lewis argues that the purely given cannot be a possible object of knowledge. The given cannot be known because all our knowledge involves concepts, which is something that we ourselves bring to the given. As with Locke's *substratum*, we can only say of it *that* it is, not *what* it is.[3] In Lewis's words, "The given is *in*, not before, experience" (MWO:55). Following Royce (and Peirce), Lewis argues that it can only be interpreted.

The given must further be distinguished from the *object* that is given. As Lewis explains in *Mind and the World Order*,

> The given is presentation of something real, in the normal case at least; *what* is given (given in part) is this real object. But the whatness of this object involves its categorical interpretation; the real object, as known, is a construction put upon this experience of it, and includes much which is not, at the moment, given in the presentation.
>
> (MWO:58)

In brief, the object that is presented to me when I see Lewis's fountain pen is given to me only partially, and is interpreted by me *as* a fountain pen by relating experiences to it that are not present but which I anticipate were I to perform certain acts, such as unscrewing its cap, putting the tip on a sheet of paper, relating it with past experiences, etc. Still, the aspects thus introduced are not just products of my imagination; they relate to what is given. The baby who uses the fountain pen to soothe the discomforts of teething just as well discovers that there is ink in the pen as the scholar who gently puts it to paper.

The given should also not be confused with reality. Aligning himself with Peirce and James, Lewis writes, "experience as it comes to us contains not only the real but all the content of illusion, dream, hallucination, and mistake. The *given* contains both real and unreal, confusingly intermingled" (CL:236). Only by applying a conceptual system—that is, by positioning what is directly experienced within a framework that is *not* thus experienced—can we say that something is real or unreal. Reality, for Lewis, is a conceptual construction created by the human mind to fit its aims in scientific reasoning and its need, as a social animal, for a "common world." For instance, we call an oasis at the horizon that disappears when we approach it unreal because it does not meet the criteria that we have found conducive to satisfying our interests. Nothing in the content of the experience itself—that is, the experience still uncontaminated by *any* conceptual system—gives us any ground for calling the oasis unreal. As Lewis puts it in "The Pragmatic Conception of the *A Priori*,"

> Failure to behave in certain categorical ways marks it as unreal. Uniformities of the type called "natural law" are the clues to reality and unreality. A mouse which disappears where no hole is, is no real mouse; a landscape which recedes as we approach is but illusion. . . . That the uniformities of natural law are the only reliable criteria of the real, is inescapable. But such a criterion is ipso facto *a priori*. No conceivable

experience could dictate the alteration of a law so long as failure to obey that law marked the content of experience as unreal.

(CL:236)

For Lewis, the determination of reality, the classification of phenomena, and the discovery of natural law are all connected. The distinction between the real and the unreal is moreover essential to the act of interpretation: "It is only because the mind is prepared to judge it real or unreal according as it bears or fails to bear certain marks, that interpretation of the given is possible at all, and that experience can be understood" (MWO:13). One way to look at Lewis's conceptual pragmatism is as a systematic attempt at developing an epistemology from the phenomenology of James and Peirce.

Lewis's take on the given makes him conclude that we cannot have any knowledge of external reality unless we first add something ourselves—that we cannot be mere disinterested spectators. To see a fountain pen on the desk or a flock of geese fly over, we must connect what is directly presented to us as given with a certain structure within which what is given can be understood as a fountain pen or as a flock of geese. What we add ourselves, Lewis calls the "a priori." Since Lewis understands the a priori to be a free creation of our mental activity, he equates it with being analytic.[4] Lewis thereby draws a sharp distinction between the given and the a priori—between the synthetic and the analytic. Having thus separated the a priori from the given, Lewis next seeks to bridge the divide pragmatically, in a move reminiscent of Royce, through the interpretative act (7.2). For Lewis, it is in the interpretative act that the a priori and the given are brought together.

Although Lewis accepts the received view that the a priori is both necessary and independent of experience, he comes to it in an unusual way, which results in a new conception of the a priori. First, Lewis rejects the generally held opinion that the a priori is necessary because the mind is forced to accept it as true. According to Lewis, the situation is the exact opposite. The a priori is necessary not because the mind is forced to accept it no matter what experience will bring, but because it represents the free attitude of the mind, so that it does not matter whether experience agrees with it or not. As Lewis explains,

Definitions and their immediate consequence, analytic propositions generally, are necessarily true, true under all possible circumstances. Definition is legislative because in some sense arbitrary. . . . If experience were other than it is, the definition and its corresponding classification might be inconvenient, fantastic, or useless, but it could not be false.

(CL:233)

For Lewis, it is not the a priori that the mind is forced to accept as true, but the given. Hence, Lewis contrasts necessary truth with what is factually contingent, but not with what is voluntary in thought and action.

Regarding the *independence* of the a priori, Lewis makes a similar observation. Traditionally, what makes the a priori independent of experience is that it was regarded as a product of the "inner light" of a reason that is absolute, even if instilled imperfectly in us humans. Experience was either assumed to fit this product or miraculously agreed with it, as with Leibniz's preestablished harmony. Lewis again takes the almost exact opposite view: The a priori is independent of experience precisely because it "prescribes *nothing* to experience" (MWO:197). The a priori does not anticipate the given, but our attitude to it:

> The thought which both rationalism and empiricism have missed is that there are principles, representing the initiative of mind, which impose upon experience no limitations whatever, but that such conceptions are still subject to alteration on pragmatic grounds when the expanding boundaries of experience reveal their infelicity as intellectual instruments.

> (CL:239)

Having alternatives becomes, for Lewis, even a trademark of the a priori. The a priori can be distinguished from the given precisely by recognizing that it has alternatives; or, as Lewis puts it, "by the ordinary criteria of responsibility in general—that a different mode of acting is possible and makes a discoverable difference" (MWO:232).

It is important to note that Lewis does not think that the a priori precedes all experience, as with the rationalist's innate ideas, which were assumed to be carried within us from birth. Rather, the a priori schemes through which we seek to interpret a *particular* experience must be formulated in advance of that experience.

Lewis sees the a priori as distinctly analytic, thereby rejecting the Kantian notion of synthetic a priori knowledge (MWO:231). That is, in contrast to Kant, Lewis maintains that a priori knowledge cannot tell us anything about the given; it only gives us the means through which we can give, for ourselves, some order to the given, for instance, defining the moment of death. Once we define death as having stopped breathing, no empirical observation can show us that this definition is false. What may happen, as it did when death was defined this way, is that the definition conflicts with some other deeply ingrained a priori principle (such as the notion that death is irreversible) or that it fails to serve us well (for instance, by causing us to bury people alive). Both call for a revision of the definition. Historically, the definition was indeed replaced, first by one in terms of a stoppage of the flow of blood, and later by one that makes the absence of brain activity the dominant sign of death. In both cases, the new definition does not prove its predecessor false, but simply causes us to abandon it.

Mathematics has shown us that elaborate a priori systems can be developed, and Lewis makes this the basis for his more general observation that all our knowledge contains "an element of just such logical order which rise from our definitions" (CL:244). Like Peirce and Schiller, Lewis is keenly aware of the development within nineteenth-century mathematics to replace axioms with postulates, and his own view of the a priori is in part inspired by it.

Interpretation, finally, involves the application of a priori conceptual systems to the given, thereby imposing an order upon it. For Lewis, this is something *we* bring to experience. We can do this because we confront the given with certain ready-made distinctions and systems of classification. When we pronounce someone dead, for instance, we do so by applying our preestablished conception of death to what we encounter in experience.

In Lewis's view, knowledge, or understanding, commences precisely "when some conceptual pattern of relationships is imposed upon the given by interpretation" (CL:250). To know, Lewis explains, "is to find what is presented significant of what is not, just now, so presented" (MWO:44). Lewis hereby rejects a copy-theory of knowledge. We do not attain knowledge when we somehow furnish ourselves with a copy of what is presented; rather, we know something when we can proceed from what is given to something that is not. To know that there is an oasis at the horizon, or that the object on the desk is a fountain pen, is to know how to act toward it and with what results.

Within interpretation, there are two ways in which what is immediately presented can be related to what is not: it can be related to future actual and possible experiences, or it can be related to our own interests and actions. Errors occur when I relate what is presently given to a future experience that fails to occur, or when I predict that something will serve my interest when it doesn't. Regarding the first direction, Lewis argues that there is some structure inherent to the given. The given cannot be a "smooth undifferentiated flux," Lewis observes, because in that case attention would not be able to mark any boundaries (MWO:58). What the boundaries are, however, can be learned only from experience, and only in a manner that is inseparably wound up with our aims and actions:

> That the rug is on the floor or the thunder follows the flash, is as much given as the color of the rug or the loudness of the crash. But that I find this disjunction of rug and floor possessed of a meaning which the wrinkles in the rug do not have, reflects my past experience to taking up and putting down rugs.
>
> (MWO:59)

Recall that the given itself cannot be known, at least not in any substantial sense. It is that buzzing and blooming confusion we seek to give some order to by imposing a priori schemes on it. Even to identify the rug as an object, to object-ify it, is already to impose a conceptual scheme on what is presented. The point is, however, that when we perceive what we have come to recognize as rugs, there is something to what is given that makes it natural for us to separate rugs from floors in a way that we cannot separate rugs from wrinkles or colors.

This brings us to the second direction Lewis distinguishes, namely, where the given is related not to future possible or actual experiences, but to our own aims and interests. Here, how we categorize the given depends on whether we expect the interpretation to lead us to the result we desire. As Lewis puts it, "What the mixed and troubled experience will be—that is beyond me. But what I shall do with it—that is my own question, when the character of experience is before me" (MWO:265). Faced with what is given, I am free to impose any category upon it I want, Lewis argues, and I am likely to pick those categories that best serve my purposes.

How we classify a certain experience is thus determined by a learned relation that connects it to other experiences and to action. Whether a certain interpretation is successful depends on whether it matches our future experiences and serves our interests. In brief, the issue of interpretation is a thoroughly pragmatic one.

9.2 Pragmatism, Truth, and Valuation

Since, for Lewis, knowledge results from the successful application of an a priori conceptual system to the given, knowledge is for him always relative to a conceptual system. For Lewis, scientific as well as everyday knowledge is a product of deeply rooted attitudes and interpretative habits of thought, and it is the past success of conceptual schemes that guides us in our understanding of the world within which we live. The result is a thoroughly pragmatic theory of truth:

> There can be no more fundamental ground than the pragmatic for a truth of any sort. Nothing—not even direct perception—can force the abandonment of an interpretative attitude . . . except some demand or purpose of the mind itself.
>
> (MWO:266f)

On this account, alchemy is replaced by modern chemistry not because alchemy has been proven false, but because the alchemist's categories and principles no longer connect with the given in a way that serves our purposes. Some pragmatists interpret this in terms of new truths replacing old truths, but Lewis finds this an unfortunate expression. It is more accurate to say that an old scheme for interpreting the given is replaced by a new one. In this process the old scheme is not found to be false but simply abandoned.

Lewis is very critical of the pragmatism of James and Dewey, whom he accuses of neglecting the a priori. Because of this, they "seem to put all truth at once at the mercy of experience and within the power of human decision" (MWO:266). For Lewis, one must not begin as a pragmatist, but one must begin by constructing a priori systems, a process during which one is guided by intellectual motives that go well beyond the practical and the expedient—motives such as consistency, simplicity, and completeness. Without a well-developed a priori, Lewis insists, the acquisition of knowledge remains a random leap in the dark. Any pragmatism that ignores this aspect of knowledge acquisition, Lewis continues, is no more than "a cheerful form of skepticism" (MWO:271). For Lewis, it is not in the *construction* of a priori systems, but only *in their application to the given* that one is to be a pragmatist. "We must all be pragmatists," Lewis writes, "but pragmatists in the end, not in the beginning" (MWO:267).

Lewis's pragmatist answer to the question of how to connect a priori conceptual frameworks with the given bestows a central place to value judgments. A priori schemes are chosen with a concrete purpose in mind, or because they best serve our needs in general and in the long run. Both entail an appeal to what we value. As Lewis explains in *An Analysis of Knowledge and Valuation*,

> Knowledge, action, and evaluation are essentially connected. The primary and pervasive significance of knowledge lies in its guidance of action: knowing is for the sake of doing. And action, obviously, is rooted in evaluation. For a being which did not assign comparative values, deliberate action would be pointless; and for one which did not know, it would be impossible.
>
> (AKV:3)

When acting deliberately, I act from the belief that the situation I find myself in can be altered according to my will to meet a present aim. For instance, I can walk to the apple tree across the road to pick some of its apples. Taken this way, Lewis's pragmatism comes down to the view,

> that all problems are at bottom problems of conduct, that all judgments are, implicitly, judgments of value, and that, as there can be ultimately no valid distinction of theoretical from practical, so there can be no final separation of questions of truth of any kind from questions of the justifiable ends of action.
>
> (CL:108)

A value-neutral pragmatism—or at that, a value-neutral philosophy—is a contradiction in terms.

Since what a priori system to adhere to involves a judgment as to its value, the value judgment must be made independently of the system whose value is being judged. Doing otherwise would beg the question. Lewis's way out of this predicament is to make value judgments a species of empirical judgments. In fact, the central thesis of *An Analysis of Knowledge and Valuation* is that value judgments are empirical judgments—a view that implies that they are capable of verification. Later, we see Hilary Putnam make a similar move when discussing the fact–value distinction (12.1).

To get a better sense of how Lewis understands empirical knowledge, it is useful to consider his division of empirical knowledge into expressive statements, terminating judgments, and non-terminating judgments. *Expressive statements* are mere articulations of what is immediately presented in experience, without any commitment as to whether their object is real, a phantasm, or a representation of something else. The claim "I see what *looks like* a marble staircase down the hall," Lewis considers an expressive statement, as I am restricting myself wholly to describing what is encountered in experience (AKV:179). The situation is different for the apparently similar statement "I see a marble staircase down the hall," as now I am making a judgment about how the world is. Roughly speaking, the difference is the following: Discovering that the staircase is part of an elaborate *trompe l'oeil* falsifies the second statement but does not affect the first one, as the later discovery does not alter the initial impression. It still *looked* like a marble staircase. For Lewis, expressive statements are thus non-falsifiable. They cannot be proven wrong. What is more, they are also unverifiable. No corroboration with any other fact can add anything to the initial impression that is being captured in the expressive statement. Getting close to the stairs and finding that the steps are really there does not strengthen the original impression that it looked like a marble staircase. Since expressive statements cannot be falsified or corroborated, Lewis denies that they can be properly classified as knowledge. However, they do allow us to refer to the basic facts of experience.

Besides expressive statements, Lewis distinguishes between terminating judgments and non-terminating judgments. *Terminating judgments* are typically of the form,

> Given that I have a direct experience S, then if I do A, I will have a direct experience E; where S and E are experiences that can be captured in expressive statements.

Terminating judgments find their cue in what is immediately given, but what determines their meaning and truth is not given. Such terminating judgments, however, can be verified, and they can be verified conclusively. Moreover, they are verified *not* by putting them under closer scrutiny, but by performing the act that connects S with E.[5] Hence, in contrast to expressive statements, terminating judgments can be shown to be true or false. Lewis considers the verified terminating judgment the paradigm of empirical knowledge. Terminating judgments, he observes, admit of "decisive and complete verification or falsification" (AKV:181).

The second type of judgments Lewis calls *non-terminating* on the ground that,

> while there is nothing in the import of such objective statements which is intrinsically unverifiable, and hence nothing included in them which is not expressible by some terminating judgment, nevertheless no limited set of particular predictions of empirical eventualities can completely exhaust the significance of such an objective statement.
>
> (AKV:184)

The statement that there is a marble staircase down the hallway is for Lewis a *non*-terminating judgment. Although nothing included in the statement is intrinsically unverifiable, no finite set of terminating judgments can fully capture its meaning. This because no finite number of terminating judgments—if I do A, I will experience E—would be sufficient to fully exhaust the empirical significance of a non-terminating judgment, as the number of possible actions that bear upon the issue is endless. In Lewis's view, the class of non-terminating judgments comprises most of the empirical statements we habitually make (AKV:185). "Jupiter has four moons," "Most Americans are overweight," and "Mario married Maria" are all examples of non-terminating judgments.

Although no finite set of terminating judgments can fully capture the empirical significance of a non-terminating judgment, non-terminating judgments can be verified or confirmed in terms of the terminating judgments they entail. In other words, the knowledge conveyed by a non-terminating judgment is always probable knowledge where its probability is a function of the verification of the terminating judgments it entails. For Lewis, non-terminating judgments can be said to be "practically certain" when the degree of their verification is such that "no later confirmation can render what is presently judged more certain than it is at the moment" (AKV:181).

Lewis's discussion of empirical knowledge betrays his pragmatist slant. His notion of terminating judgments clearly breathes the spirit of the principle of pragmatism, on which the meaning of a judgment is a function of its conceivable practical consequences. Moreover, since non-terminating judgments are cast in terms of the terminating judgments they entail, the same can be said for them.

Importantly, since for Lewis terminating judgments can be decisively and completely verified by reducing them to (non-falsifiable) expressive statements, it is ultimately the given that determines which terminating judgments are true and which are false, and by the same token, which non-terminating judgments are probably so. As we will see later in this chapter, the idea that the given can perform such a function is rejected by Davidson and Goodman.

9.3 Logical Positivism

Around the same time, a school of thought emerges in Europe called logical positivism (or logical empiricism). The logical positivists subscribe to the central thesis of the empiricists, that only statements about sensory phenomena are genuine, and they take this as their guide when discussing meaning, truth, and inquiry. For the logical positivists, there are essentially only two types of meaningful empirical statements: statements cast directly in observational language, and statements that can be reduced to (or translated into) statements cast directly in observational language. They further maintain that these observation statements are indubitable and incorrigible, so that they can be considered a secure foundation of our knowledge. However, in contrast to Lewis, the logical positivists do not distinguish between statements such as "This object looks red" and "This object is red," thereby combining two very different kinds of statements under the rubric of observation sentences. Recall that, for Lewis, the former are indubitable and incorrigible, but the latter are not.

In the logical positivist's view, any statement containing a theoretical term such as "electron," "gravity," or "hardness" must be translatable into a set of statements that are equivalent to it, while containing only observation terms. In response to the question of how to establish this translation, the logical positivists point to Russell and Whitehead, who in their *Principia Mathematica* sought to reduce mathematics to logic and set theory, and to Wittgenstein's *Tractatus Logico-Philosophicus*. Put briefly, the translation, or reduction, must abide by the transformation rules of first-order predicate logic, which must be taken to be strictly tautological—i.e., analytic—so that they would add nothing whatsoever to the observation sentences they connect. In this way, the logical positivists seek to avoid having to admit that claims about the world are somehow, whether wholly or in part, mind dependent, which would undermine their empiricist stance. In contrast, if we were to stick with Peirce's normative logic (6.5) or Dewey's experimental logic (8.1), both of which are far from tautological, our claims about the world would be at least partially mind dependent.

Carnap's 1928 *Der logische Aufbau der Welt* is the most ambitious product of the logical positivist era. Here Carnap tries to do for epistemology what the *Principia* tried to do for mathematics. The aim of the book, Carnap explains, is to reduce all claims about reality to claims about the given. For Carnap, this means showing how each meaningful statement is in effect a logical construction of so called observation sentences, which are sentences that capture raw, unanalyzed perceptual data, without any conceptual pollution.

In light of this, the logical positivists' answer to the search for meaning is relatively straightforward. The meaning of any statement, word, etc., consists of the observation statements into which it can be translated, while giving particular attention to the *relations* between those observation statements. Regarding the second point, *logical* positivists differ from earlier forms of positivism, such as Comte's, and empiricism more generally. Modern logic, they argue, gives us a perfect and transparent medium through which those relations can be precisely and unambiguously expressed. For the logical positivists, knowledge is a matter of grasping these relations. It is not concerned with the *content* of our experience—which is private and non-communicable—but with the (logical) *structure* of our experience, which *can* be communicated. It is this logical structure that renders our concepts intersubjective. Hence, it is not someone's unique and private experience of some particular fact that constitutes knowledge, but how this experience fits within a larger structure that *is* communicable.

For the linguistically oriented logical positivists, this comes down to the question of how to relate experience to a language (the medium through which we express and communicate our thought), where "language" is to be interpreted broadly as "a set of symbols which are to be combined in accordance with a definite logical syntax" with the purpose "to mirror or express facts."[6] For the logical positivists, a statement *expresses* a fact, not by eliciting certain sensations, but through its *structural similarity* with the fact. A statement is true when its components correctly reflect the components of the fact it expresses; it is false when they don't. This idea of knowledge as a mirror of reality (which was inspired by a focus on the *structure* of experience, rather than its content) is radically rejected by the pragmatists. It is explicitly criticized by Dewey, and it becomes the focal point for Richard Rorty in *Philosophy and the Mirror of Nature* (Chapter 11) and of Hilary Putnam in his rejection of metaphysical realism (Chapter 12).

9.4 Pragmatism and Pragmatics

A session at the 1934 International Congress of Philosophy on the importance of logical analysis for epistemology brings the pragmatists Ferdinand Schiller and Charles Morris together with the logical positivists Otto Neurath and Rudolf Carnap.[7] The session has considerable impact. While Schiller remains more or less an outsider, Morris, Carnap, and Neurath gravitate to one another. Consequently, when Carnap is forced to flee the Nazis,

Morris arranges for him to come to the University of Chicago, and shortly thereafter the three begin coediting the *International Encyclopedia of Unified Science*.

In his own contribution to the session, Morris, a student of Mead, seeks to show that pragmatism and logical positivism are "essentially complementary," adding that "much is to be expected from a conscious cross-fertilization of the two" (LPP:23). According to Morris, the connection between the two is strongest where they address the issue of meaning. At face value, pragmatists and logical positivists appear seriously at odds on this issue. Whereas pragmatists seek to connect the meaning of, say, a proposition with the expectations of the person who uses it, logical positivists connect it with the syntactical rules of the language that determine its (legitimate) use. For the logical positivists, when studying the meaning of a proposition, one must look not at those who use it and the mental states they connect with it, but at how the proposition fits within the language that is being used. On the latter view, the meaning of a proposition "becomes the non-analytic propositions which logically follow from it, i.e., which the syntax of the language allows" (LPP:27).

According to Morris, far from being mutually exclusive, the two views are complementary, addressing different aspects of the meaning situation. Building on Peirce's triadic semiotics (6.7), Morris observes,

> Symbols have three types of relation: to a person or persons, to other symbols, and to objects; meaning has three corresponding dimensions . . . the biological aspect (meaning as expectation), the formalist aspect (meaning as that expressible in a particular speech), and the empirical aspect (meaning as functional substitutability for objects).
>
> (LPP:27f)

Here we find the root of the influential distinction between pragmatics (the relation of symbols to persons), syntax (the relation of symbols to other symbols), and semantics (the relation of symbols to objects). Further elaborating on the complementarity of pragmatism and logical positivism, Morris continues,

> If we say that the meaning of a symbol is the expectation it arouses, this is practically equivalent to saying that the meaning of a symbol is its possible extension (i.e., all the objects to which it can be applied), and this in turn is similar to saying that the meaning of a symbol is determined by the specification of those characters which an object must have for the symbol to be applied. And then since these characters must in turn be specified by the use of other symbols, we find ourselves led to the formalistic position that the meaning of a symbol is determined by its

syntactical connections with other symbols (i.e., by the grammatical rules of its usage).

(LPP:28)

The first part, where the meaning of a symbol is related to the expectations of its users, is addressed by the pragmatists; while the second part, where the meaning of the symbol is related to the grammatical structure of a language, is addressed by the logical positivists. Hence, the complementarity.

Carnap accepts Morris's triadic distinction between pragmatics, semantics, and syntax, adding, with an explicit reference to Peirce, that a complete theory of language must address all three. As Carnap explains in his *Introduction to Semantics*,

> In semiotic, the general theory of signs, three fields are distinguished. An investigation of a language belongs to pragmatics if explicit reference to a speaker is made; it belongs to semantics if designata but not speakers are referred to; it belongs to syntax if neither speakers nor designata but only expressions are dealt with.

Thus, pragmatics, for Carnap, is that part of a theory of language that concerns the relation between language and speaker: "If in an investigation explicit reference is made to the speaker, or, to put it in more general terms, to the user of a language, then we assign it to the field of *pragmatics*."[8] About the relation with pragmatism, Carnap notes, "It seems to me there is agreement on the main points between the present views of the *Vienna Circle* . . . and those of *Pragmatism*, as interpreted e.g. by Lewis" (TM:427).

Carnap's main contribution to pragmatics (although the term itself is absent) is in "Testability and Meaning," which appeared in the journal *Philosophy of Science* in 1936 and 1937—two years after Carnap met Morris, and shortly following Carnap's emigration to the US. In "Testability and Meaning," Carnap addresses the question, What makes a statement verifiable, confirmable, testable? According to Carnap, this is an empirical question, not a logical one. It belongs to "a biological or psychological theory of language as a kind of human behavior, and especially as a kind of reaction to observations" (TM:454). Rejecting the possibility of absolute verification, Carnap considers the issue of confirmation and testing a practical one (TM:426). Consequently, it pertains to the relation between speaker and language, and hence belongs to pragmatics.

There are other moves toward pragmatism in Carnap's thought. In the controversy surrounding the analytic–synthetic distinction, Carnap makes a distinct shift toward Lewis, who drew the analytic–synthetic distinction along pragmatic lines.[9] Whether the sentence "All ravens are black" is analytic or synthetic depends on what we decided the meaning of our terms to be—in this case, whether we have decided to make "being black" part of the meaning of "raven." Carnap holds a pragmatic view of explicit definitions, contextual definitions, reduction sentences, and even of entire linguistic frameworks:

> The introduction of . . . new ways of speaking does not need any theoretical justification because it does not imply any assertion of reality. To be sure, we have to face at this point an important question; but it is a *practical*, not a theoretical question; it is the question of whether or not to accept the new linguistic forms. The acceptance cannot be judged as either true or false because it is not an assertion. It can only be judged as being more or less expedient, fruitful, conducive to the aim for which the language is intended.[10]

In his 1934 *Logical Syntax of Language*, Carnap captures this attitude in his famous "principle of tolerance," which states that in philosophical analysis, one may opt for any linguistic framework one wishes. For Carnap, as for Lewis, there are no fundamental logical principles, no privileged representational systems, and no fundamental ontological objects. As he puts it, quite in contrast to Peirce, "In logic there are no morals. Everyone is at liberty to build up his own, i.e., his own form of language, as he wishes."[11] The choice is a pragmatic one: one picks the framework that works best. And each framework comes with its own ontological commitments—commitments that reveal themselves in the observation sentences. From the logical positivist's perspective, the inability to separate out expressive statements (as Lewis had done) was no oversight.

9.5 Verificationism

The logical positivists see an intimate connection between meaning and verification—a connection that goes well beyond the general observation that before you can verify a statement you must first know what it means. They maintain the much more radical thesis that questions of meaning and verification come down to the same[12]—to know the meaning of a sentence is to know what the state of affairs would be if that sentence were true. This view entails that "if for two sentences the conditions under which we would have to take them as true are the same, then they have the same meaning" (TM:420). In brief, for the logical positivists, the meaning of a proposition is its method of verification. This view is known as *verificationism*, and the logical positivists' criterion of meaning is called the *verifiability principle* or the *verification principle*. This principle plays a role similar to that of the pragmatic maxim, albeit not without significant differences. Whereas the verification principle is decidedly about propositions—it is meant to establish whether a proposition has meaning or not, and this is a binary all-or-nothing affair—the pragmatic maxim concerns objects of the mind more broadly, and, for

Peirce at least, reflects only the highest of three grades of clearness (2.4). It is not as if the pawnbroker, who has reached only the first grade of clearness with respect to gold, does not know what "gold" means; quite the contrary.

Initially, the logical positivists maintain a strong version of the principle on which a statement is meaningful if and only if it can be conclusively shown true or false by relating it to direct observations—i.e., by translating it into observation sentences. For example, "This teacup is fragile" would mean "If this teacup is dropped on the floor, it will break." In Lewis's terms, this implies that for non-terminating judgments to have meaning, they must first be reduced to terminating ones. This version of the verification principle quickly proves too restrictive. For instance, all statements about the past and the future become meaningless because they cannot be conclusively verified. Even claims as mundane as "I was born" must be rejected, as it is clearly impossible to go back to the situation where you were born, which alone would allow you to conclusively verify the claim that you were born, thereby giving it meaning.

Later versions of the principle relax the requirement that for a statement to be meaningful, we must be able to conclusively show it true or false. It is to this more moderate version of the principle that Carnap and Neurath ascribe. As Carnap explains, "If by verification is meant a definitive and final establishment of truth, then no (synthetic) sentence is ever verifiable" (TM:420). According to Carnap, we can only *confirm* a sentence more and more, thereby increasing our confidence that the sentence is true. For Carnap, a sentence is confirmable if we know what conditions would confirm the sentence. Besides confirmability, Carnap also introduces the stronger notion of testability. A sentence is testable if we can produce experiments at will that would lead to its confirmation or disconfirmation. The notion of confirmability is wider, as not all sentences that are confirmable are also testable. The claim that there is life on planets in other galaxies is confirmable, as we know the conditions that would confirm it, but it is not testable.

At which point a specific claim is sufficiently confirmed to justify our accepting it as true, Carnap considers a pragmatic issue (TM:426). This makes Carnap conclude that the acceptance or rejection of a non-analytic sentence always includes a conventional element, though not without being acutely aware that there is also a nonconventional element that generally plays the dominant role. Carnap is further well aware that for most practical purposes, and even within scientific research, a sufficient level of certainty is reached after a few positive instances, after which no additional experiments are needed—a view he shared with Peirce.

Our inability to conclusively verify sentences is, for Carnap, not a mere practical hindrance—one that could be overcome given sufficient time and resources. Like Lewis, Carnap concedes that universal sentences, most markedly those expressing natural laws, can never be fully verified because the number of instances that they refer to is open-ended.

9.6 Quine's More Thorough Pragmatism

W.V.O. Quine (1908–2000) is a student of Lewis at Harvard, and while still in his early twenties he comes in close contact with logical positivism. He meets with the Vienna Circle and visits Carnap in Prague. After absorbing many of the logical positivists' views, Quine comes to reject the view he ascribes to Lewis and Carnap, on which the pragmatic element is limited solely to the choice of a language or conceptual system, suggesting that everything else can be treated non-pragmatically. For Quine, this view hinges on two dogmas that he seeks to dispel in his influential 1951 "Two Dogmas of Empiricism." They are the dogma of reductionism and the dogma of the radical separation of the analytic and the synthetic.[13] Abandoning these two dogmas, Quine argues, causes "a shift toward pragmatism" (LPV:20); in fact, it leads to a "more thorough pragmatism" than that of Lewis or Carnap (LPV:46).

According to Quine, the notion of analytic statements stems from the realization that truths generally depend not only on facts about the world (sometimes referred to as extralinguistic facts), but also on facts about language. To use Quine's example, the statement "Brutus killed Caesar" would be false not only if the world had been different in certain respects, but also if the English word "killed" had meant something altogether different. That there are these two radically different components has led to the conviction that when analyzing a statement—e.g., to determine whether or why the statement is true—we can neatly separate these components. This conviction then spurred the notion that there could be sentences for which the extralinguistic component is nil, resulting in statements for which no extralinguistic fact can have any effect on their truth value. These are the so-called "analytic statements." In "Two Dogmas," Quine argues that we have no evidence at all that we can separate these two components or that there are any statements for which the extralinguistic component is nil.

Whether there are any analytic statements is, for Quine, an empirical question, and he examines several options. He begins by distinguishing two kinds of analytic statements. First, there are those that are *logically* true, which means that they are true solely because of their logical syntax. An example is "All unmarried men are unmarried," which is true no matter what meaning one ascribes to "unmarried" or to "men." Next, there are statements that can be turned into the first, as Quine puts it, by a substitution of synonyms. The statement "All bachelors are unmarried" belongs to this second kind. It can be translated into the first statement by substituting "unmarried men" for "bachelors" on the ground that being male and unmarried belongs to the concept of a bachelor. Here, *the identity in meaning* of "bachelor" and "unmarried man" justifies the substitution. Hence, even though not *logically* true or false, statements of this second kind, like the first, can be said to be true or false independently of any extralinguistic facts.

Quine focuses on the second, more interesting kind and examines various attempts at justifying the substitution. I will look at one of them, namely the view that the substitution is justified because "bachelor" is explicitly *defined* as an unmarried adult male. Quine observes that although it is relatively easy to justify substitutability by reference to a definition, it is something altogether different to derive the analyticity of a statement from the fact that the substitution is based on a definition. Definitions, Quine observes, are not framed in a vacuum, but they are formed against an unquestioned background of beliefs without which they could not convey any meaning. It is an empirical fact that we call unmarried adult men bachelors, and this fact requires that the terms constituting the definition have meaning—i.e., that "male," "adult," and "unmarried" have meaning. That we call unmarried adult males bachelors, and that in the past substitution of one for the other has always worked, allows us to predict that substitution will continue to work in the future. However, at the same time, we cannot guarantee that it will *always* work—that no exceptions are possible. In fact, it appears that we can truly rule out the very possibility of failed substitution *only* by tacitly relying upon analyticity, but that implies that we cannot use definition *to prove* the possibility of analyticity, as then we would be arguing in a circle. The other attempts to establish analyticity that Quine discusses fail for similar reasons, which in his view shows "how stubbornly the distinction between analytic and synthetic has resisted any straightforward drawing" (LPV:41). Quine therefore calls it a *dogma* of empiricism. Empiricists have accepted it, often uncritically, without having any empirical justification for doing so.

The idea of substitution is caught up with a view on meaning that Quine derisively calls the museum myth of meaning—the idea that our mind is like a museum filled with mental exhibits. The words we use are then like the labels that name or describe each exhibited item, and changing the labels leaves the exhibits unaffected (OR:27). On this view we have a certain mental object that we can label "bachelor" or "unmarried adult male"; we can switch the two labels without this affecting the mental object we attach them to, and it is the mental object that justifies the substitution. The museum myth plays a key role in the correspondence theory of truth. On this view, what we say is true when our mental objects line up with the facts. Instead, Quine subscribes to a behaviorist semantics: We can understand a language only by studying actual linguistic behavior—which, he adds, is also how we learned our native language. When we look at it this way, we discover that it is very unlikely that different linguistic responses can be shown to be exactly identical in meaning or reference. This makes any substitution approximate—sufficient for practical purposes, but insufficient for establishing analyticity. In rejecting this dogma, Quine distances himself from Lewis and Carnap, effectively reestablishing the pragmatisms of Peirce, James, and

Dewey. The views of the latter three do not hinge on this dogma; in fact, they all three reject it.

The second dogma Quine addresses is that of *reductionism*. For Quine, this dogma builds on the first. In its radical form, reductionism goes back to the early logical positivists who held that any meaningful statement not about direct observations can be translated, at least in principle, into simple statements about direct observations using transformation rules that are analytic. Following this line of argument, the logical positivists maintain that the entire empirical import of our knowledge "boils down to a range of confirmatory experiences" (LPV:41). With the analytic–synthetic distinction exposed as a dogma, this view is no longer defensible, as it requires us to identify certain claims as analytic; in fact, Quine argues, both dogmas are "at root identical" (ibid). With the analytic–synthetic distinction gone, a distinction that typically accompanies it, namely that between necessary and contingent statements (as statements are often considered necessary precisely because they are a priori or analytic), goes out the window too.

Having unmasked the analytic–synthetic distinction and reductionism as dogmas of empiricism, Quine, a committed empiricist, rejects them, as any empiricist should. All our claims are synthetic and contingent. The result is a moderate holism where the emphasis shifts from statements, or sentences, to theories:

> A whole sentence is ordinarily too short a text to serve as an independent vehicle of empirical meaning. It will not have its separable bundle of observable or testable consequences. A reasonably inclusive body of scientific theory, taken as a whole, will indeed have such consequences.
>
> (PPE:26)

These theories, or conceptual systems, however, are underdetermined. One and the same set of experiences can support a variety of explanations. Consequently, when faced with what Quine called "recalcitrant experiences," one generally has recourse to multiple readjustments, or, as Quine puts it metaphorically,

> Total science is like a field of force whose boundary conditions are experience. A conflict with experience at the periphery occasions readjustments in the interior of the field. Truth values have to be redistributed over some of our statements. Reëvaluation of some statements entails reëvaluation of others, because of their logical interconnections. . . . But the total field is so underdetermined by its boundary conditions, experience, that there is much latitude of choice as to what statements to reëvaluate in the light of any single contrary experience.
>
> (LPV:42)

This view inspired what is now called the Duhem–Quine thesis: we cannot test a scientific hypothesis in isolation, as doing so typically requires one or more background assumptions (also called auxiliary assumptions or auxiliary hypotheses) to be true. This means that, when a hypothesis fails the test, we can usually retain it by rejecting or modifying certain background assumptions instead. Consequently, the best we can do is to test the hypothesis together with the background hypotheses that it relies on. This implies that we will not be able to identify which hypothesis is the culprit were the test to fail. Similarly, we cannot say that a hypothesis is true were the test to succeed, as the test only confirms a set of hypotheses in toto. In practice this comes down to testing a conceptual scheme, or some significant part of it, rather than any singular statement or hypothesis within it, thereby refuting the verification principle of the logical positivists we looked at earlier.

Because our theories are underdetermined by the empirical data on which they rest, we must make choices, as the data allow for multiple, possibly even contradicting theories. As a result, we are "largely the author rather than discoverer of truth" (PPE:34). As Quine explains,

> As an empiricist I continue to think of the conceptual scheme of science as a tool, ultimately, for predicting future experience in the light of past experience. Physical objects are conceptually imported into the situation as convenient intermediaries—not by definition in terms of experience, but simply as irreducible posits comparable, epistemologically, to the gods of Homer. Let me interject that for my part I do, qua lay physicist, believe in physical objects and not in Homer's gods; and I consider it a scientific error to believe otherwise. But in point of epistemological footing the physical objects and the gods differ only in degree and not in kind. Both sorts of entities enter our conception only as cultural posits. The myth of physical objects is epistemologically superior to most in that it has proved more efficacious than other myths as a device for working a manageable structure into the flux of experience.
>
> (LPV:44)

This notwithstanding, Quine maintains that the physical objects we arrive at are real, "down to the most hypothetical of particles," because

> we are always talking within our going system when we attribute truth; we cannot talk otherwise. Our system changes, yes. When it does we do not say that truth changes with it; we say that we had wrongly supposed something true and have learned better. Fallibilism is the watchword, not relativism.
>
> (PPE:33f)

As with Lewis, logic is no exception. Even the most deeply ingrained laws of logic are open to revision, and Quine cites as an example a proposal to revise the law of excluded middle to simplify quantum mechanics.

The beauty of the concept of analyticity was that it enabled us to identify our own contribution to knowledge; it enabled us to separate what was of our own making as opposed to what we (passively) received through the senses. However, with analyticity no longer defensible, we can no longer do so. In all our knowledge, what we find and what we contribute are inseparably interweaved, and when we separate the two in thought, it will always be a fallible empirical judgment. What is more, because of the under-determination of theory by data and our inability to test each statement in isolation, this judgment holds only within a certain conceptual system. When we move to a different conceptual system, our judgment about what we do or do not contribute may pan out differently as well. Consequently, we can no longer identify what is a product of the mind and what is not, as different theories, or different conceptual schemes, will give us different answers. Quine rejects Peirce's notion of a final opinion—we are fated to be fallibilists till the bitter end.

Quine's treatment of conceptual systems is distinctly pragmatic: They are tools for predicting future experience through past and present experience. The pragmatic aspect tells us what to settle on when a recalcitrant experience allows for alternative readjustments, as is often the case: "The edge of the system must be kept squared with experience; the rest, with all its elaborate myths or fictions, has as its objective the simplicity of laws" (LPV:45). For Quine, science is normative, with simplicity as one of its core values, and its aim is to help us cope with the world. Hence, Quine concluded "Two Dogmas" as follows:

> Each man is given a scientific heritage plus a continuing barrage of sensory stimulation; and the considerations which guide him in warping his scientific heritage to fit his continuing sensory promptings are, where rational, pragmatic.
>
> (LPV:46)

Quine proves a reluctant pragmatist, however, and his references to pragmatism become increasingly rare. In "The Pragmatists' Place in Empiricism," written in part in reply to an article in the *Times Literary Supplement* in which he was called the last pragmatist,[14] Quine depicts the pragmatists as empiricists, but as followers rather than leaders, who have only a cursory relation to what Quine identified as the five milestones of modern empiricism (PPE:37). Although Quine concedes that pragmatism has its attractions, his largely nominalistic interpretation of the pragmatic maxim causes him to consider it as merely a version of the verification principle, which by that time has been all but refuted. Uncomfortable with the myriad of tendencies within pragmatism, Quine limits his loyalty to what he calls pragmatism's two best guesses: the doctrine, that truth is to a high degree human-made, and its behaviorist semantics (PPE:37). Quine's pragmatism, however, is nonetheless more thorough than Lewis's or Carnap's in that we must be pragmatists in the beginning as well as in the end.

9.7 On Worlds and World Making

Nelson Goodman (1906–1998), also a student of Lewis, explores situations where conceptual schemes imply statements that contradict statements implied by other conceptual schemes. Take the geocentric view, on which Earth is the unmoving center of the universe.[15] It states that "The Earth does not move." In contrast, the heliocentric view, which positions the Sun at the center, states that "The Earth does move." Since these two statements contradict, if one is true, the other must be false. Now it is tempting, Goodman, continues, to resolve this contradiction as follows:

> The Earth does not move according to the geocentric view.
> The Earth does move according to the heliocentric view.

This does not work, he writes, for the simple reason that whereas the original two claims were about Earth, the latter two are not. This becomes clear when we realize that the truth of "The Earth does not move according to the geocentric view" is independent of whether the Earth moves or not, as it is a claim only about what the geocentric view asserts. Now we can say that the geocentric and heliocentric views are two different versions (or conceptual schemes) for describing reality. But given what we have seen so far, we have to admit that we cannot describe reality independently of any version whatsoever. Consequently, the claim "The Earth moves" must always be understood as belonging to some version or other, as without it the claim would have no meaning. But if there is no truth to the matter independently of some version, then it cannot be used to adjudicate which version to favor when faced with competing versions that make contradictory claims. Put differently, in the absence of such version-independent facts, we have no non-arbitrary ground on which to claim which of them truly describes the world. All we can say is that they cannot possibly describe the same world, because they contradict. This leads Goodman to state that versions come with worlds and that where versions contradict, assuming they can be considered adequate, they must describe different worlds. Broadly speaking, we can say that a version is correct when there is a world that fits it. That, however, does not entitle us to conclude that there must be one world that fits all versions. In fact, contradictions like the one just discussed suggest that this is most likely not the case. If theories are underdetermined by data, as Quine argues, then there is likely to be a plurality of worlds. In fact, it is not entirely clear how versions relate to worlds, or for that matter, what these worlds are made of. Since we can only think about a world through some version, we cannot really say that a version is true to a world, as the reverse is equally true—namely, that the world is true to a version.

Goodman further differs from Quine and the logical positivists in that he does not privilege physics, or natural science more generally, as giving us the true—or at least the truest—description of the world. For Goodman, it makes no sense to say that physical optics gives us a truer description of sunsets than Monet's *San Giorgio Maggiore at Dusk*. Rather, these descriptions belong to different versions. Various criteria can be used to determine what version to choose. However, the claim that one version describes "the world" better than the other version cannot be one of the criteria.

Goodman's arguments not only undermine Lewis's claim that the given can somehow help us determine which version to accept (as we can only compare versions with other versions), but it also undermines the idea, held most notably by Peirce, that in the long run we can come to a final opinion, the object of which is reality, as it is very likely that we would eventually end up with multiple versions that contradict one another. Rather, in a more Jamesean fashion, we must conclude that we partake in multiple worlds at once.

9.8 Davidson and a Third Dogma

In 1974, Donald Davidson publishes a paper in which he identifies a third dogma of empiricism: the dogma that we can neatly separate a conceptual scheme from its (uninterpreted) content—that we can neatly separate an organizing system from what is waiting to be organized—a dogma Davidson believes Quine failed to shed.[16] Again, the idea is that we can isolate what we encounter (the given as it is, independently of any conceptualization) from what we add to it (the scheme through which this given is conceptualized).

The scheme–content distinction has induced conceptual relativism (the idea that our statements about the world are always relative to some conceptual system) and allowed for the existence of alternative, equally justifiable conceptual systems that are incommensurable—implying that translation of one into the other is impossible, not just in practice, but in principle. This view has been ascribed to certain cultural anthropologists, such as Benjamin Whorf, and certain historians of science, such as Thomas Kuhn.[17] For Whorf, Hopi Indians who are exposed to the same given as native English speakers *conceptualize* this given differently, and consequently they can be said to live in a different world. Both these worlds contain different facts, as facts emerge only at the conceptual level. As with reductionism, once we have bought into the analytic–synthetic distinction, the scheme–content distinction follows naturally—especially when we also reject the synthetic a priori.

According to Davidson, for there to be a conceptual scheme that is truly different from ours, it is necessary that it cannot be translated into ours, as intertranslatability shows that at a deeper level both belong to the same conceptual scheme. Consequently, there can be multiple conceptual schemes *only* when they are incommensurable. Davidson then continues by arguing that the idea that we can get face to face with a conceptual scheme that is so alien to ours that it is *fully* untranslatable is incoherent. Not only would we be unable to recognize it as a conceptual scheme, but more importantly, we would be conceptualizing it as such while simultaneously denying that conceptualizing it is possible.

This still leaves us with a vast range of partially intertranslatable conceptual schemes (though Davidson prefers to speak of interpretation rather than translation). In such situations, there are some concepts that agree with how we carve up the world, whereas there are others we cannot make to agree at all. However, since we are recognizing it as a conceptual scheme, it is natural for us to presuppose that in virtue of its being a conceptual scheme, it bears, in some broadly similar way, some relation to what *our* scheme bears a relation to as well. This causes Davidson to argue that in trying to understand what people mean, we must presuppose that most of their beliefs are true. We would be quite at a loss to translate, say a string of Hopi sounds, without taking this for granted. We do so even when a speaker of our own language says something that we think is true even though he is using what we take to be the wrong word. Davidson mentions someone who mistakenly calls a passing ketch a yawl. Hence, in contrast to the classical view where the establishment of meaning solidly precedes the establishment of truth, we now begin by ascribing truth to someone's claims and, *on the basis of that*, try to figure out what he must have meant. Only if that fails do we identify the claim as false. In other words, we have to be charitable when interpreting the claims of others. This charity "is forced on us;—whether we like it or not, if we want to understand others, we must count them right in most matters."[18] If truth and meaning are thus interdependent, the notion that a conceptual scheme can be purely a priori, and hence analytic, is no longer tenable; and with that, conceptual relativism goes out the window as well. We will return to this last point with Rorty in Chapter 11.

With the scheme–content dogma gone, Davidson believes that there is not much left of empiricism. This is because empiricism relies on the notion that there is something neutral and common that lies outside all conceptual schemes and determines which schemes are correct or more expedient. Like Carnap, Quine, and Goodman before him, Davidson denies that we can use the given—i.e., the world as it precedes any conceptualization of it—that way. We cannot determine which scheme is correct, or even which one is preferable, on pragmatic grounds, by comparing it to the given, or to experience. We can only compare conceptual schemes with other conceptual schemes. When we verify or falsify a hypothesis, we are not testing it against the unconceptualized given, but we are testing it against other conceptual schemes, including those that constitute the background that gave the theory that contained the hypothesis its meaning. Put into more Peircean terms, we share a great many common beliefs against the backdrop of which doubts and disagreements emerge, and in terms of which these doubts and disagreements are both understood and resolved.

In this chapter we saw that, for Lewis, conceptual schemes are a priori, hence analytic, and that empirical knowledge results from the application of such schemes to the given—a process where the decision of which scheme to choose is justified on pragmatic grounds. Something similar was found in Carnap. Quine argues that this approach presupposes an indefensible dogma, that of the analytic–synthetic distinction. Because of this, Quine argues for "a more thorough pragmatism" (LPV:46). By this he means that whereas Carnap and Lewis limited pragmatism to the choice of a conceptual system only, with the analytic–synthetic distinction gone, this is no longer an option. Pragmatic choices have to be made in the development of such systems as well. In other words, pragmatism is what empiricism becomes without the dogmas.

Peirce would likely agree with Davidson's rejection of the third dogma. Recall that, for Peirce, the meaning of our concepts is cast in terms of their conceivable practical consequences. When inquiry progresses, these conceivable practical consequences are bound to change, so that the meaning of our concepts will change over time as well. We mean something quite different with gold today than we did during the Middle Ages, when it was still considered a mixture of sulfur, mercury, and salt. Hence, when we identify truth with the opinion all would agree upon at the end of inquiry, as does Peirce, and we imagine this opinion to contain the claim that gold is malleable, what is meant by gold then is unlikely to be what was meant by it in the Middle Ages, or, for that matter, what we mean by it today. Because of this, the idea of conceptual schemes will be too static and artificial for Peirce, and he would likely agree that the distinction that the third dogma aims to capture is a chimera.

Notes

1. For an intellectual biography, see Murray Murphey, *C.I. Lewis, the Last Pragmatist* (New York, 2005).
2. See especially Lewis's "The Structure of Logic and Its Relation to Other Systems," *Journal of Philosophy* 18 (1921): 505–16.
3. John Locke, *Essay Concerning Human Understanding* (Oxford, 1975), II.xiii.19.
4. Lewis here rejects the Kantian notion of the synthetic a priori, which concerns claims about the world that are true independently of experience because we cannot think them otherwise than that we do (e.g., all color is extended). For Lewis, who wants to separate out the contributions that we as knowing agents make to empirical knowledge, this would rather be an empirical fact about the mind.

5. Note that, for Lewis, the truth of a conditional is independent of the truth of its antecedent, so its truth can be asserted even when the antecedent is false.

6. Albert Blumberg and Herbert Feigl, "Logical Positivism: A New Movement in European Philosophy," *Journal of Philosophy* 28 (1931): 281–96, p.287.

7. The papers for this session, as well as a partial transcript of the discussion, appeared in *Actes du huitième congrès international de philosophie à Prague 2–7 Septembre 1934* (Prague, 1936), pp.121–60.

8. *Introduction to Semantics,* op. cit., p.9.

9. Rudolf Carnap, "Meaning Postulates," *Philosophical Studies* 3 (1952): 65–73.

10. Rudolf Carnap, "Empiricism, Semantics, and Ontology," *Revue International de Philosophie* 11 (1950): 20–40, p.31f; emphasis added.

11. Rudolf Carnap, *Logical Syntax of Language* (London, 1937), p.52.

12. On verificationism and its relation to pragmatism, see Cheryl Misak, *Verificationism: Its History and Prospects* (New York, 1995); C.I. Lewis, *Collected Papers of Clarence Irving Lewis* (Stanford, 1970); W.P. Alston, "Pragmatism and the Verifiability Theory of Meaning," *Philosophical Studies* 6 (1955): 65–71.

13. W.V.O. Quine, "Two Dogmas of Empiricism," LPV:20–46; originally published in 1951. See also Morton White, "The Analytic and the Synthetic: An Untenable Dualism," in Morton White (ed), *Pragmatism and the American Mind* (London, 1973); Stanley Munsat, *The Analytic-Synthetic Distinction* (Belmont, 1971). For Lewis's view on analyticity, see AKV:35–163.

14. Ernest Gellner, "The Last Pragmatist: The Philosophy of W.V. Quine," *Times Literary Supplement* (25 July 1975): 848–53.

15. Nelson Goodman, *Ways of Worldmaking* (Indianapolis, 1978), p.2ff.

16. Donald Davidson, *Inquiries into Truth & Interpretation* (Oxford, 1984), pp.183–98.

17. See e.g., Benjamin Lee Whorf, "The Relation of Habitual Thought and Behavior to Language," in Leslie Spier (ed), *Language, Culture and Personality: Essays in Memory of Edward Sapir* (Menasha, 1941); Thomas Kuhn, *The Structure of Scientific Revolutions* (Chicago, 1970). Both were profoundly influenced by the logical positivists.

18. Ibid., p.197.

Chapter 10

The European Reception Revisited

In the previous chapter we looked primarily at some developments within American philosophy related to the advent of logical positivism. The focus was on Lewis, Carnap, Quine, and Davidson. In this chapter, we return to developments in Europe. As noted in the Introduction, the European reception of pragmatism was initially quite hostile. There were exceptions, and we examined some of them, most notably Ferdinand Schiller and the Florentine pragmatists. We also saw that there were tendencies within European thought that paralleled pragmatism, raising the question of affinity versus influence. In this chapter we look at the influence of pragmatism on some key British and German philosophers. In both countries, the early reception of pragmatism ran through Schiller and James. Only later do European philosophers become acquainted with Peirce and, especially in Germany, with Mead and Dewey.

10.1 From Russell, to Ramsey, to Wittgenstein

In 1903, Peirce begins corresponding with Victoria Lady Welby, who is well connected in British intellectual circles. The correspondence lasts until her death in 1912.[1] Circulating copies of letters she receives, Welby introduces Peirce's mature thought to Bertrand Russell and others. This material includes Peirce's semiotics, his derivation of the categories, and his existential graphs. One of Welby's correspondents is a young philosopher and linguist named C.K. Ogden, who incorporates an extensive discussion of Peirce, with excerpts from the letters, in an influential book that he co-authors with I.A. Richards: *The Meaning of Meaning*.[2] Ogden also arranges for the first collection of Peirce's papers, *Chance, Love, and Logic* edited by Morris Cohen, to appear on the British market.[3] Both works appear in 1923, exposing British philosophers to a brand of pragmatism that differs significantly from the James and Schiller variety.

Initially, Russell harshly attacks pragmatism, mostly that of James and Schiller, which he sees as too closely allied with idealism, his main target.[4] In his review of James's *Pragmatism*, after acknowledging that as fellow empiricists they have much in common, he writes that the book "is like a bath with hot water running in so slowly that you don't know when to scream."[5] The analytic philosophers, Russell among them, and the pragmatists are both looking for ways to make our ideas clear. However, whereas Peirce and the pragmatists aim to do so by connecting thought with action, the analytic philosophers try to do it through a logical analysis of propositions. A key obstacle for Russell, and one that prevents him from embracing pragmatism, is his insistence that truth be independent of our epistemic situation. This clashes directly with James, who instead insists that "the trail of the human serpent is . . . over everything"—we can never escape our epistemic situation (WJ:384). Hence, much of Russell's criticism centers on the pragmatists' notion of truth, especially its relation to the will to believe. As Russell puts it, "Some practice in the will to believe is an almost indispensable preliminary to the acceptance of pragmatism; and conversely pragmatism, when once accepted, is found to give the full justification of the will to believe."[6]

When spending the fall of 1914 at Harvard, however, where Royce is still teaching, Russell becomes more broadly exposed to the pragmatists, including Peirce, who died just months before. In the years that followed, Russell came to embrace James's neutral monism, pragmatism's behaviorism, and the realization that language, far from a neutral medium, shapes what we speak of. As for the third, Russell explains,

> I imagined that logic could be pursued by taking it for granted that symbols were always, so to speak, transparent, and in no way distorted the objects they were supposed to "mean."[7]

Whereas Russell formerly held that belief and action had to be clearly separated, accusing the pragmatists, who failed to do this, of muddying the waters, he now no longer believes this. The result is a much more pragmatic account of cognition. At the same time, Russell continues to reject the pragmatic notion of truth, and he remains a committed foundationalist, holding that we can derive a true picture of the world from sense data—a view that results in the notion that propositions are true when they mirror, or resemble, the facts.

In the 1920s, Russell also makes significant concessions to the pragmatists' notion of truth:

> Pragmatism . . . realizes that the truth that *we* can attain to is merely human truth, fallible and changeable like everything human. What lies outside the cycle of human occurrences is not truth, but fact (of certain kinds). Truth is a property of beliefs and beliefs are psychical events. Moreover their relation to facts does not have the schematic simplicity which logic assumes . . . Beliefs are vague and complex, pointing not to

one precise fact, but to several vague regions of fact. Beliefs, therefore, unlike the schematic propositions of logic, are not sharply opposed as true or false, but have a blur of truth and falsehood; they are of varying shades of grey.[8]

In brief, even though we see in Russell an initial reluctance to embrace pragmatism, an outright hostility even, over time we see him clearly moving in a pragmatist direction.

10.2 The Pragmatism of Frank Ramsey

Frank Ramsey (1903–1930) is a brilliant young mathematician and philosopher who is close to Ogden, Russell, and Wittgenstein, and who during his short life (he dies at twenty-six) makes significant contributions to a variety of fields. It is Ogden who exposes Ramsey to Peirce and, though familiar as well with the work of James and other pragmatists, Ramsey develops himself more and more into a Peircean pragmatist, especially after the 1923 publication of *Chance, Love, and Logic*.[9]

Pragmatism's main value, Ramsey writes, is "to fill a gap" in Wittgenstein's system (ibid). By this Ramsey means Wittgenstein's *Tractatus Logico Philosophicus*, a work Wittgenstein himself came to reject, in part because of Ramsey's criticisms.[10] In the *Tractatus*, Wittgenstein draws a distinction between what we can talk about (which, as it turns out, is very little) and what we cannot talk about but merely hint at (which happens to include pretty much everything we find important). Ramsey rejects Wittgenstein's picture theory of meaning, on which, using Ramsey's words, "the sense of a proposition is that the things meant by its elements (the words) are combined with one another in the same way, as are the elements themselves, that is logically."[11] For Ramsey, this means that Wittgenstein fails to provide a complete account of what it means for a proposition to have sense. It is pragmatism that points Ramsey to a more comprehensive way of talking about meaning. Pragmatism, Ramsey writes, is the view "that the meaning of a sentence is to be defined by reference to the actions to which asserting it would lead, or more vaguely still, by its possible causes and effects," carefully adding "of this I feel certain, but of nothing more definite."[12] Though Ramsey explicitly acknowledges that he obtained his pragmatism from Russell, it is not difficult to see in it some version of Peirce's maxim.

The shift in the conception of meaning we encounter here leads to a different conception of truth: from true propositions picturing or mirroring the facts, we shift to *beliefs* being true when they meet our (epistemic) ends. The picture theory only deals with the relationship between a proposition and the world it purports to depict, and it does so without any reference to the person whose picture it is. Consequently, even though Ramsey accepts a redundancy theory of truth—that for any sentence S, the sentence

"S is true," means exactly the same as (adds nothing to) the sentence S itself, making the add-on "is true" redundant—he also argues that such a theory must be supplemented with a theory of truth that pertains to mental states (beliefs, judgments, assertions, etc.). Hence, Ramsey takes another cue from Russell. He shifts from talking about propositions to talking about beliefs: "any set of actions for whose utility p is a necessary and sufficient condition might be called a belief that p, and so would be true if p, i.e. if they are useful."[13]

The result is the rejection of a single-minded emphasis on linguistic analysis, which had resulted in a rather thin notion of definition, and a move toward Peirce's third grade of clearness (2.4). Often, Ramsey observes, we encounter terms that we cannot define, but we can only "explain the way in which they are used."[14] For Ramsey, this means that philosophy must not neglect the "subjective side."[15]

Ramsey's pragmatist turn takes additional shape in a paper called "Truth and Probability," in which he seeks to apply probability theory to the fact that we can have degrees of belief, and explores how this relates to action: "Whenever we go to the station we are betting that a train will really run, and if we had not a sufficient degree of belief in this we should decline the bet and stay home."[16] From this Ramsey moves to a view about logic close to Peirce's; a view on which logic is a normative theory, a theory about how we should reason (6.5)—which bets we should accept, which we should decline, and why—rather than a branch of mathematics as had been suggested by Russell's work, especially the *Principia Mathematica*.

Briefly put, much of Ramsey's philosophical endeavor involves his rejecting the view that only what is reducible to sense data and logic can count as knowledge, and in his seeking to develop a serious alternative. Recall that Russell, the logical positivists, and Wittgenstein all call everything that does not fit the procrustean bed of logic and sense data nonsense, albeit that Wittgenstein at least admits that this includes some very important nonsense, like ethics and religion. For Ramsey, pragmatism, and especially Peirce, seem to be a way out. Unfortunately, his search for a way out comes to an abrupt halt, when he dies from surgical complications at the age of twenty-six.

10.3 Ludwig Wittgenstein: Meaning as Use

After completing his *Tractatus*, Ludwig Wittgenstein (1889–1951) becomes a schoolteacher in a remote Austrian village, convinced he has solved all philosophical problems. It does not last long. Soon he gives up on the *Tractatus*, in part due to Ramsey's criticisms, and he returns to philosophy a few years later. The most influential work to come out of this later period is the

Philosophical Investigations, published posthumously. In this later period, we discern a certain shift toward pragmatism, albeit more an issue of similarity than one of influence. Wittgenstein's sole contact with pragmatism is through James's *Principles of Psychology* and his *Varieties of Religious Experience*. Wittgenstein is reluctant, however, to associate himself with pragmatism. In *On Certainty*, a series of remarks written shortly before his death (and also published posthumously), he states, somewhat to his own surprise, that he is "trying to say something that sounds like pragmatism," adding, rather cryptically, "here I am being thwarted by a kind of *Weltanschauung*" (OC§422). It seems that what is holding Wittgenstein back is his belief that pragmatism reduces the value of everything to its favorable practical consequences—James's famous cash value. As Wittgenstein had put it almost two decades earlier,

> If I want to carve a block of wood into a particular shape any cut that gives it the right shape is a good one. But I don't call an argument a good argument just because it has the consequences I want (Pragmatism).[17]

Wittgenstein's shift to pragmatism is related to his increased awareness that knowledge and action are deeply interconnected. Wittgenstein and pragmatists both come to define meaning in terms of practice. For the pragmatists, this is some version of Peirce's pragmatic maxim; for Wittgenstein, it is the claim that "for a *large* class of cases—though not for all—in which we employ the word 'meaning' it can be defined thus: the meaning of a word is its use in the language" (PI§43), or more precisely, in a language-*game*—a term Wittgenstein uses to denote "the whole, consisting of language and actions into which it is woven" (PI§7). In brief, for Wittgenstein, to understand a word, or a sentence, is knowing how to use it. However, whereas for the pragmatists, the maxim functions as a prescription (it is a signpost that tells us how to move forward), for Wittgenstein, it points to a limit beyond which philosophy cannot go. Though there are exceptions, the meaning of our linguistic expressions is typically determined by how we use them. Now, people do what they do for a variety of reasons, but any explanation of these reasons comes down to a narration of variously arbitrary contingent facts and the relations among them—a narration that we can endlessly refine but cannot step out of (PI§124). Thus, for Wittgenstein, there is in the end no philosophical explanation for the things we do. Quite the contrary, philosophical explanations are derivatives thereof, so that they must somehow be grounded in what we do while what we do remains itself ungrounded. As Wittgenstein observes, this practice of giving grounds must come to an end somewhere. However, this end is not reached in some indubitable proposition, such as Descartes's "I think, therefore I am," or in ungrounded presuppositions—propositions *more* certain than any grounds we could give them—such as G.E. Moore's claim that he knows that he has a hand;[18] it is rather to be found in our "ungrounded way of acting" (OC§110):

> Giving grounds, however, justifying the evidence, comes to an end;— but the end is not certain propositions' striking us immediately as true, i.e., it is not a kind of *seeing* on our part; it is our *acting*, which lies at the bottom of the language-game.
>
> (OC§204)

Like Mead had done earlier, Wittgenstein subscribes to Goethe's rejection of the Gospel of John—in the beginning was not the word, but the act. And acts, in contrast to propositions, are not the kind of things that can be true or false. They just are.

The pragmatists, of course, would add that, though acts may not be true or false, they can be successful or unsuccessful, thus opening up the possibility of grounding knowledge in *successful* acts or in the circumstance that there are such things as successful acts. Here, however, Wittgenstein and the pragmatists part ways. For Wittgenstein, the ground of our knowledge is not specific acts that were proven successful. Rather, the ground of our knowledge lies in the rather simple realization that there are things that we trust:

> I really want to say that a language-game is only possible if one trusts something (I did not say "can trust something").
>
> (OC§509)

The parenthetical comment is crucial. Wittgenstein only acknowledges that this is something we do: there are things we trust—for instance, that I have never been on the moon, that the earth exists, that my feet have always been with me, etc. We trust such things because it is unreasonable not to, even though we cannot prove them because any proof will be less certain than they are. They are, rather, instinctual, in that they are not taught and often remain unarticulated. Now, Wittgenstein observes, many of these things are not particularly useful. For instance, our trust that the earth really exists doesn't typically feature in the explanations and proofs of science or engineering. Things like that are not useful, in the narrow sense that they direct us to successful action—action that gives us the things we want. Rather, they constitute the general background that makes (successful) action possible, and that allows us to formulate those wants to begin with. As Wittgenstein puts it, "Much seems to be fixed and it is removed from the traffic"— like train carriages parked on dead-end sidetracks (OC§211). "We just *can't* investigate everything," Wittgenstein writes shortly after, "If I want the door to turn, the hinges must stay put" (OC§343). This does not mean that those things never change, but they change rather in the way a riverbed changes with the river (OC§97)—there is no one-to-one correspondence with our wants and their relief. This all means that, for Wittgenstein, though the ultimate ground of our knowledge does reside in the practical, it does not reside in successful action, as he thinks the pragmatists claimed. For Wittgenstein, there is something deeper than that.

10.4 Pragmatism and Phenomenology

Notwithstanding a sheer unanimous rejection of pragmatism in Germany, James's 1890 *Psychology* had a significant impact on German phenomenology.[19] A key figure is Carl Stumpf, who meets James in 1882 and introduces James's *Principles of Psychology* to Edmund Husserl, who is generally considered the founding father of phenomenology. Husserl is attracted to James's notion of a stream of thought, his doctrine of fringes, and James's views on intersubjectivity and intentionality. Husserl also thinks highly of Peirce's logic, but is mostly unaware of his pragmatism and his phaneroscopy, and Husserl thinks highly of Royce. The person I will focus on, however, is Max Scheler (1874–1928), whose 1926 *Erkenntnis und Arbeit* (knowledge and work) comes to shape the reception of pragmatism in Germany for much of the twentieth century. Scheler's work plays a pivotal role also in phenomenology and in philosophical anthropology and critical theory, which makes him a key figure.[20]

In Scheler's view, pragmatism, like phenomenology, is not merely a tool for doing philosophy but is a way of being in the world. More specifically, pragmatism is a way of being where our relation to the world is primarily, if not exclusively, defined in terms of domination and adaptation. Pragmatism's great contribution, Scheler argues, is having shown that modern science is not at all trying to discover the world as it reveals itself, but is only interested in the world insofar as we can control it; that is, insofar as we can make it serve our purposes: "*the primary relation of man*—indeed of all organisms—*to* the world is not at all theoretical but *practical*."[21] There is no "natural worldview" independent of practical considerations. We developed sense organs not so we could acquire disengaged theoretical knowledge about the world, but to steer our actions. In fact, Scheler sees a theory of perception that is grounded in our embodied drives (a *triebmotorische Wahrnehmungstheorie*) as the most secure element of pragmatism.[22]

The German phenomenologist Adolph Reinach (1883–1917) makes a similar point when he writes in his obituary of James that the pragmatists have shown,

> that science in no way consists in a simple "picturing" of its objects, but that it everywhere forms and shapes its material, simplifying and modifying it according to its own particular lights. The colourless, odourless and tasteless world of natural science is not a depiction of our world.[23]

Reinach continues by drawing an implication that he believes pragmatists failed to draw: "there remains the task of filling in those parts which the individual sciences have left open."[24] Reinach takes this to mean that "a science must be developed which is separate from these and which does not go beyond the phenomena by forming and shaping them, but rather has the single aim of adequately and faithfully grasping these phenomena themselves."[25] Hence, in the eyes of Reinach, pragmatism paves the way and lends legitimacy to phenomenology.

Scheler is less positive than Reinach because he worries that the pragmatists fail to acknowledge that there are other forms of knowledge besides knowing how to master our environment—Herrschaftswissen, as he called it—a view he sees confirmed in James's repeated claim that truth is the cash value of our ideas. For Scheler, such a single focus on Herrschaftswissen, of which he also accuses the positivists, is not only one-sided but also dangerous. As he explains,

> Even when techno-positive science should be completed, man as a spiritual being would still be absolutely empty—indeed, he might lapse back into barbarism . . . [and] barbarism supported systematically by science would be the most dreadful barbarism that we can think of.[26]

In response, Scheler distinguishes two additional types of knowledge: Bildungswissen (cultivation) and Erlösungswissen (knowledge for salvation)—arguing that a true philosophy embraces all three, while also seeking to harmonize them. Bildungswissen relates to one's development as a person; Erlösungswissen is inspired by what Scheler calls an "irresistible urge . . . to be in knowing contact with a reality that is intuited as overpowering and holy."[27] It is knowledge that "derives from God and remains in God's service" (von der Gottheit und für die Gottheit).[28] In developing his conception of knowledge, Scheler returns to an Aristotelian notion where knowing an object entails participating in its Sosein—its being what it is on its own accord, not as a tool that can serve some purpose of ours. For Scheler, this type of knowing is a relationship of being, or Seinsverhältnis, which is characterized by humility and self-effacement, rather than by domination and control. Getting to know another being, or the world, requires openness and a willingness to become like it—that is, to participate in its Sosein. Such a knowing relationship, Scheler argues, can only be described as love, and Scheler finds this in the phenomenological attitude, with its desire to see the world simply as it lights up before us:

> It will be like the first step into a flowering garden of a man who had stayed for years in a dark prison. The prison is our human environment confined by an intellect that has turned toward the merely mechanical and whatever can be mechanized.[29]

As shown in the previous chapters, the notion that pragmatism embodies a worldview where all knowledge reduces to a mechanical-like mastery is surely unfair and is in part due to Scheler's cursory and uneven exposure to the pragmatists. There is most certainly a close affinity between Scheler's own approach and Peirce's critique of the calculating rationality of the economists and his embracing of *agapasm* as a cosmic and epistemic force in "Evolutionary Love" (EP1:352ff), with Royce's Christian-inspired philosophy of loyalty,[30] Dewey's insistence on the esthetic in his *Experience and Nature*, and the great naturalness with which pragmatists have come to develop their own versions of phenomenology. Moreover, Scheler's insistence on the primacy of the natural world—the world of experience within which we move and have our being, and to which we must always return[31]—dovetails neatly with the biologically inspired views of Mead and Dewey. Finally, there is an issue with the word "science." When Peirce says that philosophy is a positive science and Scheler argues that philosophy should be distinguished from science, it is important to recognize that they have very different ideas about what science is, and that rather than contradicting each other, their views are actually very close.

Scheler's views exert a profound impact on a variety of philosophers. This includes Martin Heidegger (1889–1976), who joins Husserl as an assistant before coming to reject the central tenets of Husserl's view and develop his own views in his 1927 *Sein und Zeit* (*Being and Time*). Crucial to Husserl is the idea that whenever we are conscious, we are conscious of something. This property of consciousness—its always being about something—Husserl calls its intentionality. Husserl next seeks to identify what we experience when we are conscious of something by excluding, through a process of phenomenological reduction, all preconceptions about external causes and consequences. Next, because there is no reason to assume that phenomenon and being are not identical, Husserl argues that we are directly conscious of the things themselves, and he thinks that in this way we can provide a proper grounding to the sciences—that is, make science truly rigorous. Heidegger rejects Husserl's brand of phenomenology on the ground that the neutral stance that Husserl envisions, far from being neutral, is already a theoretical construct. According to Heidegger, we first need to examine what makes this intentionality possible—what *it* is grounded in. This brings Heidegger to a study of the pre-theoretical conditions that make intentionality possible, and he finds this in a particular way of being which he calls *Dasein* (being-there). Crucially, we are present in the world before we reflect upon that world, and while being present, we are actively engaged with that world as well—taking up some tasks rather than others, adopting certain goals rather than others, etc. For Heidegger, this pre-theoretical engagement with the world forms the basis for any understanding of that world. Things initially manifest themselves such that they match our tasks and goals; that is, they manifest themselves in terms of the activities in which they are put to use. Their basic characteristic is that they are something-for-something, like a hammer is for hammering, straw for roofing, fire for cooking, etc. Heidegger calls this type of being *Zuhandensein* (being-available). The availability of things structures our world by directing our attention. It is here that we find the source of intentionality. Hence, we find with Heidegger a phenomenology of things as they manifest themselves within the activities where they are put to use. The kind of being Husserl focuses on, and which Heidegger calls *Vorhandensein* (being-present), is in the end an unnatural derivative of this more fundamental *Zuhandensein*. Moreover, it is something that can be understood only in terms of the latter. Making being-present more fundamental than being-available mistakenly suggests that the former represents how things truly are, and that the latter must be understood in terms of the former. The real situation, for Heidegger, is the reverse: how things appear as merely present *is a derivative*, and a rather unnatural one, from how they appear as being available. In brief, any cognitive grasp of the world is derivative of our practical interaction with that world, which is to a large extent, and originally, pre-cognitive.

All of this appears to align Heidegger not only with Scheler, but also with pragmatism.[32] Heidegger, however, forcefully rejects pragmatism, which he associates with a *rechnendes Denken*—a calculating rationality that makes everything subject to our desires and demands, while those desires and demands are themselves not subject to anything:

> "*Pragmatism*"—is the doctrine that the true must be sought in, and posited as, the useful. This usefulness is conceived as the furthering and securing of that state of human life which one takes over as present-at-hand [*Vorhanden*] and given or . . . demands as given and immutable.[33]

Pragmatism, Heidegger continues, leads to "an abyssal lack of meditation and an impotence for questioning."[34] As he puts it later, it reflects a way of thinking that "blocks the path to contemplating what is characteristic of modern technology."[35] Pragmatism exemplifies a scientific-technological understanding of the world in which everything is so wholly understood as a means to an end that it is unable to question its own end(s) other than in terms of means. Heidegger thinks he can find the solution instead in National Socialism, even identifying it as "the inner truth and greatness of that movement."[36] Without apparently giving up entirely on National Socialism, much of Heidegger's later work is devoted to the questions that the calculating rationality of pragmatists, positivists, and the sciences do not ask and cannot answer.

10.5 Pragmatism and Philosophical Anthropology

Scheler's 1928 *Die Stellung des Menschen im Kosmos* (*The Human Place in the Cosmos*),[37] which appeared two years after his book on pragmatism, is typically considered the founding document of a school of thought called philosophical anthropology. Inspired by phenomenology, philosophical anthropology also aims to establish a new beginning for philosophy. It centers on the question: what is man? As Scheler explains,

> In our ten-thousand-year history we are the first age in which man has become completely and unreservedly problematic: in which he no longer knows what he is, while at the same time knowing that he doesn't know.[38]

Since it is we as humans who are asking the question, philosophical anthropology is ultimately an exercise in self-reflection. The religious-inspired Scheler assigns to us a special place within the cosmos on the ground that we are endowed with mind (*Geist*), as a result of which we are not confined to our biological environment. Instead we are, as Scheler puts it, world-open (*weltoffen*): we can transcend our biological environment and create, so to speak, our own world.

The central figure of twentieth-century philosophical anthropology, however, is Arnold Gehlen (1904–76), especially his 1940 *Der Mensch: Seine Natur und seine Stellung in der Welt*.[39] Gehlen starts off from an idea he found in Nietzsche, namely, that we are "the not-yet-determined animal."[40] Gehlen interprets this to mean that we are not fully adapted to a specialized environment and as a result enjoy a high degree of plasticity, or freedom, which enables us to make choices—we are, to use Scheler's term, world-open. However, because we are poorly equipped (we are not particularly fast or strong, and our senses are not very sharp) we face a world that presents itself as unpredictable and full of surprises, from which we must seek relief. Unable to lose ourselves in the here and now, we had to become anticipatory beings. In this orientation to the future, we not only had to master nature but also had to discipline ourselves, as only by transforming nature and ourselves could we create a human world, one governed by human-made institutions, which then could become, so to speak, our "second nature."

Like Mead and Heidegger, Gehlen puts the idea of action front and center: We are forced to act; that is, we have no other option but to create the conditions necessary for our survival. Thus, for Gehlen, humans are first and foremost acting beings, not minds with bodies, as Descartes and most of modern philosophy had it. By focusing on the act, Gehlen circumvents the mind–body dualism that still plagued Scheler:

> human consciousness (and animal consciousness as well) can only be understood in relation to *behavior*, such that it may be defined as a *phase of action*. This basic tenet of pragmatism, founded by Peirce and James, is doubtlessly correct.[41]

In fact, Gehlen sees pragmatism as "the only branch of philosophy to view man as an acting being."[42] Moreover, in line with his conception of man as an anticipatory being, he subscribes to a pragmatist conception of truth:

> Truth is never inherent to a sentence but is rather the mark of a function or service the sentence performs. As far as consciousness is concerned, the sentence as such is always hypothetical and "undecided" . . . It is possible, however, to prove the truth of a sentence and this always involves setting it in motion: we trace it back to its origin in experience, we ascertain its effectiveness by determining its future usefulness, or we compare it to other sentences in order to see what pattern emerges. . . . An isolated sentence, as the mere object of reflection, cannot even be questioned as to whether it is "true or false."[43]

Though Gehlen sees pragmatism as a great step forward compared with rationalism and empiricism, he fears, like Scheler and Heidegger before him, that it relies "too strongly on an instrumental understanding of knowledge," while also calling out Dewey for being "overly optimistic."[44] More specifically, Gehlen argues that pragmatism ignores "the silent processes that unfold unconsciously in the social setting," such as the bureaucratization of society, and the paradoxical situation we find ourselves in: a situation in which our need to act extends beyond our ability to know—a situation that calls for a non-experimental form of action, one that is grounded in tradition, instinct, habit, or convention. In brief, for Gehlen, pragmatism is too experimentalist, too progressive:

> Pragmatism fails to see—not on a fundamental level, but in the interpretation of its standpoint—that experience is far richer and broader than what can be readily translated into "controlled behavior."[45]

In sum, although Gehlen is far more positive about pragmatism than Scheler and especially Heidegger, he shares their concern that pragmatism is too instrumentalist. Moreover, as with Heidegger, Gehlen too is drawn to National Socialism as a way of breaking free from the overly instrumental way of thinking that had come to define industrial society, and as a way of giving human beings a place to dwell.

10.6 Critical Theory Rejects Pragmatism

Seeking to apply Marxism to the challenges of the twentieth century, and forcefully rejecting National Socialism, the Frankfurt School (*Frankfurter Schule*) also heavily criticizes instrumental reasoning and how it has come to shape us. The Frankfurt School originates in 1924 as the Institute for Social Research (*Institut für Sozialforschung*) and is considered the birthplace of critical theory. Critical theory holds that traditional social and political theories are unable to address the power structures and means of domination that exist in liberal capitalist societies. In exposing this, critical theory aims at creating, as Max Horkheimer (1895–1973) puts it, "a world which satisfies the needs and powers" of human beings.[46] Though the Institute originated as a Marxist research center, the school comes to distance itself from traditional Marxist theories, finding them too inflexible, and it does so in part by returning to Marx's Hegelian roots. Horkheimer, who takes the helm of the Institute in 1930, is a central figure. In this discussion of the relationship between pragmatism and the Frankfurt School, I will focus on Horkheimer and Jürgen Habermas.

In 1935, having been forced into exile by the Nazis, Horkheimer and the Institute settle at Columbia University, where John Dewey is still active, even though he retired five years earlier.[47] Despite clear affinities with pragmatism, proximity does not engender dialogue. The Institute is isolationistic and sticks to its European roots, both culturally and philosophically. The latter includes the standard European views about pragmatism discussed earlier. Most of the Institute's interactions are with the sociology department, which is primarily interested in the Institute's contributions to empirical social research.

Pragmatism, especially its Deweyan stripe, and critical theory both aim at creating, to repeat Horkheimer, "a world which satisfies the needs and powers" of human beings. As Dewey puts it in 1946,

> Humane liberalism in order to save itself must cease to deal with symptoms and go to the causes of which inequalities and oppressions are but the symptoms . . . instead of using social power to ameliorate the evil consequences of the existing system, it shall use social power to change the system.

> (LW11:287)

However, despite their shared aim, there are significant differences in outlook. Some of these come to light during heated discussions between the Institute and Sidney Hook (1902–89), a Marxist-inspired former student of Dewey, who teaches at nearby New York University.[48] Hook starts as a Marxist who is enthusiastic about the Soviet Union, and he becomes a prominent expert on Marxist philosophy. However, in 1933, Hook begins to distance himself from Marxism, as he feels that it leads to authoritarianism and fascism. Hook's disenfranchisement with Marxism does not cause him to give up on socialism, however, and he comes to argue for a democratic form of socialism—a shift that was largely enabled by his exposure to Dewey's pragmatism. As with Dewey, Hook takes Peirce's notion of scientific inquiry—understood as the selfless search for truth by a community of inquirers inspired by the right attitude—as his model for a well-functioning democracy. Put briefly, Hook, like Dewey, believes that a community of free citizens who are educated, informed, and inspired by the right attitude could shape society such that most, if not all, can flourish. In consequence, for Hook and the pragmatists more generally, the way of thinking that defines science, when conceived broadly, can be applied also to improve society.

The critical theorists see things rather differently. Whereas Hook and the pragmatists favor liberal democratic solutions, the Frankfurt theorists have a dim view of the promise of democracy. In their estimation, it too leads to authoritarianism and fascism. As Herbert Marcuse puts it shortly after the Nazis won the German election, "we can say that liberalism 'produces' the total authoritarian state out of itself, as its own consummation at a more advanced stage of development."[49] The main culprit, they argue, is a narrowing of the faculty of reasoning to a technocratic instrumentalism; a narrowing that is accelerated by capitalism, for which everything, including humans, reduces to means of production, and of which the pragmatists, so the critical theorists believe, seek to give a philosophical justification.

A key accomplishment of this period is Horkheimer and Adorno's *The Dialectic of Enlightenment* (1944), which explores the causes of what they see as the failure of the age of enlightenment—the period, beginning roughly in the seventeenth century, during which reason triumphed over religion and modern science emerges. The book occasions a series of lectures by Horkheimer at Columbia. These lectures force him to take a more direct stance on pragmatism, and they are subsequently published as *The Eclipse of Reason*.[50] In this book, Horkheimer distinguishes between objective and subjective reasoning, arguing that the latter completely crowds out the former, with devastating consequences. Subjective reasoning—which in its more extreme form becomes instrumental reasoning—is a means–end reasoning, where the value of everything is determined by the end it serves. Now, if all reason reduces to subjective reason, Horkheimer argues, it can no longer be used to evaluate the ends themselves, as we can only evaluate them in terms of how they serve some further end, and this *ad infinitum*. Even "a hike that takes a man out of the city," Horkheimer writes, "is reasonable only if it serves another purpose, e.g., health or relaxation, which helps to replenish his working power. In other words, the activity is a mere tool, for it derives its meaning only though its connection with other ends."[51] Because of this, Horkheimer argues,

> The acceptability of Ideals, the criteria for our actions or beliefs, the leading principles of ethics and politics, all our ultimate decisions, are made to depend upon factors *other* than reason. They are supposed to be matters of choice and predilection, and it has become meaningless to speak of truth in making practical, moral, or esthetic decisions.[52]

To the exiled critical theorists, this explains how National Socialism emerged as a natural outcome of the enlightenment. With reason unable to give us a sense of purpose, the National Socialists found it in Romanticism, a movement that the Romantic poet Friedrich Schlegel once aptly described as a fantastic representation of the emotional. Horkheimer sees his view confirmed in the logical positivists and others. If what cannot be reduced to simple statements about sense impressions is meaningless, then reason is useless when we are trying to answer questions on how to improve society. Horkheimer subsequently connects this type of reasoning with pragmatism:

> Modern thought has tried to make a philosophy out of this view, as represented in pragmatism. The core of this philosophy is the opinion that an idea, a concept, or a theory is nothing but a scheme or plan of action, and therefore truth is nothing but the successfulness of the idea.[53]

It is not hard to see that Horkheimer is interpreting pragmatism mostly through a Jamesean lens, confounding, even more so than James had done himself, pragmatism with the doctrine of the will to believe (3.2). It is also not hard to see from the handful of pages devoted to pragmatism in *The Eclipse of Reason* that Horkheimer's knowledge of the movement is painfully limited. What we get is at best a crude caricature. For instance, he makes much of Peirce's claim that pragmatists like to look at everything as if it were "thought of in the laboratory":[54]

> Pragmatism, in trying to turn experimental physics into a prototype of all science and to model all spheres of intellectual life after the techniques of the laboratory, is the counterpart of modern industrialism, for which the factory is the prototype of human existence, and which models all branches of culture after production on the conveyor belt, or after the rationalized front office.[55]

The effect of this, Horkheimer maintains, can be exemplified by the mindset of a criminologist who maintains "that trustworthy knowledge of a human being can be obtained only by the well-tested and streamlined examining methods applied to a subject in the hands of the metropolitan police."[56] Pragmatism, for Horkheimer, reduces reasoning to a type of experimentation that takes its own ends and the status quo for granted, and for which truth "is to be desired not for its own sake but insofar as it works best."[57]

In sum, Horkheimer sharply attacks Hook's attempted solution—that the way science works, at least in its ideal form, shows us how we should go about improving society. Science, Horkheimer argues, has come of age as the handmaiden of an industrial society. Its disinterested search for truth is long abandoned for a utilitarian means–end reasoning that takes the ends themselves for granted. Far from being a servant of truth, science has come to serve the means of production, and blindly so; much the same can be said for democracy. Inspired by Hegelian dialectic—which seeks to resolve the tension that arises when an idea (or thesis) occasions its rejection (or antithesis) by forming a synthesis of the two—the critical theorists seek to rescue rationality from the hegemony of this subjective or instrumental reasoning.

From the perspective of the pragmatists, there are several problems with the critical theorist's approach. Not only do the critical theorists lack a clear statement of what this objective reasoning entails (the thesis), but they also reduce subjective reasoning (the antithesis) to a straw man, lumping all pragmatism under it. Not only do they thereby prematurely exclude pragmatism from partaking in the resolution (the synthesis), but it also results in a paternalistic authoritarian intellectual elitism that runs counter to the pragmatist's ideal of a free, egalitarian society of informed citizens capable of working together for the good of all.

10.7 Jürgen Habermas: Critical Theory Turns to Pragmatism

In the early 1960s a new wave of critical theorists, most notably Karl–Otto Apel and Jürgen Habermas, begin to take pragmatism seriously.[58] Habermas (b. 1929) first joins the Institute (which by then had returned to Frankfurt) in 1956. Though he shares many of the concerns of Horkheimer and Adorno, he is far more positive about the prospect of improving democratic societies. Habermas sees the modern capitalist democratic society as a major historical achievement and acknowledges that its liberal institutions are essential for genuine criticism. To save the enlightenment—with its focus on reason as the primary source of knowledge, and with worthy ideals such as liberty, toleration, and equality—critical theory must find a way to cure the democratic process from the distortions it has suffered within a capitalist society, and much of Habermas's work is devoted to this.

Habermas's first systematic discussion of pragmatism is found in his 1968 *Knowledge and Human Interests*. In this work he seeks to show that "a radical critique of knowledge is possible only as social theory."[59] According to Habermas, positivism flattened epistemology to philosophy of science, so that there is no longer any knowledge that is not scientific knowledge. In this way we acquired an image of "a self-subsistent world of facts structured in a lawlike manner" that conceals how these laws and facts were constituted.[60] Habermas credits pragmatism, as represented by Peirce, for breaking out of this, not by attacking it from without, but by transcending its self-imposed boundaries from within—something Peirce does by pragmatically redefining truth and meaning, and broadening the scientific method into a communal logic of inquiry that is structured by abduction, deduction, and induction.[61] The communal aspect especially attracted Habermas to Peirce, and his later familiarity with Mead and Dewey made him realize the profound implications of Peirce's ideas for critical theory.

Going back at least to Descartes, the paradigm case for knowledge, Habermas observes, is that of the solitary individual who applies the faculty of reasoning (which is the same in everyone) to transform the world that confronts him into a rational, objective whole—much like farmers transform their natural surroundings into plots of land capable of efficient food production. This way of thinking, Habermas continues, ignores the fact that at its very core, reasoning is not a solitary affair—one that pits a singular individual against the world—but a communal and therefore communicative affair. This leads to a different type of reasoning, which Habermas calls communicative rationality. This communicative rationality carries with it, Habermas writes,

> connotations based ultimately on the central experience of the unconstrained, unifying, consensus-bringing force of argumentative speech, in which different participants overcome their merely subjective views and, owing to the mutuality of rationally motivated conviction, assure themselves of both the unity of the objective world and the intersubjectivity of their lifeworld.[62]

Beliefs, statements, and acts can be said to be more rational the more defensible they are against criticism. This view resonates with Peirce's theory of inquiry and with Dewey's views on the prospects of democracy, which, as Dewey puts it, rest "upon persuasion, upon ability to convince and be convinced," and upon "the improvement of the methods and conditions of debate, discussion and persuasion" (LW2:365). This view also resonates with Dewey's notion of warranted assertibility (8.5), as it is clear that being able to give reasons for one's views does not make them true. We can further add that for Peirce, Royce, and especially Mead, even an isolated individual is always engaged in communicative reasoning—interpreting its past self while addressing its future self.

When social theory brings the communicative aspect of reasoning to the fore, language reveals itself first and foremost as a medium for coordinating action. This coordination through language demands that speakers adopt a practical attitude in which they aim for mutual understanding. This makes communicative action possible; that is, action grounded in a deliberative process wherein individuals interact and coordinate their acts based on matching or agreed-upon interpretations of the situation. In other words, communicative action requires that the participants recognize the intersubjective validity of the different claims on which social cooperation depends. Much of this we already encountered in Mead. The result is a pragmatist theory of meaning wherein the meaning of an utterance, or speech act, is determined not by how well it copies, or represents, "the world," but by its "acceptability conditions":

> we understand a speech act when we know the kinds of reasons that a speaker could provide in order to convince a hearer that he is entitled in the given circumstances to claim validity for his utterance—in short, when we know *what makes it acceptable.*[63]

To illustrate this point, Habermas quotes an example of someone who requests a saucer of mud:

> To want simply a saucer of mud is irrational, because some further reason is needed for wanting it. To want a saucer of mud because one wants to enjoy its rich river-smell is rational. No further reason is needed . . . for to characterize what is wanted as "to enjoy the rich river-smell" is itself an acceptable reason for wanting it and therefore this want is rational.[64]

The added reason makes the request acceptable, which the bare request did not, and one counts as rational when one, under suitable circumstances, can provide such reasons. What counts as a reason is a function of the shared, pre-interpreted background that constitutes our intersubjective lifeworld. In the end, it is in such reasons that agreement is grounded, as it enables the discussants to take an affirmative stance toward claims that are being made.[65] Habermas hereby avoids the conclusion that reasoning is always about means and never about ends.

As with Peirce, where application of the method of science generates the norms inquirers use to guide themselves and to evaluate the claims of others, communicative action also shapes its own norms.[66] Any communicative act that is aimed at reaching understanding, Habermas argues, must be solely motivated by the desire to reach a rational consensus. Habermas calls the situation where this is met an "ideal speech situation."[67] Early on, he extracts from this a consensus theory of truth that identifies truth with what would be agreed upon in an ideal speech situation.[68] Later on, he shifts to a "pragmatic epistemological realism" on which the objective world, rather than ideal consensus, is the truth-maker.[69] Habermas is here facing the same problem that Peirce faced earlier, which is showing how something that purportedly holds in the indefinitely long run, or in some envisioned ideal situation, can be relevant for what people are actually doing today.

There is, however, also something else going on, which is that this non-coercive consensus-building force found in free public discourse is situated within an environment where communication is systematically distorted by other ways social interaction is shaped. One only has to look at how the media shape a lifeworld against which the opinions voiced by individuals are interpreted as rational or not. In general terms, communicative action tends to atrophy into fixed modes of coordination, so that one does not have to repeatedly reinvent the wheel. Prime examples of such modes are markets, mass media, and bureaucracies. However, once in existence, these modes of coordination tend to become subject to their own laws, and what began as a relief for communicative action can grow into an unyielding obstacle. Now, whereas pragmatism proves useful to Habermas when developing an "action-theoretic" framework, he finds it less useful when developing a framework for understanding the system-theoretic aspects of society and their effect on reasoning and knowledge acquisition. In Chapter 15, we see similar criticisms from Cornel West.

From the pragmatist's perspective, Habermas can be seen as drawing too sharp a divide between action and discourse, and as focusing too one-sidedly on the latter. In the following chapter we see a similar turn in Richard Rorty. The result is a privileging of linguistic communication that leads to an impoverished notion of experience compared to that of the traditional pragmatists. It ignores the intricate interplay of action and discourse that Peirce found in the laboratory and which he thought was exemplary of what pragmatism stands for. It also ignores the relationship between actions and institutions, and how this shapes individuals, found in Mead. In the next chapter, though, we focus on Rorty.

Notes

1. The correspondence is published as *Semiotic and Significs: The Correspondence between Charles S. Peirce and Victoria Lady Welby*, edited by Charles Hardwick (Bloomington, 1977).
2. C.K. Ogden and I.A. Richards, *The Meaning of Meaning* (London, 1923), esp. Appendix D.
3. Charles S. Peirce, *Chance, Love and Logic: Philosophical Essays* (London, 1923).
4. An excellent and extensive discussion of the reception of pragmatism in Cambridge, England, is found in Cheryl Misak, *Cambridge Pragmatism: From Peirce and James to Ramsey and Wittgenstein* (Oxford, 2016).
5. Bertrand Russell, "Transatlantic Truth," *The Albany Review* 10.2 (1908): 393–410, p.393; reprinted as "William James's Conception of Truth," in Bertrand Russell, *Philosophical Essays* (London, 1910), but with the quoted sentence omitted.
6. Russell (1910), p.92.
7. Bertrand Russell, "Review of Ogden & Richard's *The Meaning of Meaning*," *The Dial* 81 (August 1926): 114–21, p.114.
8. Bertrand Russell, *Basic Writings* (London, 2009), p.240.

9. For a comprehensive discussion of Ramsey's pragmatism, see Misak (2016), chapter 6.

10. See esp. Ramsey's Critical Notice of the *Tractatus, Mind* 32.128 (1923): 465–78.

11. Ibid., p.469.

12. Frank Ramsey, *Philosophical Papers* (Cambridge, 1990), p.51.

13. Ibid., p.40.

14. Ibid., p.5.

15. Ibid., p.6.

16. Ibid., p.79.

17. Ludwig Wittgenstein, *Philosophical Grammar* (Berkley, 1974), p.185, written in the early thirties; cf. *Remarks on the Philosophy of Psychology* (Oxford, 1980), 1:266.

18. Moore is talking about propositional knowledge: *I know that* "This is my hand."

19. See e.g., Herbert Spiegelberg, *The Phenomenological Movement: A Historical Introduction* (The Hague, 1982), pp.62–4, 100–4, 128–30; James M. Edie, "William James and Phenomenology," *Review of Metaphysics* 23.3 (1970): 481–526.

20. For detailed discussions on Scheler in relation to pragmatism, see Matthias Müller and Michael Gabel, *Erkennen, Handeln, Bewähren: Phänomenologie und Pragmatismus* (Nordhausen, 2015).

21. Max Scheler, *Gesammelte Werke*, vols. 11 (Berne and Bonn, 1971–1997), 8:239; emphasis in original. Unless stated otherwise, translations from the German are my own.

22. Scheler (1971–1997), 8:282ff.

23. Adolf Reinach, "William James and Pragmatism," in Kevin Mulligan (ed), *Speech Act and Sachverhalt: Reinach and the Foundations of Realist Phenomenology* (Dordrecht, 1987), pp.291–8, p.298.

24. Ibid.

25. Ibid. Reinach appears unaware of Peirce's work in this area.

26. Scheler (1971–1997), 8:211.

27. Ibid., 8:65.

28. Ibid., 8:211.

29. Ibid., 3:339; quoted from Spiegelberg (1982), p.278.

30. Josiah Royce, *The Philosophy of Loyalty* (Nashville, 1995).

31. Max Scheler, *Selected Philosophical Essays* (Evanston, 1973), p.225.

32. See e.g. Mark Okrent, *Heidegger's Pragmatism: Understanding Being and the Critique of Metaphysics* (Ithaca, 1988), albeit that it makes only the skimpiest reference to the pragmatists.

33. Martin Heidegger, *Ponderings XII—XV: Black Notebooks 1939–1941* (Bloomington, 2017), p.31.

34. Ibid.

35. Martin Heidegger, "Nur noch ein Gott kann uns retten," *Der Spiegel* 30 (May 1976): 193–219, p.214; a September 23, 1966, interview with Heidegger, published posthumously.

36. Martin Heidegger, *An Introduction to Metaphysics* (New Haven, 1959), p.199; originally a lecture of 1935.

37. Max Scheler, *The Human Place in the Cosmos* (Evanston, 2009).

38. Max Scheler, "Die Sonderstellung des Menschen im Kosmos," *Der Leuchter, Weltanschauung und Lebensgestaltung* 8 (1927): 162.

39. Arnold Gehlen, *Man: His Nature and Place in the World* (New York, 1988).

40. Ibid., p.4; Friedrich Nietzsche, *Beyond Good and Evil: Prelude to a Philosophy of the Future* (Cambridge, 2002), fragment 62.

41. Gehlen (1988), p.54.

42. Ibid., p.288.

43. Ibid., p.289.

44. Ibid., p.297.
45. Ibid.
46. Max Horkheimer, *Critical Theory* (New York, 1972), p.246.
47. For a detailed discussion, see Thomas Wheatland, *The Frankfurt School in Exile* (Minneapolis, 2009).
48. See esp. Wheatland (2009), chapter 3.
49. Herbert Marcuse, "The Struggle Against Liberalism in the Totalitarian View of the State," in *Negations: Essays in Critical Theory* (Boston, 1968), pp.3–42, p.19.
50. Max Horkheimer, *The Eclipse of Reason* (New York, 1947).
51. Ibid., p.37.
52. Ibid., p.7f; emphasis added.
53. Horkheimer (1947), p.41f.
54. Ibid., p.47; Horkheimer is quoting from the opening paragraph of Peirce's 1905 *Monist* paper "What Pragmatism is" CP 5.411.
55. Horkheimer (1947), p.50.
56. Ibid., p.49.
57. Ibid., p.45.
58. For Karl-Otto Apel, see e.g. his *Understanding and Explanation: A Transcendental-Pragmatic Perspective* (Cambridge, 1984).
59. Jürgen Habermas, *Knowledge and Human Interests* (Boston, 1971), p.vii.
60. Ibid., p.69.
61. Ibid., p.113ff.
62. Jürgen Habermas, *The Theory of Communicative Action* (Boston, 1984–7), p.10.
63. Jürgen Habermas, *On the Pragmatics of Communication* (Cambridge, 1998), p.232.
64. Habermas (1984–7) quoting Richard Norman, p.16.
65. Habermas (1984–7), p.297.
66. Also, Mead: "when the process of evolution has passed under the control of social reason" (PA:508), it "becomes not only self-conscious but also self-critical" (MSS:255).
67. Jürgen Habermas, "Discourse Ethics: Notes on Philosophical Justification," in Christian Lenhart and Shierry Nicholson (eds), *Moral Consciousness and Communicative Action* (Cambridge, 1980), p.86.
68. Jürgen Habermas, *Toward a Rational Society* (Boston, 1970), p.91f.
69. Jürgen Habermas, *Truth and Justification* (Cambridge, 2003), p.7.

Chapter 11

The Neopragmatism of Richard Rorty

Within America, pragmatism returns visibly to the forefront in the last part of the twentieth century largely because of Richard Rorty's influential *Philosophy and the Mirror of Nature* (1979). Rorty's rather radical take on pragmatism is not uniformly accepted, however, and this results in a division into two rather loose pragmatist groupings: neopragmatism, which originates with Rorty, and which comes to define itself roughly in opposition to analytic philosophy; and new pragmatism, which rather aims to use pragmatism to broaden analytic philosophy. A discussion of new pragmatism, in which Hilary Putnam is the central figure, follows (Chapter 12).

Richard Rorty (1931–2007) grows up in a pragmatist milieu. His parents belong to the New York City circle of leftist intellectuals that we encountered earlier in the clash between Sidney Hook and the exiled Frankfurt School.[1] At age fifteen, Rorty attends the University of Chicago, where the tide had since turned against pragmatism. At Chicago, Rorty later writes, pragmatism was considered "vulgar, 'relativistic,' and self-refuting" (RR:503). It was a school of thought that missed something important:

> They pointed out over and over again, Dewey had no absolutes. To say, as Dewey did, that "growth itself is the only moral end," left one without a criterion for growth, and thus with no way to refute Hitler's suggestion that Germany had "grown" under his rule. . . . Only an appeal to something eternal, absolute, and good . . . would permit one to answer the Nazis, to justify one's choice of social democracy over fascism.
>
> (ibid)

This search for absolutes is precisely what attracted the young Rorty, who was eagerly looking for a way to "hold reality and justice in a single vision" (RR:503). The result is disillusion. Philosophy fails to deliver, and Rorty spends the rest of his life "looking for a coherent and convincing way of formulating [his] worries about what, if anything, philosophy is good for" (RR:505). It leads him back to his roots, most importantly Dewey and pragmatism. In 1967, Rorty publishes *The Linguistic Turn*, an anthology that surveys the most recent attempt at finding absolutes: linguistic philosophy. Rorty's final evaluation is pessimistic. Like all earlier attempts to put philosophy on a secure footing, this one too is failing, and this realization segues into his 1979 *Philosophy as the Mirror of Nature*. In this book Rorty identifies Wittgenstein, Heidegger, and Dewey as the most important philosophers of the twentieth century because by rejecting the idea that philosophy needs a foundation, they "brought us into a period of 'revolutionary' philosophy . . . by introducing new maps of the terrain (viz., of the whole panorama of human activities) which simply do not include those features which previously seemed to dominate" (MN:5ff). At the same time, the strong emphasis on language inspired by the linguistic turn remains with him.

11.1 The Idol of the Mirror

The absolute that Rorty takes issue with in *The Mirror of Nature* is the representationalism that had already attracted much of the pragmatists' fire. It is the view which Dewey dubbed the spectator theory of knowledge (8.2). Rorty phrases the issue as follows:

> The picture which holds traditional philosophy captive is that of the mind as a great mirror, containing various representations—some accurate, some not—and capable of being studied by pure, nonempirical methods. Without the notion of the mind as mirror, the notion of knowledge as accuracy of representation would not have suggested itself.
>
> (MN:12)

Note that the mirror metaphor goes significantly further than the spectator metaphor. Whereas a spectator can still interpret what she sees, a mirror is wholly dumb—it blindly and indiscriminately reflects everything. This does not mean that mirrors don't distort, but if they do, they do it along established principles (such as the laws of optics) that can be discovered, analyzed, and duly corrected for.[2] In *The Linguistic Turn*, language is the mirror and philosophical analysis the tool for removing its distortions.

Rorty believes that our desire to give our knowledge secure footing is what prompted the mirror metaphor, as it lends a sense of neutrality to our sense impressions. As Rorty sees it, however, this desire is entirely misguided:

> The desire for a theory of knowledge is a desire for constraint—a desire to find "foundations" to which one might cling, frameworks beyond which one must not stray, objects which impose themselves, representations which cannot be gainsaid.
>
> (MN:315)

Rorty dismisses such a quest for foundations, claiming that it only perpetuates old superstitions and human insecurities. By calling them constraints, Rorty seems to be thinking primarily of the logical positivists and the early Wittgenstein, who dismissed so much of what we say as nonsense, rather than Mead, Dewey, and the later Wittgenstein, who preferred to talk of handlebars and hinges rather than constraints.

Rorty's main objections to the mirror metaphor are similar to those voiced by the classical pragmatists. Most significantly, picturing reality is not really what we are after when we seek knowledge, and where knowledge matters, the metaphor is of little or no help. As Rorty aptly observes,

> Nobody engages in epistemology or semantics because he wants to know how "this is red" pictures the world. Rather we want to know in what sense Pasteur's views of disease picture the world accurately and Paracelsus' inaccurately. . . . But just here the vocabulary of "picturing" fails us.
>
> (RR:113)

As Rorty observes in *The Mirror*, "The notion of 'accurate representation' is simply an automatic and empty compliment which we pay to those beliefs which are successful in helping us do what we want to do" (MN:10). In its place Rorty proposes a shift "from metaphors of isomorphism, symbolism, and mapping to talk of utility, convenience, and likelihood of getting what we want" (RR:113). In effect, this is a shift toward pragmatism, as knowledge acquisition becomes itself a mode of acting: "When the contemplative mind, isolated from the stimuli of the moment, takes large views, its activity is more like deciding what to *do* than deciding that a representation is accurate" (ibid). In fact, as Rorty puts it elsewhere, "Disengagement from practice produces theoretical hallucinations."[3]

Ridding philosophy from the idol of the mirror also has deeper ramifications. The mirror metaphor implies the possibility of a neutral vantage point—one that is independent of our wishes, desires, preoccupations, and idiosyncrasies—and makes it the standard. The idea is that when we approach things from such a neutral vantage point, then we will see them as they truly are. Rorty denies that such a neutral vantage point—assuming that it can be attained—can be a guarantee for truth: "The pragmatist tells us that it is useless to hope that objects will constrain us to believe the truth about them, if only they are approached with an unclouded mental eye, or a rigorous method, or a perspicuous language" (RR:115).

11.2 The Impact of Sellars and Quine

Rorty doesn't come to his central criticism of the mirror metaphor through the classical pragmatists, but through the analytic tradition in which he was trained, and which forms the main target in *The Mirror of Nature*. In Rorty's eyes, this tradition, which so forcefully rejected pragmatism, is now gradually transforming itself into a species of it. For Rorty, Wilfrid Sellars's attack on the given and Quine's attack on analyticity (and with that on [logical] necessity) caused some serious cracks in the mirror, cracks that are beyond repair and cannot be hidden.

Traditional philosophy, as Rorty understands it, presupposes that within our knowledge we can separate what is given from what is added by the mind. The idea that sense impressions cannot be wrong—they are just what they are, that they are purely given—has led many to believe that they can be made into a secure foundation for knowledge. Sellars objects to this by arguing that this belief results from confusing sense impressions with so-called basic propositions; that is, propositions the truth or falsity of which is wholly determined by the occurrence or non-occurrence of the sense impressions they express. As indicated earlier, the central aim of the logical positivists, but also of analytic philosophy more generally, was to ground all knowledge claims in such basic propositions. Sellars agrees that sense impressions cannot be wrong (they are what they are), but he denies that they can count as knowledge. Propositions *about* sense impressions can be counted as knowledge, but they lack the quality of indubitability, or givenness, of sense impressions. They can be wrong, even though up to now, as Rorty explains, "nobody has given us any interesting alternatives which would lead us to question [them]" (MN:175). Sellars's critique of the given is presaged by Peirce when he claims that perceptual judgments are unconscious abductive inferences (6.8).

Rorty doesn't deny that we have sense impressions; that we see patches of red, have pains, experience hunger, feel content, etc. What he does deny is that such sense impressions count as beliefs, or that they can play any role in justifying our beliefs. They are mere stimuli. Those who seek to ground our beliefs in sense impressions, Rorty contends, confuse the *formation* of a belief with its *expression* or its *justification*. Although the formation of the belief may be due to something pre- or non-propositional, its expression (which allows it to be communicated to others or to one's future self) and justification both take place entirely within language. For Sellars, for instance, "science is rational not because it has a foundation, but because it is a self-correcting enterprise which can put any claim in jeopardy, though not all at once."[4] Of course, this is precisely Peirce's scientific method combined with his notion of fallibilism (2.3).

A second blow to the mirror metaphor comes from Quine in his rejection of the analytic–synthetic distinction (9.6). According to Rorty, with the analytic–synthetic distinction gone, we can no longer distinguish between the "necessary," which is entirely "within" the mind, and the "contingent," which is at least in part independent of it (MN:169). Rorty's observation here parallels his rejection of the view that basic propositions cannot be wrong. As with basic propositions, "a necessary truth is just a statement such that nobody has given us any interesting alternatives which would lead us to question it" (MN:175).

Rorty draws a radical conclusion from the criticisms of Sellars and Quine, namely that there is no neutral ground on which to stand, and that there is no other way to assess philosophical views but from a study of existing criticisms and defenses of those views. As a result, the criteria for evaluating any belief become purely conversational ones. In the absence of a neutral ground (the given, or the analytical), "the True and the Right are matters of social practice" (MN:178). Since the justification of a belief—of *all* belief—takes place within language, which is a social practice, justification—*any* justification—is ultimately also a matter of social practice. When entering a linguistic community, we submit ourselves to its epistemic rules—the rules through which its members frame questions, utter warnings, give orders, express emotions, form justifications, etc. In sum, for Rorty, the justification of belief is always a social affair, one that is guided by established practice.

11.3 From Correspondence to Conversation

Rorty's rejection of representationalism colors his take on inquiry. For the representationalists, inquiry has a clearly defined purpose, which is to discover the truth, and we attain it when our beliefs accurately represent their objects. This approach gives us a rather solid criterion on which to judge how well or badly a specific inquiry is conducted. Good inquiry causes our beliefs to adequately represent reality. Epistemic practices that do not lead to this are bad, unsound, or unscientific.

For Rorty, the aim of inquiry is not to *represent* reality, but to *use* reality to obtain what we want; that is, to bring us what we set out to achieve when we started the inquiry. Having rejected representationalism, Rorty embraces a causal theory of knowledge, arguing that the world "causes us to hold beliefs, and we continue to hold the beliefs which prove to be reliable guides to getting what we want" (PSH:33).

What we want, however, is highly multifarious. Consequently, it makes little sense to speak of "the aim of inquiry" as if inquiry has a single, clearly defined goal. Inquiry may have many aims, all with different ramifications, including moral, social, and political ones. For the pragmatist, Rorty explains, "the pattern of all inquiry—scientific as well as moral—is deliberation concerning the relative attractions of various concrete alternatives" (CP:164). Because of this, Rorty rejects the idea of a scientific method, if by this is meant some fixed recipe, or algorithm, that allows us to "avoid the need for conversation and deliberation and simply tick off the way things are" (ibid).

For Rorty, the rejection of representationalism radically opens up the playing field. We are no longer constrained by the requirement that we must adequately mirror reality. Rorty seeks to stretch this playing field as far as it will let him, arguing that the *only* constraints set upon inquiry are conversational ones, a view he identifies with pragmatism. Referring explicitly to Peirce, Rorty explains that "the only sense in which we are constrained to truth is that, as Peirce suggested, we can make no sense of the notion that the view which can survive all objections might be false" (CP:165). However, since objections are always cast in language, Rorty, taking his cues from Davidson (9.8), interprets this to mean that all constraints upon inquiry are conversational. Recall that, for Davidson, we can only compare our conceptual schemes with *other* conceptual schemes, not with the world as it purportedly is in and of itself. Earlier, in *The Mirror of Nature*, Rorty already remarked that justification is a matter of conversation: "Justification is not a matter of a special relation between ideas (or words) and objects, but of conversation, of social practice" (MN:170). Successful inquiry is inquiry that keeps the conversation going. Consequently, the search for truth makes way for a search for solidarity. In *Consequences of Pragmatism*, Rorty characterizes pragmatism entirely in conversational terms, calling it,

> the doctrine that there are no constraints on inquiry save conversational ones—no wholesale constraints derived from the nature of the objects, or of the mind, or of language, but only those retail constraints provided by the remarks of our fellow-inquirers.
>
> (CP:165)

Rorty is correct in observing that there is an affinity between this view and that of the classical pragmatists, but how much is certainly open for debate. True, Peirce maintained that truth is identical with the final opinion, but what makes this opinion final for Peirce is not that the inquirers agree, but that they all are forced to accept the same conclusion and that any future inquiries will again give us that very same conclusion. In Peirce's view, it is not *a search for agreement* that drives inquiry; rather, having competent peers agree with you is a sign, often a welcome one, that what you believe to be true might actually be so. The agreement that Peirce has in mind, however, is distinctly not a product of mere conversation, but is the result of a prolonged interaction with a world that is there and that does not budge. This connection with the world is absent, or at best well disguised, in Rorty. In fact, with its sole focus on agreement and conversational constraints, Rorty's interpretation undercuts the very distinction that Peirce seeks to draw between the a priori and the scientific methods (2.3).

The notion that something extra-linguistic might influence the formation of our beliefs is again conspicuously absent in the following passage from *Objectivity, Relativism, and Truth*:

> For pragmatists, the desire for objectivity is . . . simply the desire for as much intersubjective agreement as possible . . . Insofar as pragmatists

make a distinction between knowledge and opinion, it is simply the distinction between topics on which such agreement is relatively easy to get and topics on which agreement is relatively hard to get.

(PP1:23)

For Rorty, the inquirer does not even aim for anything more than that others approve of his beliefs, and philosophy comes down to "a study of the comparative advantages and disadvantages of the various ways of talking which our race has invented" (CP:xl). Rorty hereby shifts the attention from thinking in terms of a scientific method that prescribes how people should conduct their inquiry, no matter what the inquiry is about or from what motives it began, toward a study of the vocabularies people use and in which they cast their problems, their aims, and their findings. What makes Galileo's physics superior to Aristotle's, Rorty writes provocatively, is not that Galileo made a better use of the so-called "scientific method," but because "Galileo was using some terminology which helped, and Aristotle wasn't" (CP:193).

As for the question of how Galileo arrived at this new and successful terminology, Rorty's answer is as simple as it may be disappointing: "He just lucked out." It just turned out that Galileo's vocabulary worked better in bringing us the things we want than did Aristotle's. As to the question of what makes it so, Rorty admits that pragmatists like him have no answer, but neither do they need one. Rather, they reject the question. The different vocabularies are not made true or false by "the world," but they are like different tools that have alternative uses. For a change of vocabulary, such as the switch from Aristotle's way of speaking to Galileo's, no more arguments are required than for choosing, say, a Phillips screwdriver over a flat one. All that matters in the end is that it works better. Rorty denies, however, that the improvements of vocabularies, like the one of Galileo over Aristotle, mark an objective course of progress. All we can say is that the new vocabularies work better in giving *us* what *we* want.

Rejecting representationalism for a form of instrumentalism, Rorty argues that "one should stop worrying about whether what one believes is well grounded and start worrying about whether one has been imaginative enough to think up interesting alternatives to one's present beliefs" (PSH:34). What is needed in science and philosophy is the vision and drive of an entrepreneur, rather than the myopic precision of a forensic accountant. The attitude of the Rortyan scientist and philosopher is not that of submission to an immanent teleology, as with Peirce, but a desire of being astonished and exhilarated (PSH:28). When scientists and philosophers have become pragmatists, Rorty remarks, "There would be less talk about rigor and more about originality. The image of the great scientist would not be of somebody who got it right but of somebody who made it new" (PP1:44).

At the same time, Rorty does not deny that there is something like an external world, but its role seems almost negligible, and we always encounter it under a certain description. As Rorty put it in *Philosophy and Social Hope*,

> We can never be more arbitrary than the world lets us be. So even if there is no Way the World Is, even if there is no such thing as "the intrinsic nature of reality," there are still causal pressures. These pressures will be described in different ways at different times and for different purposes, but they are pressures none the less.

(PSH:33)

Rorty further agrees with Peirce that such causal pressures cannot be seen as truth-makers, epistemic anchors, or neutral foundations, but he rejects Peirce's idea that we have little option but to postulate that the opinions we form of them, assuming we inquire into them long enough (where "long enough" may take trillions of years) would ultimately lead to a shared and conclusive agreement. Nor does he seem to agree with James, who in his discussion of the will to believe acknowledges that "the squeeze is so tight that there is little loose play for any hypothesis" (WJ:436). Since, for Rorty, all we encounter must be captured under a certain description before it can be counted as knowledge, and because theories are underdetermined by data so that there are numerous, incommensurable descriptions for any datum (including scientific, poetic, and religious descriptions), Rorty rejects the idea that any description can be privileged or seen as representative and be called the true one. Rorty, in good pragmatist fashion, thus rejects the idea that it is somehow our job to *represent* this world—assuming there is indeed "One Way the World Is." It is our job, rather, to cope with these causal pressures.

It is not entirely clear, though, how we should interpret Rorty's insistence that, with representationalism gone, the only constraints upon inquiry are conversational ones. If theories are tools, they must prove their worth in action, but that is hardly a mere conversational affair. Surely, I could try to convince you by means of some abstract mathematical narrative, waxing eloquently about straight lines, planes, triangles, etc., that a Phillips screwdriver works better for that screw than a flat one, but nothing beats the simple practice of showing that one fits snugly while the other doesn't. And what to do about the experimental scientist who, late at night, struggles to identify strands of protein under a microscope? We would surely call this inquiry, but it is hard to cast it wholly in terms of conversational constraints. It is difficult to deny, it seems, that there is a microscope, and that there is something under it that at least in part dictates what the scientist sees and predates any descriptions of it and thus contributes to their formation. As Jay Rosenberg once aptly put it,

> There's something that counts as getting it wrong. . . . Finding out whether one has gotten a pudding recipe right does. The proof of the pudding is in the eating. . . . If it's got lumps in it, then something non-linguistic has gone wrong.[5]

In response, it could be argued that Rorty's conception of language is too narrow and that something like Peirce's triadic semiotics provides a better way. Such semiotics explicitly brings in the so-called dynamic object (6.7) and relates much more seamlessly with our perception of the world, which is semiotic too—like the dark clouds signaling an approaching storm. We can even say that, notwithstanding all his talk about Galileo, it seems that Rorty truly sides with Francesco Sizzi, the Florentine astronomer who refused to look through Galileo's telescope because he already knew that what Galileo claimed it showed (namely that Jupiter has four moons) could not possibly be true—it did not fit the conversation. So, let's look a bit closer at Rorty's views on truth.

11.4 Against Truth

With representationalism out of the window, the notion of truth as correspondence with reality must be abandoned too, and a new conception of truth, if any, is being called for. For Rorty, the crucial issue is not whether a belief is true, but whether we are justified in believing something, which for him comes down to the question of whether we can defend the belief against the objections of others. Once we have finished talking about the justification of our beliefs, Rorty contends, there is nothing of substance left to say about truth, because we have no way of talking about truth other than in terms of the justification of belief. Hence, in *The Mirror of Nature*, Rorty boldly claims that truth is "what our peers will, *ceteris paribus*, let us get away with saying" (MN:176). Rorty thus follows Dewey in abandoning truth for warranted assertibility, but he also pushes it further, associating truth "with the consensus of a community rather than a relation to a nonhuman reality" (PP1:23). Note further that Rorty speaks of *a* community rather than, as Peirce had done, *the* community. A problem with Rorty's view is that it fails to adequately capture what we mean when we claim that a certain statement of ours is true. This, because we are not satisfied when we are merely "preaching to the choir"; that is, to our peers. We want *everyone* to agree.

The main problem Rorty sees with philosophical accounts of truth is that "truth is not the sort of thing one should expect to have a philosophically interesting opinion about" (CP:xiii). Even if some characteristic is shared by all true statements, there is such a diversity among true statements that it is unlikely that anything of value or interest can be said about it. Rorty holds the same view for moral goodness. There is such a wide variety of good acts that the notion of goodness, as something all good acts somehow have in common, is as good as empty. Pragmatists, Rorty argues, reject the traditional attempts of isolating the true and the good as if these were the two most precious gems of philosophy. In its place they do not propose a rival theory of truth. Quite the contrary, pragmatists declare the whole enterprise of seeking theories of truth outdated. One might as well continue to insist that chemical compounds be analyzed in terms of the four basic elements: earth, fire, air, and water. Pragmatists, Rorty contends, propose a more radical revision. Traditional philosophy, he claims, is as outmoded as alchemy. Its subject, its techniques, and its vocabulary need serious overhaul. As Rorty puts it in *Consequences of Pragmatism*, "As long as we see James or Dewey as having 'theories of knowledge' or 'theories of morality' we shall get them wrong" (CP:160). There is also no need for a theory of truth:

> Inquiry and justification have lots of mutual aims, but they do not have an overarching aim called truth. Inquiry and justification are activities we language-users cannot help engaging in; we do not need a goal called "truth" to help us do so, any more than our digestive organs need a goal called health to set them to work.
>
> (PSH:37f)

This leads us quite far from Peirce's insistence that inquiry is a conscious activity that calls for self-discipline and hence for norms that we should seek to live up to.

The preceding notwithstanding, Rorty rejects the idea that being justified in believing that p entails that p is true. However, since justified belief is only as far as we can go, the gap between the two is, as he puts it, "forever unbridgeable."[6] But this does not rid us of truth altogether. For the non-representationalist Rorty, the notion of truth comes to play a different and far more modest role. He accepts Tarski's disquotational use, which allows us to make metalinguistic comments, such as, "The sentence *Snow is white* is true, if and only if snow is white." In addition, the word "truth" can be used in a cautionary sense, as in "This belief is justified, but is it really true?" Or it can be used to praise a belief. For instance, Rorty interprets James's famous comment that the true is only the expedient in our way of thinking to mean that the word "true" is not used to explain what distinguishes true from false propositions, but to endorse a proposition by praising it. To say that a statement is true is merely to give the successful inquirer "a rhetorical pat on the back" (CP:xvii). To make anything more of it by trying to "clarify" this philosophically by developing a *theory* of truth, Rorty argues, only leads to trouble. In its place, Rorty advocates a sort of epistemological emotivism, which again means that in the end he sees Peirce's a priori method as the proper (or the only attainable) way of fixing belief.

11.5 Solidarity, Ethnocentricity, and Irony

Having thus dismissed traditional theories of truth and the notion of inquiry as something that leads us to truth, the question becomes, what is it that we are doing when we claim we are acquiring knowledge? Rorty's answer is that we are engaged in a conversation aimed at generating agreement—or, at least, interesting disagreement—in a way that helps us cope with life. As Rorty puts it in *Consequences of Pragmatism*, "In the end, the pragmatists tell us, what matters is our loyalty to other human beings clinging together against the dark, not our hope of getting things right" (CP:166). The metaphor is revealing. The darkness against which we are clinging together is at once impenetrable and threatening. Since nothing external or extralinguistic can generate agreement—since all that we encounter can be adjusted for in innumerable ways—we can in the end only count on each other. Consequently, what we need is solidarity.

It is not entirely clear, however, how we are to frame this idea of solidarity, which is a solidarity with "our peers." As we saw with Mead, the individual self is a composite of roles connected to different games (7.5). So one can think of a physicist who is also a devout Christian. Perhaps we should rather think of our peers in terms of the questions we are asking. For questions of cosmology, they would be other physicists; for questions regarding premarital sex, they would be (at least for our Christian physicist) other Christians. There is a sense in which this brings Rorty close to Peirce, who argued for a natural classification of the sciences. Here, a particular science, like quantum electrodynamics, is defined as "the actual living occupation of an actual living group of men" (R1334:13)—it is the product of certain people gravitating toward one another because of shared interests, beliefs, experiences, etc.[7] This may be a viable approach when the various roles are in relative harmony, but much less so when they conflict—which ties in with James's discussion of reality in the context of his phenomenology in Chapter 3. In fact, one of the criticisms that Rorty receives is that when he talks about solidarity and ethnocentricity, he seems to presuppose a stable, rather homogeneous society—one he further models on himself, an educated American liberal white male, rather than a truly pluralistic one. From Mead's perspective, the question is rather whether, and if so to what degree, a robust "generalized other" can emerge, especially within a pluralistic sociocultural environment, and whether such a generalized other is culture bound or can be more universal (7.5).

For Rorty, however, solidarity can only be culture dependent. There is no super-cultural vantage point. The best we can aim for is to compare and contrast alternative cultural traditions from the perspective of the tradition that we grew up in. Inquiry cannot be truly disinterested, and it always takes place within and against the backdrop of a particular culture. Rorty denies, however, any charge of cultural relativism. As he writes in *Objectivity, Relativism, and Truth*, "The pragmatist, dominated by the desire for solidarity, can only be criticized for taking his own community too seriously. He can only be criticized for ethnocentrism, not for relativism" (PP1:30). For instance,

> When we say that our ancestors believed, falsely, that the sun went around the earth, and we believe, truly, that the earth goes around the sun, we are saying that we have a better tool than our ancestors did. Our ancestors might rejoin that their tool enabled them to believe in the literal truth of the Christian Scriptures, whereas ours does not. Our reply has to be, I think, that the benefits of modern astronomy and of space travel outweigh the advantages of Christian fundamentalism. The argument between us and our medieval ancestors should not be about which of us has the universe right. It should be about the point of holding views about the motion of heavenly bodies, the ends to be achieved by the use of certain tools. Confirming the truth of scripture is one such aim, space travel is another.
>
> (PSH:xxv)

Our way of talking about the world and our medieval ancestors' way of talking can be described, using a phrase of Wittgenstein, as two different language games. Even if they turn out to be equally acceptable on their own terms, as Rorty suggests they are, we can still maintain, as Rorty also proposes, that the best way of talking about the world is how *we* talk about the world. Consequently, Rorty argues that he is not a cultural relativist (in which case he would refuse to privilege one culture, his own, above the others), nor is he an objectivist (in which case he would admit of certain extra-cultural criteria of truth or purpose), but he is an ethnocentrist. He is aware of the relativity of *our* culture, while at the same time privileging it because doing so is our best, if not our only, option:

> We must, in practice, privilege our own group, even though there can be no noncircular justification for doing so. We must insist that the fact that nothing is immune from criticism does not mean that we have a duty to justify everything.
>
> (PP1:29)

Note that Rorty is not telling us to take our culture for granted or to declare it the gold standard by which to measure other cultures. The point is, rather, that we cannot really escape our culture; we can only criticize it piecemeal, and from the inside. Continuing this trajectory, Rorty argues that philosophers should become cultural critics, all-purpose intellectuals who address current problems, not from the aspect of eternity but in a historicist manner, something he himself aims to do in *Achieving Our Country*. Thus, whereas Peirce shied away from what he called "topics of vital importance" because philosophy is too ill equipped to deal with them, Rorty sees them as all we should be talking about, albeit that he agrees with Peirce that we should not use philosophy when we do so (at least not as it is traditionally conceived). No doubt there are still people interested in doing philosophy, but like those who still want to practice religion, their activity should be relegated to the private domain; it is something you do at home, or in select company, and with the curtains closed. Interestingly, Rorty's ethnocentrism still allows him to speak of the external world in the same way as the objectivist does, as in Western culture, we do tend to speak about the world in the objectivist's vocabulary. Opponents of Rorty, however, including, as we will see, Hilary Putnam, have argued that ethnocentrism fails to escape cultural relativism because it still makes truth dependent upon the actual cognitive practices within a specific epistemic community, and the mere circumstance that we have no choice but to privilege our own practices does not make the result any less relativistic.

If Rorty is right, however, then how do we convince people from other cultures that we are right and they are wrong? Rorty's answer is that we do this by changing their vocabulary; by making them see things as we see them. We could, for instance, teach the alchemist about modern chemistry. This is more than telling him that his views are false. The alchemist must come to see the physical world in an entirely different way. Moreover, for Rorty, changing how one *sees* the world means changing how one *speaks* about it. Such a change of vocabulary is, moreover, not a logical affair. Quite the opposite: Logic applies only within the confines of an already set language that determines what moves are permitted and what are not.

What, then, about our own vocabulary? Can we change that as well? We obviously cannot seek to change our vocabulary—our own way of seeing things—by exposing ourselves to our own vocabulary (i.e., to how we see things). In an important sense, what Royce held true of logic (9.1), Rorty holds true for our language as well: it is final and self-justifying. We cannot put our own language up for discussion because that same language will always be the medium and benchmark for all we say and think, including any reflections upon our own vocabulary and grammar. Of course, we can be made to change our mind by being exposed to the languages of others, but that is a different issue. The question here is whether we can be genuinely critical toward our own language and change it, as it were, from within. Rorty thinks we can, at least up to a point, and the method he suggests is that of irony—a method that goes back to Socrates and that we encountered earlier with Bourne (8.7). Since our language is its own benchmark, Rorty maintains, we can put it up for discussion only by knowingly and willingly violating some of its rules. That is to say, when we feign ignorance or consciously misapply it with the deliberate purpose to provoke and unmask. Rorty calls this the method of irony, and those who practice it he calls "ironists," adding that apart from the confrontation with foreign grammars and vocabularies, it is only through irony that we can escape our ethnocentrism.

Ironists, Rorty explains, are people who are "never quite able to take themselves seriously because [they are] always aware that the terms in which they describe themselves are subject to change, always aware of the contingency and fragility of their final vocabularies, and thus of their selves" (RR:279f). The opposite of irony, Rorty explains, "is common sense. For that is the watchword of those who unselfconsciously describe everything important in terms of the final vocabulary to which they and those around them are habituated" (RR:280). In line with this, Rorty considers the later Wittgenstein an ironist "who cheerfully tosses out half-a-dozen incompatible metaphysical views in the course of the *Investigations*" (CP:21). There is a sense in which Rorty's irony can be seen as an alternative to Peirce's *critical* common-sensism (6.4), but if so, it would be one that keeps the extra-linguistic world (which was so important to Peirce), safely at bay. In fact, one gets a strong impression that by reducing philosophy to rhetoric, dialectics, and literary criticism (PP:283), Rorty is handing over pragmatism to what Peirce had called the "lawless rovers of the sea of literature" (CP5.449). In Chapter 15 we will see Rorty apply the method of irony to feminism.

One could object to Rorty's approach that the pragmatist has other ways of escaping ethnocentrism. Mead, Dewey, and Gehlen all looked at our biological side, observing that there are certain more or less universal human characteristics. Rorty dismisses all that. To him, Dewey would have been a better philosopher had he not written *Experience and Nature*, and "no such discipline as 'philosophical anthropology' is required as a preface to politics, but only history and sociology" (RR:245).

In a paper called "The Priority of Democracy to Philosophy," Rorty further applies his views to what he considers one of the greatest accomplishments of Western civilization: democracy. When developing their political theories, the Enlightenment thinkers relied on the idea that we as human beings possess a conscience which furnishes us with human dignity and rights, and that we possess reason, so that "free and open discussion will produce 'one right answer' to moral as well as scientific questions" (RR:240). For Rorty, there is no evidence that we possess either. Quite the opposite. Consequently, traditional philosophy has it backwards when it looks for a *philosophical* foundation for democracy. It is democracy that forms the foundation for philosophy. The contingent emergence of the free exchange of ideas enabled by democracy forms through a process of deliberate mutual adjustments a certain coherence in belief, and that's all there is to it. Social policy, Rorty remarks, "needs no more authority than successful accommodation among individuals, individuals who find themselves heir to the same historical traditions and faced with the same problems" (RR:247). The terms that we settle on do not refer to any "essences," and no additional justification for democracy or philosophy is called for, or even possible. In fact, we cannot be truly devoted to democracy as long as we believe "that we can have knowledge of an 'objective' ranking of human needs that can overrule the result of democratic consensus" (RR:449)—which was precisely why the critical theorists could not commit to democracy (10.6).

The consequences of Rorty's view are sobering. Without any extra-linguistic underpinnings to rely on, he has to say that we do not *possess* human rights—as if such rights are somehow part of our nature, or essence. Instead, the phrase "human rights" is merely an expression we currently agree upon using to condemn or commend certain actions or beliefs. Unsurprisingly, this strong nominalistic view makes Rorty pessimistic about the future of such social accomplishments as democracy and human rights. They may be hard fought, but they are easily lost. With nothing to keep them in place, they are vulnerable to the full force of the mood swings that are so characteristic of Peirce's a priori method. As Rorty expresses it in an interview with Lewis-Kraus: "If I had to lay bets, my bet would be that everything is going to go to hell, but, you know, what else have we got except hope?"[8] "Modern, literate, secular societies," Rorty writes, are isolated in time and space "surrounded by misery, tyranny, and chaos" (PP:289), and all we have in defense of them is the hope that they can make life "freer, less cruel, more leisured, richer in goods and experiences, not just for our descendants but for everybody's descendants" (ibid). But, for Rorty, this remains a hope that can be grounded

> in nothing more profound than the historical facts which suggest that without the protections of something like the institutions of bourgeois liberal society, people will be less able to work out their private salvations, create their private self-images, reweave their webs of belief and desire in the light of whatever new people and books they happen to encounter.
>
> (PP:288)

In conclusion, one could object that Rorty's entire take on pragmatism is hampered by his starting point. Notwithstanding his criticism of the linguistic turn as the latest instantiation of a philosophy in search of a foundation, Rorty ends up pretty much buying into the turn itself, as is revealed by his continual focus on language. A pragmatist can easily retort, that he should have rejected—or better perhaps, revolutionized—the linguistic turn, for instance by advocating a semiotic turn instead (6.7). Especially if this is a triadic semiotics, such as Peirce's, the result will be a more robust philosophy that avoids the problems of representationalism without falling prey to relativism or subjectivism, as some have argued happened to Rorty. Among those who have argued that Rorty succumbed to relativism, we find Hilary Putnam, to whom we turn in the next chapter. It is not altogether clear, however, whether Putnam himself succeeds in deflecting the same charge.

Notes

1. For a biography of Rorty, see Neil Gross, *Richard Rorty: The Making of an American Philosopher* (Chicago, 2008).
2. Dewey too refers to the mirror metaphor (e.g., MW3:318); see also Francis Bacon, *New Organon* 1.41.
3. Richard Rorty, *Achieving Our Country: Leftist Thought in Twentieth-Century America* (Cambridge, 1998), p.94.
4. Wilfrid Sellars, *Science, Perception, and Reality* (New York, 1963), p.170.
5. Jay Rosenberg, "Raiders of the Lost Distinction: Richard Rorty and the Search for the Last Dichotomy," *Philosophy and Phenomenological Research* 53 (1993): 195–214, p.201.
6. Herman Saatkamp (ed), *Rorty and Pragmatism: The Philosopher Responds to His Critics* (Nashville, 1995), p.149.
7. E.g., de Waal (2013), p.10ff.
8. Gideon Lewis-Kraus, "An Interview with Richard Rorty," *The Believer*, June 2003. Cornel West, to whom we return in Chapter 15, speaks of hope without optimism.

Chapter 12

Hilary Putnam
Philosophy With a Human Face

Hilary Putnam starts his philosophic journey as a metaphysical realist. On this view, there exists a real world composed of a fixed totality of objects—a world that can be captured, at least in principle, within a single and complete description that can be called the truth. In a sense, truth is how an all-knowing god would see and describe the world. One reason why Putnam holds on to this view is that the predictive success of the sciences would be an absolute miracle if its theories were not (at least) approximately true—if they did not represent the world more or less correctly.[1] This is often referred to as the no-miracles argument. Though, as we will see, Putnam comes to reject metaphysical realism, he steadfastly holds on to a realism of sorts as it remains the best, if not the only, explanation for the successes of the sciences. Putnam thus rejects Rorty's ethnocentrism. Science works, not because scientists agree with one another, but because theories reflect how the world truly is. Putnam, however, rather quickly discovers that metaphysical realism is not a tenable position, and this brings him first to internal realism and later to a natural or commonsense realism. It is here that we see him taking significant steps in the direction of pragmatism. Part of what motivates Putnam is a rejection of the reductionism that many metaphysical realists, including someone like Quine, feel comfortable with, which is the idea that our beliefs and impressions of the ordinary world of trees, cats, tables, etc., are mistaken, because the only true description of them is the one given by particle physics. In this chapter we look at Putnam's trajectory from metaphysical to commonsense realism, as well as some of the back and forth between Putnam and Rorty.

Like Rorty, Putnam (1926–2016) grows up in a politically active left-leaning household and is trained as an analytic philosopher. He makes significant contributions to the philosophies of mind, mathematics, and science before turning to pragmatism in the late 1980s. A distinctive trait of Putnam is that he habitually subjects his views to vigorous scrutiny, which often causes him to modify his position. Consequently, Putnam, like Peirce, is best studied chronologically. In 1962, Putnam marries Ruth Anna Jacobs, who is also a philosopher. Her work focuses on William James, and it is James who comes to play the lead role in Putnam's pragmatism. Here, Putnam differs from Rorty, who put Dewey center stage. Both find Peirce much less promising, as they take him as still defending a correspondence theory of truth. Putnam openly distances himself from pragmatism, mainly because he rejects its conceptions of truth. Rorty's frequently calling himself a pragmatist may also have been a factor, as Putnam is very critical of Rorty's ethnocentrism, which he sees as indistinguishable from cultural relativism. This notwithstanding, Putnam takes pragmatism very seriously. He likes its fallibilism (Peirce), its rejection of paper doubt (Peirce), its commitment to pluralism (James), and its rejection of worn-out dichotomies (Dewey). The last include the theory–practice, analytic–synthetic, and fact–value dichotomies.

A good way of approaching Putnam's pragmatism is by looking at the view he rejects, the metaphysical realism we touched on previously (RHF:30). As we saw, metaphysical realism builds on the idea, suggested by common sense, that the world consists of a fixed totality of objects and maintains that this totality can be captured in a single true and complete description. Metaphysical realism further assumes that we can distinguish what belongs to the world from inventions of the mind. Finally, it assumes that we can describe the former as it is in and of itself—that is, uncolored by the knower's situation, mood, aims, desires, etc. In short, it presumes that a God's-eye view, though perhaps not humanly attainable, is at least in principle possible and can be made the benchmark of truth. Truth on this view is a correspondence between the world and its description—it is how an all-knowing and totally disinterested God would describe it.[2] To a significant degree, this is the kind of view that Rorty criticizes in *The Mirror of Nature*, that Dewey objects to when he rejects the spectator theory of knowledge, that motivates Lewis and others to think in terms of conceptual schemes, and that James derides by suggesting that it would imply that "a race of dogs bred for generations, say in the Vatican . . . ought to become, if time were given, accomplished *connoisseurs* of sculpture" (PP1:403).

According to Putnam, rejecting metaphysical realism, however, does not force us to embrace relativism, nor does he think that the classical pragmatists were relativists. On both points, Putnam differs from Rorty. For Rorty, rules of inference are, like the rules of chess, ultimately products of culture-specific social conventions, as there are no external standards to fall back on. An obvious way to try to avoid such relativism is by pointing at the natural and biological aspects of human existence. As already noted, there are various ways of doing this. One can point at Gehlen's philosophical anthropology (10.5). One can point at Heidegger's *Dasein* and how it structures our being in the world (10.4). One can point at Mead and Dewey and their focus on the problem situation and how this involves the whole person (7.6). Or one can point at Peirce, for whom cultural differences would be part of the idiosyncrasies that would be filtered out eventually in the course of inquiry (2.6). In short, Rorty's cultural differences may conceal a deeper unity, which arguably puts the burden upon the non-relativist to disclose what this supposedly deeper unity consists in. Putnam agrees that there is something deeper, but determining what it is exactly and how a belief in it can be justified remains a constant struggle.

In *Realism with a Human Face* (1990), Putnam seeks to deflect relativism by extrapolating upon Dewey's "warranted assertibility" (8.5). Putnam presents five insights, or principles, as he calls them, related to warrant and justification, which he thinks are generally subscribed to by pragmatists, going all the way back to Peirce's earliest writings (RHF:22):

1. In ordinary circumstances, there is usually a fact of the matter as to whether the statements people make are warranted or not.
2. Whether a statement is warranted or not is independent of whether the majority of one's cultural peers would *say* it is warranted or unwarranted.
3. Our norms and standards of warranted assertibility are historical products; they evolve over time.
4. Our norms and standards always reflect our interests and values. . . .
5. Our norms and standards of *anything*—including warranted assertibility—are capable of reform. There are better and worse norms and standards. (RHF:21)

From these principles we can see that, in contrast to Rorty, Putnam embraces Peirce's fourth method of fixing belief, the method of science, while also subscribing to Peirce's notion that what counts as good inquiry (the norms and standards) is not something externally imposed upon inquiry, but emerges from within inquiry itself.

Recalling the problem of the underdetermination of theory by data and the possibility of incommensurability (both discussed in Chapter 9), Putnam's first principle does not in itself allow us to escape relativism. In such a situation we still have no means for privileging our view above those of others. What is further needed is a robust account of the norms and standards of warranted assertibility, one that fits within the confines of principles 3–5, which all have a decidedly relativistic ring to them.

Putnam addresses the second principle with the observation that when we say that a statement is warranted, we clearly do not mean just that the majority of our peers agree with us, as we clearly allow for situations where we think we are right and everyone else is wrong. That is, we in fact do believe that statements can be warranted even when the overwhelming majority of our peers believe that they are false. Although relativists officially reject this, Putnam keenly observes that they also subscribe to it, at least in practice, as they continue to defend their own views even when the vast majority of scientists, theologians, and philosophers dismiss them. In short, their actions betray their word—in defending their view, they refute it by tacitly relying on non-relativist norms or standards, the very possibility of which they deny. So, let us turn to these norms or standards by looking at them under the more general auspice of values.

12.1 The Collapse of the Fact–Value Distinction

Earlier, we discussed the demise of the analytic–synthetic dichotomy, with Quine arguing that we cannot make sense of analyticity. The result is that for any statement we can make about the world, we cannot disentangle what we ourselves contribute to that statement from what is purely given to us (9.6). However, merely rejecting the analytic–synthetic distinction still enables us to maintain that we can give a purely *factual* account of the world. Putnam, by rejecting the fact–value dichotomy, goes a step further: statements about the world always contain both factual and value components, and they do so in a way that does not allow us to disentangle them. This implies that, for Putnam, statements about the world are always value laden. There are no statements for which the value component is truly zero.

The fact–value distinction goes back to David Hume's claim that you cannot derive ought from is, or for that matter, is from ought. That people do something does not mean that they ought to do it, nor does it follow from the fact that people ought to do something that they will do it. Hume's claim assumes, and reinforces, a strict separation of facts and values. The logical positivists subsequently collapse the resulting dichotomy, either by reducing all value statements to factual statements (as in emotivism, where statements of value are reduced to expressions of emotion), or by outright rejecting them on the ground that, since they are not factual (because they cannot be tested), they must be cognitively meaningless. Either way, we are left only with factual statements. The fact–value dichotomy is in like manner collapsed in Rorty, as he equates what we should believe with what the majority of our peers actually do believe.

The logical positivists do not deny that we can *distinguish* facts from values. Quite the contrary, they rely on that very distinction when they demand that facts be value-free. Putnam, in contrast, denies that we can truly distinguish them. Facts are always infused with values, and values are always infused with facts. There are no value-free facts, nor are there any fact-free values. (Putnam rejects the idea of a priori values.) This means that we cannot neatly shave off the value components, leaving us only with factual components, or the other way around. Consequently, the idea that the world consists of a totality of facts that can be described neutrally (a core presupposition of metaphysical realism) proves untenable. Putnam does not deny that there are situations where drawing the distinction is useful, but he does deny that we can draw any metaphysical conclusions from it, which is what the metaphysical realist tries to do.

Part of what engenders the demise of the fact–value distinction is the realization that with the advance of science, Hume's notion of a fact as what can be directly observed is no longer tenable. We routinely accept things as facts even though we cannot observe them, treating them instead as basic presuppositions or as conclusions from arguments that may or may not have old-fashioned Humean facts as part of their premises. Consequently, we should say that it is *the scientific system as a whole* that has factual content, not individual statements denoting clear and distinct observables (a view the early logical positivists still held on to). In fact, what makes us believe that the latter represent facts is the wider system they are part of. This becomes clear from cases where our senses are deceived, as when a stick partially submerged in water *looks* bent even though it is not. The *fact* of the matter is that the stick is straight, because that's what the theory says it should be.

Theories, Putnam further observes, are not value neutral. For instance, when we compare two empirically equivalent but conflicting theories about the world to determine which one is correct, we often invoke qualities such as coherence and simplicity. As Putnam observes, these qualities are values, because they function as action-guiding terms: "To describe a theory as 'coherent, simple, explanatory' [is] to say that acceptance of the theory is *justified*," which means that "one ought to accept" the theory (RHF:138). Such terms are prescriptive, not descriptive. Similarly, Ockham's famous razor is not a statement about what the world is like, but it says something about what we find important in our explanations of the world. As with Peirce's conception of logic as a normative science (6.5), Putnam argues that we cannot ignore epistemic values when discussing theories.[3] That being said, such epistemic values tend to have a more objective ring to them than, say, aesthetic values. We do not typically say that simplicity lies in the eyes of the beholder.

The same holds for observation sentences, the last stronghold of the empiricists. Even when all I say is "That is an oak!" I'm relying on classifications that have been independently justified. On top of that, I'm paying attention to something at the expense of other things, which is a valuation too.

The germ of Putnam's view lies in four theses he learned from one of his undergraduate professors, Edgar Singer Jr., a pragmatist who briefly worked with James at Harvard:

1. *Knowledge of facts presupposes knowledge of theories*, where the latter include generalizations. For example, to know that something is an oak tree, one must have a background that makes this classification possible.

2. *Knowledge of theories presupposes knowledge of facts*—there are no generalizations about the world that we can know a priori.

3. *Knowledge of facts presupposes knowledge of values*, meaning: (i) justifying factual claims presupposes value judgments, and (ii) such value judgments are objective, not subjective.

4. And, conversely, *knowledge of values presupposes knowledge of facts*; there are no a priori values.[4]

The four theses smartly capture how anything we think of is always an amalgam of fact and value. This is further confirmed when we look at "thick" ethical concepts, like rudeness or cruelty. For instance, the claim that Caligula was a cruel emperor, Putnam aptly points out, is not neatly factorable into its descriptive components and its value components—cruelty cannot be described in wholly value-neutral terms before pronouncing it bad, nor can one say that it is bad independently of any description of it.[5]

12.2 Whether Our Norms Are All Subjective

If we cannot disentangle facts from norms and values, and norms and values are subjective, or at least culturally determined, then the question becomes whether objective knowledge is possible at all. As we saw in the previous chapter, Rorty denies that it is. The most we can do is to privilege our own culture and become ethnocentric. To Putnam, this does not sound right. For instance, whether a leg-prosthesis is good (which is a value judgment) depends primarily on its ability to replace a human leg—by how well it fits, how heavy it is, whether it allows us to do the things we normally do with our legs, etc. None of this seems particularly subjective or culturally determined; rather, they are fairly straightforward questions of biomechanical engineering. True, we can say, as does Rorty, that our norms and values merely reflect our interests, but that only shows that they are conditional; it does not show that they're not objective.

To simplify things, I will focus on epistemic warrant, i.e., what justifies us in believing something or in calling it true (which are two different things). Recall that Rorty equates truth with what our peers let us get away with, and this claim is Putnam's prime target. According to Putnam, Rorty's claim does not truthfully represent what we mean when we call a statement or belief justified. More precisely, Rorty fails to distinguish between a claim being justified and our *believing* that it is justified. It is not uncommon for us to *believe* that a claim is justified, when in fact it is not. The prevalence of a great variety of logical fallacies certainly testifies to this, as does the psychological fact that we are all too easily swayed by claims that agree with what we already believe. There are certainly moments when we say to ourselves, "I can't believe I fell for that." In sum, there is an important practical distinction to be drawn between a statement being justified and our *believing* that it is justified, and we typically want to retain that distinction *even* in situations where a belief is uniformly held.

The same is true where the reform of norms and values is at issue. Recall Putnam's observation that we believe that some norms and standards are better than others (principle 5 presented earlier). Partially in light of this, we reform our norms and values. This applies even to something as seemingly timeless as mathematical proofs and our idea of mathematical rigor.[6] Here too, we distinguish between a reform being successful and our *believing* that it is successful. As Putnam observes, giving credit to Nelson Goodman,

> norms, standards, and judgments about particular cases often *conflict*. When this happens, we are often pushed to a special kind of philosophical reflection which we might call *reconstructive reflection* [and] we can learn a great deal from partial and even fragmentary reconstructions, and we can learn a great deal from reconstructing our beliefs in alternative ways.
>
> (RHF:25)

Even where there is no conflict between norms, their mere application can invite reform: "relying on our existing norms and standards of warrant, we discover facts which themselves sometimes lead to a change in the pictures that inform those norms and standards" (ibid).

Again, the norms and what they apply to cannot be neatly separated. Though we may be able to disentangle them up to a point, after the fact, and *in abstracto*, they originally emerge together as one. As we saw earlier, Peirce takes a similar stance about inquiry. It is within inquiry that norms of what counts as good or bad inquiry develop, rather than that these norms are somehow externally imposed upon inquiry. For Putnam, and pragmatists more generally, we can no longer rely on the old notion of a neutral, God-given (hence, superhuman) rationality, which effectively reduces our task to that of discovering our own mistakes. To this we can add that what is true for inquiry also applies to mathematical proofs, a history that spans a great variety of cultures over a long stretch of time.[7] Consequently, it is hard to see how it could all be just a matter of what culture one resides in. And it is not just science and mathematics. In Chapter 14, we will see that the law provides an interesting example of it as well.

Arguments like these suggest to Putnam that relativism (what counts as true depends entirely on one's culture) is not a viable alternative to metaphysical realism (what counts as true is wholly independent of one's culture) and this is true also for Rorty's ethnocentrism. In Putnam's view, it is pragmatism that can provide a viable middle way, but it has to be a pragmatism different from Rorty's. This pragmatism comes to the front in a view that Putnam calls "internal realism," one he later modifies into a natural realism.

12.3 Pragmatism and Internal Realism

Internal realism aims to show that we can have it both ways: reject the metaphysical realist's notion of a complete and neutral description of the world, while at the same time maintaining that there is an objective world out there that is independent of language and mind and to which our descriptions should conform.[8] In short, Putnam seeks to show that conceptual relativity and realism are compatible.

Putnam begins by observing that we cannot talk about what is really out there without making conceptual choices. You cannot say, for instance, that trees exist, let alone anything else about them, without first explaining what counts as a tree. To illustrate this, Putnam asks us to imagine a world wherein we can identify three individual objects: x_1, x_2, and x_3 (ibid). Next, he observes that we can describe that same world so that it contains not three but seven objects, namely, by counting any sum of multiple objects also as an object. In that case we get, in addition to x_1, x_2, x_3, also $(x_1 + x_2)$, $(x_2 + x_3)$, $(x_1 + x_3)$, and $(x_1 + x_2 + x_3)$. If this strikes you as odd, you can think of the Big Dipper. We typically call the Big Dipper an object—and one that we believe to be really "out there"—mostly because it is easy to spot and can be used to locate the North Pole Star, which is not so easy to spot. And we happily do so while calling the stars within the Big Dipper objects too.

Putnam's example shows that even when we go down to the most basic notions we have about the world—what does it mean to be an object, what does it mean for something to exist, etc.—we have to make choices. Moreover, there is nothing about the world itself that is telling us that we should go with the three-object version rather than the seven-object version, or vice versa. Consequently, the question "So how many objects are there really, three or seven?" does not make sense to Putnam; the answer depends on what you mean by object—that is, it depends on how you *conceptualize* the world, and there are different ways of doing that. It is important to keep in mind that such different conceptualizations are still taken to refer to the same world. For instance, even though young-earth creationists and geologists conceptualize the world differently, so that their claims cannot be true at the same time, they are still referring to the same object. That is to say, when the geologist rejects the young-earth creationist's claim, she does so on the presumption that both are referring to the same thing, namely Earth.

There is nothing about the world itself, however, that requires that the different descriptions we give of it can all be seamlessly translated into one another, or that they can be reduced to a single description. Consequently, for Putnam, our inability to reduce our commonsense objects to the language of particle physics does not force us to then say that only the latter truly describes what is real, which is what the metaphysical realist requires us to do. (In addition to his earlier self, Putnam sees both Wilfrid Sellars and Bernard Williams as making this move [PWL:37f]). For Putnam, consistency is rather a value that we impose upon our conceptualizations because it helps us in making sense of things. There is no reason to assume it to be absolute, or that it mirrors how things really are.

All of this puts Putnam close to James's initial insights in the *Psychology*, which we discussed in Chapter 3. The key question, though, remains: how are we to avoid succumbing to relativism? Clearly, Putnam observes, we are not relativists in practice. When we visit a doctor, we accept how the doctor conceptualizes our condition, *even* when we do so differently (or even *experience* it differently), as we tend to think that where our health is concerned, the doctor's way of seeing things is better than our own. Hence, in practice, we do not believe that all conceptualizations are equal, and what causes this seems to be something about the world itself. It is this that inspires Peirce to move from the third to the fourth method for fixing belief, and leads James to conclude "The Will to Believe" by saying that even though you can (and sometimes must) choose freely, if you choose wrongly, you'll pay the price, sometimes dearly so (WJ:735). As Putnam puts it, "in ordinary circumstances, there is usually a fact of the matter as to whether the statements people make are warranted or not" (RHF:21). That is to say, "knowledge is not a story with no constraints except internal coherence," as the relativist makes it out to be (RTH:54). There are external inputs. The crucial point is that when such external inputs enter our knowledge, they are always already conceptually contaminated.

Earlier, we saw Putnam rejecting that norms and values are subjective or relative to a culture, something he thinks is true especially for epistemic norms. That our peers disagree with us is not necessarily a reason for giving up on what we think is right, true, or worthy of believing. In the context of this, Putnam revives Dewey's notion of warranted assertibility as a way of determining which ways of conceptualizing are more representative of the world, albeit that he calls it rational acceptability. With this, Putnam has in mind the circumstances under which we have reason to accept that a certain statement or system of statements is true. What is rationally acceptable, for Putnam, is not the product of some universal faculty called reason that must be ascribed to every single one of us, nor is it what our peers agree on as being reasonable, but is determined rather by the inquiry we are engaged in (Peirce) or the indeterminate situation we are responding to (Mead and Dewey).

Putnam is careful to point out, however, that rational acceptability is not to be identified with truth. As the history of thought has painfully shown, there have been plenty of situations where we were justified in accepting a statement as true when in fact it was false. On top of that, a statement can be true even when we are not in the least justified in accepting it as such. Though Putnam rejects Peirce's notion of truth in terms of the belief we would reach at the end of inquiry (2.6), he does introduce the idea of "ideal rational acceptability." Though Putnam believes that such a situation is as unattainable as the frictionless surfaces that physicists talk about, he does think that it can be approximated "to a very high degree." So, rather than functioning as a regulative ideal for inquiry—which is what Peirce had in mind—Putnam is thinking rather in terms of a postulate that allows us to develop a theory of knowledge that reconciles conceptual relativism with realism: Just as you can develop a theory of physics on the assumption that surfaces are frictionless (even though they are not), you can develop a theory of knowledge on the assumption that ideal rational acceptability is feasible (even when it is not).[9] Later, Putnam relaxes his notion of ideal rational acceptability, writing, "a statement is true if and only if its acceptance would be justified were epistemic conditions good enough" (PWL:29).

None of this seems to force Putnam into going back to the metaphysical realist's notion that ultimately there can be only one description of reality, and that ideally this description will be a *full* description as well. There is no need, Putnam continues, to posit some God's-eye point of view. It suffices to say that there are only "the various points of view of actual persons reflecting various interests and purposes that their descriptions and theories subserve" (RTH:49f). Since, as we saw, ideal rational acceptability pertains to the "ideal coherence of our beliefs with each other and with our experiences *as those experiences are themselves represented in our belief system*" (RTH:50), there can be multiple descriptions which, as long as they do not conflict too blatantly in our practical lives (which includes the practical lives of scientists when they are in the process of trying to figure something out) are acceptable representations of the world.

It is important to keep in mind that, writing after Quine and Davidson, Putnam rejects the three dogmas of empiricism—the analytic–synthetic distinction, reductionism, and the scheme–content distinction. To these Putnam adds his own rejection of the fact–value distinction. Consequently, when we conceptualize the world as we find it, so to speak, what we ourselves contribute to the result (our conceptualization) cannot be identified, let alone be separated out. Everything comes together as one, with all its peculiarities—including the realization that we seem to be able to provide multiple descriptions of that world that all seem to be representative of it even though they do not quite add up.

Unsurprisingly, Rorty remains skeptical of Putnam's commitment to realism. For Rorty, the demise of metaphysical realism leaves us no choice but to also let go of the notion of truth.[10] He sees little use in Putnam's attempt at redefining it in terms of warranted assertibility or rational acceptability, as it fails to reflect what the term meant originally. What we have left is at best the empty shell of a concept. As we saw in the last chapter, to say that a statement or theory is true is, for Rorty, nothing but "a compliment paid to beliefs which we think so well-justified that for the moment further justification is not needed" (RR:230). And it is an empty compliment to boot, because it does not add anything. Rorty is further critical of Putnam's attempt to think of truth as *idealized* acceptability. For Rorty, this is either too abstract to be of any use (making it yet another empty compliment), or if it is not, it is rooted in *our* practices (as what other practices could they be rooted in), in which case Putnam's internal realism collapses into Rorty's very own ethnocentrism. Put differently, though Rorty commends Putnam for rejecting the God's-eye view, he sees him as sliding back when he clings to the idea of "a limit-concept of ideal truth" (RTH:216).[11] "What is such a posit supposed to do," Rorty wonders not without sarcasm, "except to say that from God's point of view the human race is heading in the right direction?" (RR:230). Rorty continues,

> To say that *we* think we're heading in the right direction is just to say, with Kuhn, that we can, by hindsight, tell the story of the past as a story of progress. To say that we still have a long way to go, that our present views should not be cast in bronze, is too platitudinous to require support by positing limit concepts.
>
> (RTH:232f)

Rorty hereby accepts Putnam's claim that whether a statement is warranted or not does not depend on whether the majority of our peers would *say* it is warranted or not. The history of science reveals as much. What Rorty denies is that there is any deep philosophical story to be told here, whether it is the metaphysical realist's story about a God-like description, or the internal realist's story about idealized rational acceptability.

12.4 Natural Realism

In the 1990s Putnam's views begin to shift away from internal realism, though not without giving up on it entirely and without returning to metaphysical realism. Putnam devotes much of his 1994 Dewey Lectures to this shift, aiming, as he explains, "to make clear what I'm keeping from my own past positions and where I feel I went wrong in the 'internal realism' that I have been defending."[12] Following James (WJ:194), Putnam terms the result natural realism.

The problem Putnam finds himself running into is one that Peirce also noted when developing his pragmatic notions of truth and reality, namely the problem of buried secrets (2.6). We can reasonably ask whether it is true that Cleopatra sneezed five times on her fifth birthday while simultaneously conceding that our epistemic conditions will never be good enough to determine this. From the example given, it is moreover easy to see that the number of true statements is likely going to be vastly greater than the number of statements that meet Putnam's standard of idealized rational acceptability. For instance, we can ask the same question not just for any other day in Cleopatra's life, but also for every day in the lives of everyone who has ever lived. And that's just one question. That we can endlessly multiply such cases suggests that truth cannot be identified with ideal rational acceptability.

Putnam's response to the buried secrets problem is to concede that the notion of truth, as held by metaphysical and internal realists alike, is construed too narrowly, and he advocates instead for a return to a more commonsense conception of truth and reality. For Putnam, this means giving up on the idea of representationalism. Metaphysical realism and internal realism are essentially representationalist theories: truth consists in *representing* something correctly. The problem for metaphysical realism is that we can never know whether our representations are correct because we cannot compare them with the God's-eye view. The problem with internal realism, as we just saw, is that even under ideal epistemic conditions, there is still an enormous discrepancy between what is true and what is rationally acceptable. With his natural realism, Putnam is now moving away from representationalism altogether, embracing a direct realism instead. The transition runs largely through Putnam's changing views on perception. Putnam long held on to the representational view of perception that shaped much of modern philosophy—the view that we perceive the world through a veil of ideas. Descartes, for instance remarked that the senses "do not, except occasionally and accidentally, show us what external bodies are like in themselves,"[13] and Locke similarly observed,

> It is evident the mind knows not things immediately, but only by the intervention of the ideas it has of them. Our knowledge therefore is real only so far as there is a conformity between our ideas and the reality of things.[14]

James's *Psychology* and his radical empiricism, Peirce's phaneroscopy and his scholastics-inspired semiotics, Dewey's rejection of the spectator view of knowledge, and Husserl's phenomenology are all attempts to break loose from this view.

Part of what fueled the representationalist view was the advance of physics, which caused properties such as colors to be located in the mind of the perceiver—rubies are not really red; that's just how *we* see them. Moreover, our experience with dreams and hallucinations shows us that we can see something even when there is nothing there. All this suggests that what is presented to the mind when we have a sensory impression is not the object we are seeing, but a mental representation of that object. A key problem for representationalists is that having separated knowledge from its object, they cannot reconnect the two.

In his move toward direct perception, Putnam builds largely on James. Like James's earlier rejection of British empiricism, Putnam too wants to return to how we actually experience things. Once we do that, he argues, we will quickly realize that the problem with both metaphysical and internal realism is their representationalism. Combining James's empiricism with Wittgenstein's claim that understanding a language is being able to use it (10.3), Putnam argues that in order to understand a sentence like "The bathroom is down the stairs to your right," you must be able to use the sentence, and that is very different from conjuring up a mental image that correctly maps a deeper reality to which we have no immediate access. Moreover, we can use the sentence only when we accept many things about our day-to-day world as being real and true—that there really are such things as bathrooms and stairs, that they can stand in that kind of relation to each other, that staircases don't disappear once you step on them, etc. And in the end, these notions about what is true or real constitute the final touchstone for any philosophical claims about what is true or real. In other words, we can make sense of our commonsense world only when we accept that many of the things we encounter are real and that many of our beliefs about them are true, while also recognizing that we can be wrong about any single one of them. Hence, Putnam, like Peirce, is a fallibilist. Earlier, we saw Davidson make a similar move: we can understand a language only when we assume that most of what its users say is true (9.8).

The central problem with representationalist theories, from Putnam's perspective, is that they separate the mind from the world, after which they cannot reconnect the two in any meaningful way. Natural realism, or commonsense realism as Putnam also calls it, shows both

> the needlessness and the unintelligibility of a picture that imposes an interface between ourselves and the world. It is a way of completing the task of philosophy, the task that John Wisdom once called a "journey from the familiar to the familiar."
>
> (TC:10)

It is needless, because our direct experience already places rational constraints upon our thinking—that is, constraints that we can think and deliberate about with our human capacity for reasoning. It is unintelligible, because the resulting "real world" cannot play any role in our representations (since we have no independent access to what our representations are presumed to represent; all we have is our representations) while at the same time it is assigned the essential role of separating truth from fiction.

For Putnam, to understand a claim—say, that the bathroom is to your right—is to be able to successfully move around in a language game (the phrase is Wittgenstein's, but we can also think of Mead). Now, we use language for a variety of reasons. Admittedly, one of them is to describe reality. Even there, though, describing reality is never a mere copying—it involves choices, including conceptual ones. In Wittgenstein's words, seeing is always a seeing as. Importantly, whatever our choices may be, the result must be answerable to reality. As Putnam remarks, "our words and life are constrained by a reality not of our own invention" (TC:9), and whenever we do anything, we take much of that world for granted. For the natural realist, what this reality is, is being revealed to us in our daily going about. To quote Wittgenstein, "If I make an experiment I do not doubt the existence of the apparatus before my eyes. I have plenty of doubts, but not that" (OC§337).

The philosophers' mistake, Putnam explains, is to presuppose "that the term *reality* must refer to a single superthing instead of looking at the ways in which we endlessly negotiate—and are *forced* to renegotiate—our notion of reality as our language and our life develop" (TC:9).

None of this means we have to give up altogether on the idea of identifying truth with ideal rational acceptability; hence, Putnam's natural realism is not a radical departure from his earlier internal realism. Not only does it often suffice, but it is also, Putnam points out, "a conceptual prerequisite of our being able to understand a language at all" (PWL:29). It is a hinge, not between language and the world, as the metaphysical and internal realist had it, but between language and our understanding of it, and he calls this "a partial vindication of pragmatism" (ibid). A Peircean could further add here that we should look at all of this as a triadic relationship—one that connects a dynamic object with and immediate object through an interpretant (6.7).

In the previous chapter, we saw that Rorty's rejection of traditional philosophy led him to conclude that democracy cannot be grounded in philosophy without begging the question, because philosophy itself is grounded in the actual exchange of ideas, which takes the form of a democracy. Putnam's rejection of metaphysical realism leaves him in a similar predicament: we cannot justify democracy in terms of something that goes beyond the experience and values which the members of a community happen to share. Putnam and Rorty both hold that democracy is preferable to other socio-political systems, and they both take democracy to be self-justifying. Where they differ is that Putnam still believes that we can give a philosophical justification for this claim, whereas Rorty has given up on that. For Putnam, we can still give an epistemological justification of democracy. Democracy, he argues, "is the precondition for the full application of intelligence to the solution of social problems" (RP:180). This brings us back to Dewey's idea that democracy is to be fashioned in the image of a community of inquiry aimed at solving "the problems of men." Ideally, it brings together an indefinite community of participants that each come with their experiences and values, while actively preventing obstructions that block or distort the course of their deliberations and attempts at problem solving—like censorship, or propaganda. Since the aim is not "to control the enemies of the community or its shirkers, but, by giving reason to people already disposed to hear it, to help in creating a community continually held together by that same disposition," there is, Putnam observes, no need to refer to anything beyond this (RP:181). The aim is to improve society, not to have it match some universal ideal.

To conclude, what seems to enable Putnam to avoid lapsing into relativism is his rejection of the subjectivity or cultural dependency of values. What counts as good inquiry is determined by certain characteristics of the inquiry, not by certain specifics of the situation it is conducted in, like one's culture, or who is willing to listen. Moreover, we do *experience* those characteristics. They are internal to the inquiry itself, and we feel guided by them. For instance, we may continue to hold on to our ideas on how to improve society, even when our peers disagree, even when we lose the election by an overwhelming margin. For Rorty, as we saw, Putnam's strategy does not work. It either smuggles back in the God's-eye view, or it is merely a disguised form of ethnocentrism. In the last two chapters, we also saw that whereas Rorty's main inspiration is Dewey, Putnam's main inspiration is James. In the next chapter, we will look at someone who is inspired primarily by Peirce: Susan Haack.

Notes

1. Hilary Putnam, *Mathematics, Matter and Method* (Cambridge, 1975), p.73.
2. Putnam ascribes such a view to Bernard Williams, especially in his book on Descartes (PWL:37).
3. Hilary Putnam, *The Collapse of the Fact/Value Dichotomy* (Cambridge, 2002), p.30.
4. PWL:19; paraphrased for brevity.
5. Putnam (2002), p.34ff.
6. See e.g., Israel Kleiner, "Rigor and Proof in Mathematics: A Historical Perspective," *Mathematics Magazine* 64.5 (1991): 291–314.
7. E.g., Karine Chemla's *The History of Mathematical Proof in Ancient Traditions* (Cambridge, 2012) covers a wide variety of cultures and time periods.
8. Hilary Putnam, *The Many Faces of Realism* (LaSalle, 1987), p.33.
9. From Peirce's perspective the analogy is problematic, as it is precisely the friction caused by secondness that distinguishes knowledge from reverie.
10. For Rorty's criticism of Putnam's internal realism, see e.g., "Solidarity or Objectivity?" (RR:227–38); see also Paul Foster, "What Is at Stake Between Putnam and Rorty?" *Philosophy and Phenomenological Research* 52.3 (1992): 585–603.
11. Quoted by Rorty, RR:232.
12. Published as *The Threefold Cord* (TC).
13. René Descartes, *Principles of Philosophy*, Pt. 2, Sect. 3, in *The Philosophical Writings of Descartes*, 3 vols. (Cambridge, 1984–91), 1, p.224.
14. John Locke, *Essay Concerning Human Understanding* (Oxford, 1975), IV.iv.3.

Chapter 13

Susan Haack
Reclaiming Pragmatism

Susan Haack (b. 1945) is sometimes called the intellectual granddaughter of Peirce, which is an apt description. The key elements of Peirce's thought, including his realism, his critical common-sensism, his theory of perception, and his fallibilism, are all prominent in Haack, as are his care for terminology, his focus on inquiry, and his insistence on "the will to learn." Sometimes Peirce's views return with a twist, sometimes his views are developed further and updated for our time (like the addition of fake reasoning as a special form of pseudo inquiry). Where Rorty campaigns for the Deweyan side of pragmatism, and Putnam is deeply inspired by James, Haack represents the Peircean strand.

The title of Haack's third book, *Evidence and Inquiry* (1993) concisely captures the central tenet of her thought, which is to examine what makes evidence stronger or weaker and inquiry better or worse conducted. The issues of evidence and inquiry are also central to her later books, *Manifesto of a Passionate Moderate* (1998), *Defending Science—Within Reason* (2003), and *Scientism and Its Discontents* (2017), and they form a core theme of her venues into philosophy of law, as in *Evidence Matters: Science, Proof, and Truth in the Law* (2014). (A discussion of her philosophy of law is postponed to the next chapter.)

From the outset, it is important to point out that the question of what makes *inquiry* better or worse conducted is very different from the question of what makes *evidence* better or worse. Though often confused, the two are, as Haack puts it, "as different as . . . criteria for judging roses are from instructions for growing them (unlike the former, the latter would, for example, inevitably mention horse manure)" (M:105). A common fallacy that follows from the failure of properly distinguishing the two is to conclude from the observation that there is more than one way that an inquiry can be conducted and that there must be different criteria by which to evaluate the result. We might call this *the pluralist fallacy*: a pluralism of legitimate methods of inquiry is taken to entail a pluralism of standards of evidence. Pragmatists, who see a close connection between inquiry and truth, must be particularly attentive to this fallacy. Siding with Peirce, Haack embraces pluralism with respect to good methods of inquiry, while rejecting pluralism regarding criteria of good evidence.

13.1 The Empirical Justification of Beliefs

In *Evidence and Inquiry*, which aims to provide a pragmatist reconstruction of epistemology,[1] Haack addresses two classic questions of epistemology: "What counts as good, strong, supportive evidence for a belief?" and "What is the connection between a belief being well-supported by good evidence, and the likelihood that it is true?" The first leads to what she calls the project of explication, the second to the project of ratification (EI:1).

The two classic theories that deal with the first project, that of explication, are foundationalism and coherentism. *Foundationalists* make a distinction between basic and derived beliefs, adding that basic beliefs are those that can be justified independently of any other beliefs. Descartes's clear and distinct ideas are examples of such basic beliefs, as are beliefs expressed in Lewis's expressive statements (9.2) or in Carnap's observation sentences (9.3). What makes these beliefs basic is that they are not justified in terms of other beliefs but by the subject's sensory experience, direct intuition, being self-justifying, etc. All our other beliefs are then justified by deriving them from these basic beliefs.

For *coherentists*, in contrast, beliefs are justified not by relating them to so-called "basic beliefs"—as no beliefs can be called basic—but by their being part of a coherent set of beliefs. This means that for the coherentist, justification is wholly a matter of relations among beliefs: all beliefs are justified in terms of other beliefs; that is, they mutually support each other. In contrast to coherentists, foundationalists allow for nonbelief input in the justification of beliefs (as this is how basic beliefs are justified). They also hold that justification is one-directional: basic beliefs justify derived beliefs, but derived beliefs cannot justify basic beliefs or even contribute to their justification. This one-directionality is a consequence of how foundationalists distinguish (and define) basic beliefs, namely as beliefs that are justified *independently* of any other beliefs.

According to Haack, coherentism and foundationalism do not exhaust the options. One can conceive, she argues, of a theory that "allows the relevance of experience to justification, but that requires no class of privileged beliefs justified exclusively by experience with no support from other beliefs" (EI:19). And it is along such lines that Haack develops her own view, which she names "foundherentism." As the name indicates, foundherentism combines elements from *found*ationalism with elements from *coherentism*.

Foundherentism can be captured roughly in terms of the following two theses (EI:19):

(FH1) A subject's experience is relevant to the justification of his empirical beliefs, but there need be no privileged class of empirical beliefs justified exclusively by the support of experience, independently of the support of other beliefs.

(FH2) Justification is not exclusively one-directional, but involves pervasive relations of mutual support.

Since, for Haack, the subject's experience plays a distinctive part in empirical justification, she shifts her focus deliberately to the process of inquiry, construing knowledge as a product of it. For Haack, justification is not merely a matter of *what* you believe, making justification wholly a matter of analyzing the belief content, but also of *why* you believe it, which is in turn related to *how* you came to believe it.

As to *how* we come to believe something, Haack further differentiates between the initiating causes (i.e., those that historically led to the belief) and the causes that are operative when the question of justification comes up (EI:75). The latter often differ from those that initially caused the belief. To use Haack's example, you may be first convinced of the innocence of the accused because he has an honest face, and later because you find out that he has a watertight alibi. In this case the justification will be *not* in terms of what initially caused the belief (seeing his honest face), but in terms of the watertight alibi learned of later.

Haack further observes that justification is a gradual affair. It comes in degrees, running from a rough first approximation (like an educated guess) to deeply entrenched beliefs, and proceeding generally through what she terms a method of "successive approximation," which is neither wholly logical nor wholly empirical. Haack's foundherentism is not the only alternative to foundationalism and coherentism. Other more recent "third options" include the later Wittgenstein (10.3), Rorty's ethnocentrism (11.5), and Putnam's internal realism (12.3).

13.2 The Analogy of the Crossword Puzzle

According to Haack, the crossword puzzle is a better analogy for representing the structure of relations of evidential support than the traditional analogy of a mathematical proof. Mathematical proofs reveal how complicated theorems can be derived from a few simple axioms, and it is the proof that justifies the theorem. Euclid's *Elements*, the standard mathematics textbook for about two millennia, has in effect become the paradigm for how to justify knowledge claims. According to Haack, those who make mathematical proof the model for empirical justification have a mistaken view of the aim of inquiry. The aim of inquiry is not an isolated conclusion, as with mathematical proofs and their focus on theorems, but rather having important parts of one's puzzle filled in. The analogy of the crossword puzzle, Haack continues, gives a more apt representation of what knowledge is and how it is acquired than the traditional analogy of the mathematical proof. As she explains,

> How reasonable a crossword entry is depends on how well it is supported by its clue and already intersecting entries; on how reasonable those entries are, independent of the entry in question; and on how much of the crossword has been completed. Similarly, what makes evidence stronger or weaker, a claim more or less warranted, depends on how supportive the evidence is; on how secure it is, independent of the claim in question, and on how much of the relevant evidence it includes.
>
> (DS:24)

In contrast to a mathematical proof, which is one-directional, a crossword puzzle allows for a pervasive mutual support among beliefs and shows how this is possible without lapsing into vicious circularity.

As we saw, Haack maintains a pluralism regarding the conduct of inquiry. This view returns in the crossword analogy:

> There can no more be rules for when a theory should be accepted and when rejected than there could be rules for when to ink in a crossword entry and when to rub it out; "the" best procedure is for different scientists, some bolder, some more cautious, to proceed differently.
>
> (DS:25)

Haack's crossword analogy extends Peirce's rope analogy in interesting and important ways. Recall that Peirce rejected the Cartesian notion of chain reasoning (a classic representation of mathematical proof) where every step is deductively linked with those before and after it. In its stead, Peirce gave the analogy of a rope. On this analogy, an argument is like a multitude of thin and fragile strands that, when twined together, become a strong and durable rope. In contrast to a chain, which breaks with its weakest link, a good rope retains its strength even when several strands were to pop.

The crossword analogy has a far richer texture than the rope analogy. For instance, it allows for the fact that not all strands are equal; it shows why and where a particular strand may be woven into the rope; it reveals the fundamental interconnectedness of facts; and, as solving a crossword puzzle involves inquiry, which rope making does not, it better exemplifies inquiry. The crossword analogy also shows the interplay of the two theses of found-herentism: FH1 is represented by the relation the entry has to its clue, while FH2 is represented by the relation the entry has to other entries, some of which are already filled in while others are still blank. The analogy even allows for Kuhnian-style paradigm shifts and does so in a manner that combines the possibility of wide-scale scientific revolutions with a robust and more continuous notion of evidential support. When it becomes increasingly difficult to fill in the smaller peripheral entries of the puzzle, this may force us to erase a larger and more central entry and replace it with another, causing a ripple effect through part of the puzzle.

As with any analogy, the analogy of the crossword puzzle also has its limits. After explaining that the purpose of an analogy is heuristic—that is, "to suggest ideas, which then have to stand on their own feet," Haack continues, "scientific evidence isn't like a crossword puzzle in every respect: there will be nothing, for example, corresponding to the appearance of a solution in tomorrow's paper; nor . . . is there a person who designs it," etc. (DS:58).

13.3 Standards of Inquiry

Inquiry is the focal point of Haack's thought. Siding with Peirce and against Rorty, she maintains that there are certain core standards of well-conducted inquiry. Although the sciences are exemplary in maintaining such standards, and people often speak with reverence of the "scientific method," the standards are by no means unique to the sciences but apply to any type of inquiry. As Haack observes,

> As far as it is a method, it is what historians or detectives or investigative journalists or the rest of us do when we really want to find something out: make an informed conjecture about the possible explanation of a puzzling phenomenon, check how it stands up to the best evidence we can get, and then use our judgment whether to accept it, more or less tentatively, or modify, refine, or replace it.
>
> (DS:24)

Scientific inquiry is best seen, and here she approvingly quotes Gustav Bergmann, as "the 'long arm' of common sense" (DS:95).

As to what makes inquiry good, Haack sides with Peirce, who remarked that science "does not so much consist in knowing, not even in 'organized knowledge,' as it does in diligent inquiry into truth for truth's sake, without any sort of axe to grind . . . from an impulse to penetrate into the reason of things."[2] Good inquiry is not just a matter of using the right methods, but first and foremost one of having the right attitude. In well-conducted inquiry, the researcher is genuinely interested to discover how things really are; that is, in discovering what is true. As Haack puts it,

> The genuine inquirer is not a collector of true propositions, nor is he a worshiper of an intellectual ideal. But he does want the true answer to his question: If he is inquiring into whether smoking causes cancer, he wants to end up believing that cigarette smoking causes cancer if cigarette smoking causes cancer, and that it doesn't if it doesn't.
>
> (M:9)

And if the situation is more complicated than that, the inquirer wants to know that too (EM:29).

Well aware that inquiry is not always conducted with this in mind, Haack distinguishes two types of pseudo inquiry: sham reasoning, which she takes from Peirce, and fake reasoning. In *sham reasoning*, the inquirer does not seek to discover how things truly are, no matter where the search will lead him, but seeks to support a proposition he is already deeply committed to, and that is nonnegotiable. The sham reasoner can be a creationist who seeks to square empirical findings with a literal interpretation of the book of Genesis, or a molecular biologist who is guided by the expectations of the commercial interests that fund her research. The characteristic feature of sham reasoning is, Haack explains, the professed inquirer's *"prior and unbudgeable commitment* to the proposition for which he tries to make a case" (M:8f).

Fake reasoning goes even further. The *fake reasoner* is driven neither by a genuine desire for truth nor by a desire to show that certain cherished beliefs are true, but he is indifferent to truth. The fake reasoner is driven by other considerations, such as a wish for promotion, money, fame, or even notoriety. As Haack observes, "In some areas of contemporary academic life a clever defense of a startlingly false or impressively obscure idea can be a good route to reputation and advancement" (M:9). What Peirce dismissively called "studying in a literary spirit" also falls under this second type. The aim is not to find or to convey true answers, but to write something that is clever and artistically pleasing.

But why should one not be a sham or fake reasoner? Why is intellectual integrity important? Certain pragmatists, and others too, have argued that inquiry should be subservient to our needs; that one should not care too much about such abstract and grandiose notions as "truth" and "getting it right." Haack's answer is a pragmatic one:

> There is instrumental value in intellectual integrity, because in the long run and on the whole it advances inquiry, and successful inquiry is, by and large, instrumentally valuable.

Compared with other animals, we humans are not especially fleet or strong; our forte is a capacity to figure things out, and hence to anticipate and avoid danger.

(M:13)

This is not to say that our capacity for figuring things out is infallible, nor that in certain circumstances believing a falsehood may not be more advantageous. Nonetheless, over-belief (believing more than is warranted by one's evidence), and under-belief (not believing when one's evidence warrants belief), are things for which one might be held morally culpable, as would be the case with the ship owner in Clifford's example (M:14; also 3.2).

13.4 Justification and Truth

In addition to the question of what counts as strong evidence for a belief (the project of explication), Haack addresses the relationship between a belief being justified and it being true (the project of ratification). As we saw, for Haack, the genuine inquirer wants to know the answer to the questions he asks. The goal of inquiry "is substantial, significant, illuminating truth" (EI:203). Hence, in the search for criteria of good justification, we focus specifically on those that increase the likelihood that justified beliefs are true.

The notion of truth that Haack has in mind conforms to Aristotle's insight that to say of what is that it is, or of what is not that it is not, is true,[3] and to Peirce's insight that whether a claim is true is wholly independent of what you or I or anyone in particular may think about it. To say that a certain proposition is true must thus not be identified with the claim that people are justified in believing it, but with the claim that things really are as the proposition says they are. As we already saw with Putnam, these are not the same. There are truths that never become justified beliefs, and there are situations where one is justified having beliefs that are not true. The young child playing by itself in the park is better off believing, wrongly, that all toadstools are poisonous than believing, rightly, that some of them taste really good. The question then becomes whether there is any relationship between a belief being justified and that same belief being true, and if so, what that relationship is and under what circumstances we are entitled to say that certain justified beliefs are true.

There are those, like Rorty, who deny that there is such a relation, arguing that having justified beliefs is the highest we can ever aspire to. Calling a justified belief true does not really add anything, Rorty notes, as we can talk about truth only in terms of the justification of beliefs. From this, he draws the conclusion that to call a justified belief true is merely to give it a rhetorical pat on the back by ascribing to it a character that, though void, is of noble ancestry—much like an atheist calling a superb bottle of wine "divine."

As Haack sees it, the problem is that many critics of the project of ratification, and this includes Rorty, set their standards for truth too high and then complain that truth is unattainable or that the entire notion of truth is misconceived. Haack, for her part, denies that we can do without truth, observing that even those who explicitly reject truth cannot avoid making implicit appeals to it. (Recall that Putnam made similar observations.)

Haack's own approach to truth is a modest one. She seeks not to prove that some of our beliefs must be true, as the foundationalist does, but merely to give "reasons for thinking that, if any truth-indication is possible for us, the foundherentist criteria are truth-indicative" (EI:205). In broad outline, her argument is Peircean. She argues that within inquiry, we can only proceed in the hope that there is a true answer to the questions we ask; that is, we can only proceed in the hope that theories that are well supported are truth-indicative.

The question that remains is this: assuming it is possible to find truths, what makes evidence, as the foundherentist explains it, truth-indicative? Haack's answer is in part an empirical one. Relativists, neopragmatists, conventionalists, postmodernists, etc., all have made much ado about what they consider evidence for a plurality of standards of evidence. People at different times and in different cultures or subcultures, they say, count different things as evidence. A physician and an astrologer, for instance, use very dissimilar facts to explain someone's chronic fatigue—the presence of certain microscopic organisms in a blood culture for the first, and the constellation of the planets in relation to the subject's birth for the second. Their reliance on evidence so divergent is then taken to imply that they must also maintain very different standards of evidence. Not so, says Haack. It is not that their *standards* of evidence are different; rather, their background beliefs diverge so much that they disagree on what to accept as evidence. However, when defending their respective views, the physician and the astrologer engage in parallel explanations about observations, causal connections, commonsense intuitions, logical relations, analogous cases, etc., revealing that deep down, they maintain the same type of standards about what counts as evidence and why. Briefly put, the wide variety of ways in which groups of people defend their views reflects differences in background beliefs more than differences in standards of evidence.[4]

Instead of making her own culture the benchmark for good evidence, as Rorty does, Haack makes human nature the benchmark of good evidence, siding rather with philosophical anthropologists such as Arnold Gehlen (10.5). As she phrases it herself,

> I would not say that "all men by nature desire to know," in the sense Aristotle intended; but a disposition to investigate, to inquire, to try to

figure things out, *is* part of our makeup, though not, for many people, an overriding part.

(EI:215)

For Haack, inquiry is a distinctly *human* affair, not a distinctly Western-European affair or a distinctly white-males-in-lab-coats affair. Concern for experiential anchoring and explanatory integration is part of our being, and not, as she puts it, "a local quirk of 'our' criteria of evidence, in any parochial sense of 'our'" (EI:209). More concisely, dismissing Rorty's ethnocentric approach, Haack advocates, like Peirce, for an anthropocentric epistemology:

> I see these standards—essentially, how well a belief is anchored in experience and how tightly it is woven into an explanatory mesh of beliefs—as rooted in human nature, in the cognitive capacities and limitations of all normal human beings.[5]

Foundherentism fits this bill. Regarding its truth-indicativeness, all it requires is that "our senses give us information about events around us and that introspection gives us information about our own mental goings-on" (EI:213). If we accept Haack's fallibilism (that we can be mistaken about anything, but not about everything), we cannot but assume this to be true whenever we engage in inquiry. Were we to believe that neither our senses nor introspection would yield us any information—assuming we could even make sense of such an assumption—inquiry as we know it would be utterly pointless. And any theory that takes such a position puts itself, to repeat Lewis's phrase, "beyond the pale of plausibility."

13.5 Against Vulgar Pragmatism

What Haack calls "vulgar pragmatism" is a particularly vocal branch of pragmatism that has received a wide following, especially among non-philosophers. The vulgar pragmatists, for whom Haack considers Rorty the main spokesperson, maintain that the justification of our beliefs has nothing to do with truth—a view that they seek to give extra weight by explicitly allying themselves with the classical pragmatists, most specifically James and Dewey (although they seem closer to Schiller and the magical pragmatists Papini and Prezzolini). It is a *vulgar* pragmatism because of its appeal to the common people, as opposed to philosophy professors, its preference for the vernacular, as opposed to philosophy's (and logic's) technical jargon, and its consequent lack of cultivation (it tills the soil only lightly) and lack of refinement (there is little interest in precision and exactness). Put briefly, the vulgar pragmatists stress the common association of pragmatism with expedience rather than with principle. Note that it is precisely this association of pragmatism with expediency that made Peirce shy away from the word and that clouded the early European reception of pragmatism.

Haack argues that the conversationalist turn that Rorty set in motion is the product of a misreading of the classical pragmatists; a misreading that is made possible by raising what may justifiably be called a false dichotomy: either accept a mirror-like correspondence view, or else a nonrepresentational conversationalism. On the latter view, inquiry no longer aims at discovering how things really are, but at ensuring that the conversation continues, preferably in new and exciting venues.

This dichotomy is surely problematic. It leaves no room, for instance, for Dewey's "more sophisticated" correspondence theory (8.5), for Mead's institutional approach to knowledge (7.5), or for Haack's foundherentism. One must either accept a rather simplistic copy theory of knowledge or give up altogether on the project of ratification. Either our knowledge mirrors reality, or there can be no standards of evidence other than the approval of our peers. Who these peers are is always historically determined, and in the absence of independent standards, we have no other option but to treat all of them as equal. We have no ground to separate the inquirers from the inquisitors, or the lone voice of reason from the angry mob. What counts is the approval of the strongest, of those who are socially and politically best situated to carry forward the conversation to which we are contributing. Eloquence trumps truth.

Once the dichotomy is drawn like this, pragmatism, which really belongs somewhere in the middle, easily tips toward conversationalism. Consequently, some pragmatists side with Rorty in rejecting Haack's project of ratification, arguing that all there is to the justification of belief is the approval of our peers, of people whom *we* believe are competent to judge our beliefs. If such conversationalism is granted, ethnocentricity is hard if not impossible to avoid. None of this is to deny the psychological temptation of ethnocentricity or of seeking refuge within epistemic bubbles where one can float peacefully on the pleasant hum of like-mindedness.

Haack dismisses this approach as disingenuous and cynical because the aim of inquiry is no longer guided by a genuine desire to have one's questions answered, but to find answers that will be approved by one's peers. Justification becomes a matter of convention. It's like paper money: I accept your dollar bills because you accept mine, and vice versa; and it is this and nothing else that gives them value. For the vulgar pragmatists, beliefs are justified this way. The justification of belief, like the value of paper money, is a social institution propped up by convention. It is entirely a product of our choices, not something dictated by things over which we have at best only limited control. The vulgar pragmatist's approach is cynical because the inquirer inquires *knowing* that the questions she asks cannot be answered, but that only, and in lieu of it, some agreement can be reached on what to say in response to them.

One way to look at this is by noting that Haack seeks to wedge a more reasonable option between two more extreme views that have become fashionable. The first, which she calls old deferentialism, is the view that is found among many logical positivists and the scientistically inclined. The focus is on "the logic of science," rationality, objectivity. It includes Putnam's metaphysical realists. The second view, which she calls new cynicism, which is found among the vulgar pragmatists, focuses on very different aspects, such as power, politics, and rhetoric. Whereas old deferentialists revere science, new cynics are deeply suspicious of it. To them, all this talk about objectivity and scientific method is only a disguise for a policy of exclusion. For instance, in *Rethinking History*, Keith Jenkins writes, "History is a discourse, a language game; within it 'truth' and similar expressions are devices to open, regulate and shut down interpretations. Such truths are really 'useful fictions' that are in discourse by virtue of power."[6] For people such as Jenkins, there are no objective standards, only power games.

In *Defending Science, within Reason*, Haack further develops her outlook into a philosophy of science that is grounded in the practice of inquiry rather than in its products or the methods used. Albeit well aware of deferential attitudes toward science, she there directs most of her critique against the new cynics—those who conclude from the fallibility of science that scientific knowledge is impossible and reduces to (male-dominated) politics and power. In *Scientism and Its Discontents* and "Six Signs of Scientism," she addresses the other side—those who take "a kind of over-enthusiastic and uncritically deferential attitude towards science, an inability to see or an unwillingness to acknowledge its fallibility, its limitations, and its potential dangers."[7] Besides a propensity to use the term "science" as a badge of honor, Haack identifies the following indicators for scientism:[8] a focus on scientific vocabulary, numerical precision, and mathematical expression even when it does not contribute; a fixation on questions of demarcation so that we can distinguish genuine science (the real thing) from pseudoscience; a focus on the scientific method when explaining why the sciences are so successful; and a tendency to hold that all true questions can be solved by science, which leads to an accompanying denigration of all other ways in which we may try to understand the world. Such scienticists seem to ignore the existence of bad science and that non-scientific ways of knowing can be more valuable than scientific ones, for instance when studying such topics as Renaissance music, causes of mental anxiety, or the consequences of displacement in urban development. In fact, it can be said that scienticists exemplify precisely the sort of narrow, calculating rationality that we encountered before and from which pragmatists, as well as many others, tried to distance themselves.

For Haack, Peirce's critical common-sensism provides a *via media* between deferentialism (old and new) and new cynicism. Like the deferentialist, the critical common-sensist maintains that there are objective standards of better and worse evidence and of better and worse conducted inquiry. However, as the preceding account of Haack's views testifies, it sees those standards as more flexible and less formal than the deferentialist does, and she rejects a sharp separation of science from our other epistemic enterprises. Simultaneously, critical common-sensism meets halfway the concerns of the cynics by acknowledging that science is a human enterprise within which inquirers have all sorts of motivations and in which observation is always already theory (and thereby value) laden. However, in contrast to the cynics, the critical common-sensist does not see these aspects of inquiry as an impediment to the process of understanding how things truly are. Quite the contrary, the social nature of inquiry and the stubbornness of the world of facts tend to filter out personal idiosyncrasies and group biases. Hence, for Haack, pragmatists should be common-sensists who are driven by the will to learn while remaining keenly aware of their fallibility.

Notes

1. For the expanded edition of *Evidence and Inquiry* (Amherst, 2009), Haack changed the subtitle from *Towards Reconstruction in Epistemology* to *A Pragmatist Reconstruction of Epistemology*.
2. Peirce, CP7.49, 1.44; cited in M:49.
3. *Metaphysics* 1011b25.
4. In *Defending Science*, Haack details foundherentism by looking at the evidence that led to the discovery of the double-helix model of DNA (DS:77–82).
5. Susan Haack, "A Foundherentist Theory of Justification," in Ernest Sosa and Jaegwon Kim (eds), *Epistemology: An Anthology* (Oxford, 2000), p.233.
6. Keith Jenkins, *Re-thinking History* (London, 1991), p.32.
7. Haack (2009), p.40.
8. Ibid., p.41.

Chapter 14

Legal Pragmatism

Historically, there exists a close link between pragmatism and the law, as four of the Metaphysical Club members are lawyers: Oliver Wendell Holmes Jr., Nicholas St. Johns Green, John Fiske, and Joseph B. Warner. It is Green who introduces the club to Bain's definition of belief, as "that upon which a man is prepared to act." As we saw in Chapter 1, this definition contains the seed of pragmatism. Moreover, like Peirce and James, Holmes, Green, and Fiske are deeply influenced by the idea of evolution. Fiske becomes a central player in the popularization of Darwin in the US, and both Holmes and Green develop theories that depict the law as a historically grown human-made instrument for adjudicating conflicting desires among people who are essentially engaged in a struggle for existence. In doing so, Holmes and Green reject traditional views of the law where the laws we create derive their authority either from reason itself, or from divine or natural law. For Holmes and Green, there is no such authority.

In this chapter, we look at a number of pragmatic contributions to legal theory, ranging from Green and Holmes to Richard Posner and Susan Haack.

14.1 Green's Pragmatic Reading of Causation

Peirce calls Nicholas St. Johns Green (1830–76) the grandfather of pragmatism (CP5.12). He especially appreciates Green's attempts to cure the legal profession of its propensity to make, as Peirce puts it, "the decisions of living men's real rights and interests . . . hang upon the emptiest scholastic distinctions."[1] This includes the distinction between proximate and remote causes with which Francis Bacon had opened his 1636 *Rules and Maximes of the Common Lawes of England*. Green's criticism of the distinction provides a good example of how pragmatism can be set to work.

As Green points out, the distinction between proximate and remote causes goes back to Aristotle's distinction between knowing *that* a thing is and knowing *why* it is. For Aristotle, knowing *why* something is comes down to knowing what caused it, as he put it, "τὸ πρῶτον αἴτον."[2] The schoolmen subsequently translated this Greek phrase into Latin as *causa proxima*, or proximate cause (PRC:4). Aiming to put the legal practice on an empirical, scientific footing, Bacon demanded that in law too, one should look for the proximate cause. By this Bacon meant that when asking for the cause of an event, courts should only go back *one* link in the chain of causation and settle on the event that immediately preceded the result.[3] By the middle of the nineteenth century, Bacon's rule was giving way to one that was inspired by Newtonian mechanics. On this view, the proximate cause refers to the *first* clearly identifiable event that set into motion the chain of events that culminated in the end result. To give a crude example, if a watchman on a ship nods off and the ship runs on a sandbar, the cause of the ship's damage is, on Bacon's rule, the ship running aground, as that was the last thing that happened, whereas for the Newtonians it would be the watchman nodding off. The notion of proximate cause, however, is the same for both. As Green formulates the distinction between proximate and remote causes,

> A proximate cause is one in which is involved the idea of necessity. It is one the connection between which and the effect is plain and intelligible; it is one which can be used as a term by which a proposition can be demonstrated, that is, one which can be reasoned from conclusively . . . A remote cause is one which is inconclusive in reasoning, because from it no certain conclusion can be legitimately drawn. In other words, a remote cause is a cause the connection between which and the effect is uncertain, vague, or indeterminate.
>
> (PRC:4)

Hence, the distinction between proximate and remote causes has "nothing to do with their relative distance from the effect either in space or time" (PRC:5)—it is rather that the former provides certitude, whereas the latter doesn't. This means that the proximate cause could be understood, as the Newtonians did, as "the last cause, looking backward from the effect, from which the effect . . . necessarily follows" (ibid). In fact, we can say that, compared to Bacon, the Newtonians were simply more optimistic about their ability to at least partially traverse back the causal chain without compromising the certitude that allows them to still call it a proximate cause. It is precisely this underlying notion of a singular causal chain, however, that Green considers problematic:

> It raises in the mind an idea of one determinate cause, followed by another determinate cause, created by the first, and that followed by a third, created by the second, and so on, one succeeding another till the effect is reached.
>
> (PRC:11)

As Green observes, "There is nothing in nature which corresponds to this. Such an idea is a pure fabrication of the mind" (ibid). In its stead, Green argues that "there is but one view of causation which can be of practical service":

> To every event there are certain antecedents, never a single antecedent, but always a set of antecedents, which being given the effect is sure to follow, unless some new thing intervenes to frustrate such result. It is not any one of this set of antecedents taken by itself which is the cause. No one by itself would produce the effect. The true cause is the whole set of antecedents together . . . But when a cause is to be investigated for any practical purpose, the antecedent which is in the scope of that purpose is singled out and called the cause, to the neglect of the antecedents which are of no importance to the matter in hand.
>
> (PRC:11f)

The proper metaphor is thus not a chain, but a net: effects and their causes are "mutually interwoven . . . as the meshes of a net are interwoven" (PRC:13). Earlier we saw Peirce make a similar distinction between rope and chain reasoning (6.4), a view that is further developed by Haack in her crossword analogy (13.2). Moreover, Green continues, what we take from this and identify as a cause or an effect is relative to the purpose of the inquiry, which in law is "to determine the rights and liabilities of the respective parties to the proceedings" (PRC:14). For instance, in insurance law, we can say that a loss counts as "a proximate consequence of a peril insured against [when] the parties intended that such a loss should be covered by the policy" (PRC:15). However, when a homeowner is said to have been negligent, say, because he stored open bottles of gasoline near an open flame, its proximate cause would be "those results which a prudent foresight might have avoided" (PRC:16) rather than anything explicitly stated in the insurance policy. Moreover, when we look more closely at those contracts and insurance policies themselves, we will see that they too are guided, in their construction, by prudent foresight regarding their desired and undesired implications. More generally, we can therefore say that "the law makes us responsible for those effects of voluntary acts which might reasonably have been foreseen" (PRC:16). Consequently, Green argues,

> The use of [Bacon's] maxim is liable to lead to error by withdrawing the attention from the true subject of inquiry. We cannot add clearness to our reasoning by talking about proximate and remote causes and effects, when we mean only the degree of certainty or uncertainty with which the connection between cause and effect might have been anticipated.
>
> (PRC:16f)

Hence, rather than require that the law focus on those causes where the connection with the event in question is plain and intelligible, as Bacon did—even invoking concepts like necessity and certainty—we should require that the law focus on what someone ought to have foreseen as a consequence of their action. This is, of course, very much in the spirit of Peirce's pragmatic maxim, which more generally connects the meaning of our terms with their conceivable practical consequences.

14.2 Oliver Wendell Holmes on Legal Liability

From the lawyers that join the Metaphysical Club, Oliver Wendell Holmes Jr. (1841–1935) becomes most prolific. Like Green, Holmes aims to ground the law in the actual dealings of man. About a decade after his first involvement in the club, Holmes publishes *The Common Law*, in which he seeks to present "a general view of the common law" (CL:1).[4] In it Holmes criticizes the idea that the law can be treated like mathematics—that is, as a logical system grounded in self-evident truths, a view also known as formalism. As Holmes points out, "the life of the law has not been logic: it has been experience" (CL:1). Part of what prompts his criticism is a rejection of the Cartesian notion of clear and distinct ideas, a criticism that partly parallels Peirce's. Descartes maintained that when we clearly and distinctly perceive an idea—whether through the senses or by introspection—that idea must be true.[5] On this view, a clear intuition that something is good or just constitutes *sufficient* proof that it is so. This Cartesian view inspired the legal notion "*conviction intime*"—a notion that became popular in the French Revolution to counter the stiff scholasticism that had come to dominate legal proceedings. On this view, the (subjective) internal conviction of the judge forms the ground for conviction in criminal cases. In attacking this idea of a private grounding of belief, Holmes follows Peirce, but he does so only partially. Whereas Peirce's criticism of Descartes applies to all we can possibly think of, Holmes applies it to the law (a person's *legal* liability), which he takes to fall within the public, objective domain, but not to morality (a person's *moral* culpability), which he still places within the private, subjective domain, albeit without giving us much of an argument for why that would be so.

Holmes takes the view that *legal* liability—i.e., whether one can be held legally accountable—is public and objective on the ground that it is something that can be assigned only by rules that are shared by members of a community. With Cartesianism firmly rejected, we can no longer give a private or *internalist* justification for legal liability—that is, a justification based on our intuitions, including our intuitions about morality, logic, and self-evidence. The reason for this is that if having clear and distinct ideas cannot be considered a sign of truth, then any internal justification will be unable to break out of the private subjective domain. Consequently, Holmes points out, we need a fully *externalist* justification for legal liability, and this he sets out to develop in *The Common Law*.

Holmes begins by observing that when we say that a person acted maliciously, we typically mean that he acted intentionally while wishing to cause harm, or suffering, for its own sake. In other words, we do not call an act malicious when the harm or suffering is a byproduct of some *other* goal that was the true intent of the act. For instance, we do not call a physician malicious for vaccinating a child, because the child's suffering was not the intent of the act. For the purpose of the law, however, this second aspect (wishing to cause harm or suffering for its own sake) is irrelevant. As Holmes puts it, "It is just as much murder to shoot a sentry for the purpose of releasing a friend, as to shoot him because you hate him" (CL:53). This leaves us only with the intent of the act. Regarding this intent, we can further distinguish between the *foresight* that certain consequences will follow and the *desire* that these consequences occur. Again, Holmes observes that the second aspect is not relevant to his purpose, and he gives the following example to support it:

> a newly born child is laid naked out of doors, where it must perish as a matter of course. This is none the less murder, that the guilty party would have been very glad to have a stranger find the child and save it.
>
> (CL:30)

Hence, all that is relevant in legally adjudicating a malicious act is that the act was intentional, by which is meant that it was done with the foresight that certain consequences would follow or were likely to follow. With respect to this foresight, we can further distinguish between what the actor actually foresaw and what "a man of reasonable prudence would have foreseen" (CL:54). What matters for the law, Holmes argues, is the latter, not the former:

> If the known present state of things is such that the act done will very certainly cause death, and the probability is a matter of common knowledge, one who does the act, knowing the present state of things, is guilty of murder, and the law will not inquire whether he did actually foresee the consequences or not.
>
> (CL:53f)

In brief, what determines legal guilt is something public, not something private. It is whether the act is such that a "man of reasonable prudence" would have foreseen that it would have certain consequences (such as injury, death, etc.) that one can be held legally accountable for and for which the law provides a certain punitive response (like a fine or jail time). Again, the affinity with the pragmatic maxim is clear.

Holmes's approach raises at least two new questions: What is "the law"? And how should we interpret this "man of reasonable prudence"? First, what is the law? As with Peirce's theory of inquiry, Holmes's starting point is not some idealized beginning, but the actual situation he encounters. For Holmes, the law reveals itself as a historical artifact that is actively being used and is continuously modified in light of current needs and demands. When later reminiscing on his early studies, he confesses that "the law presented itself as a ragbag of details"—the product of centuries of push and pull that he found so far removed from a neat, logical system that he even doubted "whether the subject was worthy of the interest of an intelligent man."[6] These early struggles lead him to the view with which he opens *The Common Law*: the law "embodies the story of a nation's development through many centuries" (CL:1); it is a set of opinions, or rules, derived from custom and historical precedent. Consequently, Holmes continues, to know what the law is, "we must know what it has been, and what it tends to become" (ibid).

Because of the law's historical nature, two very different aspects come into play when it is exercised: the demands set upon it, and the mechanisms it provides to meet those demands. As Holmes puts it,

> The substance of the law at any given time pretty nearly corresponds, so far as it goes, with what is then understood to be convenient; but its form and machinery, and the degree to which it is able to work out desired results, depend very much upon its past.
>
> (CL:1f)

The former, oblique as it often is, Holmes considers the lifeblood of the law:

> The very considerations which judges most rarely mention, and always with an apology, are the secret root from which the law draws all the juices of life. I mean, of course, considerations of what is expedient for the community concerned.
>
> (CL:35)

To adjudicate between these two aspects of the law requires practical knowledge or life experience. Moreover, since Holmes has argued that we cannot rely on our private sense of truth and justice, our views must be subjected to the community, exposing them to critical evaluation by others. Briefly put, the exercise of the law is a *communal* affair that requires *practical* rather than theoretical knowledge. This practical and communal element is most visible in the role of the jury. For Holmes, the jury embodies the community as a group of individuals who test their interpretation of the facts, and of the defendant's liability—a view close to Peirce's notion of scientific inquiry. Their function is to determine "what are the teachings of experience" regarding the liability resulting from this or that conduct (or the absence thereof) under these or those circumstances, and in situations where there are no existing standards in place to serve as a precedent—or where the standards are unclear or outdated—to set a (new) standard that defines the conduct as justifying a certain legal response (CL:134ff). In Holmes's view, the agreement reached by a group of citizens is more likely than the opinion of a singular judge "to correspond with the actual feelings and demands of the community, whether right or wrong" (CL:40). And this is the most that can be asked for given the strictures of time put upon legal proceedings.

It is thus in the practice of law that the law progresses. It progresses through the adjudication that is called for when existing laws face new situations by "able and experienced men, who know too much to sacrifice good sense to a syllogism" (CL:36). In this process, which is marked by a constant tendency to transcend private moral judgments and reach external standards, the law tends toward becoming consistent—a tendency which, like Peirce's views on the progress in science, goes in leaps and bounds, often moving forward but at times sliding back. Whereas science aims at truth, the law, Holmes explains, aims for consistency:

> The truth is, that the law [is] always approaching, and never reaching, consistency. It is forever adopting new principles from life at one end, and it always retains old ones from history at the other, which have not yet been absorbed or sloughed off. It will become entirely consistent only when it ceases to grow.
>
> (CL:36)

To Holmes, this consistency is crucial, as above all, the law should be predictable. When one is held liable in the eyes of the law, Holmes keenly observes, one confronts "the whole power of the State" (PL:457). Consequently, it is important that citizens can predict how the law is likely to respond to their actions; especially since they cannot rely on their internal sense of what is good and just. In his 1897 "The Path of the Law," Holmes even goes as far as to write, "the prophesies of what courts will do in fact, and nothing more pretentious, is what I mean by the law" (PL:461). On this view, a legal duty "is nothing but a prediction that if a man does or omits certain things he will be made to suffer in this or that way by judgment of the court" (PL:458). This is often called the prediction theory of law. From this it follows that the best way of discovering what the law means is to read it like a bad person would—as someone who cares nothing about morality, as doing so will only distract and distort:

> If you want to know the law and nothing else, you must look at it as a bad man, who cares only for the material consequences which such knowledge enables him to predict, not as a good one, who finds his

reasons for conduct, whether inside the law or outside of it, in the vaguer sanctions of conscience.

(PI:459)

Like morally conscientious people, the bad man wants "to avoid being made to pay money and will want to keep out of jail if he can" (ibid). Hence, all that needs considered is what is captured by the pragmatic maxim: "what effects, which might conceivably have practical bearings, we conceive [the law] to have."

14.3 Legal Pragmatism in the Twentieth Century

So far, the discussion has focused mostly on common law. Common law refers to the law as it emerges from judicial decisions in courts, which are then considered a precedent for how similar cases are to be decided in the future. Past decisions thus become prescriptive, or regulative, for future decisions. In addition to this, there is statutory law. Statutory law finds its origin in formal written enactments of a legislative authority, such as the state or municipality. Statutory laws typically also lead to judicial decisions in courts, as statutes can be vague, overly general, or ambiguous, or contain gaps. Past judicial decisions regarding existing statutes thus also become prescriptive.

The importance given to precedent, paired with an inflated sense of the rationality and the good will of previous judges and legislators, has led to a mode of legal interpretation called formalism. On this view, legislative statutes and previous court decisions are considered uncontestable facts, and the adjudication of new cases is primarily an issue of identifying previous cases that resemble them, after which the decision becomes a simple modus ponens:

"If p, then q" (the prescription);
The current case is very much like p;
Hence, now too we must rule q.

In relying exclusively on deductive logic, which is ultimately tautological, we can be assured that the judge does not add anything that would cause him to stray from precedent or introduce rulings that are inconsistent.

Formalism finds its origin in another Harvard lawyer, Christopher Columbus Langdell (1826–1906), who begins teaching at Harvard Law School the same year as Green (they are even roommates for a while). Holmes vehemently rejects Langdell's approach to the law. "He represents the powers of darkness," Holmes writes rather ominously, "he is all for logic and hates any reference to anything outside of it."[7] An area in American law where formalism reigns supreme is constitutional law. The Constitution is considered a given, even sacred, and determining whether a statute violates the Constitution ideally comes down to an exercise in deductive logic with the purpose of determining whether the statute contradicts the constitution.

Broadly speaking, twentieth-century American legal pragmatism developed largely in response to formalism. Earlier in the century it affiliated itself with a movement called legal realism, which holds that jurisprudence should emulate scientific inquiry, thereby making law the empirical affair that Holmes and Green wanted it to become.[8] In contrast to the formalists, legal pragmatists emphasize the importance of context (both legal and non-legal), which brings in the empirical. This extends to even the most basic legal concepts. Far from being necessary or eternal, they too must be considered products of contingent and context-specific needs, and prone to evolve. Any extension beyond the specific needs that brought them into being may not be taken for granted but needs to be argued for. Consequently, the law is not grounded on some necessary foundation about which we can attain indubitable insight, but rather resembles Neurath's ship:

> We are like sailors who on the open sea must reconstruct their ship but are never able to start afresh from the bottom. Where a beam is taken away a new one must at once be put there, and for this the rest of the ship is used as support. In this way, by using the old beams and driftwood the ship can be shaped entirely anew, but only by gradual reconstruction.[9]

Legal pragmatists maintain further that the law must be looked upon as an instrument for resolving current and future conflicts. If the law is interpreted this way—especially when context is considered relevant and there are no fixed foundations—precedent comes to play a very different role. For the formalists, precedent can develop into a solid foundation in the form of black letter law (legal rules so well established that they are no longer subject to reasonable dispute). Legal pragmatists dispute this, not only because it ignores non-legal changes in society that may require a different ruling *even* where cases are legally the same (as with same-sex marriage), but also because of their commitment to fallibilism. This notwithstanding, precedent continues to be valuable as a guide for determining what to do in a current case. Moreover, a tendency to favor precedent furthers the consistency and predictability of the law—two aspects that, for pragmatists, are important because of a concern for the future rather than a reliance on the past. Finally, legal pragmatists reject the notion of a God's-eye view, favoring instead a perspective-based approach. Such a perspective-based approach entails the existence of multiple, possibly conflicting perspectives that need to be negotiated between, something we encountered earlier in Mead (7.7).

14.4 Dewey on Judicial Practice

Dewey discusses the law in his 1924 "Logical Method and Law" (ED1:355–62; MW15:65–77) and returns to it quite extensively in his 1938 *Logic: The Theory of Inquiry* (LW12:370ff).[10] Dewey's focus is specifically on the tension between formalism and empiricism (or realism). In fact, he sees the law as a good illustration of his theory of inquiry, as it seeks to extract general rules from practical, indeterminate situations using reasoning and logic.[11]

In his 1924 paper, Dewey seeks to show how objective legal judgments are possible. Key to his approach is the notion of the long run, which is revealed in Dewey's insistence that "the question of method to be used in judging existing customs and policies proposed is of greater moral significance than the particular conclusion reached in connection with any one controversy" (LW7:338). Moreover, as we saw, for Dewey, logic evolves over time. It is a living affair, an evolving logic of experience, which is very different from the formalists' reliance on well-worn syllogisms.

That we cannot have any timeless standards does not mean that we cannot have any standards at all, or that all standards dissolve in subjectivity. What is crucial for Dewey, as it had been for Peirce, is that inquiry is self-corrective; something that is possible in part because its results can be publicly evaluated. In short, inquiry entails that we learn from our mistakes. This means that precedents can and at times even must be overturned. More generally, for Dewey, the focus should be on *methods* of adjudication rather than the *outcomes* of past cases. What we want to ensure is that they were "the best that could have been used" given the conditions in question (ED2:156).

All of this means taking change seriously. If formal consistency with previous decisions is the driving force, then an increasing variety of cases will be treated the same. As a result, the law as a whole becomes less and less connected to the concrete situations it is supposed to govern. Dewey argues that we should instead acknowledge that in the process of adjudication, "a kind of natural selection" is taking place—a selection that occurs naturally (that is, not by conscious design) simply because some methods are found to work better than others (MW15:67). At this point, Dewey draws a comparison with language where there is the same need for consistency through change (MW15:68). Language too develops naturally. It self-adjusts in the face of changing conditions in ways that we are often barely aware of, but with precedence, consistency, and predictability all playing a role. And for both law and language, there is no preordained goal. What counts is that they continue to fulfill their purpose. For language, this is communication; for law, it is the adjudication of liability. Moreover, none of this precludes our understanding of either, makes our employment of them any less objective, or makes our reliance on it unreasonable.

In Dewey's view, what drives the non-pragmatist, especially the formalist, is the desire for a legal system in which our decisions are guaranteed to be correct, that any system that fails to provide this is ipso facto deficient, and that this deficiency can and must be rectified. For Dewey, this "quest for certainty" rests on a "confusion of *theoretical* certainty with *practical* certainty" (ED2:360). As he explains,

> There is a wide gap separating the reasonable proposition that judicial decisions should possess the maximum possible regularity in order to enable persons in planning their conduct to foresee the legal import of their acts, and the absurd because impossible proposition that every decision should flow with formal logical necessity from antecedently known premises.
>
> (ED2:360)

For Dewey, the latter kind of certainty is not only humanly unattainable, it also misconstrues the role played by facts and legal precedents. They do not *precede* the adjudication of a case, as if they were independent things to be discovered like shells on a beach; rather, they are *products* of the legal process that leads up to the decision. "The problem," Dewey writes, "is not to draw a conclusion from given premises . . . The problem is to *find* statements, of general principles and of particular fact, which are worthy to serve as premises" (ED2:359). The last phrase, "*worthy* to serve as premises," is of central importance, as the following analysis of the reasoning of a defense attorney shows:

> No lawyer ever thought out the case of a client in terms of the syllogism. He begins with a conclusion which he intends to reach, favorable to his client of course, and then analyzes the facts of the situation to find material out of which to construct a favorable statement of facts, to *form* a minor premiss. At the same time he goes over recorded cases to find rules of law employed in cases which can be presented as similar, rules which will substantiate a certain way of looking at and interpreting the facts. And as his acquaintance with rules of law judged applicable widens, he probably alters perspective and emphasis in selection of the facts which are to form his evidential data. And as he learns more of the facts of the case, he may modify his selection of rules of law upon which he bases his case.
>
> (ED2:359)

The prosecutor, from her perspective, does the same. For Dewey, the important point in all of this is that premises are *formed*, not found. This means that any account of legal reasoning must include this part, and this effectively nullifies the utility of syllogistic logic.

With the "absurd" demand for theoretical certainty rejected, Dewey continues by arguing that we should aim for *practical* certainty. By this he means "the really important issue of finding and employing rules of law, substantive and procedural, which will actually secure to the members of the community a reasonable measure of practical certainty of expectation in framing their course of conduct" (ED2:360). Moreover, rather than increasing our sense of certainty, Dewey keenly notes that the formalist's insistence on precedent is more likely to have the exact opposite effect: it becomes "a gamble which old rule will be declared regulative of a particular case" (ibid).

14.5 The Legal Pragmatism of Richard Posner

Perhaps the most prominent late-twentieth-century legal pragmatist is Richard Posner (b. 1939), who, like Holmes, spends most of his career as a judge. Posner too is no formalist. When retiring from the bench, he provocatively tells the *New York Times*: "I pay very little attention to legal rules, statutes, constitutional provisions . . . A case is just a dispute. The first thing you do is ask yourself—forget about the law—what is a sensible resolution of this dispute?"[12] At face value this sounds very much like Dewey. However, as we shall see, it lacks the situatedness that we find with Dewey. Unsurprisingly, Posner's views have been fiercely criticized by both pragmatists and their opponents.

Posner expresses the same point two decades earlier, when he presents the following definition of pragmatic adjudication: "a pragmatist judge always tries to do the best he can do for the present and the future, unchecked by any felt duty to secure consistency in principle with what other officials have done in the past" (PA:4). By the latter half, he means that legal pragmatists do not "regard the maintenance of consistency with past decisions as an end in itself but only as a means for bringing about the best results in the present case" (PA:5). This effectively implies that we are left only with the first half of his definition: "a pragmatist judge always tries to do the best he can do for the present and the future." For Posner, existing laws and precedents thus enter either as tools or obstacles into the indeterminate situation that the case represents, and which the court is being petitioned to resolve. They do not have any value in and of themselves.

It is important to point out that what Posner has in mind are novel situations, not routine cases for which existing statutes and precedent are still adequate. Though it is not impossible for new cases to be resolved purely by legal means, they often put pressure on the courts to accept non-legal elements and deviate from past decisions in light of them.[13] The problem with this is that such non-legal elements are extremely varied. They include shifts in scientific opinion on bloodstain-pattern analysis; findings that certain crimes are caused by poverty, or blatant and deliberate social inequity; the realization that legal precedents are tainted by racism, including systemic and unconscious racial bias; changing social attitudes toward abortion, euthanasia, gender, and marriage that often trigger a passionate push and pull between social conservatives and progressives; etc. In short, bringing in non-legal aspects puts very different requirements on the judge and the legal proceeding. This is an issue that we return to with Haack. A further complicating factor is that cases that hinge on such issues often arise, and need to be settled, well before an established scientific opinion on those issues is reached. This forces judges to *prejudge* scientific opinion (where scientific is taken in the broad Peircean sense) or social consensus (as with gay marriage).

Now, if the purpose of adjudication is not limited to identifying existing statutes and similar cases—with the rules that emerged through precedent—then the question becomes, what is its purpose? We saw that, for Posner, it is "to do the best [we] can do for the present and the future." In attempting to make this more precise, Posner finds his inspiration in economics. The purpose of adjudication is to maximize wealth—to make everyone collectively as well off as possible.[14] Posner further thinks that a cost-benefit analysis can show us how to make this happen: judges must decide so that it maximizes the ratio of benefits to costs as measured by the prices that all who are effected by the case are willing to pay. Importantly, since the decision sets a precedent, it is not just those who are directly affected by the particular case who must be taken into account; it reaches well beyond that.

This approach has been criticized because it puts an unreasonable burden upon judges. Not only do they have to prejudge scientific opinion and future sentiments; they are also faced with an impossible calculation of the costs and benefits for every way a case can be decided. Posner is well aware of this, and he addresses it as follows:

> When judges try to make the decision that will produce the "best results," without having any body of organized knowledge to turn to for help in making that decision, it seems they must rely on their intuitions.
> (PA:10)

In part Posner is banking here on the traditional notion of wisdom:

> at their best, American appellate courts are councils of wise elders and it is not completely insane to entrust them with responsibility for deciding cases in a way that will produce the best results in the circumstances rather than just deciding cases in accordance with rules created by other organs of government or in accordance with their own previous decisions, although that is what they will be doing most of the time.
> (PA:11f)

Judges, Posner adds, are further kept in check by the requirement that they have to "express as best they can the reasons for their decision in signed, public documents" (ibid).

Two points significantly weaken Posner's solution, as he himself admits. First, society is constantly changing, which is why Posner is allowing non-legal aspects into judicial adjudication to begin with. Now, where the past is no longer a guide to the future, wisdom becomes suspect, as wisdom is very much shaped by the past (PA:15). Second, Posner acknowledges that the US has become an increasingly pluralistic society. In a pluralistic society, judges cannot expect their decisions—or even their reasons for making them—to gain acceptance, let alone be agreed upon, by the majority or even a substantial part of society (PA:13). Moreover, for Posner, there is no independent standard of reasonableness that judges can rely on. In the absence of such a standard, it becomes hard to determine whether the judges' prejudging isn't just prejudicial, even when it receives—returning briefly to Rorty—peer approval. This is particularly pressing when a white judiciary is combined with deep racial inequities, or when a traditionally misogynic male judiciary is being called upon to adjudicate the rights of women.

Posner's focus on the future suggests that he is making pragmatism into a form of consequentialism. On this view, no principle is sacred; everything can or even must be overturned when the consequences warrant it. Critics of this type of legal pragmatism strongly object to what they see as an absolute disregard for the principled integrity of the law. One can, however, rightfully object to *both* Posner and his critics that pragmatism is not result oriented the way consequentialism is. Pragmatism, we saw when discussing the pragmatic maxim, is primarily a restriction on our use of concepts: for concepts not to be meaningless, they must be cast in terms of their conceivable practical consequences. Taking this maxim seriously has far-reaching implications, as it is to be applied to many if not all of our most basic and abstract concepts. This includes, besides philosophical notions like truth and reality, also legal concepts such as justice, fairness, causation, and liability. It may be true that, as James so aptly put it, the human serpent is over all—that when inquiring into anything, we are driven by "what we want," that wherever possible we interpret the world on *our* terms. But that is all very different from Posner's requirement that the judge in his adjudication must satisfy a certain preset teleological standard—that of maximizing collective welfare. In fact, as heirs of the theory of evolution, pragmatists reject the very idea of preset external standards and of a predetermined goal to be reached. We can go back to Dewey and his insistence that biological evolution is a process of adaptation, not the progression to some predetermined endpoint—as if the sole purpose of the tree of life was to bear humankind as its fruit.

To this, Posner responds by stating that his critics confuse his economic theory of law with utilitarianism. The economic theory, he argues, "is a theory of rights as well as of exchange," adding further that those rights "can be derived from the theory itself; they do not have to be postulated."[15] This brings him closer to Peirce and Dewey.

14.6 Haack on Evidence and Inquiry in the Law

I conclude this chapter with some of Susan Haack's contributions to philosophy of law. Well aware that legal proceedings are very different from (scientific) inquiry, Haack seeks to carry her pragmatist epistemic framework into the law, since evidence and inquiry play an important role there as well. As we saw earlier, the purpose of inquiry is to find things out. The purpose of legal cases, however, is different. It is not to *discover* whether a defendant is guilty or liable, but to *determine* whether the defendant is guilty or liable. Here, other considerations come into play. Most prominently, these include an emphasis on precedent and consistency, which has led to rights and obligations that must be upheld irrespective of the particular case at hand. Because of this, rules, laws, or regulations may overrule the process of discovering whether a defendant is guilty or liable. For instance, pertinent information may deliberately be withheld because it was obtained in an unlawful search, or a defendant's refusal to take the stand may not be used as evidence of guilt.[16]

To this we can further add that whereas inquiry is ideally a cooperative venture aimed at the shared result of having one's questions answered, the legal system, especially the American one, is decidedly adversarial. There are two parties, each making their own case, and the outcome is that the judge, or the jury, ends up choosing one side rather than the other, or that the parties end up settling without agreeing. The American sporting attitude that Bourne complained about (8.7) drives the American legal system as well. The dynamics of an adversarial process are very different from those of inquiry. As Haack explains, "inquiry starts with a question and, aiming to arrive at an answer, seeks out evidence; while advocacy, aiming to persuade, starts with a proposition to be defended and marshals the best evidence it can in its favor" (EM:91). That is to say, returning to Peirce, and also to Haack herself, if we were to look upon it purely from the perspective of inquiry, the legal profession would engage in sham reasoning (13.3).

In sum, in legal proceedings, inquiry is governed by different dynamics and constrained by independent legal considerations. More specifically, its aim is to *determine* whether the defendant is *legally* guilty or liable, not to *discover* whether the defendant is *factually* guilty or liable, albeit that considerations regarding the latter typically play a central role in determining the former.[17] Ideally, being factually guilty or liable—that is, whether the defendant actually committed the deeds he is being accused of and whether they did have the effects he is held responsible for—is a necessary even if not sufficient condition for being legally guilty or liable. And it is here that the legal system comes to rely, at times extensively, on scientific inquiry. This forces the law to reckon not only with the results of science, but also with how science works. It is here too that Haack puts her philosophy to work. She specifically aims to address those points where science and the law are (seemingly) irreconcilable and, in good pragmatic fashion, resolve conceptual confusion. The result is a "very tangled tale" (EM:93). In what follows, I highlight some of it.

Earlier, we saw that Dewey and Posner looked at legal proceedings as a means of problem-solving that goes beyond the application of past precedent to current cases. The difficulty with this is that it introduces matters, often complicated ones, that fall well without the expertise of the legal profession. It is one thing for a judge or jury to determine whether the defendant snatched a purse, as purse snatching is relatively well understood; it is something quite different to determine whether cleaning up a massive coal ash spill caused some workers to develop debilitating and deadly diseases, and if so whether (in the eyes of a reasonable person) this could have been foreseen and prevented. Here Posner's interpretation of the law in terms of "councils of wise elders" becomes less plausible. Rather, judges and juries have little other option but to rely heavily on scientific experts to help them understand the facts—whether there is a connection between coal ash and the diseases in question, whether there is a more likely alternative explanation for the occurrence of those diseases, etc.[18] What adds to the problem, as the US Supreme Court pointed out as early as 1858,[19] is that pretty much anyone can find experts that can substantiate their take on things—a situation that is further exacerbated by the adversarial nature of the judicial process. All of this raises for jurors and judges the following difficult question: How do you determine what experts to side with when you have at best a limited understanding of the subject that they are professed to be experts in? The answer, unsurprisingly, is heavily steeped in the judiciary's reliance on precedent, and this has led to what Haack calls a "troubled marriage," one that endures mostly because divorce is out of the question, as "the law can't do without scientific testimony" (EM:100). In good pragmatist fashion, Haack approaches the issue by focusing "not exclusively on the *concept* of law but on the *phenomenon* of law—law as embodied in real legal systems."[20] The law, Haack argues, is not some "brooding omnipresence in the sky" (the phrase is Holmes's), but a social institution, like the banking system or the church, and should be studied as such. Consequently, we must look at what this institution produces in terms of laws, and how those laws are enacted.

In her analysis of the role of scientific evidence and expert testimony, Haack focuses on the American legal system, and specifically on two landmark US Supreme Court cases—*Frye v. United States* (1923) and *Daubert v. Merrill Dow Pharm., Inc.* (1993)—as well as the 1975 Federal Rules of Evidence, or FRE (revised in 2000).

The *Frye* ruling shifted the debate from the reliability of the expert to the content of the testimony by holding that "the scientific principle of discovery" on which the testimony is based must be "sufficiently established to have gained general acceptance in the field to which it belongs."[21] FRE does not have this restriction, requiring instead that the testimony be "based upon sufficient facts or data," is "the product of reliable principles and methods," and is reliably applied to the specific case at hand—all of this, as long as the testimony is not otherwise legally excluded.[22] Consequently, scientific testimony may be accepted on FRE even when it fails *Frye*, which may cause a defendant to be found guilty on one but not the other *even* when the facts, as established by science, are exactly the same.

One such case led to the 1993 *Daubert* decision. In *Daubert*, the US Supreme Court rules that FRE supersedes *Frye*, but it also explains how we should understand these "reliable principles and methods," insisting that they be scientific, that is, "derived by the scientific method," which the court further describes as the practice of "generating hypotheses and testing them to see if they can be falsified."[23] In doing this, the *Daubert* decision makes it in effect the responsibility of the judge to *determine* what constitutes scientific knowledge and what does not (and to allow only the former to be heard in court). In making this determination, the tool to be used comes down to a rather crude version of Popper's falsificationist philosophy of science on which a theory which is falsifiable but not falsified is considered reliable (EM:122ff)—a view Popper would be unlikely to agree with.[24]

In her discussions of *Daubert* and the role of evidence more generally, Haack brings in her mostly Peirce-inspired pragmatism. For instance, she agrees with Peirce that there is no such thing as "the scientific method," adding that the demand that methods be "scientific" runs the further risk of catering to prevailing deferential attitudes to science or encourages a predilection for the so-called hard sciences. However, even if you were to talk of methods more broadly and in the plural, you still must find ways to determine which of them are reliable/scientific and which of them are not. This issue came to the fore in *Joiner v. General Electric*, where attorneys for the plaintiff gathered a large amount of disconnected scientific claims about the relation between Robert Joiner's exposure to PCBs and his lung cancer, each in themselves inconclusive, and concluded from it that *when it is all taken together*, the evidence *is* conclusive—a view the Supreme Court rejected.[25]

The *Daubert* decision, Haack adds, mistakenly equates science with reliability, and reliability with not being falsified. Apart from the fact that what has not been falsified is not necessarily reliable, Haack points out that the idea of falsifiability is used ambiguously as well: as "empirical testing in a laboratory or in the field," or as "in-court 'testing' through cross-examination" (EM:142). Especially for scientific disciplines that cater specifically to the legal system, like bloodstain pattern analysis or forensic psychiatry, this can engender a litigation-driven research agenda the findings of which get tested only within court proceedings—reliable evidence then becomes evidence that sways juries (EM:180ff).[26] Here we are quite far removed from science as it is commonly understood. It is moreover quite clear that being reliable and being scientific are two different things: a reliable friend is not necessarily a scientific one, and a cutting-edge scientific technique is not necessarily reliable. What counts in the end, Haack continues, is that the testimony is reliable—meaning that we may expect that its conclusions are at least probably true—not that it is scientific. With *Kumho Tire Co. v. Carmichael*—a product-liability case where the expert testimony, though highly technical (concerning tire design) was not scientific—the Supreme Court shifts to this position as well.[27]

The *Daubert–Joiner–Kumho* trifecta, which comes to represent the Supreme Court's view on evidence, far from resolved the epistemological question of who can be considered an expert and why, and along the way it introduced quite a bit of confusion. It is here that pragmatism can still be put to work. The crux of the matter is that we want to ascribe legal guilt or liability only when defendants are factually guilty or liable—that is, when they really did what they are being accused of. As reasonable as this sounds, it does entail several presuppositions that are not self-evident but need to be argued for. As Haack points out, there has to be such a thing as factual truth, this truth must be objective and not subjective, and we must be able to discover it. This last point, Haack continues, calls for "objective standards of better and worse evidence" and, moreover, that if a claim meets those standards this is "at least a fallible indication" that the claim is true.[28]

Haack addresses the first presupposition by distinguishing truth, by which she means "the phenomenon of being true," from truths, by which she means true propositions (EM:294). She argues that

> Some truths, i.e., some true propositions, are indeed relative: that banks close by 3:30 p.m., for instance, can be true only in a society where there are banks. But it obviously doesn't follow from the fact that some *truths* are relative that *truth itself* is relative.[29]

In fact, we can say that even when people claim that all truth is relative, or subjective, they are making a general statement about truths while still tacitly holding on to truth. As Peirce put it a century ago, "Every man is fully satisfied that there is such a thing as truth, or he would not ask any question" (CP5.211).

Haack further observes that at least some truths are made (recall that Schiller held that all truths are made). For instance, when a legislature issues a law that makes jaywalking illegal, then it is true within that jurisdiction that jaywalking is illegal. However, Haack continues, it doesn't follow from this that therefore it must be subjective. Whether jaywalking is illegal clearly doesn't depend on whether you or I or anyone *believes* that it is illegal. It is a fact, and one that can be discovered by studying the laws of that jurisdiction. The same can be said for the claim that Richard jaywalked. Again, whether or not he did so has little to do with our beliefs about it. This is true too for the claim that Joiner's cancer was caused by PCBs. The question remains, though, whether we can determine whether something is true or not. If one were to respond that truths like the last one may be undiscoverable *in principle*, then one is parting ways with the pragmatist—it is a response without meaning (2.4). If it is merely undiscoverable *in practice*, then all we have is a practical problem—one that is typically resolved by acquitting the accused.

In general, we discover that something is true by means of evidence. Consequently, our next task is to show that what makes evidence better or worse is not some arbitrary convention. Here Haack returns to her foundherentism (13.1). We saw that what makes evidence stronger or weaker on this view is determined by three things: the evidence *supports* the claim that is being made; the evidence is *secure*, meaning that its truth is well established and is so independently of the claim that it is taken to be evidence for; and the evidence is *comprehensive* in terms of how much it includes of what is relevant. Returning to the crossword analogy, what counts as good evidence is pretty much the same as what makes a good answer in a crossword. The likelihood that you got it right is determined by the clue, whether the word fits the puzzle, and by how much of the puzzle has been completed. Recognizing that your answer matches those criteria, then, justifies your saying that it is reliable, that you can depend on it being true, even if fallible, as the answer can still be false.

Returning to *Joiner*, we can say that the question that needs to be asked is whether the evidence presented matches a "ramifying, crossword-like structure" (EM:115). Whether a set of disconnected and each in themselves inconclusive scientific claims add up to evidence that *is* conclusive, as was claimed in the case of Mr. Joiner's cancer, depends on how those claims hang together. It is here that foundherentism has a clear edge over correspondence and coherence theories, and most definitely over a *Daubert*-inspired falsificationism. Not that it is going to be easy for complicated tort cases like *Joiner*. However, we cannot conclude from this that there is no truth to the matter, or that we are in principle unable to discover it, so that the only possible adjudication is a subjective one or that we need to rely on something as opaque as the wisdom of the elders.

Haack's view has various consequences. In line with pragmatism and Peirce's theory of inquiry, a move to foundherentism means abandoning the notion that method can be neatly separated from content, as *Daubert* had assumed. Moreover, whereas falsificationism carries with it an air of definiteness, Haack's foundherentism is self-admittedly fallible, something that conflicts with the law's eagerness for finality. Foundherentism can further be used to flesh out existing legal notions, such as the requirement that the defendant's guilt must be proven "beyond a reasonable doubt," or by a "preponderance of evidence."

Notes

1. Charles Peirce, *The Illustrations of the Logic of Science by Charles S. Peirce* (Chicago, 2014), p.189.
2. Aristotle, *Posterior Analytics*, Bk.I, Ch.13.
3. Immediately following the maxim on proximate and remote causes, Bacon writes, "IT were infinite for the law to judge the caufes of caufes and their impulfions one of another, therefore it contenteth itfelfe with the immediate caufe and judgeth of acts by that, without looking to any further degree." *Rules and Maximes of the Common Lawes of England* (London, 1636), p.1.
4. An excellent discussion of *The Common Law* in relation to Peirce's early philosophy is found in "Holmes, Peirce and Legal Pragmatism," *Yale Law Journal* 84.5 (1975): 1123–40.
5. René Descartes, *The Philosophical Writings of Descartes,* 3 vols. (Cambridge, 1984–91), 2, p.24.
6. Oliver Wendell Holmes, *Collected Legal Papers* (New York, 1952), p.301.
7. Letter to Pollock, April 10, 1881, *Holmes-Pollock Letters*, 2nd ed. (Cambridge, 1961), 2:17.
8. See John Dewey, "Logical Method and Law," *Cornell Law Review* 10 (1924): 17–27. See also Benjamin Cardoso, Holmes's successor on the US Supreme Court, *The Nature of the Judicial* (New Haven, 1921).
9. Otto Neurath, *Empiricism and Sociology* (Dordrecht, 1973), p.199.
10. See also John Dewey, "My Philosophy of Law," in *My Philosophy of Law: Credos of Sixteen American Scholars* (Boston, 1941), pp.73–85.
11. For an extensive discussion, see Mark Mendell, "Dewey and the Logic of Legal Reasoning," *Transactions of the Charles S. Peirce Society: A Quarterly Journal in American Philosophy* 30.3 (1994): 575–635.
12. Adam Liptak, "An Exit Interview with Richard Posner, Judicial Provocateur," *New York Times*, September 11, 2017.
13. See e.g. Posner's discussion of the commercial availability of oil and gas as new natural resources (PA:6f).
14. See e.g. Richard Posner, *Economic Analysis of Law* (Boston, 1973); Richard Posner, "Utilitarianism, Economics and Legal Theory," *Journal of Legal Studies* 8 (1979): 103–40.
15. Posner (1979), p.109.
16. Fourth and Fifth Amendments to the US Constitution. It is the latter, the privilege against self-incrimination, that moved the US Supreme Court to state that the purpose of a trial is the *determination* of truth, rather than the discovery of truth (Tehan *v.* Shott, 382 U.S. 406 [1966]; also, EM:306).
17. In the US, a police officer may be factually liable for misconduct without being legally liable because of the doctrine of "qualified immunity," especially after *Harlow v. Fitzgerald* (457 U.S. 800 [1982]), effectively making the question of factual liability moot.
18. See e.g., Austyn Gaffney, "'They Deserve to Be Heard:' Sick and Dying Coal Ash Cleanup Workers Fight for Their Lives," *The Guardian*, August 17, 2020.
19. Winans *v.* NY & Erie R.R. Co., 62 US 88, 101; quoted in EM:81.
20. Susan Haack, "The Pragmatist Tradition: Lessons for Legal Theorists," *Washington University Law Review* 95.5 (2018): 1049–82, p.1050.
21. Frye *v.* United States, 293 F.1013 (D.C. Cir., 1923).
22. US Federal Rules of Evidence, Rule 702, Pub. L.93–595, §702, 2 Jan. 1975, 88 Stat. 1926.
23. Daubert *v.* Merrell Dow Pharm., Inc., 509 US, 579.
24. For Popper's views, see his *The Logic of Scientific Discovery* (London, 1959).

25. Gen. Elec. Co. *v.* Joiner, 522 U.S. 136 (1997).
26. On bloodstain pattern analysis, see e.g., Leora Smith, "How a Dubious Forensic Science Spread Like a Virus," *Pro Publica*, 13 December 2018.
27. Kumho Tire Co. *v.* Carmichael, 526 U.S. 137 (1999).
28. Susan Haack, "Justice, Truth, and Proof: Not So Simple, After All" (unpublised, 2014), p.1f.
29. Ibid., p.3.

Chapter 15

Prophetic Pragmatism and Feminist Inspirations

With its emphasis on pluralism and its critical attitude toward received notions, the philosophy of the early pragmatists carries significant promise for addressing the interests and concerns of excluded groups. That pragmatism carries this promise, however, must not be taken to imply that early pragmatists were actually attentive to such issues. In fact, notwithstanding their focus on pluralism (James), democracy (Dewey), the importance of idiosyncratic viewpoints (Peirce), and taking the perspective of the other (Mead), the classical pragmatists seem to have been strangely oblivious to issues of gender and race, and to oppression and power dynamics more generally. For instance, when reviewing John Stuart Mill's *The Subjection of Women*, James objects to Mill's notion that men and women should live together as equals because it is, as he puts it, "clearly inimical to the conception of a wife as a possession"—a conception he visibly prefers.[1] With respect to race, Cornel West observes that "if a Martian were to come down to America and look at the American pragmatist tradition, they would never know that there was slavery, Jim Crow, lynching, discrimination, segregation in the history of America."[2]

In this chapter, we first look at pragmatist feminism, addressing issues of pluralism, embodied experience, and personal identity. Next, we move to the pragmatism of Alain Locke and the prophetic pragmatism of Cornel West. The latter two are deeply inspired by the African American experience.

15.1 Feminist Pragmatism

From its inception, Western culture (of which pragmatism is a product) has been dominated by white males who in passing made themselves the benchmark for what it means to be human. Women and non-European men, insofar as they *differ* from this, are not truly human—not truly rational. Feminism, broadly speaking, aims to give women their rightful place in humanity, which inspires more broadly a new and more inclusive conception of what it means to be human. As such, feminists also come to take up the cause of other marginalized groups, like people of color and people with a different sexual orientation or gender identity.

A key contemporary feminist pragmatist is Charlene Seigfried.[3] Seigfried cites three core themes in feminist research originally identified by Sandra Harding: it proceeds from women's experiences, aims to benefit women, and acknowledges that researchers are never neutral. Next, Seigfried observes that "support for and the development of these themes can be found throughout pragmatist philosophy,"[4] albeit that pragmatism advocates for pluralism more generally rather than for a specifically woman-centered perspective. In fact, a recurring question that pragmatists struggle with, Seigfried argues, is precisely how to develop unity out of diversity without losing diversity, or how to preserve diversity without losing unity. In short, how do we prevent that "either aspect of this unstable equilibrium becomes dominant"?[5]

Seigfried sees the aim of feminist pragmatism as threefold: show how unexamined preconceptions about women affected the arguments of the (early) pragmatists, bring back the voices of the women that featured in the development of pragmatism but were unduly ignored (most significantly, Jane Addams),[6] and use pragmatism thus enriched to develop a more inclusive pragmatist philosophy and to contribute to contemporary feminist thought. In this chapter, I focus primarily on the third. What complicates the situation is that some feminists self-describe as pragmatists because they advocate shifting away from the traditional notion of a purely curiosity-inspired science toward "research that alleviates human needs, especially those traditionally attended by women."[7] As we saw, such a shift from pure to applied science does not cover what the classical pragmatists argue for. In discussing feminist pragmatism, it is also important to keep in mind that neither women nor men, for that matter, constitute a homogenous group, and that what is at play is not just an issue of biological differences but also of how culturally assigned gender roles shape experience.

It is fair to say that when the early pragmatists shift their emphasis from the individual to the community, the community they envision is essentially one of Western white males. In doing so they commit, notwithstanding their penchant for pluralism, the fallacy of presuming that their own perspective is the only perspective—the perspective everyone should have.[8] Traditional philosophers were particularly susceptible to this because they failed to realize that their way of looking at the world was even a perspective to begin with. Having long conceived of truth in terms of an all-knowing God who shaped us in his image, philosophers come to see themselves in the image of God; that is, as detached, wholly transparent conduits through which truth can shine undistorted. When we add to this the socioeconomic reality that science, philosophy, and theology have long been the prerogative of affluent people who engaged in inquiry out of wonder rather than need, then what Dewey called the "spectator view of knowledge" becomes a natural outcome—a view that can be said to have given us a false sense of objectivity.

With this in mind, let us return to the pragmatists' idea of community. As we saw, this conception originates with Peirce, who thinks of it primarily as a community of inquiry. (Later, this idea is broadened by Dewey and others. I therefore begin with Peirce's idea of a community of inquiry.) As Peirce explains it, the aim of inquiry is to have one's questions answered. In this process, the role of the community is to filter out the idiosyncrasies of the individual inquirers, with the expectation that in the long run (and assuming the community incorporates all perspectives) this will cause them to eventually arrive at an agreed-upon answer. As we saw, Peirce is skeptical of our ability to challenge our own biases, making the confrontation with the views of others crucial. As Peirce also argues, we can call the answer thus arrived at true when we have reached a point where no future inquiry can cause us to change it, and this idea of truth may then become a regulative ideal. For a more precise account I refer back to Chapter 2, but for our current purpose this rudimentary description suffices. Importantly, having this as an ideal prohibits us from blocking the road of inquiry.

In light of Peirce's theory of inquiry, we can now ask if it matters whether inquirers are male or female. (For the purpose of the discussion, I begin by taking for granted the traditional male–female distinction.) Since we are focusing specifically on inquiry, this comes down to the question of whether sex or gender plays a constitutive epistemic role. Do women have something to contribute epistemically qua women? Or is gender accidental to inquiry, like the color of one's pants or what one had for breakfast?

An answer that quickly presents itself is that the female perspective *does* matter, even if only to determine whether there is a male cognitive bias affecting inquiry. Moreover, it can be fairly argued that, like any other empirical question, this is something that can be truly settled only in the long run. Importantly, since everyone brings their idiosyncrasies to inquiry, it would be wrong to exclude or censor a particular constituency, say women, by declaring upfront that their way of looking at things is insufficient or flawed. Nor, on this view, should women censor themselves by trying to remove their "female bias." We see similar sentiments among contemporary feminist philosophers, such as Elizabeth Anderson. In addressing the question of bias, Anderson discusses, for instance, the concept of Gross Domestic Product (GDP), which economists developed in the 1930s to describe the course (and health) of a nation's economy, and which became the factual ground for governmental macroeconomic and monetary decision making. By leaving out unpaid labor, economists made the contributions by women to the economy practically invisible, thereby generating a fact about the economy that, far from being gender neutral, is very much shaped by the male perspective. Anderson makes similar observations regarding IQ tests.[9]

If there is a male bias, which is hard to deny, then the female perspective will be crucial in revealing how this bias manifests itself, with what consequences, and how to prevent it. Here, we should look at not only how it affects the answers that are found, but also the *questions* that are being asked. Since inquiry proceeds from actual doubt or concrete indeterminate situations, and since the decision regarding what conceptual framework to apply is fraught with practical considerations, people with different practical experiences may opt for different frameworks, and some of these experiences may be gender inspired.

Biologists, for instance, traditionally, and mostly unwittingly, interpreted social interactions along patriarchal lines. The now-debunked belief that gorillas are solitary animals, for instance, was inspired by an overly strong focus on male gorillas and making them the model for what gorillas are truly like.[10] The patriarchal paradigm even reaches down to the molecular level. As Anderson explains,

> The constitutive parts of an individual cell cooperate because they are ruled by a wise and benevolent patriarch, the "master molecule" DNA, which autonomously tells all the other parts of the cell what to do, solely on the basis of information it contains within itself.[11]

What Anderson suggests is that the male perspective on familial relations implicitly steered our understanding in the field of molecular genetics. In principle, there is nothing wrong with this. Knowledge often advances through poignant analogies. Newton's famous inverse square law, for instance, is heavily inspired by the idea that the force of gravity spreads like a cone of light. But analogies are easily overextended, especially when one does not realize that it is an analogy to begin with. Feminists argue that this happens here too. The patriarchy paradigm engenders a penchant for monocausal explanations (as with DNA), which prevents researchers from appreciating the existence of mutual and reciprocal relationships—such as Dewey's transactional epistemology (8.2) and what Green described in terms of the meshes of a net (14.1). Feminists, Helen Longino explains,

> explicitly reject theories or explanatory models that attempt to identify one causal factor in a process, whether that be a dominant animal, or a "master molecule" like DNA. This virtue favors accounts of fertilization, or gametic fusion, for example, which treat the process as an interaction between egg and sperm, rather than the active sperm acting on the passive egg.[12]

In sum, it appears that the female perspective can play the kind of correcting role that inspired Peirce to shift from the solitary researcher to a community of inquiry.

Part of what enables Longino to argue for feminist-inspired science is the idea that theories are underdetermined by data—that different conceptual frameworks can be equally successful in describing the very same event (see especially Chapter 9). Moreover, when discussing Putnam in Chapter 12, we saw that descriptions are never value neutral to begin with. Describing something always involves making choices that hinge upon epistemic value judgments (things we find important) such as empirical adequacy, consistency, simplicity, and fruitfulness. Besides putting some question marks to these traditional epistemic values (the demand for consistency, for instance, tends to reinforce existing biases), Longino argues that even with these values in place, there is still room to maneuver, meaning that other values can play a role also. For instance, if the only values we allow are virtues such as empirical adequacy, simplicity, consistency, clarity, and fruitfulness, then the claim "a woman was raped" and "a man raped a woman" can be seen as describing the very same event and doing it equally well. At the same time, however, the first claim, which is the more prevalent one, shifts the focus from the perpetrator to the victim and, by making her the subject of the sentence, is more prone to shift the responsibility for what happened in her direction as well. Consequently, it seems that there is still room for including other factors that make a difference, and a case is to be made that pragmatism, which interprets the meaning of either claim in terms of the practical consequences that we can conceive to follow from holding the claim for true, can provide tools for determining what factors to include. In her work, Longino shows that we can address such factors in ways that need not interfere with the aim of inquiry as pragmatists envision it. These factors include virtues such as ontological heterogeneity, mutuality of interaction, and applicability to human needs.[13]

An objection to this view—one that goes back to Peirce and Haack—is that it invites sham reasoning (13.3). Harding's claim, cited earlier, that feminism should aim to benefit women suggests as much, as does Longino's claim that science should shift its focus to "research that alleviates human needs, especially those traditionally attended by women."[14] To alleviate human needs, important as it is, is not the same as having one's questions answered, and there are certainly situations where a false answer may best serve human needs. It is in part because of this that Peirce separates the sciences of discovery from the practical sciences and confines his theory of inquiry to the former. There is certainly an economical argument to be made regarding resource allocation (why study this rather than that), and it is also true that existing power structures favor male interests, but that is different from the question of whether introducing values like Longino's when choosing hypotheses or conceptual frameworks makes science, or inquiry more generally, prone to sham reasoning. Longino's commitment to empirical adequacy and her balanced approach to the other traditional epistemic values suggests otherwise. Pragmatists can further add that the degree to which such values are to be considered is something that must be settled within inquiry itself and is not something to be imposed externally. Expressed more generally, a diversity of perspectives (or standpoints) seems the best way for tackling hidden biases and preconceptions, as it constantly challenges the community of inquiry from a multitude of vantage points. The degree to which such challenges should be taken seriously is then to be settled within inquiry itself (rather than externally imposed on it), where in the short term other regulative principles—such as the principle of the economy of research—may provide guidance on where to focus our attention.

Pragmatism emerges during a time of growing awareness that science can help improve society. Dewey responds to this by arguing that scientific inquiry, as the pragmatists see it, can be applied to social issues as well. Moreover, Dewey rejects the view that society has grown so complex that its problems are better left to specialists, a view that separates science (including the social sciences) from society. Crediting Alexis de Tocqueville, Dewey remarks, "the man who wears the shoe knows best that it pinches and where it pinches, even if the expert shoemaker is the best judge of how the trouble is to be remedied" (LW2:364).

When applying scientific inquiry to society, Dewey welds together three elements: problematic situations, the scientific attitude, and a community defined in terms of a participatory democracy. The result is a way of life, inspired by a critical optimism, or meliorism. By this he means the belief that through intelligent effort we can improve the conditions we find ourselves in (MW12:181f). Importantly, where democratic participation is concerned, Dewey thinks that those who wear the shoes must have a seat at the table. And that should include people with a different race, gender, or socioeconomic standing from those in power. Within the pragmatist tradition, those who best exemplify this way of life, by actually living it, are the women of Hull House. Recall that Addams sees the settlement as "an experimental effort to aid in the solution of the social and industrial problems which are engendered by the modern conditions of life in a great city,"[15] with a special focus on problems faced by women, and that the place she chooses for the settlement is a very diverse immigrant neighborhood. The aim is to use science not to accumulate truths about the world, but to resolve concrete problematic situations, preferably those that exemplify broader problems.

Peirce, when discussing the doubt–belief mechanism that first inspired his theory of inquiry, says that the aim of inquiry is belief, and that when we attain it, inquiry naturally comes to an end—that is, until something else comes along that casts new doubt on the issue. As we saw, this possibility of new doubt causes Peirce to identify truth with a situation where our belief can no longer be shattered by new insights or events, and this then becomes a regulative ideal for inquiry. Something similar can be said when we apply the theory of inquiry to concrete social problems. Here, inquiry also comes to an end when the problem is resolved—and again, it does so only until fresh doubt is cast on the solution. This can be because the problem did not really go away or resurfaced elsewhere, because the solution caused new, possibly worse problems, etc. Here, the regulative principle becomes that of creating a social–political environment that actively involves everybody, as doing so puts us in the best position for solving the problems we currently face, as well as future ones, the nature of which we cannot yet imagine. The prohibition against blocking the road of inquiry thus becomes a prohibition against silencing the marginalized and the oppressed.

In brief, by putting inquiry front and center, a process that makes us active participants rather than mere witnesses, and by focusing on active doubts or experienced problems rather than abstract questions, pragmatists are well positioned to look at the process of knowledge acquisition as something that involves the body. This carves out a role for a pragmatist–feminist epistemology, philosophy of science, political theory, etc., aiming to ensure that the human perspective is not quietly taken to be the male perspective.

15.2 The Social Self and the Male–Female Dichotomy

Related to the theory of inquiry is the pragmatists' broadening of the concept of experience. Descartes's strict separation of mind and body inspires a one-sided identification of the knowing individual with mind—a mind that turned out to be oddly detached from the world. On this view even the very existence of the world demands proof.[16] Peirce's insistence on firstness, James's radical empiricism, Mead's focus on the act, and Dewey's notion of lived experience all seek to drive home the point that epistemic agents are embodied individuals, not disembodied spirits. As a result, a long-held argument for excluding the female perspective, namely that women are driven by feeling—thereby implying that they "think" with their bodies—loses its ground. In fact, it now becomes a reason for including them.

Pragmatists add to this that it is only *within* experience, conceived as an embodied transaction of the organism with its environment, that subject and object emerge. Subject and object do not exist fully formed before experience commences, as Descartes had it, but are products of it, and they are moreover intrinsically related. This also means that someone's gender or race—insofar as it pertains to the perception of one's self or the perception of others—is also a product of such interaction. They are not preexisting (meta)physical categories. If gender—how people with certain biological sexual characteristics come to understand themselves—is a product of experience, then there is no a priori ground for assuming that one way in which people understand themselves is to be privileged.

Beginning with Peirce, pragmatists take an externalist rather than an internalist view of mind, self, individuality, personhood, etc.[17] Mental states enter into consciousness just like everything else, and in the process our mind becomes "a thing" in the same way we come to discern things in general—like car keys, mountains, home mortgages, or exercise routines. For instance, in "Does Consciousness Exist?" James rejects the view that consciousness is some special kind of substance, advocating instead for a functionalist view (WJ:170). In part, James can do this because, in a phenomenological vein, he replaces dead matter as the primeval substance, with pure experience:

> My thesis is that if we start with the supposition that there is only one primeval stuff or material in the world of which everything is composed, and if we call that stuff "pure experience," then knowing can easily be explained as a particular sort of relation . . . into which portions of pure experience may enter.
>
> (WJ:170)

It is then the clumping together of experiences—which, importantly, includes experiences of the body—that gives rise to personal identity. Peirce takes a similar stance when he calls matter "effete mind," or "mind hidebound with habit." The result is a very different conception of mind and of personal identity. In feminist circles we find similar observations in Carol Gillian and her ethics of care. Gillian develops her views in response to Lawrence Kohlberg and his theory of moral development, which causes her to reject mainstream ethical theories with their emphasis on individuals, individual rights, universal principles, and the tabulation of consequences. Instead, ethics of care sees individuals as relational and situated. As a result, the emphasis shifts to context, interdependence, relationships, and responsibilities to concrete others. This shift brings the ethics of care close to Dewey, as can be seen especially in the work of Nel Noddings.[18]

In Chapter 7, we looked at Mead's theory of society, mind, and self, and his argument that the latter two emerge from the former through a process of role-playing. Consequently, for Mead, we understand ourselves through our interactions with others—interactions that tend to solidify into patterns, or games, as Mead called them. When this happens, we come to see ourselves in terms of the roles we play in certain games. Here it is the game, not the individual playing the game, that determines what the role entails and whether it is being played correctly. Importantly, such roles include gender-defining ones, like being a girl or boy, wife or husband, mother or father, etc. We can further add that what holds for gender identity holds also for racial or ethnic identity.

In sum, when pragmatists point at the importance of community, what they have in mind is not a gathering of fully formed individuals, but that these individuals are themselves products of the community they are participating in. This puts pragmatism in a good position to address gender and racial identity and to walk the fine line between biological characteristics and predispositions on the one hand and sociocultural constructs on the other, and to do it in a way that takes the latter as seriously as the former. Realizing that race and gender are inherently part of the self, and that they are to a large extent social constructions, shifts the demand from one of reconstruction to that of re-evaluating and re-imagining one's self and society, as well as the selves of others—a demand that extends to everyone, not just the underprivileged.

More recently, Rorty makes this kind of move as well, although he focuses largely on language, in effect reducing the issue to an exercise in redescription. Rorty denies that words like "woman" or "human" name some "unchanging essence, an ahistorical natural kind with a permanent set of intrinsic features" (RR:337f). Therefore, he rejects the idea that feminists should first unveil a women's true nature and then demand that justice be done to her (on the ground that true natures come with inalienable rights). Instead, Rorty argues, "we have to take seriously the idea that what you experience yourself to be is largely a function of what it makes sense to describe yourself as in the languages you are able to use" (RR:344).

As Rorty observes, however, these languages are far from neutral. History is not only written by the victors; it is also written in their language. This leads to a situation, Rorty notes, where the oppressed "sound crazy— *even to themselves*—if they describe themselves as oppressed" (RR:331). Arguments for their rights, Rorty continues, are bound to fail as long as they have to rely on emancipatory premises that even they themselves cannot take seriously. In a society where a wife is long considered the property of a husband, spousal rape and domestic violence "sound crazy." One could rape someone else's wife (which would be a violation of *his* rights) but not one's own wife—with her marriage vows, she had given him her irrevocable consent. This makes it difficult for women to see themselves as victims of rape or domestic violence, let alone see it as a situation that calls for a social remedy. As Rorty puts it, "only where there is a socially accepted remedy can there have been a real (rather than crazily imagined) injury" (RR:331n).

Societies, however, are not static. They evolve. And with this, languages evolve as well. Changes in social practices, which are often slow, uneven, and multifarious (and seldom logical), result in new descriptions. Rorty speaks of "creative misuses" of language, which he sees as "*causes* to change one's belief, even if not *reasons* to change them," adding that "most moral and intellectual progress is achieved by non-'logical' changes in belief" (RR:339n). In light of this, Rorty argues, the pragmatist feminist "will see herself as helping to create women rather than attempting to describe them more accurately," which implies, almost paradoxically, "that women are only now coming into existence, rather than having been deprived of the ability to express what was deep within them all the time" (RR:344). In all of this, it is important to keep in mind that Rorty is not imagining there to be some kind of ideal and just situation from which the people in the past were further removed than we are now, and to which we need to get even closer. For Rorty, that's a chimera: "evolution has no purpose and humanity no nature" (RR:334); all we can do is "to modify our practices so as to take account of new descriptions of what has been going on" (RR:333). We have no basis for claiming that either the oppressor or the oppressed is "on the side of the really real."[19] The oppressed, Rorty writes, "have different purposes and wants from their oppressors, but they do not have deeper insight into reality. They just want to relieve suffering, to change things for the better."[20]

The pragmatists' social conception of the self and the realization that how we conceive of men and women (as well as boys and girls) is in the end the product of a social construction (which is not to deny that there is significant biological basis to it) also open up the possibility of looking at people differently than in terms of a traditional male–female dichotomy. This too is reinforced by the pragmatists' shift from thinking about things in terms of fixed Platonic categories to thinking about them in terms of evolution. In fact, the pragmatists' objection to dualisms of all sorts and Peirce's doctrine of synechism (the view that "continuity governs the whole domain of experience in every element of it" [EP2:1]), puts them in a relatively good position to address issues of transsexuality and being transgender. Rather than a biological bifurcation of humans into two "opposite" sexes—each with its own essence—they see a multifarious continuity. Moreover, if gender—how we have come to understand ourselves and others because of certain biological characteristics—is to a large extent a sociocultural construction, then what pragmatists have to say about the formation of the self, and how we conceptualize the world and our roles within it, can provide powerful tools for rethinking our notions of gender identity without having to fall back on an outmoded male–female dichotomy. And, with Rorty, we can say that non-binary feelings about gender and sexual identity call for a process of redescription that is crucial for self-understanding and social acceptance.

15.3 Alain Locke on the New Negro

Similar moves are made earlier in the twentieth century by Alain Locke (1885–1954) regarding questions of race. Locke, who had been a student of Royce at Harvard, can rightly be called the first African American pragmatist, and he is deeply concerned with what was then called the Negro question. Locke rejects the idea that there is something like an essence or true nature to being Negro, and this allows him to reject the need to restore something like the Negro's true identity after centuries of subjugation, slavery, and colonialism. "The Old Negro," Locke writes in his preface to *The New Negro*,

> has been a stock figure perpetuated as an historical fiction partly in innocent sentimentalism, partly in deliberate reactionism . . . for generations in the mind of America, the Negro has been more of a formula than a human being—a something to be argued about, condemned or defended, to be "kept down," or "in his place," or "helped up."
>
> (NN:3)

What is called for instead, he writes, is a New Negro. For Locke, American blacks had to invent themselves anew, and he found in Harlem the fertile soil for the creation of a new black identity. As Locke explains,

> So what began in terms of segregation becomes more and more, as its elements mix and react, the laboratory of a great race-welding. Hitherto, it must be admitted that American Negroes have been a race more in name than in fact, or to be exact, more in sentiment than in experience. The chief bond between them has been that of a common condition rather than a common consciousness; a problem in common rather than a life in common. In Harlem, Negro life is seizing upon its first chances for group expression and self-determination.
>
> (NN:7)

And a few pages down, Locke writes, "The pulse of the Negro world has begun to beat in Harlem" (NN:14). Having spent a year at Oxford on a Rhodes scholarship, which brings him in close contact with black intellectuals from African colonies, Locke's outlook is cosmopolitan rather than American, and Harlem at the time was a brimming melting pot of black culture that attracted international attention.

Rejecting biological essentialism and with a strong focus on esthetics, Locke sees the creation of a race identity primarily in terms of artistic expressions and literature—an identity he does not expect "to be radically different, but only to be distinctively composite and idiomatic, though basically American" (PAL:213). As a committed pluralist, Locke is keen to reject, however, the idea that there is "a type Negro who, either qualitatively or quantitatively, is the type symbol of the entire group" (PAL:210).

Locke's position on race fits in with his general epistemology. Demanding that empiricism incorporates value judgments, Locke argues for what he calls a "systematic relativism" (PAL:55). Though he rejects the external imposition of a priori claims derived from abstract (and, in his view, outmoded) metaphysical systems, he does not take that to mean that, therefore, values must be subjective or arbitrary. They can still be objective. As he puts it, "we are able to discover through objective comparison of basic human values certain basic equivalences among them, which we may warrantably call 'functional constants,'" adding that this can "take scientifically the place of our outmoded categoricals and our banned arbitrary 'universals'" (PAL:55). These "functional constants," for Locke, come to "stand out as pragmatically confirmed by common human experience," which in his view gives them a far surer footing than anything externally imposed (PAL:55f). One consequence of this is that "value disciplines . . . take on the tentative and revisionist procedure of natural science"—a process wherein a value assertion would be "a tolerant assertion of preference, not an intolerant insistence on agreement or finality" (PAL:57). Locke's conception of pragmatically established objective values and the tolerance that it entails also allows him to reconcile democracy with pluralism, which then becomes the ground for personal and racial identity.

15.4 Cornel West's Prophetic Pragmatism

Within pragmatism, the issue of race is taken up again by the African American philosopher and political activist Cornel West (b. 1953), a student of both Putnam and Rorty. West finds in pragmatism an approach to philosophy that skillfully evades the long-standing obsession of philosophers with certainty and indubitable foundations of knowledge. West details this view in his 1989 *The American Evasion of Philosophy: A Genealogy of Pragmatism*. With the term "genealogy," West is referencing the French philosopher Michel Foucault. According to Foucault, the problems we face today (both theoretical and practical) are in part a product of how we resolved the problems we faced in the past. What Foucault shows by studying the past is that our solutions to these earlier problems could have been different, were often deficient, and were not always well intended. In *The American Evasion*, West is aiming to apply this to pragmatism with the aim of shedding new light on the problems pragmatists focused on (and which ones they ignored), how they answered or responded to these problems, and how this shaped the direction of pragmatism as a whole. For West, this poignantly includes their silence on class, gender, race, and empire (WR:545). What comes out of this genealogical evaluation is what West calls a prophetic pragmatism, a view that blends pragmatism with a Foucauldian methodology and (Afro-American) liberation theology.

According to West, giving up on the quest for certainty profoundly changes the nature of philosophy. Rather than "putting forward solutions to perennial problems in the Western philosophical conversation initiated by Plato," the focus shifts to "providing a continuous cultural commentary or set of interpretations that attempt to explain America to itself at a particular historical moment" (AE:5). Hence, we see with West, as we did with Schiller and Prezzolini, a return to the Sophists and, as with Rorty, the true role of the philosopher becomes that of cultural critic. Moreover, since we can no longer rely on the traditional conception of knowledge, we cannot use logic to determine what is wrong with society or what our future should look like. We need a different tool to help us. Whereas Rorty resorted to irony as a way to break free from our entrenched ways of thinking, West finds his solution in the Christian notion of prophesy.

West's notion of a prophet comes out of the black church tradition. West is specifically looking at Martin Luther King Jr., whom he sees as merging "Christian themes of deliverance and salvation with political ideals of democracy, freedom, and equality" (WR:426). West sees the origin of the prophetic black church itself as an appropriation of Christianity by black slaves who sought to extract from their lived reality—a reality where they had no other worth than as commodities to be bought, used, and sold—a sense of hope that could neither be rationally nor empirically justified.[21] Christianity, West argues, allowed black slaves to envision themselves as equals in the eyes of God, which gave them "a special self-identity and self-esteem in stark contrast with the inferior roles imposed upon them in American Society" (WR:435f). The prophet in this context becomes someone who leads us in reimagining the world as through the character of God. In this act of reimagination, the prophet is not drawing upon some privileged source of understanding but is directing his audience to things to which they tend to remain blind—a blindness that can be caused by a desire not to see. Given West's pragmatism and his accompanying denial of the traditional concept of knowledge, such prophetic reimaginations will always be fallible and experimental. Reflecting back on previous chapters, this brings West close to Sorel and critical theory, as they too focus on the need to reimagine the world in ways that open up real possibilities. And, returning to Alain Locke, West can be seen as criticizing Locke for not giving the Old Negro enough credit.

West derives much of his own prophetic imagination from left-wing romanticism. With romanticism, he means in this context,

> the preoccupation with Promethean human powers, the recognition of the contingency of the self and society, and the audacious projection of desires and hopes in the form of regulative emancipatory ideals for which one lives and dies.
>
> (AE:215)

Romanticism, however, as West realizes, also has its dark side. Historically, romantic ideals have been the cause of tremendous human suffering. The romantic ideals of Christianity inspired numerous religious conflicts and wars, Marx and Engels led to Stalin's Gulags, and the ideals of the American Revolution sanctioned genocide, state-sanctioned slavery, and white supremacy. West is further weary of romantic ideals that are inspired by a calculated, science-driven instrumentalism that he believes is out of touch with those who need help most: the wretched of the earth. That is, he rejects "the arrogant scientistic self-privileging or haughty secular self-images of many modern philosophers and intellectuals" who "demand that all peoples mimic their version of critical intelligence" (AE:232). It is in part because of this dark side to romanticism that West seeks to weld pragmatism with Christian and socialist ideas, with a focus on the gospel of love, and inspirational prophesy as its method (AE:227). If pragmatism "is ever to become more than a conversational subject matter for cultural critics in and out of the academy," West argues, "it must inspire" (AE:234). In contrast to someone like Blondel, however, who considered Catholicism the only worthy experiment (5.1), West does not require that prophetic pragmatism be Christian, or even religious. This same dark side to romanticism, referred to by West, causes Rorty to remark that philosophers and cultural critics alike better stay out of the business of prophesy.

In addition to the charge that pragmatists fail to connect with the majority of people in the world, West also warns that pragmatism fails to take seriously the anonymous forces that operate within society, largely outside of the consciousness of individual subjects, like the bureaucracies that shape not only who we are but also what can be thought, how we understand ourselves, and what we can conceive as possible. It is again the perspective of the prophetic black church tradition that inspires West, as the social forces faced by African Americans—from state-sanctioned slavery, through Jim Crow laws and racial segregation, up to the mass incarceration of black males—have all been so formidable as to leave little room for anything but dread and despair. In his discussion of institutional constraints with their anonymous force, West brings in the work of Foucault. Foucault shares West's charge that the traditional conception of knowledge has been proven an illusion. What Foucault concludes from his genealogical approach is that we have only a very limited grasp of the institutions that we ourselves create—we don't fully understand them, and we don't fully control them. For instance, in *Discipline and Punish*, Foucault details how shifts in the penal system that birthed the modern prison came to shape modern society as a whole.[22] Factories, hospitals, and schools all became modeled after the prison, but they did so by semi-conscious encroachment rather than by conscious design. It is this aspect of the history of humanity, West argues, that pragmatists tend to overlook.

At the same time West criticizes Foucault for focusing too strongly on how disciplinary power leads to the subjection and objectivization of human beings (EA:224), and for what West considers a mistaken reification of discourses and disciplines which results in a passive view of power that fails to give the individual its due. "The key to pragmatism," West writes,

> the distinctive feature that sets it apart from other philosophical traditions—and maybe its unique American character—is its emphasis

on the ethical significance of the future . . . the future has ethical significance because human will—human thought and action—can make a difference in relation to human aims and purposes.

(WR:177)

Hence, for West, we have an ethical obligation to actively try to improve our lot, even when we are in the thralls of deepest despair and convinced of the futility of our thoughts and actions. "Pragmatism," West continues, "is in need of a mode of cultural criticism that keeps track of social misery, solicits and channels moral outrage to alleviate it and projects a future in which the potentialities of ordinary people flourish and flower" (WR:187). For this, West argues, prophets are direly needed.

While pragmatic feminists and discussions about race and ethnicity by Locke, West, and others made pragmatism more inclusive, the intersection of the two groups, black women and their voices, still fares poorly. Historically, feminists focused on emancipating white middle-class women, while the black liberation movement was essentially about black men. In this context, black feminism emerges to articulate the experience—not just of being left out, but of being racially oppressed by feminists while sexually oppressed by the black liberation movement. This shows that there is a space for a pragmatic black feminism. Returning to Mead and Dewey and their focus on the indeterminate situation, one could say that the challenges faced by black women differ significantly from those faced by black men or white women, and that the best way of showing this is by examining these different situations in terms of the practical consequences we can conceive to follow from each of them. The plight of black women further reveals that Mead's theory of role-playing cannot be taken to imply that the various roles we play are neatly separable. American black women cannot play the role of being a woman without also playing the role of being African American, and vice versa. That the situation faced by black women is not factorable into a female part and a black part, so that we cannot use what we have learned about those two groups and claim that it accurately depicts their situation as well, reinforces the idea that there is a conceptual space for black feminism—that they should have their own seat at the table. Although current black feminism finds most of its inspiration within critical social theory, which has a strong focus on embedded power structures, their focus on lived experience and dialogue brings it close to pragmatist approaches as well.[23]

Notes

1. William James, *Essays, Comments, and Reviews* (Cambridge, 1987), p.253.
2. Interview with Bill Lawson, in B.E. Lawson and D.E. Koch (eds), *Pragmatism and the Problem of Race* (Bloomington, 2004), p.225.

3. Several of Seigfried's early essays are found in Charlene Seigfried, *Pragmatism and Feminism: Reweaving the Social Fabric* (Chicago, 1996). A collection of work by recent pragmatist feminists is found in Maurice Hamington and Celia Bardwell-Jones (eds), *Contemporary Feminist Pragmatism* (Routledge, 2012).

4. Seigfried (1996), p.37.

5. Charlene Seigfried, "Shared Communities of Interest: Feminism and Pragmatism," *Hypatia* 8.2 (1993): 1–14, p.2.

6. This includes more recent pragmatists, such as Cornel West, who in *The Evasion of American Philosophy,* all but ignores Jane Addams, even though of all the pragmatists, she is closest to his prophetic pragmatism.

7. Helen Longino, "Feminist Epistemology as a Local Epistemology," *Proceedings of the Aristotelian Society* (Supplementary Volume 71) (1997): 19–35, p.23.

8. In a different context, James hints in this direction when discussing the psychologist's fallacy (PP:1.161f).

9. Elizabeth Anderson, "Feminist Epistemology: An Interpretation and a Defense," *Hypatia* 10.3 (1995), p.71, 77f.

10. See e.g. Sarah Hrdy, *The Woman that Never Evolved* (Cambridge, 1981).

11. Anderson (1995), p.67.

12. Longino (1997), p.22f.

13. Ibid.

14. Ibid., p.23.

15. Jane Addams, *The Second Twenty Years at Hull-House, September 1909 to September 1929, With a Record of a Growing World Consciousness* (New York, 1930), p.125.

16. René Descartes, *Meditations Concerning First Philosophy* (1641), Second Meditation, in *The Philosophical Writings of Descartes,* 3 vols. (Cambridge, 1984–91), 2, pp.16–23.

17. For a concise discussion of Peirce's view, see de Waal (2013), pp.151–5.

18. Nel Noddings, *Starting at Home: Caring and Social Policy* (Berkeley, 2002); see also Maurice Hamington, "Care Ethics, John Dewey's 'Dramatic Rehearsal,' and Moral Education," *Philosophy of Education Yearbook* (2010): 121–8.

19. Richard Rorty, "The Professor and the Prophet," *Transition* (1991): 70–8, p.73.

20. Ibid.

21. For an overview of the African American prophetic tradition, see Christopher Hobson, *The Mount of Vision* (Oxford, 2012).

22. Michel Foucault, *Discipline and Punish: The Birth of the Prison* (London, 1977).

23. For black feminism, see Patricia Hill Collins, *Black Feminist Thought: Knowledge, Consciousness, and the Politics of Empowerment* (New York, 2000); for a connection with pragmatism, see Denise James, "Theorizing Black Feminist Pragmatism: Forethoughts on the Practice and Purpose of Philosophy as Envisioned by Black Feminists and John Dewey," *Journal of Speculative Philosophy* 23.2 (2009): 92–9.

Chapter 16

Pragmatism and the End(s) of Philosophy

Where do we go from here? Reflecting on the previous chapters, we can say that pragmatists seek to grapple with a situation where reliable philosophical staples such as truth, reality, and reason can no longer be taken for granted, but must be humanized—a demand that is being put upon us precisely when the question of what it means to be human is up for grabs as well. The sciences have brought us to a point where the old answers no longer apply, and many of the old questions are no longer relevant either. In fact, much of twentieth-century philosophy comes down to various attempts at reckoning with this. Pragmatism, we found, is one such attempt, and one that shows considerable promise.

In this concluding chapter, I want to extract some of the main tenets of pragmatism as they surfaced throughout the book with the aim of finding out whether we should, as Rorty and West so boldly declared, give up on philosophy with its faith in truth, reality, and reason, or whether philosophy, as intimated at the close of the Introduction, should become pragmatic—an approach that entails a critical and often radical rethinking of our most basic philosophic notions, including the three I just mentioned (truth, reality, and reason). Briefly put, the question is, have we reached the end of philosophy, or should philosophy recalibrate itself, a process that may lead it in different directions toward different ends?

Pragmatism has aptly been called the first postmodern philosophy.[1] Modern philosophy held on to the idea that since we are all equally endowed with reason and we are all exposed to the same reality, we eventually arrive at the same beliefs, and we can even say that these beliefs represent the truth. In developing this view, early modern philosophers invoked God—a being that they saw as all-knowing, all-powerful, and entirely good. In fact, what they ended up doing was to turn medieval cosmology upside down. Instead of trying to prove the existence of God from certain general observations about the world, as Thomas Aquinas had done, Descartes relied on certain general observations about God to prove that the world exists.[2] Both projects failed. However, when the moderns came to reject this God, all they did was to evict him. In this way they left wide open a vacancy that they could envision filling themselves. What they left fully intact was Reality as what God would encounter, Truth as what God would believe, and Goodness as how God would comprehend it. When pragmatists talk about humanizing reality, truth, and reason, they are rejecting modern philosophy with its attempts at seeking to conceive of everything as if through the eyes of an all-knowing God, while trying to develop an alternative. The alternatives they came up with range from a radical rejection of the philosophical notions they inherited from the tradition, to attempts at making them suit our circumstances. Their broader challenge was that of rejecting an outmoded objectivism without thereby falling into relativism or subjectivism. The preceding chapters chronicle part of this.

Key to humanizing truth, reality, and reason is to connect them, not to a detached divine viewpoint—like an epistemic deism—but directly to the world we find ourselves in, which from the beginning to the end is a world that forces us to act. Pragmatists thus reject the idea that we can know reality independently of our human needs and interests, or, to use a phrase of Dewey, as what a disinterested spectator would see. In fact, they deny that there is such a reality to begin with. What we normally call reality is instead a human product, formed from the buzzing and blooming confusion we found ourselves in when we first opened our eyes and began to take stock of the world—a process that is shot through and through by practical considerations, a process from which we cannot neatly separate out our own contributions, and which is a deeply social affair. The same holds for truth and goodness.

Where does this leave us? Despite Schiller's claim that there are as many pragmatisms as there are pragmatists, the preceding chapters show that there are a number of common traits that we can associate with pragmatism. Let's recapitulate some of them.

First, pragmatists are on the whole anti-foundationalist. We have no access, they claim, to some bedrock of necessary truths or self-evident premises that can give us the ultimate justification for our beliefs. We rather find ourselves, as Peirce notes, "walking upon a bog, and can only say, this ground seems to hold for the present. Here I will stay till it begins to give way" (CP5.589). Peirce's metaphor also nicely illustrates a second, related commonality, namely, that pragmatists are not skeptics but fallibilists. Fallibilists do not say, as skeptics do, that we cannot know anything because there is not a single thing we can know for certain; rather, pragmatists hold that we can be certain that many of our beliefs are true, even though we cannot say this for any single one of them. And they do so on the ground that if the vast majority of our beliefs were to be false, we would not survive, we would not be able to stay on top of that bog, we would not even be able to entertain skepticism. Admittedly, the far majority of these beliefs are too pedestrian to be philosophically exciting: that drinking water does not kill you, that you have ten toes, that hot coffee may burn your lips, that your bicycle is where you left it, that when you step on a chair it does not collapse, etc. However, from the fact that every single one of these beliefs can be false—drinking water can kill you, bikes do get stolen, chairs do collapse—it does not follow that *all* such beliefs can be false. To this the pragmatists will add that most of these beliefs are practical. They concern our immediate dealings with the world we find ourselves in, adding that the farther we move away from such practical beliefs, the more we run the risk of getting things wrong, as there is nothing (or very little) to set us straight. So, it is truly in our *practical* beliefs that we ground our beliefs more generally. Consequently, the third commonality is the belief that this bog that we are walking on is not the familiar one of water, peat, and heather, but is made of practical beliefs. It is this that inspires pragmatists to embrace in some form or other what is now called the pragmatic maxim—the fourth commonality. Pragmatists insist that we cannot understand what we cannot know, so that any claims we make about it are meaningless and should be dismissed as bad philosophy. This includes attempts at grounding our knowledge in "the unknowable," as Herbert Spencer tried to do in his *Synthetic Philosophy*, in Kant's "things in themselves," or in what God sees (or would have seen had He existed). Instead, pragmatists argue that the *meaning* of any intellectual conception we might entertain in philosophy, science, religion, or elsewhere cannot be anything but the effects that we can conceive the objects of that conception to have, where those effects are further restricted to those that can affect conduct. The reason for the latter restriction is that insofar as philosophy has a purpose, rather than that it is just an aimless musing around, doing philosophy is purpose-directed. This makes philosophy a type of voluntary and self-controlled conduct. The same is true for science and religion.

The demand that philosophical conceptions pass the pragmatic maxim has profound consequences for philosophy as a whole, as philosophers are now being asked to rethink much if not all of their vocabulary. They need to rethink their conceptions of truth, reality, and reason; their conceptions of what, where, and who we are; their conceptions of morality, law, race, gender, science, religion, and fact; and so on. In the process, some time-honored notions may be proven vacuous, whereas others may change in meaning, sometimes even dramatically. The same, again, holds for science and religion.

In sum, once the pragmatic maxim is granted, applying it to our existing conceptions may cause us to look at many things quite differently, and it will do so in ways that are both refreshing and connect directly with our being in the world. For instance, as we saw, pragmatists reject the idea of the individual self that we inherited from Descartes, explore new ways of dealing with the given element in experience, put inquiry (what scientists actually do, or should do) at the center of their philosophy of science, and rather than engaging in the traditional pursuit of giving a philosophical foundation to democracy, they argue that this puts the cart before the horse.

Pragmatism's rejection of the individual as a self-sufficient rational agent who enters the world pretty much like Athena—fully grown and dressed for battle—results in a shift to the social. Inquiry is inherently communal—not, as so much of philosophy is still today, "playing alone together." The result is a social epistemology. Knowledge, far from being a private treasure, is always public; it is a communal asset.

The pragmatists' insistence on practical consequences positions them firmly within the empiricist camp, albeit an empiricism that is very different from that of the modern philosophers—whether they side with Locke, Berkeley, and Hume, or with Scottish common-sensists like Reid and Hamilton. The pragmatist's empiricism is, to use James's phrase, a *radical* empiricism, one that connects more closely to phenomenology than to traditional empiricism. Pragmatists, moreover, tend to agree with Husserl that for science, philosophy, and religion to be rigorous, they must be grounded in phenomenology, albeit that they have a different view of what this phenomenology entails. Both Peirce's phaneroscopy, with the derivation of the categories, and James's radical empiricism are ways of returning to the life world, and we see similar moves in Royce and Lewis, and in the philosophical anthropology of Mead and Dewey. Pragmatists further agree that philosophy should not be looked upon as a domain separate from science, as if philosophers have some privileged access to knowledge that is closed off to scientists. That philosophy is part and parcel of the sciences broadly conceived is clearly visible in Peirce's division of the sciences and his call for something as seemingly bizarre as a scientific metaphysics. (Recall that the logical positivists dismissed all metaphysics as nonsense.)

As we saw, the pragmatists' rejection of the old notions of truth, reality, and reason puts them at risk of lapsing into subjectivism or relativism—two charges frequently levied against them. We also saw that those charges are not entirely unjustified. As the previous chapters reveal, however, most pragmatists, old as well as new, aim to steer between relativism and absolutism. Even though they deny that we can ever know reality as it truly is, that is, independently of *any* convention or *any* value judgment (epistemic or otherwise), they do not lose sight of the fact that our control over what enters the mind is very limited—that there is much to which we must bend. As James warned us, the squeeze is very tight. The point pragmatists are trying to make is a different one; namely, that what we must bend to cannot be captured in its pristine self—that is, *independently* of what we contribute to it through the act of knowing. That is, pragmatists deny that we can neatly separate what is truly found from what we contribute; a view they see confirmed by the collapse of many well-worn dichotomies (internal/external, analytic/synthetic, fact/value, etc.).

That we cannot neatly separate the two—that the trail of the human serpent is over everything, as James puts it—does not by itself make pragmatism subjectivist or relativist. As Schiller points out, the mere fact that we *make* reality does not make it any more subjective than suspension bridges or legal codes, just to mention two other things we also make. What pragmatists are pointing out is, rather, that we come to comprehend what affects us by encapsulating it within our conceptions, and we do so by tracing its conceivable practical consequences—that is, all the ways in which we can *conceive* that it might affect us. And pragmatists take this view without any preconception that the result must somehow mirror (or represent) a reality to which we have no direct access ourselves, and that the result must somehow be evaluated in terms of how well it does that. Nor do they demand that these conceivable practical consequences serve some pre-existing and independently formulated practical goal. Pragmatists are not utilitarians.

As for the charge of relativism, the pragmatist can point out that what it is relative to is not the perspective of an individual inquirer, or of any group of inquirers, but the concrete doubts or indeterminate situations from which our knowledge originates. For most pragmatists, the knowledge we seek is thus considered relative to—or, better perhaps, contingent upon—the inquiries we engage in, the doubts we seek to relieve, or the problems we try to resolve, rather than the culture that we grew up in or the people who surround us (together with the beliefs that they happen to have). For Peirce especially, the social nature of inquiry ensures (ideally, or in the long run) that the beliefs people bring to the table are always put up for discussion and are liable to be modified or corrected when it is being called for by the inquiry itself. The point pragmatists are making is again the same: that we cannot step outside of this and somehow envisage reality independently of our struggles to find our ways within it—struggles during which the approval of our peers may be the only thing to guide us in situations where experience does not set us straight. Furthermore, if we go with Mead, those peers are to a large extent within us, so that—still going with Mead—the problem of relativism comes down at least in part to the question, to what extent is the formation of a generalized other possible? Our knowledge, then, becomes relative precisely to the extent that it becomes human knowledge, rather than just Western European knowledge, or male knowledge, or my knowledge.

What is not yet addressed is James's doctrine of the will to believe and how it is entangled with pragmatism. If we make reality, and if in doing so we are guided by what we want, then it seems that James and those following his footsteps believe that we can make reality what we want it to be. Recall that Papini even told us to become gods! In fact, James's focus on the will to believe, together with his claim that truth is the cash value of our ideas, was one reason why pragmatism initially received such a poor reception in Europe. James's focus on the will to believe and Peirce's insistence on the will to learn also bifurcated the pragmatists themselves—separating those maintaining that pragmatism and the will to believe are inescapably conjoined from those who hold that they should be kept separate, because one can be one without the other.

In all of this, James's insistence that his will-to-believe argument applies only to so-called genuine options (and his explicitly *excluding* science from this) often went unnoticed, as did Peirce's arguments that philosophy is ill-suited for dealing with such genuine options—or vitally important topics, as he preferred to call them. In taking this view, however, Peirce effectively relegated our dealings with them to his first three methods for fixing belief. We can cling to them tenaciously, subject ourselves to authority, or just go by what sounds right. None of these seems particularly promising.

When looking at the issue of James's will to believe, we must also consider the pragmatists' rejection of what Putnam called "metaphysical realism"— the view that the world is a finished product that can be captured within a single and complete description (even if this means describing the world as four-dimensional space-time). For James, in contrast, the world is profoundly unfinished, which makes such a complete description impossible. Peirce, similarly, believed that there is real chance in the world—a view that caused him to develop an evolutionary cosmology. And Dewey and Mead reemphasized that evolution also teaches us that there is no predetermined endpoint. All of this means that we have still room to act, we have options, even if they are very limited. The result is a shift in focus: instead of making our ideas conform to the world as much as we can, we should make the world conform our ideas as much as the world lets us.

That there is still room for deliberate action that profoundly affects us seems certainly true within our lived experience where genuine options habitually appear. Moreover, as Dewey realized, this importantly includes sociopolitical issues as well as the implementation of new technologies. We can further add that over the last two hundred years or so, we *did* change our world considerably, trying to make it conform to our ideas and our needs with variable success.

Since pragmatism wants us to recast the meaning of our conceptualizations in terms of conceivable practical consequences, since we do not value all practical consequences equally, and given that the world is unfinished, a case is to be made that James's will to believe and pragmatism are more closely connected than some are willing to believe, and that this, again, is not something that causes a lapse into subjectivism or a vicious relativism.

Reflecting on the aforementioned tenets, we can say that pragmatism presents us with a philosophy that can account for our being active knowers who learn by doing in an open-ended universe, and who reap the benefits, or pay the price, depending on where the chips fall. It almost seems as if the early modern thinkers were so much taken in by the new science of optics, that when they saw themselves as created in the image of an all-knowing, all-powerful, and entirely good god, they utterly failed to realize that if such a god did create us in his image, he must have created us as co-creators—albeit co-creators with very limited options (we are not all powerful), who are deeply fallible (we are not all-knowing), and are of dubious morality (we are not entirely good). Moreover, since we cannot take in everything at once, but need to choose where to direct our attention, we can never be truly disinterested. We focus on what gets us further, either in our practical affairs or in our understanding.

This brings us to the next criticism often levied against pragmatism, namely, that it is narrowly instrumentalist. That it single-mindedly focuses on domination and control. That it sees everything as a resource to be exploited, its value determined by what you can get out of it. As Bertrand Russell put it at the beginning of the twentieth century, the pragmatist's outlook robs life "of all that gives it value, and [makes] Man himself smaller by depriving the universe which he contemplates of all its splendour."[3]

As we saw in Chapter 5, James appears to confirm such reading when he casts truth in terms of its cash value and by his enthusiasm for Papini. At the same time, however, we saw that James cautions that the squeeze is very tight, that we pay the price for choosing wrong when faced with a genuine option, and that in the domain of science we are more recorders than creators of truth. To this, people like Addams, Dewey, Locke, and West can further add that the purpose of knowledge is to improve humanity, not to provide us with a detached graphic description of poverty, sickness, and despair no matter how accurate such a description may be. Again, what we can do is limited, and it will differ greatly depending on the issue or the problem at hand. In fact, a main impetus behind Hull House was precisely that of finding out what we can and cannot do, what works and what doesn't work.

Perhaps the fullest response to Russell's indictment comes from Peirce, who distinguishes three classes of men:

> The first consists of those for whom the chief thing is the qualities of feelings. These men create art. The second consists of the practical men, who carry on the business of the world. They respect nothing but power, and respect power only so far as it [is] exercized. The third class consists of men to whom nothing seems great but reason. If force interests them, it is not in its exertion, but in that it has a reason and a law. For men of the first class, nature is a picture; for men of the second class, it is an opportunity; for men of the third class, it is a cosmos, so admirable, that to penetrate to its ways seems to them the only thing that makes life worth living.
>
> (CP1.43)

Peirce sees the pragmatist as truly belonging to the third class, which is precisely why he worked so hard to distance himself from those who tried to make pragmatism a philosophy for the second class, that of practical men.

What further defines this third class, Peirce argues, is an insistence on the will to learn. Peirce thereby continues to align himself with the leading motto of the Enlightenment, Kant's *sapere aude* (dare to know), albeit with significant humility. We must open ourselves up to the world that we find ourselves in and be willing to learn from it, be willing to let it teach us. And, as Dewey so poignantly insists, this calls for an active knower. Our understanding of the world is a creative enterprise. We are not painting by numbers. We must fashion our own concepts—they do not come to us "ready-made." Moreover, in doing so, we must cast these concepts in terms of how they might affect deliberate, self-controlled conduct. This is because when trying to find out how things are, this is precisely what we are doing. In short, to be an inquirer of any kind (philosopher, scientist, or other) one has no choice but to be a pragmatist.

Notes

1. See e.g., David Ray Griffin et al., *Founders of Constructive Postmodern Philosophy: Peirce, James, Bergson, Whitehead and Hartshorne* (Albany, 1993); John Deely, *Four Ages of Understanding* (Toronto, 2001).
2. St. Thomas Aquinas, *Summa Theologica* (1265–74), Part 1, Question 2, Article 3; Descartes (1641), Second Meditation.
3. Russell (1910), p.110.

Annotated Reading Guide

Nothing beats original sources. Like good literature, philosophical texts carry such an abundance of meaning that rereading them never feels like repetition. You always learn something new, and when you grow intellectually, they grow with you. To truly understand what drives the pragmatists, what their hopes are, and what they envision, you really must read their work firsthand. Reading good philosophical texts, however, can also be daunting. They are typically not written for the beginner, and the author's main commitment tends to be to the subject that the author is grappling with, not to the reader. Philosophers are not priests. They are searchers for knowledge—they do not claim to already possess it, ready to convey it to others in easily digestible bits with the self-assured overtone of people who already know that they know the answers. Reading a text in philosophy is therefore more like hiking through treacherous terrain with an experienced guide who is still fascinated and inspired by it all, rather than sitting in a classroom eager to learn what will be on the next exam.

The reading guide provided centers on primary sources that are easily accessible, are relatively short, and relate directly to what is discussed in the chapters. Together, they can be taken as a companion reader to the current introduction. The bibliographic references and bibliographic abbreviations used can be found in "References and Select Bibliography." Though quite a few of the essays listed can be found freely online (just search for the title), the references here are confined to more authoritative renditions, preferably to those that provide a relevant context. For the two survey chapters on the European reception of pragmatism, no natural candidates present themselves, and the reader is referred to the notes for those chapters.

Peirce and the Principle of Pragmatism

The Essential Peirce vol. 1 (EP1) contains the key philosophical texts of the early Peirce. Included are "The Fixation of Belief" and "How to Make Our Ideas Clear," which mark the origin of pragmatism and which are also often considered key early texts of analytic philosophy and philosophy of science.

William James: Pragmatism and the Will to Believe

The Writings of William James (WJ) offers a broad selection of James's philosophical papers. They include James's 1898 Berkeley address, "Philosophical Conceptions and Practical Results," where James, building on Peirce, presents his take on pragmatism, a view that he further develops in "What Pragmatism Means." Also included is James's "The Will to Believe," which contains his often-misunderstood will-to-believe argument.

The Pragmatic Humanism of F.C.S. Schiller

A comprehensive collection of Schiller's writings appeared as *F.C.S. Schiller: On Pragmatism and Humanism*. Schiller's view on pragmatism and how it relates to humanism is found in "The Definition of 'Pragmatism' and 'Humanism,'" and his views on truth are found in "The Making of Truth."

Peirce Revisited: The Normative Turn

The Essential Peirce vol. 2 (EP2) contains the key philosophical texts of the later Peirce. Two central texts that show Peirce's later take on pragmatism are "What Pragmatism Is" and "Issues in Pragmaticism." In these seminal texts, Peirce distances himself from the views of James, Schiller, and others, renames it pragmaticism, and restates his original maxim in semiotic terms.

Josiah Royce and George Herbert Mead

An extensive collection of Royce's writings is the two-volume *Basic Writings of Josiah Royce*. Not included in this collection, but of particular interest, is "Some Psychological Problems Emphasized by Pragmatism" (*Popular Science Monthly* [1913]: 394–411). Most of Mead's work was published posthumously in the form of lecture notes, most importantly *Mind, Self, and Society*. Mead gives a fairly comprehensive account of his views in "The Genesis of the Self and Social Control," which is included in the *Selected Writings* (SW).

Pragmatism and the Problems of Life: Dewey, Addams, and Bourne

A well-chosen collection of Dewey's enormous oeuvre is the two-volume *Essential Dewey* (ED1). It includes "The Development of American Pragmatism," where Dewey positions himself in relation to James and Peirce; "Existence, Value, and Criticism," where he develops his view on philosophy as a critic of culture; and "Does Reality Possess Practical Character," where he discusses the general complaint that pragmatism reduces to a form of subjectivism. Jane Addams gives a clear description of her ideas for social settlements in Chapter 6 of *Twenty Years at Hull House*, "Subjective Necessity for Social Settlements."

Conceptual Pragmatism From Lewis to Davidson

C.I. Lewis details his conceptual pragmatism in "The Pragmatic Conception of the *A Priori*," which is included in his *Collected Papers* (CL). W.V.O. Quine's criticism of this approach is found in "Two Dogmas of Empiricism" (included in *From a Logical Point of View*), where he denies that we can make sense of the notion of purely a priori knowledge on which the philosophy of Lewis, and also Carnap, hinges. A significant blow to any facile interpretation to the notion of conceptual schemes is found in Donald Davidson's "On the Very Idea of a Conceptual Scheme," which is included in *Inquiries into Truth & Interpretation*.

The Neopragmatism of Richard Rorty

The easiest go-to source for Rorty is *The Rorty Reader*. It includes his own survey of pragmatism in "Pragmatism, Relativism, and Irrationalism," as well as his classic "Pragmatism as Romantic Polytheism." Further of interest is the introduction to *Consequences of Pragmatism* (CP)

Hilary Putnam: Philosophy With a Human Face

The core of Putnam's pragmatism is found in *The Many Faces of Realism*, especially in the second lecture, "Reality Without the Dichotomies," and in *Realism with a Human Face* (RHF), which contains a good selection of Putnam's papers. For Putnam's later views, see *Pragmatism as a Way of Life*.

Susan Haack: Reclaiming Pragmatism

A concise account of Haack's foundherentism is found in "A Foundherentist Theory of Justification." Two broad collection of her essays are *Manifesto of a Passionate Moderate* and *Putting Philosophy to Work*. For her take on philosophy of science, see her "Six Signs of Scientism," as well as *Defending Science—Within Reason*.

Legal Pragmatism

The Common Law, especially its opening chapter, is a good introduction to Oliver Wendell Holmes's pragmatic approach to the law. Dewey discusses the law in his "Logical Method and Law" (included in *The Essential Dewey*, vol. 1) and he returns to it quite extensively in chapter 19 of his *Logic: The Theory of Inquiry* (LW12). A collection of Haack's papers is found in *Evidence Matters*. The first one contains an outline of her position and is titled "Epistemology and the Law of Evidence: Problems and Projects."

Prophetic Pragmatism and Feminist Inspirations

For pragmatic feminism, Elizabeth Anderson's "Feminist Epistemology: An Interpretation and a Defense" is a good starting point. Rorty's "Feminism and Pragmatism" is included in *The Rorty Reader* (RR). An excellent collection of Alain Locke's work is found in *The Philosophy of Alain Locke: Harlem Renaissance and Beyond* (PAL). For West, *The Cornel West Reader*, well represents his philosophical contributions. Especially recommended are "On Prophetic Pragmatism" and a section containing mostly shorter pieces on prophetic Christian thought.

References and Select Bibliography

Abel, Reuben. *The Pragmatic Humanism of F.C.S. Schiller* (New York, 1955).

Addams, Jane. "A Function of the Social Settlement." *Annals of the American Academy of Political and Social Science* 13 (1899): 33–55.

———. *Democracy and Social Ethics* (New York, 1902).

———. *Twenty Years at Hull House* (New York, 1910).

Aikin, Scott, and Robert Talisse (eds). *The Routledge Handbook of Pragmatism* (New York, forthcoming).

Anderson, Elizabeth. "Feminist Epistemology: An Interpretation and a Defense." *Hypatia* 10.3 (1995): 50–84.

Aune, Bruce. *Rationalism, Empiricism, and Pragmatism* (New York, 1970).

Bernstein, Richard. *The Pragmatic Turn* (Cambridge, 2010).

YL   Bourne, Randolph. *Youth and Life* (Boston, 1913).

EL   ———. *Education and Living* (New York, 1917).

Brandom, Robert. *Perspectives on Pragmatism: Classical, Recent, & Contemporary* (Cambridge, 2011).

Burke, Thomas, Micah Hester, and Robert Talisse (eds). *Dewey's Logical Theory: New Studies and Interpretations* (Nashville, 2002).

TM   Carnap, Rudolf. "Testability and Meaning." *Philosophy of Science* 3 (1936): 419–71; 4 (1937): 1–40.

Conkin, Paul. *Puritans and Pragmatists* (New York, 1968).

Cooper, Wesley. *The Unity of William James's Thought* (Nashville, 2002).

Davidson, Donald. *Inquiries into Truth & Interpretation* (Oxford, 1984).

———. *Subjective, Intersubjective, Objective* (Oxford, 2001).

de Waal, Cornelis. "Eleven Challenges to the Pragmatic Theory of Truth." *Transactions of the Charles S. Peirce Society: A Quarterly Journal in American Philosophy* 35.4 (1999): 748–66.———. *On Mead* (Belmont, 2002).

———. *Susan Haack: The Philosopher Responds to Critics* (Amherst, 2007).

———. *Peirce: A Guide for the Perplexed* (London, 2013).

——— (ed). *The Oxford Handbook of Charles S. Peirce* (Oxford, forthcoming).

Debrock, Guy. *Process Pragmatism: Essays on a Quiet Philosophical Revolution* (Amsterdam, 2003).

EW   Dewey, John. *The Early Works, 1882–1898*, 5 vols. (Carbondale, 1967–72).

ED   ———. *The Essential Dewey*, 2 vols. (Bloomington, 1998).

MW   ———. *The Middle Works, 1899–1924*, 15 vols. (Carbondale, 1976–83).

LW   ———. *The Later Works, 1925–1953*, 17 vols. (Carbondale, 1981–90).

Dickstein, Morris (ed). *The Revival of Pragmatism. New Essays on Social Thought, Law, and Culture* (Durham, 1998).

Diggins, John Patrick. *The Promise of Pragmatism: Modernism and the Crisis of Knowledge and Authority* (Chicago, 1994).

Fesmire, Steven (ed). *The Oxford Handbook of Dewey* (Oxford, 2019).

Fisch, Max. *Peirce, Semeiotic, and Pragmatism* (Bloomington, 1986).

Gale, Richard. *The Divided Self of William James* (Cambridge, 1999).

Golino, Carlo. "Giovanni Papini and American Pragmatism." *Italica* 32.1 (1955): 38–48.

Goodman, Nelson. *Ways of Worldmaking* (Indianapolis, 1978).

PRC   Green, Nicholas St. Johns. "Proximate and Remote Cause," in *Essays on Tort and Crime* (Menasha, 1933), pp.1–17.

EI   Haack, Susan. *Evidence and Inquiry: Towards Reconstruction in Epistemology* (Oxford, 1993).

M———. *Manifesto of a Passionate Moderate* (Chicago, 1998).

———. "A Foundherentist Theory of Justification," in Ernest Sosa and Jaegwon Kim (eds). *Epistemology: An Anthology* (Oxford, 2000), pp.226–36.

DS   ———. *Defending Science—Within Reason* (Amherst, 2003).

———. "Six Signs of Scientism." *Skeptical Inquirer* 37.6 (2009): 40–5.

———. *Putting Philosophy to Work* (Amherst, 2013).

EM   ———. *Evidence Matters: Science, Proof, and Truth in the Law* (Cambridge, 2014).

———. *Scientism and Its Discontents* (Rounded Globe, 2017).

Haack, Susan, and Robert Lane (eds). *Pragmatism, Old & New* (Amherst, 2006).

Hickman, Larry. *Philosophical Tools for a Technological Culture: Putting Pragmatism to Work* (Bloomington, 2001).

CL   Holmes, Oliver Wendall, Jr. *The Common Law* (Boston, 1881).

PL   ———. "The Path of the Law." *Harvard Law Review* 10.8 (1897): 457–78.

Hookway, Christopher. *Peirce* (London, 1985).

———. *Quine* (Stanford, 1988).

———. *The Pragmatic Maxim: Essays on Peirce and Pragmatism* (Oxford, 2012).

Innis, Robert. *Pragmatism and the Forms of Sense: Language, Perception, Technics* (University Park, 2002).

MT   James, William. *The Meaning of Truth* (Cambridge, MA, 1975).

———. *Pragmatism* (Cambridge, MA, 1975).

WJ   ———. *The Writings of William James: A Comprehensive Edition* (Chicago, 1977).

EPh   ———. *Essays in Philosophy* (Cambridge, MA, 1978).

WTB   ———. *The Will to Believe and Other Essays in Popular Philosophy* (Cambridge, MA, 1979).

PP   ———. *The Principles of Psychology*, 3 vols. (Cambridge, MA, 1981).

———. "G. Papini and the Pragmatist Movement in Italy." *Journal of Philosophy* 3.13 (1906): 337–41.

Ketner, Kenneth. *A Comprehensive Bibliography of the Published Works of Charles Sanders Peirce*. 2nd ed. (Bowling Green, 1986).

Kitcher, Philip. *Preludes to Pragmatism: Toward a Reconstruction of Philosophy* (Oxford, 2012).

Klein, Alexander (ed). *The Oxford Handbook of William James* (Oxford, 2018).

Kuklick, Bruce. *The Rise of American Philosophy* (New Haven, 1977).

MWO   Lewis, C.I. *Mind and the World Order: Outline of a Theory of Knowledge* (New York, 1929).

AKV   ———. *An Analysis of Knowledge and Valuation* (La Salle, 1946).

CL   ———. *Collected Papers of Clarence Irving Lewis* (Stanford, 1970).

NN   Locke, Alain. *The New Negro* (New York, 1968).

PAL   ———. *The Philosophy of Alain Locke: Harlem Renaissance and Beyond* (Philadelphia, 1989).

Maddalena, Giovanni, and Giovanni Tuzet (eds). *The Italian Pragmatists: Between Allies and Enemies* (Leiden, 2021).

Margolis, Joseph. *Reinventing Pragmatism: American Philosophy at the End of the Twentieth Century* (Ithaca, 2002).

PP   Mead, George Herbert. *The Philosophy of the Present* (La Salle, 1932).

MSS   ———. *Mind, Self, and Society from the Standpoint of a Social Behaviorist* (Chicago, 1934).

PA   ———. *The Philosophy of the Act* (Chicago, 1938).

SW   ———. *Selected Writings* (Chicago, 1964).

LEC   ———. *The Individual and the Social Self: Unpublished Work of George Herbert Mead* (Chicago, 1982).

Menand, Louis. *The Metaphysical Club: A Story of Ideas in America* (New York, 2001).

Misak, Cheryl. *Verificationism: Its History and Prospects* (New York, 1995).

——— (ed). *The Cambridge Companion to Peirce* (Cambridge, 2004).

——— (ed). *New Pragmatists* (Oxford, 2007).

———. *The American Pragmatists* (Oxford, 2013).

———. *Cambridge Pragmatism: From Peirce and James to Ramsey and Wittgenstein* (Oxford, 2016).

LPP   Morris, Charles. *Logical Positivism, Pragmatism, and Scientific Empiricism* (Paris, 1937).

———. *The Pragmatic Movement in American Philosophy* (New York, 1970).

Mounce, H.O. *The Two Pragmatisms: From Peirce to Rorty* (New York, 1997).

Murphey, Murray. *C.I. Lewis, the Last Pragmatist* (New York, 2005).

Murphy, John. *Pragmatism: From Peirce to Davidson* (Boulder, 1990).

Novak, Michael (ed). *American Philosophy and the Future: Essays for a New Generation* (New York, 1968).

Papini, Giovanni. "What Pragmatism Is Like." *Popular Science Monthly* 71.10 (1907): 351–8.

———. *Four and Twenty Minds* (New York, 1971).

———. *The Failure* (Westport, 1972). Published in Britain as *A Man—Finished*.

CP   Peirce, Charles. *The Collected Papers of Charles S. Peirce*, 8 vols. (Cambridge, MA, 1931–35, 1958). Cited by volume and paragraph number.

———. *Charles Sanders Peirce: Contributions to the* Nation (Lubbock, 1975).

W   ———. *The Writings of Charles S. Peirce: A Chronological Edition*, 7 vols. (Bloomington, 1982).

EP   ———. *The Essential Peirce*, 2 vols. (Bloomington, 1992, 1998).

———. *The Illustrations of the Logic of Science by Charles S. Peirce* (Chicago, 2014).

Perry, Ralph. *The Thought and Character of William James*, 2 vols. (Boston, 1935).

Pihlström, Sami (ed). *The Continuum Companion to Pragmatism* (London, 2011).

PA   Posner, Richard. "Pragmatic Adjudication." *Cardozo Law Review* 18.1 (1996): 1–20.

————. *Law, Pragmatism, and Democracy* (Cambridge, MA, 2003).

Pratt, Scott. *Native Pragmatism: Rethinking the Roots of American Philosophy* (Bloomington, 2002).

RTH   Putnam, Hilary. *Reason, Truth, and History* (Cambridge, 1981).

————. *The Many Faces of Realism* (LaSalle, 1987).

RHF   ————. *Realism with a Human Face* (Cambridge, 1990).

RP   ————. *Renewing Philosophy* (Cambridge, 1992).

————. *Pragmatism: An Open Question* (Oxford, 1995).

TC   ————. *The Threefold Cord: Mind, Body, and World* (New York, 1999).

————. *The Collapse of the Fact/Value Dichotomy* (Cambridge, 2002).

PWL   Putnam, Hilary, and Ruth Anna Putnam. *Pragmatism as a Way of Life* (Cambridge, 2017).

Putnam, Ruth Anna. *The Cambridge Companion to William James* (Cambridge, 1997).

LPV   Quine, W.V.O. *From a Logical Point of View* (Cambridge, MA, 1953).

OR   ————. *Ontological Relativity and Other Essays* (New York, 1969).

PPE   ————. "The Pragmatists' Place in Empiricism," in R.J. Mulvaney and P.M. Zeltner (eds). *Pragmatism, Its Sources and Prospects* (Columbia, 1981), pp.21–39.

————. *Theories and Things* (Cambridge, MA, 1981).

Rescher, Nicholas. *Realistic Pragmatism: An Introduction to Pragmatic Philosophy* (Albany, 2000).

Riccio, Peter. *On the Threshold of Fascism* (New York, 1929).

R Robin, Richard. *Annotated Catalogue of the Papers of Charles S. Peirce* (Amherst, 1964). References to letters as RL.

Romano, Carlin. *America the Philosophical* (New York, 2012).

MN   Rorty, Richard. *Philosophy and the Mirror of Nature* (Oxford, 1980).

CP   ————. *Consequences of Pragmatism* (Minneapolis, 1982).

————. *Contingency, Irony, and Solidarity* (Cambridge, 1989).

PP   ————. *Philosophical Papers*, 3 vols. (Cambridge, 1991–1998).

————. *Achieving Our Country: Leftist Thought in Twentieth-Century America* (Cambridge, 1998).

PSH   ————. *Philosophy and Social Hope* (London, 1999).

RR   ————. *The Rorty Reader* (Oxford, 2010).

Rosenthal, Sandra. *Classical American Pragmatism: Its Contemporary Vitality* (Urbana, 1999).

————. *C.I. Lewis in Focus: The Pulse of Pragmatism* (Bloomington, 2007).

EP   Royce, Josiah. "The Eternal and the Practical." *Philosophical Review* 13.2 (1904): 113–42.

————. *The Basic Writings of Josiah Royce* (Chicago, 1969).

————. *The Philosophy of Loyalty* (Nashville, 1995).

PC2   ————. *The Problem of Christianity*, 2 vols. (Washington, 2001).

Rumana, Richard. *Richard Rorty: An Annotated Bibliography of Secondary Literature* (Amsterdam, 2002).

Saatkamp, Herman, Jr. (ed). *Rorty and Pragmatism: The Philosopher Responds to His Critics* (Nashville, 1995).

Schiller, F.C.S. *Riddles of the Sphinx: A Study in the Philosophy of Evolution* (London, 1891).

AP ———. "Axioms as Postulates," in Henry Sturt (ed). *Personal Idealism* (London, 1902), pp.47–133.

———. *Humanism: Philosophical Essays* (London, 1903).

EB ———. "Pragmatism," in *Encyclopedia Britannica*. 11th ed. (Cambridge, 1911), pp.246–8.

———. *Formal Logic: A Scientific and Social Problem* (London, 1912).

———. *Studies in Humanism* (London, 1912).

HP ———. *Humanistic Pragmatism: The Philosophy of F.C.S. Schiller*. Edited by Reuben Abel (New York, 1966).

———. *F.C.S. Schiller on Pragmatism and Humanism: Selected Writings, 1891–1939*. Edited by John Shook and Hugh McDonald (Amherst, 2008).

Schilpp, Paul (ed). *The Philosophy of C.I. Lewis* (La Salle, 1968).

———. *The Philosophy of John Dewey* (La Salle, 1989).

Schneider, Herbert. *A History of American Philosophy*. 2nd ed. (New York, 1963).

Searles, Herbert, and Allan Shields. *A Bibliography of the Works of F.C.S. Schiller* (San Diego, 1969).

Seigfried, Charlene. *Pragmatism and Feminism: Reweaving the Social Fabric* (Chicago, 1996).

Shook, John. *Pragmatism: An Annotated Bibliography, 1898–1940* (Amsterdam, 1998).

Short, T.L. *Peirce's Theory of Signs* (Cambridge, 2007).

Sleeper, R.W. *The Necessity of Pragmatism: John Dewey's Conception of Philosophy* (New Haven, 1986).

Smyth, Richard. *Reading Peirce Reading* (Lanham, 1997).

Thayer, H.S. *Meaning and Action: A Critical History of Pragmatism*. 2nd ed. (Indianapolis, 1968).

Thompson, Paul, and Thomas Hilde. *The Agrarian Roots of Pragmatism* (Nashville, 2000).

Vailati, Giovanni. "Pragmatism and Mathematical Logic." *Monist* 16 (1906): 481–91.

———. "A Study of Platonic Terminology." *Mind* 15 (1906): 473–85.

West, Cornel. *Prophesy Deliverance! An Afro-American Revolutionary Christianity* (Louisville, 1982).

AE ———. *The American Evasion of Philosophy: A Genealogy of Pragmatism* (Madison, 1989).

———. *The Cornel West Reader* (New York, 1999).

White, Morton. *Science & Sentiment in America* (New York, 1972).

———. *Pragmatism and the American Mind* (London, 1973).

Winetrout, Kenneth. *F.C.S. Schiller and the Dimensions of Pragmatism* (Columbus, 1967).

PI Wittgenstein, Ludwig. *Philosophical Investigations* (Oxford, 1953).

OC ———. *On Certainty* (New York, 1969).

Zanoni, Candido. "Logical Pragmatism: The Philosophy of G. Vailati." Dissertation (University of Minnesota, 1968).

Index